Introduction to Emergency Management
Fourth Edition

Introduction to Emergency Management

Fourth Edition

George D. Haddow

Jane A. Bullock

Damon P. Coppola

AMSTERDAM • BOSTON • HEIDELBERG • LONDON • NEW YORK • OXFORD
PARIS • SAN DIEGO • SAN FRANCISCO • SINGAPORE • SYDNEY • TOKYO

ELSEVIER

Butterworth-Heinemann is an imprint of Elsevier

Acquiring Editor: Pamela Chester
Development Editor: Gregory Chalson
Project Manager: Julie Ochs
Designer: Alisa Andreola

Butterworth-Heinemann is an imprint of Elsevier
30 Corporate Drive, Suite 400, Burlington, MA 01803, USA

Library of Congress Cataloging-in-Publication Data
Haddow, George D.
   Introduction to emergency management / George D. Haddow, Jane A. Bullock,
  Damon P. Coppola. — 4th ed.
    p. cm.
   Includes bibliographical references and index.
   ISBN 978-1-85617-959-1 (hardcover : alk. paper) 1. Emergency management. 2. Emergency
  management—United States. 3. Communication in management.   I. Bullock, Jane A. II. Coppola,
  Damon P. III. Title.
  HV551.2.H3 2010
  363.34'80973—dc22   2010014614

British Library Cataloguing-in-Publication Data
A catalogue record for this book is available from the British Library.

ISBN: 978-1-85617-959-1

Printed in the United States of America
10 11 12 13 14   10 9 8 7 6 5 4 3 2 1

Working together to grow
libraries in developing countries

www.elsevier.com | www.bookaid.org | www.sabre.org

ELSEVIER   BOOK AID International   Sabre Foundation

For information on all BH publications visit our website at www.elsevierdirect.com/security

This book is dedicated to Lacy Suiter. Lacy taught us all the responsibility, privilege, and honor of serving people as emergency managers. He singlehandedly made emergency management an important discipline to the safety of our citizens. He was a gentleman, a mentor, a teacher, a cheerleader, and an impromptu singer, but most of all, he was the best friend anyone could ever have.

Contents

Foreword

In 1993, when I took over leadership of the Federal Emergency Management Agency (FEMA), emergency management was not a very well known or respected discipline. Many in the profession were hold-overs from the days of civil defense, and most elected officials did not see the value of emergency management until they had a major disaster in their community; and even then, the value was transitory. Throughout the 1990s, as the United States and the world experienced an unprecedented number of severe disasters, the critical role emergency management plays in protecting the social and economic stability of our communities was evidenced. Emergency management began to grow beyond the response environment and focus on risk analysis, communications, risk prevention/mitigation, and social and economic recovery. This required a new skill base for emergency managers, and colleges and universities added courses and degrees in emergency management to their offerings. This resulted in a better educated, multidisciplinary, proactive approach to emergency management. Emergency managers were valued members of a community's leadership. Emergency management became an important profession. It allowed me as Director of FEMA, to work with our state, local, and private partners to build one of the most respected emergency management systems in the world.

As the tragic outcome of Hurricane Katrina so vividly demonstrated, a strong emergency management system is vital to the safety of all of our citizens. There is no time in our recent history when the need for and understanding of the discipline of emergency management have been more important. The current risk environment we live in, from potential bioterrorist threats, increasingly severe hurricanes and floods, and more frequent wildfires, has dramatically increased the skills and knowledge required to be an effective emergency manager in today's world.

Introduction to Emergency Management is the authoritative guide on today's discipline of emergency management. It takes the reader through the historical context of emergency management to the present day evolution into the world of homeland security. This book focuses on the elements of an emergency management process while providing the policy underpinnings that support that process. It provides a comprehensive case study that examines the events and issues surrounding Hurricane Katrina. While focusing on the current changes happening to the United States system for emergency management, it provides readers with a solid background in international practices and policies for disaster management/homeland security. This book gives the reader practical, real world experiences through documented case studies and provides extensive references and Internet sites for follow up research.

My philosophy about emergency management has always been that we need to take a common-sense, practical approach to reducing the risks we face and protecting our citizens and our communities. We need to identify our risks, educate and communicate to our people about those risks, prepare as best we can for the risks, and then, together, form partnerships to take action to reduce those risks. This approach applies whether we are dealing with a flood, a tornado, a hazardous materials spill, a wildfire, a potential suicide bomb explosion, or a pandemic flu outbreak. George Haddow and Jane Bullock were my Deputy Chief of Staff and my Chief of Staff, respectively, when I was Director of FEMA. Together we worked to apply this approach to making our citizens and communities more disaster resistant and safer throughout the world. As you read and learn from this book, I hope you will keep those ideals in mind.

—James Lee Witt, James Lee Witt Associates

Acknowledgments

This book could not have been completed without the assistance of a series of valuable partners. We would like to thank Wayne Blanchard, whose vision, encouragement, and insights on effective education in emergency management have improved our work and the work of emergency managers everywhere. We are also grateful to the Institute for Crisis, Disaster, and Risk Management at The George Washington University, and its codirectors, Dr. Jack Harrald and Dr. Joseph Barbera, for their support. Greg Shaw's humor helped us to keep things in perspective.

We thank the many professors, students, and practitioners who gave us valuable feedback on different aspects of the book and provided suggestions to make the text more relevant and useful.

Finally, the authors wish to thank their respective spouses, Kim Haddow and Mary Gardner Coppola, for their enduring good humor and patience.

Introduction

No country, community, or individual is immune to the impacts of disasters. Disasters, however, can be and have been prepared for, responded to, and recovered from, and have had their consequences mitigated to an increasing degree. The profession (and academic discipline) that addresses this "management" of disasters is called *emergency management*, and this book is designed to provide the reader with a comprehensive foundation on the history, structure, organization, systems, and concerns that shape the management of disasters and other emergencies. Contained within are details and descriptions of contemporary emergency management practices and strategies, as well as descriptions of the key players involved in emergency management both within the United States and around the world. Our intent is to provide the reader with a working knowledge of how the functions of comprehensive emergency management operate and the influence they can have on everyday life.

This fourth edition represents a documentation of the current status of the discipline as it gravitates toward a state of equilibrium. The 2001 terrorist attacks set in motion a series of events that forever changed not only the way government jurisdictions at all levels (federal, state, and local) addressed the terrorism hazard but also the way members of the public, nongovernmental organizations, and businesses prepare for disaster events independent of and in concert with these agencies. Popular opinion is that these actions were mostly knee-jerk in nature and failed to preserve the positive lessons of previous years—especially those from the highly regarded James Lee Witt years of 1992 to 2000. In 2005, the failed response to Hurricane Katrina confirmed such fears, and it had the effect of recalibrating our comprehensive approach to all-hazards risk assessment by reminding all emergency management practitioners that regardless of the public, policy, and media agendas, emergency management must be guided by scientific and statistical risk analysis.

Since the third edition of this book was published, FEMA has regained many of the programs and offices it lost as a result of the creation of the Department of Homeland Security (DHS) and Secretary Chertoff's Six-Point Agenda. FEMA has regained its status as the agency responsible for the bulk of the nation's emergency management policy, direction, and federal-level operations, yet it remains stifled under the umbrella of an organization dedicated to security-based concerns. Within DHS, FEMA is subject not only to indirect access to the president and a diminished decision-making authority, but it must also conform to the strategic focus of an agency whose fundamental mission is markedly different from its own.

In 2005, we saw a national system of emergency management—once regarded as one of the most effective and emulated systems in the world—proven incompetent in responding to an event that had been long predicted, planned for, and studied: Hurricane Katrina. Five years later, FEMA is still struggling to rediscover its role while the recovery along the Gulf Coast steadily progresses. This edition examines how FEMA has evolved as a result of the legislation enacted in the aftermath of Hurricane Katrina and how a change in administrations and political ideologies has helped to direct these changes.

While the book emphasizes the U.S. domestic system of emergency management, many of the experiences discussed, lessons learned, and emerging trends are replicable to emergency management systems around the world. Emergency management in the United States has experienced every form of disaster: natural, man-made, and intentional. The lessons learned from these experiences, the changes made in response to these events, and how the system continues to evolve because of climate changes and other emerging threats provide a solid landscape to examine what emergency management is or could be.

This book, however, does not focus exclusively on FEMA. State and local emergency management organizations are the subjects of many of the case studies, and their collaborative affiliations with FEMA are discussed at length throughout the text. One full chapter, in fact, is dedicated to how emergencies are managed at the international level when the capacity of whole countries or regions falls short of what is required to manage the disaster at hand. With greater frequency, events such as the 2004 Asian earthquake and tsunami, cyclone Nargis in Burma in 2008, and the Sichuan earthquake that same year have highlighted the need for a more robust international emergency management system, and governments across the globe have focused more attention on the issue. A detailed case study of the response to the 2001 earthquake in Gujarat, India, is provided to illustrate these systems.

Chapter 1 includes a brief discussion of the historical, organizational, and legislative evolution of emergency management in the United States by tracing the major changes triggered by disasters or other human or political events, including the creation of the Department of Homeland Security. The chapter includes an analysis of the organizational, legislative, and policy changes made in emergency management both pre- and post-Hurricane Katrina. Chapter 2 identifies and defines the hazards confronting emergency management. Chapter 3 discusses the function of mitigation and the strategies and programs emergency management or other disciplines use to reduce the impacts of disaster events. Chapter 4 catalogues the broad range of programs and processes that comprise the preparedness function of modern emergency management. Chapter 5 breaks from the more traditional approach to emergency management and focuses on why communication with the public, the media, and partners is critical to emergency management of the twenty-first century. Chapter 6 focuses on the essential functions and processes of responding to a disaster event. Chapter 7 describes the broad range of government and voluntary programs available to assist individuals and communities in rebuilding in the aftermath of a disaster. Chapter 8 provides an overview of current activity in international emergency management through an examination of selected international organizations. Chapter 9 describes how the events of September 11, 2001, have altered the traditional perceptions of emergency management. Chapter 10 looks at the post-9/11, post-Katrina environment and provides insights, speculations, recommendations, and three options on where emergency management is or should be headed in the future.

Our goal in writing this book was to provide readers with an understanding of emergency management, insight into how events have shaped the discipline, and thoughts about the future direction of emergency management. The events of September 11 and the failures of Hurricane Katrina demonstrate the critical need for and value of emergency management. The evolving threats, the realities of global climate change, and our changing social, economic, and political environment demand new and innovative approaches and leadership. We hope this text will motivate each reader to accept the challenge.

The Historical Context of Emergency Management

What You'll Learn

- The early roots of emergency management
- The modern history of emergency management in the United States
- How FEMA came to exist and how it evolved during the 1980s, 1990s, and the early twenty-first century
- The sudden changes to modern emergency management that resulted from the 9/11 terrorist attacks and Hurricane Katrina
- Changes made by post-Hurricane Katrina legislation and a new administration in Washington, D.C.

Introduction

Emergency management has its roots in ancient history. Early hieroglyphics depict cave dwellers trying to deal with disasters. The Bible speaks of the many disasters that befell civilizations. In fact, the account of Moses parting the Red Sea could be interpreted as the first attempt at flood control. As long as there have been disasters, individuals and communities have tried to find ways to fix them, but organized attempts at disaster recovery did not occur until much later in modern history.

This chapter discusses the historical, organizational, and legislative history of modern emergency management in the United States. Some of the significant events and people that have shaped the emergency management discipline over the years are reviewed. Understanding the history and evolution of emergency management is important because at different times, the concepts of emergency management have been applied differently. The definition of *emergency management* can be extremely broad and all-encompassing. Unlike other, more structured disciplines, it has expanded and contracted in response to events, congressional desires, and leadership styles.

Recently, events and leadership, more than anything else, have brought about dramatic changes to emergency management in the United States. The terrorist attacks of September 11, 2001, led to massive organizational changes and programmatic shifts in emergency management. Many believe that these changes undermined the effective national system of emergency management that had evolved during the 1990s and led to the profound failure of all levels of emergency management in response to Hurricane Katrina in 2005.

A simple definition for emergency management is "a discipline that deals with risk and risk avoidance." Risk represents a broad range of issues and includes an equally diverse set of players. The range of situations that could possibly involve emergency management or the emergency management system is extensive. This supports the premise that emergency management is integral to the security of everyone's daily lives and should be integrated into daily decisions and not just called on during times of disasters.

Emergency management is an essential role of government. The Constitution gives the states the responsibility for public health and safety—hence the responsibility for public risks—with the federal government in a secondary role. The federal role is to help when the state, local, or individual entity is overwhelmed. This fundamental philosophy continues to guide the government function of emergency management.

Based on this strong foundation, the validity of emergency management as a government function has never been in question. Entities and organizations fulfilling the emergency management function existed at the state and local levels long before the federal government became involved. But as events occurred, as political philosophies changed, and as the nation developed, the federal role in emergency management steadily increased.

In the aftermath of the failed response to Hurricane Katrina, extensive discussion about emergency management, particularly the response and recovery functions, has taken place. An ever-increasing presence of nonprofit organizations delivering support to their particular constituencies after Katrina has given rise to interest on the part of the nonprofit community to take on increased responsibilities for disaster response. To date this has not materialized, but steps have been taken at the federal level to apply a top-down approach to emergency management functions, particularly relative to planning for disasters. While the Post-Katrina Emergency Management Reform Act detailed changes to how federal emergency management functioned, many of the changes included in this legislation were overlooked or were slow to be adopted by the leadership at the Federal Emergency Management Agency (FEMA) and the Department of Homeland Security (DHS). With the election of Barack Obama as president in 2008, both Congress and the emergency management community looked forward to positive changes and support for a struggling discipline.

Early History: 1800–1950

In 1803, a congressional act was passed that provided financial assistance to a New Hampshire town that had been devastated by fire. This was the first example of the federal government becoming involved in a local disaster. It was not until Franklin Roosevelt's administration used government as a tool to stimulate the economy that the federal government began to make significant investments in emergency management functions.

During the 1930s, the Reconstruction Finance Corporation and the Bureau of Public Roads were both given the authority to make disaster loans available for repair and reconstruction of certain public facilities after disasters. The Tennessee Valley Authority was created during this time to produce hydroelectric power and, as a secondary purpose, to reduce flooding in the region.

A significant piece of emergency management legislation was passed during this time. The Flood Control Act of 1934 gave the U.S. Army Corps of Engineers increased authority to design and build flood-control projects. This act has had a significant and long-lasting impact on emergency management in this country. This act reflected the philosophy that humans could control nature, thereby eliminating the risk of floods. Although this program would promote economic and population growth patterns along the nation's rivers, history has proven that this attempt at emergency management was both shortsighted and costly.

The Cold War and the Rise of Civil Defense: the 1950s

The next notable time frame for the evolution of emergency management was during the 1950s. The era of the Cold War presented the principal disaster risk as the potential for nuclear war and nuclear fallout. Civil defense programs proliferated across communities during this time. Individuals and communities were encouraged to build bomb shelters to protect themselves and their families from nuclear attack from the Soviet Union.

Almost every community had a civil defense director, and most states had someone who represented civil defense in their state government hierarchy. By profession, these individuals were usually retired military personnel, and their operations received little political or financial support from their state or local governments. Equally often, their civil defense responsibilities were in addition to other duties.

Federal support for these activities was vested in the Federal Civil Defense Administration (FCDA), an organization with little staff or financial resources whose main role was to provide technical assistance. In reality, the local and state civil defense directors were the first recognized face of emergency management in the United States.

A companion office to the FCDA, the Office of Defense Mobilization was established in the Department of Defense (DOD). The primary functions of this office were to allow for quick mobilization of materials and production and stockpiling of critical materials in the event of a war. It included a function called *emergency preparedness*. In 1958, these two offices were merged into the Office of Civil and Defense Mobilization.

The 1950s were a quiet time for large-scale natural disasters. Hurricane Hazel, a Category 4 hurricane, inflicted significant damage in Virginia and North Carolina in 1954; Hurricane Diane hit several mid-Atlantic and northeastern states in 1955; and Hurricane Audrey, the most damaging of the three storms, struck Louisiana and North Texas in 1957. Congressional response to these disasters followed a familiar pattern of ad hoc legislation to provide increased disaster assistance funds to the affected areas.

As the 1960s started, three major natural disaster events occurred. In a sparsely populated area of Montana, the Hebgen Lake earthquake, measuring 7.3 on the Richter scale, was proof that states other than California were at risk for severe earthquakes. Also in 1960, Hurricane Donna hit the west coast of Florida, and Hurricane Carla blew into Texas in 1961. The incoming Kennedy administration decided to make a change to the federal approach to such disasters. In 1961 it created the Office of Emergency Preparedness inside the White House to deal with natural disasters. Civil defense responsibilities remained in the Office of Civil Defense within the DOD.

Changes to Emergency Management: the 1960s

As the 1960s progressed, the United States would be struck by a series of major natural disasters. The Ash Wednesday storm in 1962 devastated more than 620 miles of shoreline on the East Coast, producing more than $300 million in damages. In 1964, an earthquake measuring 9.2 on the Richter scale in Prince William Sound, Alaska, became front-page news throughout America and the world. This quake generated a tsunami that affected beaches as far down the Pacific Coast as California and killed 123 people. Hurricane Betsey in 1965 and Hurricane Camille in 1969 killed and injured hundreds of people and caused hundreds of millions of dollars in damage along the Gulf Coast.

As with previous disasters, the response was passage of ad hoc legislation for funds. However, the financial losses resulting from Hurricane Betsey's path across Florida and Louisiana raised the issue of disaster insurance against future floods and a potential method to reduce continued government assistance after such disasters. Congressional interest was prompted by the unavailability of flood protection insurance on the standard homeowner policy. If this type of insurance was available, it was cost-prohibitive. These discussions eventually led to the passage of the National Flood Insurance Act of 1968, which created the National Flood Insurance Program (NFIP).

Congressman Hale Boggs of Louisiana is appropriately credited with steering this unique legislation through Congress. Unlike previous emergency management/disaster legislation, this bill sought to do something about the risk *before* the disaster struck. It brought the concept of *community-based mitigation* into the practice of emergency management. In simple terms, when a community joined the NFIP, in exchange for making federally subsidized, low-cost flood insurance available to its citizens, the community had to pass an ordinance restricting future development in its floodplains. The federal government also agreed to help local communities by producing maps of their community's floodplains.

ADDITIONAL RESEARCH

In October 2006, a report entitled *Costs and Consequences of Flooding and the Impact of the National Flood Insurance Program* was issued, which provided an overview of what the NFIP had accomplished. It is available at *www.fema.org*.

The NFIP began as a voluntary program as part of a political compromise that Boggs reached with the then senator Tom Eagleton of Missouri. As a voluntary program, few communities joined. After Hurricane Camille struck the Louisiana, Alabama, and Mississippi coasts in 1969, the goals of the NFIP to protect people's financial investments and to reduce government disaster expenditures were not being met. Change would not occur until Hurricane Agnes devastated Florida in 1972.

George Bernstein, who was brought down from New York by President Nixon to run the Federal Insurance Administration (FIA) within the Department of Housing and Urban Development (HUD), proposed linking the mandatory purchase of flood insurance to all homeowner loans that were backed by federal mortgages. This change created an incentive for communities to join the NFIP because a significant portion of the home mortgage market was federally backed. This change became the Flood Insurance Act of 1972.

It is important to note how local and state governments chose to administer this flood risk program. Civil defense departments usually had the responsibility to deal with risks and disasters. Although the NFIP dealt with risk and risk avoidance, responsibilities for the NFIP were sent to local planning departments and state Departments of Natural Resources. This reaction is one illustration of the fragmented and piecemeal approach to emergency management that evolved during the 1960s and 1970s.

CRITICAL THINKING

Can you think of any positive or negative aspects of disaster-driven evolutionary changes in the United States' emergency management system? What about for changes that occur in the absence of initiating disaster events?

The Call for a National Focus on Emergency Management: the 1970s

In the 1970s, the responsibility for emergency management functions was evident in more than five federal departments and agencies, including the Department of Commerce (weather, warning, and fire protection), the General Services Administration (continuity of government, stockpiling, and federal preparedness), the Treasury Department (import investigation), the Nuclear Regulatory Commission (power plants), and HUD (flood insurance and disaster relief).

With the passage of the Disaster Relief Act of 1974, which was prompted by the previously mentioned hurricanes and the San Fernando earthquake of 1971, HUD possessed the most significant authority for natural disaster response and recovery through the NFIP under the FIA and the Federal Disaster Assistance Administration (disaster response, temporary housing, and assistance). On the military side were the Defense Civil Preparedness Agency (nuclear attack) and the U.S. Army Corps of Engineers (flood control); however, taking into account the broad range of risks and potential disasters, more than 100 federal agencies were involved in some aspect of risk and disasters.

This pattern continued down to the state and, to a lesser extent, local levels. Parallel organizations and programs added to the confusion and the turf wars that especially occurred during disaster response efforts. The states and the governors grew increasingly frustrated over this fragmentation. In the absence of one clear federal lead agency in emergency management, a group of state civil defense directors led by Lacy Suiter of Tennessee and Erie Jones of Illinois launched an effort through the National Governors Association to consolidate federal emergency management activities in one agency.

With the election of a fellow state governor, President Jimmy Carter of Georgia, the effort gained steam. President Carter came to Washington committed to streamlining all government agencies and seeking more control over key administrative processes. The state directors lobbied the National Governors Association (NGA) and Congress for a consolidation of federal emergency management functions. When the Carter administration proposed such an action, it was met with a receptive audience in the Senate. Congress already had expressed concerns about the lack of a coherent federal policy and the inability of states to know whom to turn to in the event of an emergency.

The federal agencies involved, however, were not as excited about the prospect. A fundamental law of bureaucracy is a continued desire to expand control and authority, not to lose control. In a consolidation of this sort, there would be both losers and winners. There was a question of which federal department/agency should house the new consolidated structure. As the debate continued, the newly organized National Association of State Directors of Emergency Preparedness championed the creation of a new independent organization, an idea that was quickly supported by the Senate.

In the midst of these discussions, an accident occurred at the Three Mile Island nuclear power plant in Pennsylvania, which added impetus to the consolidation effort. This accident brought national media attention to the lack of adequate off-site preparedness around commercial nuclear power plants and the role of the federal government in responding to such an event.

On June 19, 1978, President Carter transmitted to Congress the Reorganization Plan Number 3 (3 CFR 1978, 5 U.S. Code 903). The intent of this plan was to consolidate emergency preparedness, mitigation, and response activities into one federal emergency management organization. The president stated that the plan would establish the Federal Emergency Management Agency (FEMA) and that the FEMA director would report directly to the president.

Reorganization Plan Number 3 transferred to FEMA the National Fire Prevention Control Administration (Department of Commerce), the Federal Insurance Administration (HUD), the Federal Broadcast System (Executive Office of the President), the Defense Civil Preparedness Agency (Department of Defense), the Federal Disaster Assistance Administration (HUD), and the Federal Preparedness Agency (GSA). The following emergency preparedness and mitigation functions were also transferred to FEMA:

- Oversight of the Earthquake Hazards Reduction Program (Office of Science and Technology Policy)
- Coordination of dam safety (Office of Science and Technology Policy)
- Assistance to communities in the development of readiness plans for severe weather-related emergencies
- Coordination of natural and nuclear disaster warning systems

- Coordination of preparedness and planning to reduce the consequences of major terrorist incidents

Reorganization Plan Number 3 articulated the following fundamental organizational principles:

1. Federal authorities who were to anticipate, prepare for, and respond to major civil emergencies should be supervised by one official who is responsible to the president and given attention by other officials at the highest levels.
2. An effective civil defense system requires the most efficient use of all available resources.
3. Whenever possible, emergency responsibilities should be extensions of federal agencies.
4. Federal hazard mitigation activities should be closely linked with emergency preparedness and response functions.

Subsequent to congressional review and concurrence, the Federal Emergency Management Agency was officially established by Executive Order 12127 of March 31, 1979 (44 FR 19367, 3 CFR, Comp., p. 376). A second Executive Order, 12148, mandated the reassignment of agencies, programs, and personnel into the new entity, FEMA.

Creating the new organization made sense, but integrating the diverse programs, operations, policies, and people into a cohesive operation was a much bigger task than realized when the consolidation began. It would take extraordinary leadership and a common vision. The consolidation also created immediate political problems. By consolidating these programs and the legislation that created them, FEMA would have to answer to 23 committees and subcommittees in Congress with oversight of its programs. Unlike most other federal agencies, it would have no organic legislation to support its operations and no clear champions to look to during the congressional appropriations process.

In addition, President Carter had problems finding a director for this new organization. No large constituent group was identified with emergency management, and at the time the administration was facing major problems with Congress and the public because of the Iranian hostage crisis. President Carter finally reached into his own cabinet and asked John Macy, then head of the Office of Personnel Management (OPM), to become director of FEMA.

John Macy's task was to unify an organization that was not only physically separated—parts of the agency were located in five different buildings around Washington—but also philosophically separate. Programs focused on nuclear war preparations were combined with programs focused on a new consciousness of the environment and floodplain management. Macy focused his efforts by emphasizing the similarities between natural hazards preparedness and civil defense by developing a new concept called the Integrated Emergency Management System (IEMS). This system was an all-hazards approach that included direction, control, and warning as functions common to all emergencies from small, isolated events to the ultimate emergency of nuclear attack. For all his good efforts, FEMA continued to operate as individual entities pursuing their own interests and answering to their own congressional bosses. It was a period of few major disasters, so virtually nobody noticed this problem of disjointedness.

Civil Defense Reappears as Nuclear Attack Planning: the 1980s

The early and mid-1980s saw FEMA facing many challenges but no significant natural disasters. The absence of the need for a coherent federal response to disasters, as was called for by Congress when it approved the establishment of FEMA, allowed FEMA to continue to exist as an organization of many parts.

In 1982, President Reagan appointed Louis O. Giuffrida as director of FEMA. Mr. Giuffrida, a California friend of Ed Meese, who was one of the president's closest advisors, had a background in training and terrorism preparedness at the state government level. General Giuffrida proceeded to reorganize FEMA consistent with administration policies and his background. Top priority was placed on government preparedness for a nuclear attack. Resources within the agency were realigned, and additional budget authority was sought to enhance and elevate the national security responsibilities of the agency. With no real role for the states in these national security activities, the state directors who had lobbied for the creation of FEMA saw their authority and federal funding declining.

Giuffrida also angered one of the only other visible constituents of the agency: the fire services community. Giuffrida diminished the authority of the U.S. Fire Administration by making it part of FEMA's Directorate of Training and Education. The newly acquired campus at Emmitsburg, Maryland, was intended to become the preeminent National Emergency Training Center (NETC).

During Giuffrida's tenure, FEMA faced several unusual challenges that stretched its authority, including asserting FEMA into the lead role for continuity of civilian government in the aftermath of a nuclear attack, managing the federal response to the contamination at Love Canal and Times Beach, Missouri, and the Cuban refugee crisis. Although Giuffrida managed to bring the agency physically together in a new headquarters building in Washington, D.C., severe morale problems persisted.

Dislike of Giuffrida's style and questions about FEMA's operations came to the attention of U.S. Representative Al Gore of Tennessee, who then served on the House Science and Technology Committee. As the congressional hearings proceeded, the Department of Justice and a grand jury began investigations of senior political officials at FEMA. These inquiries led to the resignation of Giuffrida and top aides in response to a variety of charges, including misuse of government funds, but the shake-up marked a milestone of sorts: FEMA and emergency management had made it into the comic strip "Doonesbury."

President Reagan then selected General Julius Becton to be director of FEMA. General Becton, a retired military general and former director of the Office of Foreign Disaster Assistance in the State Department, is credited uniformly with restoring integrity to the operations and appropriations of the agency. From a policy standpoint, he continued to emphasize the programs of his predecessor, only in a less visible manner. Becton expanded the duties of FEMA when he was asked by the DOD to take over the program dealing with the off-site cleanup of chemical stockpiles on DOD bases. This program was fraught with problems, and bad feelings existed between the communities and the bases over the funds available to the communities for the cleanup. FEMA had minimal technical expertise to administer this program and was dependent on the DOD and the Army for the funding. This situation led to political problems for the agency and did not lead to significant advancements in local emergency management operations, as promised by the DOD.

At one point in his tenure, General Becton ranked the programs in FEMA by level of importance. Of the more than 20 major programs, the earthquake, hurricane, and flood programs ranked near the bottom. This priority seems logical based on the absence of any significant natural hazards, but this situation is noteworthy in the context that it continued the pattern of isolating resources for national security priorities without recognizing the potential of a major natural disaster.

This issue was raised by then senator Al Gore in hearings on FEMA's responsibilities as lead agency for the National Earthquake Hazards Reduction Program (NEHRP). Senator Gore, reacting to a scientific report that up to 200,000 casualties could result from an earthquake on the New Madrid fault, believed that FEMA's priorities were misplaced. The legislation that created the NEHRP called on FEMA to develop a plan for how the federal government would respond to a catastrophic earthquake. This Federal Response Plan would later become the standard for all of the federal agencies' response operations. Senator Gore concluded that FEMA needed to spend more time working with its federal, state, and local partners on natural hazards planning.

An Agency in Trouble: 1989–1992

As Congress debated, and finally passed, major reform of federal disaster policy as part of the Stewart McKinney–Robert Stafford Act, FEMA's potential and its ability to support a national emergency management system remained in doubt. As the 1980s closed, FEMA was an agency in trouble. It suffered from severe morale problems, disparate leadership, and conflicts with its partners at the state and local levels over agency spending and priorities.

With a new administration in place, President George H.W. Bush named Wallace Stickney as director of FEMA. Mr. Stickney was from New Hampshire and was a friend of John Sununu, who was Bush's chief of staff. Mr. Stickney came to the director's position having been a staff person at the New England Regional Office of the Environmental Protection Agency and as a volunteer firefighter. His emergency management credentials were minimal, and his selection was poorly received by many of the state directors. At the same time, the political appointees who were named to FEMA's regional director positions—the first line of FEMA's response system—were equally lacking in emergency management experience. These appointments would prove to have dire consequences for both FEMA and the American public.

In 1989, two devastating natural disasters called the continued existence of FEMA into question. In September, Hurricane Hugo slammed into North Carolina and South Carolina after first hitting Puerto Rico and the Virgin Islands. It was the worst hurricane in a decade, with more than $15 billion in damages and 85 deaths. FEMA was slow to respond, waiting for the process to work and for the governors to decide what to do. Less than a month later, the Bay Area of California was rocked by the Loma Prieta earthquake as the 1989 World Series got under way in Oakland Stadium. FEMA was not prepared to deal with the catastrophe.

A few years later, FEMA was not so lucky. In August 1992, Hurricane Andrew struck Florida and Louisiana, and Hurricane Iniki struck Hawaii only a few weeks later. Again, FEMA wasn't ready, but with Hurricane Andrew, it was not only FEMA that failed the people of Florida, but the process and the system as well. Starting with Hurricane Hugo, public concern over natural disasters was high. People wanted, and expected, their government to be there to help in their time of need. FEMA seemed incapable of carrying out the essential government function of emergency management.

In the aftermath of Hurricanes Andrew and Iniki, there were calls for abolishing FEMA. But the incoming Clinton administration realized how important an effective response and quick recovery were to communities and to voters and was determined to fix the emergency management system.

The Witt Revolution: 1993–2001

When President Clinton nominated James Lee Witt to be director of FEMA, Witt breathed new life into FEMA and brought a new style of leadership to the troubled agency. Witt was the first director of FEMA with emergency management experience. He was from the constituency who had played a major role in creating FEMA but had been forgotten: the state directors. With Witt, President Clinton had credibility and, more important, a skilled politician who knew the importance of building partnerships and serving customers.

Witt came in with a mandate to restore the trust of the American people that their government would be there for them during times of crisis. He initiated sweeping reforms inside and outside the agency. Inside FEMA, he reached out to all employees, implemented customer service training, and reorganized the agency to break down bottlenecks. He supported the application of new technologies to the delivery of disaster services and focused on mitigation and risk avoidance. Outside the agency, he strengthened the relationships with state and local emergency managers and built new ones with Congress, within the administration, and with the media. Open communications, both internally and externally, were the hallmarks of the Witt years at FEMA.

Witt's leadership and the changes he made were quickly tested as the nation experienced an unprecedented series of natural disasters. The Midwest floods in 1993 resulted in major disaster declarations in nine states. FEMA's successful response to these floods brought the opportunity to change the focus of postdisaster recovery by initiating the largest voluntary buyout and relocation program to date in an effort to move people out of the floodplain and out of harm's way.

The Northridge, California, earthquake quickly followed the Midwest floods in 1994. Northridge tested all of the new streamlined approaches and technology advancements for delivery of services and created some more. Throughout the next several years, FEMA and its state and local partners would face every possible natural hazard, including killer tornadoes, ice storms, hurricanes, floods, wildfires, and drought.

When President Clinton made Witt a member of his cabinet, the value and importance of emergency management was recognized. Witt used this promotion as an opportunity to lobby the nation's governors to include their state emergency management directors in their cabinets.

The Oklahoma City bombing in April 1995 represented a new phase in the evolution of emergency management. This event, following the first bombing of the World Trade Center in New York City in 1992, raised the issue of America's preparedness for terrorism events. Because emergency management responsibilities are defined by risks and the consequences of those risks, responding to terrorist threats was included. The Oklahoma City bombing tested this thesis and set the stage for interagency disagreements over which agency would be in charge of terrorism.

While this debate continued, FEMA took an important step in its commitment to disaster mitigation by launching a national initiative to promote a new community-based approach called Project Impact: Building Disaster-Resistant Communities. This project was designed to mainstream emergency management and mitigation practices into every community in America. It went back to the roots of emergency management. It asked a community to identify risks and establish a plan to reduce those risks. It asked communities to establish partnerships that included all of the stakeholders in the community, including, for the first time, the business sector.

ADDITIONAL RESEARCH

"Project Impact Initiative to Create Disaster Resistant Communities Demonstrates Worth in Kansas Years Later" (*www.emergencymgmt.com/disaster/ProjectImpact-Initiative-to.html*). This article documents how preventive measures, taken by communities in Kansas as part of the Project Impact program, saved lives years later when devastating tornadoes struck across Kansas.

By building a disaster-resistant community, the community would promote sustainable economic development, protect and enhance its natural resources, and ensure a better quality of life for its citizens. Figure 1-1 shows the effects of mitigation during Hurricane Ike. As the decade came to an end, FEMA was still recognized as the preeminent emergency management system in the world. It was adopted in other countries, and Witt became an ambassador for emergency management overseas.

FIGURE 1-1 Gilchrist, Texas, August 16, 2009. These stilt homes were the only structures still standing in the town of Gilchrist after Hurricane Ike destroyed it. FEMA is still working with local, state, and federal agencies to rebuild the town.
Photo by Patsy Lynch/FEMA.

Terrorism: 2001

With the election of George W. Bush, a new FEMA director, Joe Allbaugh, was named to head the agency. As a former chief of staff to Bush when he was governor of Texas and Bush's campaign manager in the 2000 presidential race, Allbaugh had a close personal relationship with the president. As demonstrated by Witt and Clinton, this was viewed as a positive for the agency. His lack of emergency management background was not an issue during his confirmation hearings.

Allbaugh got off to a rocky start when the administration decided to eliminate funding for the popular Project Impact. Immediately after this decision was announced, the 6.8 magnitude Nisqually earthquake shook Seattle, Washington. Seattle happened to be one of the most successful Project Impact communities. The mayor of Seattle appeared on national television and gave Project Impact credit for the minimal damage from the quake. When then vice president Dick Cheney was asked why the program was being eliminated, he responded that there had been doubts about its effectiveness. As FEMA's budget proceeded through the appropriations process, Congress put funding back into Project Impact.

As part of the major reorganization of the agency, Allbaugh recreated the Office of National Preparedness (ONP). This office was first established in the 1980s during the Giuffrida reign for planning for World War III and had been eliminated by Witt in 1992. This action raised some concerns among FEMA's constituents and FEMA staff. However, this time the mission of the office was focused on terrorism.

As the events of September 11, 2001, unfolded, FEMA activated the Federal Response Plan, and response operations proceeded as expected in New York and Virginia.

The strength of the U.S. emergency management system was proven, however, as hundreds of response personnel initiated their operations within just minutes of the onset of events.

The Department of Homeland Security: 2001–2005

Almost immediately after the terrorist attacks on the World Trade Center, the president created by executive order the Office of Homeland Security within the White House. The same day that announcement was made, Tom Ridge, the governor of Pennsylvania, was sworn in to lead the office with the title Assistant to the President.

In March 2002, President Bush signed Homeland Security Presidential Directive-3 (HSPD-3), which stated the following:

> *The Nation requires a Homeland Security Advisory System to provide a comprehensive and effective means to disseminate information regarding the risk of terrorist acts to federal, state, and local authorities and to the American people. Such a system would provide warnings in the form of a set of graduated "threat conditions" that would increase as the risk of the threat increases. At each threat condition, federal departments and agencies would implement a corresponding set of "protective measures" to further reduce vulnerability or increase response capability during a period of heightened alert.*
>
> *This system is intended to create a common vocabulary, context, and structure for an ongoing national discussion about the nature of the threats that confront the homeland and the appropriate measures that should be taken in response. It seeks to inform and facilitate decisions appropriate to different levels of government and to private citizens at home and at work.*

What resulted was the widely recognizable five-color Homeland Security Advisory System code. On November 25, 2002, President Bush signed into law the Homeland Security Act of 2002 (HS Act) (Public Law 107-296) and announced that Tom Ridge would be appointed secretary of a new Department of Homeland Security (DHS) to be created through this legislation. This act, which authorized the greatest federal government reorganization since President Harry Truman joined the various branches of the armed forces under the Department of Defense, was charged with a threefold mission of protecting the United States from further terrorist attacks, reducing the nation's vulnerability to terrorism, and minimizing the damage from potential terrorist attacks and natural disasters.

The sweeping reorganization into the new department, which officially opened its doors on January 24, 2003, joined together over 179,000 federal employees from 22 existing federal agencies under a single, cabinet-level organization. The creation of DHS was the culmination of an evolutionary legislative process that began largely in response to criticism that increased federal intelligence interagency cooperation could have prevented the September 11 terrorist attacks. The White House and Congress both had recognized that a

Homeland Security czar would require both a staff and a large budget in order to succeed, and thus began deliberations to create a new cabinet-level department that would fuse many of the security-related agencies dispersed throughout the federal government.

For several months during the second half of 2002, Congress jockeyed between different versions of the Homeland Security bill in an effort to establish legislation that was passable yet effective. Efforts to incorporate many of the intelligence-gathering and investigative law enforcement agencies—the National Security Agency (NSA), the Federal Bureau of Investigation (FBI), and the Central Intelligence Agency (CIA)—into the legislation failed.

Despite these delays and setbacks, after the 2002 midterm elections, the Republican seats gained in both the House and Senate gave the president the leverage he needed to pass the bill without further deliberation (H.R., 299-121 on November 13, 2002; Senate, 90-9 on November 19, 2002). Although the passage of this act represented a significant milestone, the implementation phase presented a tremendous challenge—a concern expressed by several leaders from the agencies that were to be absorbed. On November 25, 2002, President Bush submitted his Reorganization Plan (as required by the legislation), which mapped out the schedule, methodology, and budget for the monumental task.

Although a handful of these agencies remained intact after the consolidation, most were fully incorporated into one of four new directorates: Border and Transportation Security (BTS), Information Analysis and Infrastructure Protection (IAIP), Emergency Preparedness and Response (EP&R), and Science and Technology (S&T). A fifth directorate, Management, incorporated parts of the existing administrative and support offices within the merged agencies. Secretary Ridge was given exactly one year to develop a comprehensive structural framework for DHS and to name new leadership for all five directorates and other offices created under the legislation.

In addition to the creation of the Department of Homeland Security, the HS Act made several changes to other federal agencies and their programs and created several new programs. On March 1, 2003, Joe Allbaugh, in a memo to FEMA staff, announced that he was resigning as FEMA director. Michael Brown, formerly general counsel to FEMA and acting deputy director, was named as the acting director of FEMA within the DHS Emergency Preparedness and Response directorate. Mike Brown came to FEMA because of his long, personal friendship with Allbaugh. His academic training was in law, and prior to coming to FEMA he had been the executive director of the Arabian Horse Association based in Colorado.

With the DHS establishment moving forward, in 2004 FEMA was faced with four major hurricanes that assaulted Florida. Because of that election year's overall political nature, and with Florida being regarded as key in deciding the outcome of the presidential election (as well as the fact that the president's brother Jeb was the governor of Florida), a great deal of effort was expended to ensure that the federal response to the hurricanes was efficient and effective. However, everyone was well aware that Florida had one of the most effective state emergency management systems in the country and that it was actually "calling the shots."

ADDITIONAL RESEARCH

DHS Office of the Inspector General, 2005. Audit of FEMA's Individuals and Households Program in Miami-Dade County, Florida, for Hurricane Frances. *http://www.dhs.gov/xoig/assets/mgmtrpts/OIG_05-20_May05.pdf*

One of the many issues that arose in the aftermath of the hurricanes was the allegation of widespread fraud in the handling of people receiving aid from FEMA even when they had suffered no damages to or loss of their homes. The DHS inspector general, an independent oversight group that investigates government waste, fraud, and abuse of federal programs, investigated the allegations, and this report summarizes their findings.

On November 30, 2004, Ridge announced his resignation. On February 16, 2005, Michael Chertoff was unanimously confirmed by the Senate to lead the Department of Homeland Security. On July 13, 2005, Michael Chertoff released a six-point agenda that would be used to guide a reorganization of the department aimed at streamlining its efforts. According to the six-point agenda, the following changes were to be made:

- Increase overall preparedness, particularly for catastrophic events
- Create better transportation security systems to move people and cargo more securely and efficiently
- Strengthen border security and interior enforcement and reform immigration processes
- Enhance information sharing (with partners)
- Improve financial management, human resource development, procurement, and information technology within the department
- Realign the department's organization to maximize mission performance

As part of the proposed reorganization, virtually all of the remaining preparedness capabilities in FEMA, including the U.S. Fire Administration, were moved to the new Office of Preparedness. The exception was the Emergency Management Institute (EMI). Although the EMI training function was always considered part of preparedness, the senior-level FEMA officials argued that its courses supported response and recovery. A new FEMA office was to focus exclusively on response and recovery.

Under the initial DHS organization (Figure 1-2), the Emergency Preparedness and Response directorate contained most of the pre-DHS FEMA functions and staff. Under the Chertoff reorganization, EP&R was eliminated, and the director of FEMA, who was formerly the undersecretary for EP&R, would become an office director. The reorganization was somewhat unclear regarding who would be in charge in a disaster, since the responsibility for the new National Incident Management System (NIMS) was actually vested in the director of Operations Coordination.

Under the Chertoff reorganization, the structure of federal emergency management and disaster assistance functions was returned to pre-FEMA status. The responsibilities

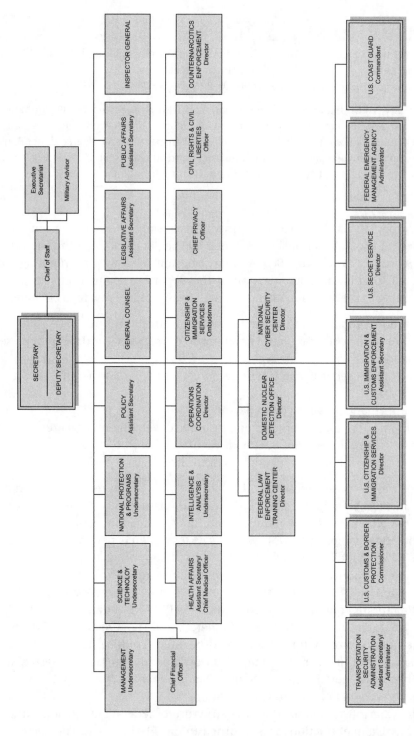

FIGURE 1-2 DHS organizational chart.

and capabilities for mitigation, preparedness, response, and recovery would now be spread out among several entities within the Department of Homeland Security. Policy decisions were exercised to focus most of the human and financial resources on catastrophic threats of bioterrorism and terrorism.

The situation at the time was very similar to the one that existed prior to the creation of FEMA in 1979. Federal emergency management and disaster assistance capabilities were located in numerous federal departments and agencies scattered across the federal government and in the White House. This time, however, instead of being scattered across the federal government, they were scattered within the fledgling Department of Homeland Security. Before this reorganization, FEMA programs were constantly being tasked and taxed to provide financial and human resources to support higher-priority programs in DHS. By taking apart the core programs of FEMA, it became even easier to reassign its resources and diminish its mission within DHS.

The Hurricane Katrina Debacle: 2005

As Secretary Chertoff proceeded with his reorganization, scientists like Max Mayfield (the director of the National Hurricane Center) predicted another active hurricane season. As always, the greatest fear was that a major storm would hit the Gulf Coast, particularly low-lying New Orleans.

Under James Lee Witt, a Category 5 hurricane impacting New Orleans was considered one of the three possible worst-case disaster scenarios. In fact, since the 1980s, FEMA funds had been used to contract multiple evacuation studies of the New Orleans area. In 1995, a national exercise of the Federal Response Plan entitled "Response 95" used a New Orleans hurricane scenario. This particular exercise was never completed because on the first day of play, a major flood event impacted the Gulf Coast (including the site of the exercise play, New Orleans) and abruptly ended the exercise.

Another disaster exercise termed "Hurricane Pam" was convened and completed in July 2004 with appropriate follow-up requirements to correct the problems and deficiencies discovered during the previous exercise. Unfortunately, the funding to support these corrective actions, which had been adequately budgeted by FEMA, became part of a funding reallocation requested of FEMA by DHS management to support other DHS priorities.

The "Senate Report on Katrina" best describes what occurred during those fateful hours and days in late August. The specific danger Katrina posed to the Gulf Coast became clear on the afternoon of Friday, August 26, when forecasters at the National Hurricane Center and the National Weather Service saw that the storm was turning west. Phone calls were immediately made to Louisiana emergency management officials, and in their 5 p.m. EDT Katrina forecast and accompanying briefings, the meteorologists alerted both Louisiana and Mississippi that the track of the storm was expected to shift significantly to the west of its original track to the Florida panhandle. The National Hurricane Center warned that Katrina could be a Category 4 or even 5 by landfall. By the next morning, Weather Service officials confirmed that New Orleans was squarely at risk.

Over the weekend, the drumbeat of warnings continued. FEMA held videoteleconferences on both days, discussing the potential dangers of Katrina and especially the risks to New Orleans. Max Mayfield of the Hurricane Center called the governors of the affected states, something he had only done once before in his 33-year career, and President Bush took the unusual step of declaring a disaster in advance of an emergency event for the states in the projected impact zone.

Hurricane Katrina made landfall in Buras, Louisiana, on Monday, August 25, 2005. At the time it was reported as a Category 4 storm when it made landfall. The National Hurricane Center would later downgrade it to a Category 3 storm. In any event, it was considered an extremely dangerous storm by weather forecasters and the National Hurricane Center. It impacted a broad geographic area stretching from Alabama to coastal Mississippi and southeast Louisiana, an estimated 90,000 square miles. In May 2006, the death toll from the storm was 1,856, with another 705 individuals listed as missing (Figure 1-3).

The storm impacted over 1.5 million people and displaced more than 800,000 citizens. The U.S. Coast Guard rescued over 24,273 people, and FEMA search and rescue teams rescued nearly 6,600 persons. Federal government disaster relief expenses are expected to exceed $100 billion, and the insurance losses are expected to exceed $35 billion. The National Flood Insurance Program paid more than $16.1 million to over 205,000 people who filed claims related to Katrina. Forty-four states and the District of Columbia received emergency declarations to cover their expenses for sheltering millions of evacuees who had to be transported out of the Gulf.

FIGURE 1-3 New Orleans, Louisiana, on September 18, 2005. This shows the damages to homes and property in the lower ninth ward due to Hurricane Katrina. The markings on these houses were made by the search and rescue teams who looked for survivors after the storm. Searchers wrote the date the house was searched, the time, which search party was involved, any survivors found, and any animals that were still in the house. From Andrea Booher/FEMA.

By any account, Hurricane Katrina was a massive storm, deadly and destructive. It served to expose severe cracks in the nation's emergency management system and its ability to respond to a catastrophic event. Government after-action reports, which are done after most disasters, and media accounts have judged the response a failure, and the recovery phase is considered to show the same level of incompetence. Changes that had been made to Louisiana's coastal landscape, particularly the loss of wetlands and increased channelization, made New Orleans and the Louisiana coast more vulnerable to hurricanes. Design and construction decisions on the levee system and inadequate maintenance of that system contributed to the impacts of Katrina.

The storm challenged the capacities and capabilities of emergency management operations at all levels of government. The lack of planning for the Superdome as the designated shelter of last resort for New Orleans and the subsequent problems that occurred in that facility provided the most visible demonstration of the failed capacities. Many of the problems of the immediate response exposed the impacts of priority focus on terrorism and homeland security in recent years and may have contributed to the decrease in these capacities and capabilities.

Elected officials at all levels of government stumbled badly as they tried to provide leadership in the face of this disaster. The business community, voluntary agencies, and nongovernmental organizations (NGOs) stepped up to provide extraordinary services to storm victims. The general public, corporations, unions, and foundations donated billions of dollars for disaster relief.

Despite the understanding of the Gulf Coast's particular vulnerability to hurricane devastation, officials braced for Katrina with full awareness of critical deficiencies in their plans and gaping holes in their resources. While Katrina's destructive force could not be denied, state and local officials did not marshal enough of the resources at their disposal. Adding to these shortfalls, years of inadequate funding of federal, state, and local emergency functions left them incapable of fully carrying out their missions to protect the public and care for victims.

ADDITIONAL RESEARCH

In the aftermath of Katrina, both houses of Congress held extensive hearings on what went wrong. The Senate report, "The Senate Committee on Homeland Security and Governmental Affairs. 2006. Hurricane Katrina: A Nation Still Unprepared," provides insight into the results of the hearings and deliberations.

http://hsgac.senate.gov/_files/Katrina/ExecSum.pdf

More than 1,800 people died from Hurricane Katrina, and tens of thousands were displaced and suffered for days in places like the Superdome, on freeway ramps, and on tops of roofs while waiting to be rescued. Thousands lost their homes and were separated from loved ones. The dislocation, chaos, and desperation that lingered for months after the storm were direct results of the failure of government at all levels to plan, prepare for, and respond aggressively to the storm. Failure can be assessed at all levels, but when

President Bush signed the federal declaration of disaster and announced it *before* Katrina even made landfall, the federal government, through DHS/FEMA, assumed the primary responsibility for the stewardship of the response to this storm's aftermath. And by any objective evaluation of the response, it was a colossal failure.

The Steps Leading to the Katrina Debacle

In many respects, FEMA's failures after Katrina were a predictable outgrowth of steps that were taken in the aftermath of September 11. FEMA lost its status as an independent agency—and its direct access to the president—when it was absorbed into the newly created Department of Homeland Security (DHS). The director of FEMA was no longer on the same level as the cabinet secretaries whom FEMA had to task and direct during disasters. At the state level, many states created their own offices of homeland security that subsumed emergency management or were competitive structures, further complicating emergency response organization.

FEMA personnel and funds, including money for preparedness and mitigation intended for state and local agencies, were redistributed to support other higher priorities within DHS. The result of these actions was that the agency was even further hollowed out. The federal response plan was restructured into the National Response Plan to accommodate the new DHS arrangements and the operational oversight role of the department's secretary. A new level of bureaucracy was added with the creation of the principal federal officer (PFO) as the new coordinator in a disaster. Where previously the director of FEMA had maintained a clear line of authority and accountability, the existence of a new PFO created confusion over who would be in charge in a disaster. As a result, the necessary civilian and military assets were not deployed to facilitate the evacuations and provide supplies to the evacuation shelters before Katrina hit.

FEMA also failed to work with the governors on how to use the National Guard. Another factor in the post-Katrina fiasco was the dramatic post-9/11 change from a focus on "all-hazards" management—in which responders prepare for calamities according to plans that apply regardless of their precise nature—to a focus on terrorism that led to significantly weakened national capabilities. At all levels of government, approximately 75 percent of available resources for emergency management activities were applied to terrorism. Preparing, mitigating, or responding to natural disasters like floods, tornadoes, or hurricanes was subordinated to a narrow, if understandable, focus on terrorism. That reprioritization depleted the capabilities to respond to disasters at all levels of government.

Post-Katrina Changes

In the rush to examine and investigate what went wrong and to take corrective actions, both the House of Representatives and the Senate engaged in extensive hearings and investigations. The White House dispatched Frances Townsend, assistant to the president

---

ADDITIONAL RESEARCH

The Bush administration's report, "The Federal Response to Hurricane Katrina: Lessons Learned," was released in February 2006. It was a weighty document and included 125 recommendations and 11 critical actions that needed to be completed by June 1, the start of the 2006 hurricane season. Most of its recommendations have still not been implemented, but it remains a unique assessment of the federal government's role in disaster relief as far as the Bush administration was concerned.

---

for Homeland Security, to conduct a thorough review of what went wrong and to generate corrective recommendations.

These organizational and leadership issues were not easily swept under the rug. Senators Clinton and Mikulski introduced legislation to restore FEMA to its independent status and make the director's position a cabinet post. This legislation went nowhere. Powerful forces on the Senate Committee on Homeland Security blocked these efforts, particularly Senator Joe Lieberman, who had been instrumental in the DHS's creation and clearly did not want his creation tampered with. Lieberman was joined by Republican Committee Chair Susan Collins, who would not even consider moving FEMA out.

The 109th Congress, in response to hearings and reports, passed legislation that revised federal emergency management policies that vested more power in the president, reorganized FEMA, and enhanced and clarified the mission, functions, and authorities of both the agency and its parent organization, DHS.

Six statutes enacted by the 109th Congress are notable in that they contain changes that apply to future federal emergency management actions. These public laws include the following:

- The Post-Katrina Emergency Management Reform Act of 2006
- The Security and Accountability for Every Port Act of 2005, known as the SAFE Port Act
- The Pets Evacuation and Transportation Standards Act of 2006
- The Federal Judiciary Emergency Special Sessions Act of 2005
- The Student Grant Hurricane and Disaster Relief Act
- The John Warner National Defense Authorization Act for Fiscal Year 2007

Most of these statutes contain relatively few actual changes to federal authorities related to emergencies and disasters. The Post-Katrina Emergency Management Reform Act of 2006 (commonly known as PKEMRA), however, contains many changes that have long-term consequences for FEMA and other federal entities. That statute reorganizes FEMA, expands its statutory authority, and imposes new conditions and requirements on the operations of the agency. In addition to the public laws just listed, Congress enacted supplemental appropriations, one-time waivers of requirements, and temporary extensions solely associated with Hurricanes Katrina, Rita, and Wilma.

ADDITIONAL RESEARCH

The Congressional Research Service's publication "Federal Emergency Management Policy Changes after Hurricane Katrina—A Summary of Statutory Provisions" is an excellent report that identifies the requirements and changes for FEMA, DHS, and federal emergency management policies and programs under PKEMRA.

http://www.fas.org/sgp/crs/homesec/RL33729.pdf

In summary, PKEMRA requires that DHS reconsolidate all of the emergency management functions (including preparedness) into FEMA, elevates the status of FEMA within the department, protects the FEMA assets from reassignment within DHS, and gives FEMA enhanced organizational autonomy. In addition, the act provides for FEMA to maintain ten regional offices. It adds to FEMA a National Advisory Council, Regional Advisory Councils, a disability coordinator, a small state and rural advocate, and regional strike teams. They provide autonomy for the FEMA administrator (formerly director) to communicate directly with Congress.

After Mike Brown resigned (or was terminated), David Paulison became FEMA administrator. Paulison had served as U.S. Fire Administrator and had a long and distinguished career in the fire service in Florida. His elevation to the top position was well received by the fire service constituencies, who had long felt that they had not received their due within FEMA and the emergency management community. Harve Johnson, a former admiral in the Coast Guard, was appointed deputy administrator.

The new leadership came with the firm mandate to prevent another Katrina. To do so, FEMA leadership took a very different approach to the emergency management partnership with both state and locals. FEMA instituted the "new FEMA"—a top-down approach in which federal requirements for response planning and operations were imposed on state and local emergency management operations as a condition of receiving federal resources.

The Integrated Planning System that was created included different planning parameters than those used by state and local emergency planners in their certifications. State and local compliance with the National Information Management System (NIMS) was made a condition for continued funding. The old system in which the federal government supplemented state and local efforts and worked in partnership was replaced by a system where in a major disaster the federal government took charge and supplanted state and local authorities. To support this change, FEMA was able to substantially increase its staff in both its headquarters and the regions, and many of the new senior managers who were hired came from organizations such as the Coast Guard and the military, where federal supremacy and authority were the normal operational parameters.

At the direction of DHS leadership, at the federal level, FEMA concentrated on remaking the National Response Plan into a National Response Framework (NRF) that blurred the lines of responsibility among the federal partners in responding to disasters. Under the new NRF, DHS/FEMA assumed many more responsibilities such as acting as the lead federal agency for Mass Care, an Emergency Support Function (ESF) previously led by the American Red Cross (ARC). On the other hand, DHS/FEMA used the PKEMRA requirements to deflect problem areas such as postdisaster housings.

PKEMRA called for a new strategy for disaster housing, and FEMA engaged other federal agencies, specifically the Department of Housing and Urban Development (HUD), in development of this strategy and taking on a major role in providing postdisaster housing. This change in responsibility was piloted during the Texas disasters of 2008 to mixed results. A more complete discussion of this follows in later chapters of the text. Although the new FEMA was never really tested, problems persisted. Major portions of the Katrina recovery continued to languish, especially in New Orleans, the morale in FEMA was at an all-time low, and a federal, state, and local partnership on emergency management still did not exist.

CRITICAL THINKING

What do you think could have been done in the years preceding hurricane Katrina to better prepare the states to deal with this kind of event? Do you think that this event was so large that only a federal response could have managed it? Explain your answer.

The Future Environment of Emergency Management

Emergency management issues did not play a prominent role in the presidential election of 2008. The issue of the failed response to Katrina and the slow recovery were certainly a part of the campaign dialogue, and both presidential nominees visited New Orleans and vowed to speed up the recovery. Barack Obama's election represented a change from the past, including a change for emergency management. Although Obama's administration discussed removing FEMA from DHS and returning it to its former position as an independent agency, this was not to be. Janet Napolitano, secretary of DHS, strongly believed that FEMA was an essential part of DHS. She was committed to finding the right administrator for FEMA and chose W. Craig Fugate, former state director of Emergency Management from Florida (Figure 1-4). Fugate brought excellent credentials and extensive operational experience to the position. Florida was one of the premier state emergency management organizations in the United States, and although Fugate had been a strong proponent of moving FEMA out of DHS, he accepted the position and was easily confirmed by the Senate.

At his confirmation hearing and in subsequent speeches, Fugate has said that he wants to make a culture of preparedness—especially personal preparedness—a hallmark of his FEMA tenure. As a result, he has changed the vocabulary of disasters, referring to individuals impacted by disasters as "survivors" instead of "victims."

His team includes several veterans of the 1990s Witt years, and he strongly supports rebuilding the partnership with state and local emergency management organizations.

FIGURE 1-4 Washington, D.C., August 10, 2009. FEMA administrator W. Craig Fugate makes opening remarks at the 2009 Conference on Community Preparedness in Arlington, Virginia. FEMA/Bill Koplitz.

His ability to rebuild FEMA into a strong, well-managed, and responsive organization, however, has yet to be determined. The 2009 hurricane season was one of the calmest in decades, and the H1N1 flu outbreak was addressed, so Fugate's agency has not yet responded to a major disaster. The recent reorganization seems to indicate a consolidation of the response-and-recovery functions under a single directorate led by Bill Carwile, an ex–federal coordinating officer with substantial response experience.

Yet, questions remain about Fugate's strategic vision for the agency. Although a strong supporter of mitigation while in Florida, the political head of the mitigation division remains unfilled a year after the presidential election, and Fugate has expressed concerns about the NFIP, whose floodplain management requirements in exchange for subsidized insurance coverage remain a primary implementing program for community mitigation.

FEMA's future role in disaster housing and long-term recovery is also cloudy. FEMA initiated activities to develop a national disaster recovery framework to complement the national response framework and to support the requirements of PKEMRA. At the same time, the White House established a White House Working Group on Recovery, with a report due to the president in early 2011. The White House Working Group is cochaired by the secretaries of DHS and HUD. If one wanted to speculate, it would be easy to see that certain, if not all, recovery programs may be moving over to HUD sometime in the future. This is an interesting turn, since many of these programs were taken out of HUD because they couldn't execute them and didn't have the connections at the state level to make them work.

Another factor that will influence the Fugate term as administrator is the continuing question of the role of the military, particularly the Northern Command (NORTHCOM), in future disasters. NORTHCOM is actively working with, and in some cases supplying

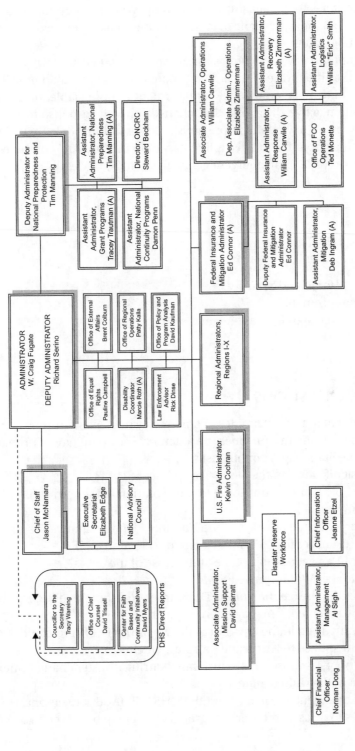

FIGURE 1-5 FEMA organizational chart.

personnel to, the states to do catastrophic planning. Whether they are looking to support disaster in other than the typical role of logistical support as performed by the Army Corps of Engineers is still in question.

In the last chapter, we will explore historical context and what recent actions and policies may suggest for the future of emergency management. The chapter will discuss possible trends that may make emergency management a more viable, proactive discipline as opposed to the reactive discipline that changes only in response to major events or disasters. Finally, as we have done in previous editions of this book, we will speculate on what the future may hold for the discipline based on the authors' combined experience of over 100 years of working in emergency management.

Important Terms

Civil defense
Department of Homeland Security
Emergency management
Federal Emergency Management Agency

Self-Check Questions

1. What are some of the first examples of emergency management?
2. According to the Constitution, does the federal government have a primary or secondary role in managing public risks?
3. What is the significance of the Flood Control Act of 1934?
4. How did the Cold War era contribute to the evolution of modern emergency management?
5. What disaster led to the creation of the National Flood Insurance Program?
6. Describe the events of the 1970s that led to the creation of FEMA.
7. Why was FEMA an agency in trouble at the close of the 1980s?
8. How did James Lee Witt improve FEMA?
9. What changes did the creation of the Department of Homeland Security bring about for the federal emergency management capacity?
10. List the steps involved in the creation of the Department of Homeland Security.
11. Why was the response to Hurricane Katrina so ineffective?
12. How did the poor response to the Hurricane Katrina disaster change emergency management in the United States?
13. What area of emergency management did DHS/FEMA seek to emphasize in 2009?
14. What changes to disaster recovery programs were being proposed in 2009?

Out-of-Class Exercise

Investigate how civil defense and emergency management evolved in your state or city. Look at such factors as when it was created, its original purpose, and what it accomplished. Find out how this organization changed following the creation of FEMA. Find out who your local or state emergency manager is, and where he/she falls within the organizational diagram of your municipal or state leadership. Is there an online profile or biography for this person? If so, what emergency management experience does he/she have that makes him/her qualified for the job?

2

Natural and Technological Hazards and Risk Assessment

What You Will Learn

- The range of natural hazards that affect the United States
- Scales and systems used to measure the magnitude of hazards and disasters
- Technological hazards and their causes and effects
- The terrorist threat, including weapons of mass destruction
- How hazard risks are assessed
- Social and economic risk factors and how they influence a community's risk profile

Introduction

A *hazard* is defined as a "source of danger that may or may not lead to an emergency or disaster" (National Governors Association, 1982), and it is named after the emergency/ disaster that could be so precipitated. Each hazard carries an associated *risk*, which is represented by the likelihood of the hazard leading to an actual disaster event and the consequences of that event should it occur. The product of realized hazard risk is an emergency event, which is typically characterized as a situation exhibiting negative consequences that require the efforts of one or more of the emergency services (fire, police, EMS, public health, or others) to manage. When the response requirements of an emergency event exceed the capabilities of those established emergency services in one or more critical areas (e.g., shelter, fire suppression, mass care), the event is classified as a *disaster*.

Hazard identification is the foundation of all emergency management activities. When hazards react with the human or built environments, their associated likelihood and consequence risk factors can be assessed. Knowledge about the risk posed by identified hazards becomes the basis of preparedness planning and mitigation actions. And it is the realization of risk, such as what occurs when an earthquake, tornado, flood, or other hazard event is experienced, that emergency response and recovery capabilities and resources are called upon. In modern emergency management, all activities are predicated on the accurate and effective identification and assessment of hazards and risks.

This chapter discusses the full range of existing hazards, both natural and technological, and the methods by which associated hazard risk may be assessed. For each hazard, a brief description of the hazard and its effects is provided, as well as information on hazard detection and classification.

Natural Hazards

Natural hazards are those that exist in the natural environment as a result of hydrological, meteorological, seismic, geologic, volcanic, mass-movement, or other natural processes, and that pose a threat to human populations and communities. Natural hazards are often intensified in scope and scale by human activities, including development and modification of the landscape and atmosphere. For example, the construction of communities in the floodplain or on barrier islands almost always increases risk associated with hurricane-force winds, flooding, and storm surge. When structures are constructed on or around seismic faults, the likelihood that they will be destroyed in a future earthquake event is greatly increased. Through better understanding of natural hazards, and the processes by which they affect the human and built environments, societies can better plan for these stressors and reduce vulnerability (Chapter 3 examines how humans can better live with hazards).

Floods

A flood is an overabundance of water that engulfs dry land and property that is normally dry. Floods may be caused by a number of factors, including heavy rainfall, melting snow, an obstruction of a natural waterway, and other generative factors. Floods usually occur from large-scale weather systems generating prolonged rainfall or onshore winds, but they may also result from locally intense thunderstorms, snowmelt, ice jams, and dam failures. Floods are capable of undermining buildings and bridges, eroding shorelines and riverbanks, tearing out trees, washing out access routes, and causing loss of life and injuries. Flash floods usually result from intense storms dropping large amounts of rain within a brief period, occur with little or no warning, and can reach full peak in only a few minutes (Figure 2-1).

Floods are the most frequent and widespread disaster in many countries around the world, including the United States, due to the prevalence of human development in the floodplain. The close relationship between societies and water is the result of commerce (the transportation of goods has most commonly been conducted by water), agriculture, and access to drinking water. The adverse implication of this relationship has been a global increase in exposure to flood events. FEMA estimates that approximately 8 to 10 million households are at risk from flooding in the United States alone, which sustain an average of $2 billion to $3 billion in losses each year. Flood losses paid by FEMA's National Flood Insurance Program in the 1990s totaled in the billions of dollars (Table 2-1).

FIGURE 2-1 Georgia, September 22, 2009. Floodwaters covered parts of roller coasters at the Six Flags Over Georgia amusement park following heavy rain on September 20–21.
Photo by Bruce Kinney.

Table 2-1 Top Ten U.S. Flood Disasters, 1900–2009 (by Total Cost of National Flood Insurance Program Losses Paid)

Event	Date	Number of Paid Losses	Amount of Paid Losses
Hurricane Katrina	August 2005	166,792	$16,075,081,110
Hurricane Ike	September 2008	45,244	$2,468,281,985
Hurricane Ivan	September 2004	27,599	$1,575,656,693
Tropical Storm Allison	June 2001	30,662	$1,103,774,388
Louisiana Flood	May 1995	31,343	$585,072,008
Hurricane Isabel	September 2003	19,853	$491,844,143
Hurricane Rita	September 2005	9,480	$465,070,605
Hurricane Floyd	September 1999	20,439	$462,270,253
Hurricane Opal	October 1995	10,343	$405,528,543
Hurricane Hugo	September 1989	12,843	$376,493,066

Source: FEMA. 2010. Significant Flood Events: 1978–January 2010. National Flood Insurance Program. http://www.fema .gov/business/nfip/statistics/sign1000.shtm

Floods are typically measured according to their elevation above standard water levels (of rivers or coastal water levels). This elevation is translated into the annualized likelihood of reaching such heights. For example, a flood depth that has a 1 percent chance of being reached or could be expected to occur once across a 100-year period would be considered a "100-year flood event." Typically, structures that are contained within areas likely to experience flooding in a 100-year flood event are considered to be within the

---

ADDITIONAL RESEARCH

The following reports provide supplemental information about annualized flood losses in the United States:

Compilation of Flood Loss Statistics (The National Weather Service):
http://www.nws.noaa.gov/hic/flood_stats/Flood_loss_time_series.shtml
Flood Damage in the United States, 1926–2000—A Reanalysis of National Weather Service Estimates (Pielke, Roger A., Mary W. Downton, and J. Zoe Barnard Miller, 2002):
http://www.flooddamagedata.org/flooddamagedata.pdf

---

floodplain. Governments in many countries maintain river and stream gauges to monitor floodwater elevations and to provide information on rising water for use in sandbagging and dyke construction. Such information also allows for early warning and evacuation to occur.

Earthquakes

An earthquake is a sudden, rapid shaking of the earth's crust that is caused by the breaking and shifting of rock beneath the earth's surface. This shaking can cause the collapse of buildings and bridges; cause disruptions in gas, electric, and phone service; and trigger landslides, avalanches, flash floods, fires, and huge, destructive ocean waves (tsunamis). Structures constructed on unconsolidated landfill, old waterways, or other unstable soil are generally at greatest risk unless seismic mitigation has been utilized. Seismicity is not seasonal or climate dependent and can therefore occur at any time of the year (Figure 2-2).

Each year, knowledge about the location and behavior of the earth's seismic zones increases thanks to improvements in seismic detection and monitoring. Over one billion people worldwide live in seismic zones. Earthquake damage can be extensive, especially when buildings have been constructed without incorporation of seismic-resistant materials and designs. Earthquakes can cause secondary fire hazards when gas lines are severed and flammable materials storage sites are compromised. These fires can spread rapidly among damaged buildings because water systems may be damaged and fire services are either unable to access the fire or are overwhelmed by other response requirements. Fire was a leading cause of thousands of deaths in 1995 when an earthquake struck Kobe, Japan, because debris from damaged and destroyed buildings blocked many access points for firefighters and equipment.

Earthquakes are sudden, no-notice events despite scientists' and soothsayers' best efforts to predict when they will occur. Seismic sensing technology is effective at measuring and tracking seismic activity, but it has yet to accurately predict a major seismic event with any degree of accuracy.

FIGURE 2-2 Atascadero, California, January 25, 2004. This home slid two feet off its foundation due to the 6.5 San Simeon earthquake.
Photo by Dane Golden/FEMA News Photo.

Each year hundreds of earthquakes occur in the United States, though the vast majority are barely perceptible. As earthquake strength increases, its likelihood of occurrence decreases. Major events, which are greater than 6.5 to 7 on the Richter scale, occur only once every decade or so, but such events have been among the most devastating in the experience of the United States. The Northridge earthquake that struck California in 1994, for instance, is the second most expensive natural disaster to ever occur in the United States as ranked by FEMA relief costs, resulting in almost $7 billion in federal funding (and second only to Hurricane Katrina).

The strength and effects of earthquakes are commonly described by the Richter and Modified Mercalli Intensity (MMI) scales. The Richter scale, designed by Charles Richter in 1935, assigns a single number to quantify the strength and effect of an earthquake across the entire area affected according to the strength of ground waves at its point of origin (as measured by a seismograph). Richter magnitudes are logarithmic and have no upper limit. The MMI also measures the effects of earthquakes, but rather than applying a single value to the event, it allows for site-specific evaluation according to the effects observed at each location. The MMI (Table 2-2) rates event intensity using Roman numerals I through XII. Determinations are generally made using reports by people who felt the event and observations of damages sustained by structures.

CRITICAL THINKING

It is possible to assign Modified Mercalli Intensity values to historical earthquakes, but Richter magnitudes cannot be retroactively assigned. Why do you think this is true? Which of these scales is more useful in terms of disaster planning? Why?

Table 2-2 Modified Mercalli Intensity Scale

MMI Intensity	Damages Sustained and Sensations Experienced	Richter Scale Equivalent
I–IV (Instrumental to Moderate)	No damage sustained. Sensation ranges from imperceptible to that of a heavy truck striking the building. Standing motor cars may rock.	≤4.3
V (Rather Strong)	Felt by nearly everyone; many awakened. Some dishes, windows broken. Unstable objects overturned. Pendulum clocks may stop.	4.4–4.8
VI (Strong)	Felt by all; many frightened. Some heavy furniture moved; a few instances of fallen plaster. Damage slight.	4.9–5.4
VII (Very Strong)	Damage negligible in buildings of good design and construction; slight to moderate in well-built ordinary structures; considerable damage in poorly built or badly designed structures; some chimneys broken.	5.5–6.1
VIII (Destructive)	Damage slight in specially designed structures; considerable damage in ordinary substantial buildings with partial collapse. Damage great in poorly built structures. Fall of chimneys, factory stacks, columns, monuments, walls. Heavy furniture overturned.	6.2–6.5
IX (Ruinous)	Damage considerable in specially designed structures; well-designed frame structures thrown out of plumb. Damage great in substantial buildings, with partial collapse. Buildings shifted off foundations.	6.6–6.9
X (Disastrous)	Most masonry and frame structures/foundations destroyed. Some well-built wooden structures and bridges destroyed. Serious damage to dams, dikes, embankments. Sand and mud shifting on beaches and flat land.	7.0–7.3
XI (Very Disastrous)	Few or no masonry structures remain standing. Bridges destroyed. Broad fissures in ground. Underground pipelines completely out of service. Widespread earth slumps and landslides. Rails bent greatly.	7.4–8.1
XII (Catastrophic)	Damage nearly total. Large rock masses displaced. Lines of sight and level are distorted. Objects are thrown into the air.	≥8.1

Source: USGS, 2009. Magnitude/Intensity Comparison. Earthquake Hazards Program. *http://earthquake.usgs.gov/learn/topics/mag_vs_int.php*

Hurricanes

Hurricanes are cyclonic storms that begin as tropical waves and grow in intensity and size. Tropical waves continue to progress in size and intensity to tropical depressions and tropical storms as determined by their maximum sustained wind speed. The warm-core tropical depression becomes a tropical storm when the maximum sustained surface wind speeds range from 39 miles per hour to 73 miles per hour (mph). Tropical cyclonic storms are defined by their low barometric pressure, closed-circulation winds originating over tropical waters, and an absence of wind shear. Cyclonic storm winds rotate counterclockwise in the Northern Hemisphere and clockwise in the Southern Hemisphere.

A hurricane is a cyclonic tropical storm with sustained winds measuring 74 mph or more. Hurricane winds extend outward in a spiral pattern as much as 400 miles around

Table 2-3   The Saffir–Simpson Scale

Category	Conditions	Effects
1	Wind Speed: 74–95 mph Storm Surge: 4–5 feet above normal	Primary damage to unanchored mobile homes, shrubbery, and trees. Some coastal flooding and minor pier damage. Little damage to building structures.
2	Wind Speed: 96–110 mph Storm Surge: 6–8 feet above normal	Considerable damage to mobile homes, piers, and vegetation. Coastal and low-lying area escape routes flood 2–4 hours before arrival of hurricane center. Buildings sustain roofing material, door, and window damage. Small craft in unprotected mooring break moorings.
3	Wind Speed: 111–130 mph Storm Surge: 9–12 feet above normal	Mobile homes destroyed. Some structural damage to small homes and utility buildings. Flooding near coast destroys smaller structures; larger structures damaged by floating debris. Terrain continuously lower than 5 feet above sea level (ASL) may be flooded up to six miles inland.
4	Wind Speed: 131–155 mph Storm Surge: 13–18 feet above normal	Extensive curtain wall failures, with some complete roof structure failure on small residences. Major erosion of beaches. Major damage to lower floors of structures near the shore. Terrain continuously lower than 10 feet ASL may flood (and require mass evacuations) up to 6 miles inland.
5	Wind Speed: Over 155 mph Storm Surge: Over 18 feet above normal	Complete roof failure on many homes and industrial buildings. Some complete building failures. Major damage to lower floors of all structures located less than 15 feet ASL and within 500 yards of the shoreline. Massive evacuation of low-ground, residential areas may be required.

Source: FEMA.

a relatively calm center of up to 30 miles in diameter known as the "eye." Hurricanes are fed by warm ocean waters. As these storms make landfall, they often push a wall of ocean water known as a "storm surge" over coastal zones. Once over land, hurricanes cause further destruction by means of torrential rains and high winds. A single hurricane can last for several weeks over open waters and can run a path across the entire length of the eastern seaboard.

Hurricane season runs annually from June 1 through November 30. August and September are peak months during the hurricane season. Hurricanes are commonly described using the Saffir–Simpson scale (Table 2-3).

Hurricanes are capable of causing great damage and destruction over vast areas. Hurricane Floyd in 1999 first threatened the states of Florida and Georgia, made landfall in North Carolina, and damaged sections of South Carolina, North Carolina, Virginia, Maryland, Delaware, New Jersey, New York, Connecticut, Massachusetts, and Maine. The damage was so extensive in each of these states that they all qualified for federal disaster assistance. Single hurricanes can affect several countries, as was the case with Hurricane Mitch, which brought death and destruction to Nicaragua, Guatemala, El Salvador, and Honduras.

Table 2-4 Top Ten Most Expensive U.S. Hurricanes, 1900–2006 (Ranked by FEMA Relief Costs)

Hurricane	Year	Category	Damage (in billions)
Hurricane Katrina—FL, AL, LA, MS	2005	3	$29,319
Hurricane Rita—TX, LA	2005	5	$3,750
Hurricane Ivan—AL, FL, GA, LA, MS, NJ, NY, NC, PA, TN, WV	2004	3	$2,431
Hurricane Georges—AL, FL, MS, PR, VI	1998	4	$2,245
Hurricane Wilma—FL	2005	5	$2,111
Hurricane Charley—FL, SC	2004	4	$1,885
Hurricane Andrew—FL, LA	1992	5	$1,814
Hurricane Francis—FL, GA, NY, NC, OH, PA, SC	2004	4	$1,773
Hurricane Jeanne—DE, FL, PR, VI, VA	2004	3	$1,407
Hurricane Hugo—NC, SC, PR, VI	1989	4	$1,307

Sources: FEMA, 2009. "Most Expensive Presidentially Declared Disasters." *http://www.fema.gov/hazard/hurricane/top10hu .shtm;* FEMA, 2009. "Top Ten Natural Disasters Ranked by FEMA Relief Costs." *http://www.fema.gov/hazard/topten.shtm.*

The costliest disaster in U.S. history in pure dollar figures (approximately $80 billion; Reuters, 2009) and one of the deadliest in terms of lives lost and injuries sustained (1,836 killed) was Hurricane Katrina (Table 2-4). Katrina reached Category 5 status with sustained winds of over 175 mph—making it the fourth strongest hurricane recorded at the time—before making landfall as a Category 3 hurricane along the Gulf of Mexico coast. With strong winds and a storm surge reaching 28 feet, Katrina devastated coastal communities in Alabama, Florida, Mississippi, and Louisiana. Flooding and near total destruction was sustained in almost 80 percent of New Orleans and much of Biloxi/Gulfport, Mississippi. The storm went on to cause further destruction in several other states as it made its way north toward Canada. Four years later, many of the Gulf Coast areas—especially hard-hit New Orleans—are still reeling from this disaster event, with full recovery years or even decades away.

CASE STUDY: THE IMPACT OF THE STORM

Hurricane Katrina impacted different areas in different ways. Along the Mississippi Gulf Coast, Katrina generated a 25- to 30-foot tidal surge that swept away structures and vehicles in its path. Hotels and casinos located on the Gulf were severely damaged, and in some cases entire communities disappeared. In New Orleans, the principle impact was the flooding caused by the breaches in the levees that left almost 80 percent of the city underwater for up to six weeks.

However, some sections of the city—notably those areas closest to the river such as the French Quarter—experienced very little if any flooding. Tidal surge was only a factor in the Lower Ninth Ward section of the city, which, together with St. Bernard Parish, experienced the tidal surge that traveled up the Mississippi River Gulf outlet. Wind and rain caused considerable damage to homes and businesses throughout the region.

Over 1.3 million people evacuated before Katrina even made landfall, and an estimated 800,000 people were displaced for an extended period of time. As of April 2010, the Census Bureau estimated the population of the city of New Orleans to be just under 355,000, or just three-quarters its pre-Katrina size (Robertson, 2010). However, the true size will not be known for certain until the 2010 Census results are released in early 2011.

Critical infrastructures such as water, power, communications, schools, hospitals, and child care were severely damaged and disrupted in all impacted areas. Government facilities and private industry suffered massive losses. The White House report on Katrina, "The Federal Response to Hurricane Katrina: Lessons Learned," estimated damage to housing at $67 billion, business property suffered $20 billion in damages, and government property suffered an estimated $3 billion in damages (Townsend, 2006). Insured losses from Katrina are estimated to be the greatest ever in U.S. history.

THE HURRICANE KATRINA TIMELINE

The following is a timeline of events starting with the initial formation of Hurricane Katrina as Tropical Depression 12 through the first days following Katrina making landfall on August 29, 2005. This timeline was compiled from several sources including FEMA, The Brookings Institution, and CNN. The U.S. Senate prepared an after-action report entitled "Hurricane Katrina: A Nation Still Unprepared."

- *Tuesday, August 23:* Tropical Depression 12 forms about 200 miles southeast of the Bahamas; what was to become Hurricane Katrina is first recognized as a potential hazard.
- *Thursday, August 25:* Tropical Storm Katrina becomes Hurricane Katrina. A Category 1 hurricane with sustained winds in excess of 74 mph moves across South Florida and into the Gulf of Mexico. Katrina is now over the warm waters of the Gulf, where it begins to strengthen, and early tracks by the National Hurricane Center show Katrina making landfall "between Mobile, Alabama, and Grand Isle, Florida."
- *Friday, August 26:* The hurricane track shifts twice during the day; first projected to make landfall on the Mississippi-Alabama border and later in the day projected to make landfall on the Louisiana-Mississippi border. The governors of both Louisiana and Mississippi declare a state of emergency and activate their state National Guards.
- *Saturday, August 27:* Katrina, now a Category 4 or 5 storm, is expected to hit New Orleans, and Governor Blanco requests a declaration of a federal state of emergency for Louisiana, which President Bush approves that same day. New Orleans Mayor Nagin declares a state of emergency, and evacuations begin in Louisiana and Mississippi.
- *Sunday, August 28:* Mayor Nagin issues a mandatory evacuation order. The Superdome opens as a shelter of last resort, and by the end of the day 10,000 people and 150 National Guardsmen are in the Dome; evacuation all along the Gulf Coast continues.
- *Monday, August 29:* Katrina, now a Category 4 hurricane with 145 mph winds makes landfall in lower Plaquemines Parish, Louisiana, between 6:00 and 7:00 a.m. CST. Major disaster declarations are signed by President Bush, levees in New Orleans are breached, and floodwaters begin to fill sections of the city. The Coast Guard begins rescue operations in New Orleans.

- *Tuesday, August 30:* Floodwaters cover up to 80 percent of the city. An estimated 50 to 100,000 people are trapped in the city, including the Superdome and Convention Center. Governor Blanco issues an order to evacuate the Superdome. The Coast Guard rescue continues, and widespread looting is reported.
- *Wednesday, August 31:* Governor Blanco and President Bush discuss military assistance and decide who should be in charge of the National Guard. The Houston Astrodome prepares to receive evacuees from Katrina.
- *Thursday, September 1:* 45,000 people are now housed in the Superdome and the Convention Center; bus evacuation of populations in New Orleans begins. DHS secretary Chertoff and FEMA director Brown indicate they were unaware of any problems at the Convention Center.
- *Friday, September 2:* President Bush makes his first visit to the disaster area, meeting with both governors and Nagin. The number of National Guard troops deployed is increased, and Congress approves $10.5 billion in immediate relief.
- *Saturday, September 3:* 40,000 National Guardsmen are now deployed to the Gulf Coast. President Bush orders 7,200 active duty military to the Gulf, and the evacuations of the Superdome and the Convention Center are completed.
- *Monday, September 5:* The gap in the levee is closed, but more levee repairs are required. The Bush-Clinton Fund is announced, and President Bush dispatches 4,700 additional active military troops.
- *Tuesday, September 6:* The Corps of Engineers begins pumping water out of New Orleans, and Mayor Nagin authorizes troops and police to remove individuals from the city.
- *Thursday, September 8:* Congress approves President Bush's request for $52 billion in additional aid.

In recent years, significant advances have been made in hurricane tracking technology and computer models. The National Hurricane Center in Miami, Florida, now tracks tropical waves from the moment they form off the coast of West Africa through their development as a tropical depression. Once the tropical depression grows to the strength of a tropical storm, the Hurricane Center assigns the storm a name. After the sustained wind speed exceeds 74 mph, the storm officially becomes a hurricane. The National Hurricane Center uses aircraft to observe and collect meteorological data on the hurricane and to track its movements across the Atlantic Ocean. It also uses several sophisticated computer models to predict the storm's path. These predictions are provided to local and state emergency officials to help them make evacuation decisions and to predeploy response and recovery resources.

Historically, high winds and flooding caused by storm surge have been the principal contributors to the loss of life and injuries and the property and infrastructure damage caused by hurricanes. Inland flooding caused by hurricane rainfall has also resulted in large losses of life and severe property damage, especially in zones of hilly or mountainous topography. Damage to the environment is another important factor related to hurricane-force winds and flooding. For instance, storm surges cause severe beach erosion, most notably on fragile barrier islands. Inland flooding from Hurricane Floyd inundated waste ponds on hog farms in North Carolina, washing the hog waste into the Cape Fear River and ultimately into the ocean. The storm surge created by Hurricane Katrina has had a profound impact on the environment—in some cases completely erasing or altering coastal areas. Dauphin Island was literally pushed toward the land by the force of the surge, and the Chandeleur Islands were completely destroyed. Breton National Wildlife Refuge, one of 16 wildlife refuges damaged by the storm, lost over half of its area. Much of this land lost served as breeding grounds for marine mammals, reptiles, birds, and fish.

Storm Surges

Storm surges, defined as masses of water that are pushed toward the shore by meteorological forces, are the primary cause of the injuries, deaths, and structural damages associated with hurricanes, cyclones, nor'easters, and other coastal storms. When the advancing surge of water coincides with high tides, the resulting rise in sea level is further exacerbated. Storm surges may reach several dozen feet under the right conditions, as was the case in Hurricane Katrina. Wind-driven turbulence becomes superimposed on the storm tide, thereby causing further damage to structures that are inundated through wave action (each cubic yard of water results in 1,700 pounds of pressure on affected structures). The surge height at landfall is ultimately dictated by the expanse and intensity of the storm, the height of the tide at the time of landfall, and the slope of the sea floor approaching land. The longer and shallower the sea floor, the greater the storm surge will be.

Because much of the United States' densely populated Atlantic and Gulf Coast coastlines lie less than ten feet above mean sea level, storm surge risk is extreme. Hurricane Katrina served as a reminder of the speed and intensity of the storm surge threat that persists in greatest part due to increasing coastal development. After crossing southern Florida, Katrina followed a westward track across the Gulf of Mexico before turning northwest toward the Gulf Coast. The storm made its second landfall as a strong Category 4 hurricane in Plaquemines Parish, Louisiana, on August 29, 2005. When the storm made its third and final landfall along the Mississippi/Louisiana border, its hurricane-force winds extended up to 190 miles from the center of the storm, and tropical storm-force winds extended for approximately 440 miles. The strength and wide geographical area affected by the storm resulted in a surge greater than anything previously recorded along the Gulf Coast. A 30-foot storm surge, combined with very strong wave action and constant high winds, resulted in a magnitude of destruction never before experienced in the United States. The enormous pressure by the force of the storm surge on the levee system that protected New Orleans caused several breaches that flooded the city with as much as 20 feet of water in some areas. *USA Today* developed an animation showing how a hurricane causes a storm surge: *http://www.usatoday.com/graphics/weather/gra/gsurge/flash.htm*.

The National Hurricane Center operates a computerized model, called SLOSH (Sea, Lake, and Overland Surges from Hurricanes), to estimate storm surge heights and winds resulting from historical, hypothetical, or predicted hurricanes. When making calculations, SLOSH takes into account pressure, size, forward speed, track, and wind.

The model's output is a color-coded map indicating storm surge heights for defined areas in feet above the model's reference level. These calculations are applied to a specific locale's shoreline, incorporating the unique bay and river configurations, water depths, bridges, roads, and other physical features. When SLOSH is used to estimate storm surge from predicted hurricanes, forecast data are entered every 6 hours over a 72-hour period and updated as new forecasts become available. SLOSH is accurate within a range of 20 percent plus or minus what is actually observed. The model accounts for astronomical tides, but it does not consider rainfall, riverflow, or wind-driven waves. However, this information can be combined with the model's output to create a more accurate analysis of at-risk areas.

Tornadoes

A tornado is a rapidly rotating vortex or funnel of air extending groundward from a cumulonimbus cloud, exhibiting wind speeds of up to 300 miles per hour. Approximately 1,200 tornadoes are spawned by thunderstorms each year in the United States. Most tornadoes remain aloft, but the few that do touch the ground are devastating to everything in their path. The forces of a tornado's winds are capable of lifting and moving huge objects, destroying or moving whole buildings, and siphoning large volumes from bodies of water and ultimately depositing them elsewhere. Because tornadoes typically follow the path of least resistance, people living in valleys have the greatest exposure to damage.

Tornadoes have been measured using the Fujita-Pearson Tornado Scale since its creation in 1971 (Table 2-5). In 2006, research indicated that tornado damage was occurring from winds of much weaker intensity than previously thought, so the National Weather Service created an enhanced scale to measure them (Table 2-6). First used in January 2007, this scale expands upon the original system's measure of damage to homes by adding 18 new damage indicators, including those that affect trees, mobile homes, and several other structures (giving a total of 28 indicators studied in the classification of a tornado). Under the enhanced Fujita-Pearson scale, a tornado that does not affect houses can still be classified.

Tornado damage occurs only when the funnel cloud touches down on land. In the United States, the states with the greatest tornado risk are Texas, Oklahoma, Arkansas, Missouri, and Kansas. Together these states occupy what is commonly known as "tornado alley." In recent years, however, tornadoes have struck in cities that are not regularly frequented by tornadoes, including Miami, Nashville, and Washington, D.C. Tornadoes can also touch down in several places in succession, as occurred in Washington, D.C. in 2001. In that event, a single tornado first touched down in Alexandria, Virginia, just south of the city and then again in College Park, Maryland, just north of D.C. Tornado season generally falls between March and August, although tornadoes can occur at any time of the year. Tornadoes tend to occur in the afternoon and evening, with more than 80 percent of all tornadoes striking between noon and midnight.

Table 2-5   Original Fujita-Pearson Tornado Scale

Category	Conditions	Effects
F-0	40–72 mph	Chimney damage, tree branches broken
F-1	73–112 mph	Mobile homes pushed off foundation or overturned
F-2	113–157 mph	Considerable damage, mobile homes demolished, trees uprooted
F-3	158–205 mph	Roofs and walls torn down, trains overturned, cars thrown
F-4	207–260 mph	Well-constructed walls leveled
F-5	261–318 mph	Homes lifted off foundation and carried considerable distances, autos thrown as far as 100 meters

Table 2-6   Enhanced Fujita-Pearson Tornado Scale

Category	Conditions	Effects
F-0	65–85 mph	Minor to light damage to structures and vegetation
F-1	85–110 mph	Moderate damage to structures and vegetation
F-2	111–135 mph	Heavy damage to structures and vegetation
F-3	136–165 mph	Severe damage to structures and vegetation
F-4	166–200 mph	Extreme damage to structures and vegetation
F-5	Over 200 mph	Complete destruction of structures and vegetation

Building collapse and flying debris are the principal factors behind the deaths and injuries tornadoes cause. Early warning is key to surviving tornadoes, as warned citizens can protect themselves by moving to structures designed to withstand tornado-force winds. Doppler radar and other meteorological tools have drastically improved the ability to detect tornadoes and the amount of advance warning time available before a tornado strike. Improved communications and new technologies have also been critical to giving people advanced warning.

Buildings that are directly in the path of a tornado have little chance of surviving unless they are specifically designed to withstand not only the force of the winds but also that of the debris "missiles" that are thrown about (Figure 2-3). "Safe room" technology developed by FEMA and Texas A&M University, which retrofits a portion of a structure to withstand such winds through engineered resistant design and special resilient materials, offers those in the path of a tornado much greater survival likelihoods (Figure 2-4). Safe rooms are often the most cost-effective way to mitigate tornado risk in communities that are already heavily developed, since they can be built into an existing (or new) structure for a small cost (estimated between $3,000 to $5,000).

In order to greatly expand the mitigation benefits of safe rooms, similar technology is being developed for use in community mass-care shelters. New technologies in building design and construction are also being developed by FEMA and others to reduce the damage to buildings and structures not located directly in the path of a tornado. Many of the same wind-resistant construction techniques used effectively in high-risk hurricane

FIGURE 2-3 Mena, Arkansas, April 15, 2009. Volunteers from a faith-based organization undertake the task of cleaning up the debris from an elderly woman's home that was destroyed on the evening of April 9 by an F3 tornado. Several western Arkansas counties were struck by five documented tornadoes that caused widespread damage that Thursday evening.
FEMA Photo by Win Henderson.

FIGURE 2-4 Tulsa, Oklahoma, November 23, 2001. Disaster Ally in the Eastland Mall. Safe rooms can be designed with many different materials. Shown are concrete block walls, formed concrete walls, and a special ceiling framing. Photo by Kent Baxter/FEMA News Photo.

areas have been found to be equally effective when applied to new and retrofitted structures located in tornado-prone areas.

Wildfires

Wildfires (often called "wildland fires") are classified into three categories: *surface fires*, the most common type, which burn along the floor of a forest, moving slowly and killing or damaging trees; *ground fires*, which are usually started by lightning and burn on or just below the forest floor; and *crown fires*, which burn through the forest canopy high above the ground and therefore spread much more rapidly due to wind and direct contact with nearby trees. Wildland fires are an annual and increasing hazard due to the air pollution (primarily smoke and ash that travel for miles, causing further hazards to health and mechanical or electrical equipment), risk to firefighters, environmental effects, and property destruction they cause.

As residential areas expand into relatively untouched wildlands (called the "wildland-urban interface"), the threat to the human population increases dramatically. Protecting structures located in or near the wildland poses special problems and often stretches firefighting resources beyond capacity. Wildland fires also cause several secondary hazards. For instance, when heavy rains follow a major fire, landslides, mudflows, and floods can strike on or downhill from the newly unanchored soil. These fires can also severely scorch the land, destroying animal habitats and causing barren patches that may persist for decades, increasing the likelihood of long-term erosion.

Several terms are used to classify the source and behavior of wildland fires:

- *Wildland fires.* Fueled almost exclusively by natural vegetation, these fires typically occur in national forests and parks, where federal agencies are responsible for fire management and suppression.
- *Interface or intermix fires.* These fires occur in or near the wildland-urban interface, affecting both natural and built environments and posing a tactical challenge to firefighters concerned with the often conflicting goals of firefighter safety and property protection.
- *Firestorms.* Events of such extreme intensity that effective suppression is virtually impossible, firestorms occur during extreme weather and generally burn until conditions change or the available fuel is exhausted.
- *Prescribed fires and prescribed natural fires.* These are fires that are intentionally set or selected natural fires that are allowed to burn for the purpose of reducing available natural fuel.

Severe drought conditions and the buildup of large quantities of "fuel" (dead trees and flammable vegetation) on the forest floors have led to a steady increase in the prevalence of wildfires in the United States. Since the National Interagency Fire Center began tracking the number and acreage of fires in 1960, the average number of fires has fallen (presumably due to fire-prevention programs), while the annual acreage burned has risen. In other words, the fewer fires that are occurring are larger and more destructive on average. Before 2004, no year had seen more than 7 million acres burned, and few experienced greater than 4 or 5 million acres burned. Yet, from 2004 to 2007, each year exceeded 8 million, and both 2006 and 2007 exceeded 9 million acres burned. In 2008 the number fell to just over 5 million, and 2009 saw approximately 6 million burned (NIFC, 2009).

Mass Movements

The general category of mass movements includes several different hazards caused by the horizontal or lateral movement of large quantities of physical matter. Mass movements cause damage and loss of life through several different processes, including the pushing, crushing, or burying of objects in their path, the damming of rivers and waterways, the subsequent movement of displaced bodies of water (typically in the form of a tsunami), destruction or obstruction of major transportation routes, and alteration of the natural environment in ways in which humans are negatively impacted. Mass-movement hazards are most prevalent in areas of rugged or varied topography, but they can occur even on level land, as in the case of subsidence. The following are the categories of mass-movement hazards:

- *Landslides.* Landslides occur when masses of relatively dry rock, soil, or debris move in an uncontrolled manner down a slope. Landslides may be very highly localized or massive in size, and they can move at a creeping pace or at very high speeds. Many areas have experienced landslides repeatedly since prehistoric times. Landslides are activated when the mechanisms by which the material was anchored become compromised (through a loss of vegetation or seismic activity, for example).
- *Mudflows.* Mudflows are water-saturated rivers of rock, earth, and other debris that are drawn downward by the forces of gravity. These phenomena develop when water rapidly accumulates in the material that is moved, like during heavy rainfall or rapid snowmelt. Under these conditions, solid or loose earth can quickly change into a flowing river of mud, or "slurry." These flows move rapidly down slopes or through channels, following the path of least resistance, and often strike with little or no warning. Mudflows have traveled several miles in many instances, growing in size as they pick up trees, cars, and other materials along the way.
- *Lateral spreads.* Lateral spreads occur when large quantities of accumulated earth or other materials spread downward and outward due to gradual hydrologic and gravitational forces. Spreads can affect rock, but they also occur in fine-grained, sensitive soils such as clays.
- *Liquefaction.* When saturated solid material becomes liquid-like in constitution due to seismic or hydrologic activity, it can exacerbate lateral spreading.
- *Rockfalls.* Rockfalls occur when masses of rock or other materials detach from a steep slope or cliff and descend by freefall, rolling, or bouncing. Topples consist of the forward rotation of rocks or other materials about a pivot point on a hill slope. Rockfalls can occur spontaneously when fissures in rock or other materials cause structural failure or due to seismic or other mechanical activity (including explosions or the movement of heavy machinery).
- *Avalanches.* An avalanche is a mass of ice or snow that moves downhill at a high velocity. Avalanches can shear trees, cover entire communities and highway routes, and level buildings in their path. Avalanches are triggered by a number of processes, including exceeding critical mass on a steep slope or disturbances caused by seismicity or human activity. As temperatures increase and snowpack becomes unstable, the

risk of avalanches increases. The primary negative consequences associated with avalanches are loss of life (mostly to backcountry skiers, climbers, and snowmobilers) and obstruction of major transportation routes. Around 10,000 avalanches are reported each year in the United States. Since tracking began in 1790, an average of 144 people have become trapped in avalanches annually, and of these an average of 14 sustain injuries and 14 die. The average annual value of structural damage is $500,000, though the secondary costs associated with disrupted commerce can be much greater.

• *Land subsidence.* Land subsidence is the loss of surface elevation caused by the removal of subsurface support. Subsidence can range from broad, regional lowering of large landmasses to severe localized collapses. The primary cause of this hazard is human activity, including underground mining, extraction of groundwater or petroleum, and the drainage of organic soils. The average annual damage associated with subsidence in the United States is estimated to be at least $125 million.

• *Expansive soils.* Soils and soft rock that tend to swell or shrink when their moisture content changes are referred to as expansive soils. These changes are extremely detrimental to transportation routes (including highways, streets, and rail lines) and structures that are built above the affected soils. The most extensive damage affects highways and streets. Two rock types that are particularly prone to expansion and that are prevalent in the United States (primarily in the West) are aluminum silicates (e.g., ash, glass, and rocks of volcanic origin) and sedimentary rock (e.g., clay and shale).

Tsunamis

A tsunami is wave or series of waves that is generated by a mass displacement of sea or lake water. The most common generative factor behind tsunamis is undersea earthquakes that cause ocean floor displacement, but large tsunamis have been caused by volcanic eruptions and landslides as well. Tsunami waves travel outward as movements of kinetic energy (rather than traveling water) at very high speeds in all directions from the area of the disturbance, much like the ripples caused by a rock thrown into a pond. As the waves approach shallow coastal waters, wave speed quickly decreases and the water is drawn upward and onto land. Tsunamis can strike at heights of up to and over 100 feet and extend onto land for a mile or more (depending upon topography). The force of the water causes near total destruction of everything in its path.

The areas at the greatest risk from tsunamis are those lying less than 50 feet above sea level and within one mile of the shoreline. Successive crests (high water) and troughs (low water) can occur anywhere from 5 to 90 minutes apart. Tsunamis travel through deep water at approximately 450 miles per hour, so the areas closest to the point of origin experience the greatest destruction and have the least amount of forewarning. Most tsunami-related deaths are the result of drowning, while the loss of services and related health problems associated with the incredible destruction of the infrastructure (including the loss of hospitals and clinics, water pollution, contaminated food and water stocks, and damaged transmission lines) adds to these statistics.

ADDITIONAL RESEARCH

The Woods Hole Oceanographic Institute has developed a highly illustrative website about the causes and dynamics of tsunamis. This website also provides significant information about mitigation techniques, historical tsunami events, warning systems, modeling, and much more. The site can be accessed at *http://www.whoi.edu/home/interactive/tsunami/*.

CASE STUDY: RECENT MAJOR TSUNAMI EVENTS

On December 26, 2004, following an earthquake off the coast of the Banda Aceh region of Indonesia that measured 8.9 on the Richter scale, a series of tsunamis devastated vast coastal regions in 11 countries as far as East Africa. The earthquake was the most powerful to occur in four decades, and it generated waves reaching as high as 60 feet on coastal shorelines. The devastation from this event in terms of the geographical range and number of people affected within the brief time frame is virtually unprecedented in modern history.

Due to an almost complete lack of regional tsunami warning capabilities, little advanced notice of the presence or severity of these impending waves was possible for the affected populations, many of whom included foreign tourists. As a result, most people had no opportunity to move to higher ground—an action that surely would have prevented the high number of injuries and fatalities that occurred. While the exact number of people killed will never be known, it is assumed to be greater than 150,000 and possibly more than 200,000. Over 500,000 injuries were reported, and ten times as many people were left homeless.

Almost five years after this terrible event, another quake struck in the nearby South Pacific region, causing large tsunamis in the islands of Samoa, American Samoa, and Tonga. These events were caused by an 8.0 magnitude earthquake near the Samoan Islands on September 29. While significant infrastructure had been put into place to detect tsunamis and warn the at-risk populations, communication failures prevented many people from being informed. Upon personally observing now-familiar telltale signs of a coming tsunami, including the earthquake itself, and changing off-tide water levels, many residents fled to higher ground. However, 189 people still lost their lives, most of whom lived in hardest-hit Samoa.

Five years after the Indian Ocean tsunami, widespread disparity exists in the rates of recovery between the affected countries and even within each affected country from region to region. Assistance from national and international development agencies and organizations, including the U.S. Agency for International Development (USAID), the Australian Agency for International Development (AUSAID), the United Nations, and others, has helped to speed recovery and ensure that tsunami-mitigation measures and practices are incorporated into rebuilding efforts. Many of USAID's recovery projects have already concluded, including work in Indonesia, Sri Lanka, India, and Thailand, while others are still working to bring about recovery.

The U.S. government is just one of many national governments that helped to bring about recovery in the affected countries, contributing over $650 million in aid, primarily to Indonesia ($405.7 million) and Sri Lanka ($134.6 million) (USAID, 2009). Recovery from the 2009 tsunami events is also expected to take time, but due to the much more limited geographic area affected and the much smaller populations on the islands that were struck, recovery will not see the complexities of the 2004 events. In fact, the U.S. government dedicated only $50,000 in assistance to Tonga and $100,000 to Samoa to assist with the cost of recovery. FEMA provided USG federal assistance to American Samoa because the islands are U.S. territory and therefore under the coverage of Stafford Act assistance. For information on USAID and FEMA involvement in these events, visit *http://www.usaid.gov/locations/asia/tsunami/, http://www .usaid.gov/our_work/humanitarian_assistance/disaster_assistance/countries/samoa/template/ index.html, and http://www.usaid.gov/our_work/humanitarian_assistance/disaster_assistance/ countries/tonga/template/index.html.*

Volcanic Eruptions

A volcano is a break in the earth's crust through which molten rock from beneath the earth's surface (magma) erupts. Over time, volcanoes will grow upward and outward, forming mountains, islands, or large, flat plateaus called "shields." Volcanic mountains differ from mountain chains formed through plate tectonics (movement of the earth's crustal plates) because they are built through the accumulation of materials (lava, ash flows, and airborne ash and dust) rather than being pushed up from below. When volcanic material exits the earth, it is called lava, and the nature of its exit determines the land formations that result. Thinner lava typically moves quickly away from the source and becomes a large shield (as in the case of the Hawaiian Islands), while thicker lava and other materials form steeper volcanic formations.

When pressure from gases and molten rock becomes strong enough to cause an explosion, violent eruptions may occur. Gases and rock shoot up through the opening and spill over or fill the air with lava fragments. Volcanoes cause injuries, death, and destruction through a number of processes, including direct burns, suffocation from ash and other materials, trauma from ejected rocks, floods and mudflows from quickly melted snow and ice, burial under burning hot "pyroclastic" ash flows, and others. Airborne ash can affect people hundreds of miles away from the eruption and influence global climates for years afterward.

Volcanic ash contaminates water supplies, causes electrical storms, and can cause roofs to collapse under the weight of accumulated material. Eruptions may also trigger tsunamis, flash floods, earthquakes, and rockfalls. Sideways-directed volcanic explosions, known as "lateral blasts," can shoot large pieces of rock at very high speeds for several miles. These explosions can kill by impact, burial, or heat. They have been known to knock down entire forests. Most deaths attributed to the Mount St. Helens volcano were a result of lateral blast and trees that were knocked down. Volcanic ash also has some positive implications because it can be used for construction or road building, as abrasive and cleaning agents, and as raw materials for many chemical and industrial uses. Ash-covered land is also rich in mineral nutrients and ideal for agricultural production.

Severe Winter Storms

Severe winter storms occur when extremely cold atmospheric conditions coincide with high airborne moisture content, resulting in rapid and heavy precipitation of snow and/or ice. When combined with high winds, the event is known as a blizzard. In the United States, these hazards originate from four distinct sources:

- In the Northwest, cyclonic weather systems originate in the North Pacific Ocean or the Aleutian Island region.
- In the Midwest and Upper Plains, Canadian and Arctic cold fronts push ice and snow deep into the heart of the nation—in some instances, traveling as far south as Florida.
- In the Northeast, lake-effect snowstorms develop when cold weather fronts pass over the relatively warm surfaces of the Great Lakes.
- The eastern and northeastern states are affected by extratropical cyclonic weather systems in the Atlantic Ocean and the Gulf of Mexico that produce snow, ice storms, and occasional blizzards.

On January 1, 2006, the federal government began to use a new scale, similar to the scales used to measure the magnitude and intensity of hurricanes and tornadoes, to measure severe winter storms. The Northeast Snowfall Impact Scale (NESIS) provides a numerical value to storms based on the geographical area affected, the amount of snow accumulation, and the number of people affected. The minimum threshold for a storm's inclusion in the scale is 10 inches of snow falling over a wide area.

NESIS values range from 1 to 5 and include associated descriptors (from most to least severe) of Extreme, Crippling, Major, Significant, and Notable. The NESIS scale differs from other meteorological indices in that it considers population data. It uses the following formula:

$$\text{NESIS} = \sum_{n=4}^{x=30} \left[\frac{n}{10} \left(\frac{A_n}{A_{mean}} + \frac{P_n}{P_{mean}} \right) \right]$$

where A equals the area affected and P equals the population affected. Table 2-7 shows the categories assigned to severe winter storms using this formula.

Drought

Drought is defined as a prolonged shortage of available water, primarily due to insufficient rain and other precipitation or because exceptionally high temperatures and low humidity cause a drying of agriculture and a loss of stored water resources. Drought hazards differ from other natural hazards in three ways:

1. A drought's onset and conclusion are difficult to determine because the effects accumulate slowly and may linger even after the apparent termination of an episode.
2. There is no precise or universally accepted determination of what conditions constitute official drought conditions or the degree of drought severity.
3. The drought's effects are less obvious and spread over a larger geographic area.

Table 2-7   NESIS Values

Category	NESIS Value	Description
1	1–2.499	Notable
2	2.5–3.99	Significant
3	4–5.99	Major
4	6–9.99	Crippling
5	10.0+	Extreme

Source: NOAA, 2006. *http://www.ncdc.noaa.gov/oa/climate/research/ snow-nesis/*

In very poor countries, drought is associated with famine, which is widespread starvation brought about by limited access to food resources. However, in the United States, where mechanisms are in place to move resources quickly from region to region, the threat of famine no longer exists.

The Climate Prediction Center of the National Weather Service monitors nationwide drought conditions and provides visual reports on a weekly basis and seasonal reports on a monthly basis. A report of current drought conditions in the United States, referred to as the United States Drought Monitor, can be viewed at *http://www.cpc.noaa.gov/ products/expert_assessment/drought_assessment.shtml.*

Extreme Temperatures

Major diversions in average seasonal temperatures can cause injuries, fatalities, and major economic impacts when they are prolonged or coincide with other natural or technological events. Extreme heat, called a heat wave, occurs when temperatures of ten or more degrees above the average high temperature persist across a geographic region for several days or weeks. Humid or muggy conditions, which add to the discomfort of high temperatures, can occur when a "dome" of high atmospheric pressure traps hazy, damp air close to the ground. Excessively dry conditions that coincide with extreme heat can provoke wind and dust storms.

When little rain occurs in conjunction with extreme heat, droughts are likely to occur. Prolonged periods of heat have resulted in hundreds of thousands of deaths in single instances, including 600 in the Chicago area in 1995 and almost 37,500 in Europe in 2003. In most years, over 1,500 people die from exposure to excessive heat in the United States, making it the number one weather-related killer of humans.

While there is no widely accepted standard for extreme cold temperatures, periods of colder than normal conditions exhibit a range of negative consequences, depending on where they occur and exactly how cold temperatures fall. Any time temperatures fall below freezing, there is the risk of death from hypothermia to humans and livestock, with the degree to which populations are accustomed to those temperatures a primary factor in resilience. Extreme cold can also lead to serious economic damages from frozen water pipes; the freezing of navigable rivers, which halts commerce and can cause ice dams; and the destruction of crops.

Coastal Erosion

Coastal erosion, which is the loss of land bordering a body of water, is measured as the rate of change in the position or horizontal displacement of a shoreline over a period of time. It is generally associated with storm surges, hurricanes, windstorms, and flooding hazards, and it can be exacerbated by human activities such as boat wakes, shoreline hardening, and dredging. The primary concern with coastal erosion is the economic damages that occur to properties constructed very close to the eroding coasts, which lose their natural protection from the water and waves.

Environmental impacts from erosion include the loss of animal habitats and aesthetic losses. Fishing industries that are dependent on coastal habitats can suffer great losses from changes caused by coastal erosion, and the loss of tourism can result in similar economic impacts. Coastal features like dunes and mangroves also provide a natural defense against several hazards, including tsunami waves and storm surges, so their loss may signal an increase in vulnerability from these hazards.

Thunderstorms

Thunderstorms are meteorological events that bring heavy rains, strong winds, hail, lightning, and tornadoes. Thunderstorms are generated by atmospheric imbalance and turbulence caused by a combination of several conditions, including: unstable, warm air rising rapidly into the atmosphere; sufficient moisture to form clouds and rain; and upward lift of air currents caused by colliding weather fronts (cold and warm), sea breezes, or mountains.

A thunderstorm is classified as severe if its winds reach or exceed 58 mph, it produces a tornado, or it drops surface hail at least 0.75 inch in diameter. Thunderstorms may occur singly, in clusters, or in lines. Thus, it is possible for several thunderstorms to affect one location in the course of a few hours. These events are particularly devastating when a single thunderstorm affects one location for an extended period. Such conditions lead to oversaturation of the ground and subsequent flash flooding and slope erosion.

Lightning is a major secondary threat associated with thunderstorms. In the United States, between 75 and 100 Americans are hit and killed by lightning each year. Many air disasters have been linked to thunderstorms due to the unpredictable and turbulent wind conditions they cause and the threat of electronic or mechanical failure caused by lightning strikes. When humans or structures are hit by lightning, the effect is devastating to both.

Hail

Hail is frozen atmospheric water that falls to the earth. Moisture in clouds becomes frozen into crystals at high temperatures and begins to fall under its own weight. Typically, these crystals melt at lower temperatures, but in the right conditions they pick up more moisture as they fall and are then lifted to cold elevations, which causes refreezing. This cycle may continue until the individual hailstones reach several inches in diameter under the right conditions. Because of the strength of severe thunderstorms and tornadoes, both can cause this cyclic lifting, and therefore they are often accompanied by hail. Hailstorms occur more frequently during late spring and early summer when the jet stream migrates northward across the Great Plains. When they fall, they can damage crops, break windows, destroy cars and other exposed properties, collapse roofs, and cause other destruction totaling nearly $1 billion each year in the United States.

CRITICAL THINKING

- Are you aware of the hazards faced by your community, including those that may only happen once every few decades (and therefore may not have occurred in your lifetime)?
- Have any of your community's natural hazards resulted in a major disaster requiring state or federal assistance?
- Do any natural hazards affect your community routinely? If so, what actions has the community taken to mitigate these recurrent hazards? Have these actions been successful in reducing the consequences or likelihood of the hazards?
- Are there any natural hazards that you or your community can ignore because your geographic location precludes you from risk? What are those hazards, and why can you ignore them?

Technological Hazards

Technological, or man-made, hazards are an inevitable product of technological innovation and human development. These hazards, which can occur after the failure of existing technology, tend to be much less understood than their natural counterparts and are increasing in number as the scope of and dependence on technology expands. The most common technological hazards arise from various components of transportation, infrastructure, industry, and buildings/structures.

Structural Fires

Studies have shown that civilizations have been fighting structural fires using coordinated governmental resources since the first century AD (Coppola, 2006). Structural fires can be triggered or exacerbated by both natural processes, including lightning, high winds, earthquakes, volcanoes, and floods, or by human origins, including accidents and arson, for example. Lightning is the most significant natural contributor to fires affecting the built environment. Buildings with rooftop storage tanks for flammable liquids are particularly susceptible. There were 1,415,500 fires in the United States in 2008. Of these, 48.3 percent were outside and "other" fires, 35.4 percent were structure fires, and 16.3 percent were vehicle fires.

Residential fires represented 27.7 percent of all fires and 78.3 percent of structure fires. 83.7 percent of all civilian fire fatalities occurred in the home, where a home is defined as a one- or two-family dwelling or an apartment. Of those, approximately 72.5 percent occurred in single-family homes and duplexes. Intentionally set structure fires occurred 30,500 times and represented 5.9 percent of structural fires and $866 million in structural property losses. Over 17,500 vehicle fires were deliberately set, causing an estimated $139 million in property damage (Karter, 2008).

Dam Failures

Dams are constructed for many purposes, the most common being flood control and irrigation. When dams retaining large quantities of water fail, there exists the potential for large-scale uncontrolled releases of stored water downstream. Dam failures pose the most extreme flood risk due to the sudden and severe impacts that can result. Dams most often fail as a result of maintenance neglect, overtopping (as in the case of a flood), poor design, or structural damage caused by a major event such as an earthquake, collision, or blast. Dams are both publicly and privately owned and maintained, so their monitoring can pose a challenge to offices of emergency management charged with assessing associated hazard risk. The United States boasts the second greatest number of dams nationwide, exceeded only by China.

Hazardous Materials Incidents

Hazardous materials are chemical substances that if released or misused can pose a threat to the environment or personal health. Such chemicals are prevalent in many industries and products, including agriculture, medicine, research, and consumer product development. Hazardous materials may be explosive, flammable, corrosive, poisonous, radioactive, or otherwise toxic or dangerous. Releases typically occur as a result of transportation accidents or accidental releases at production and storage facilities. Depending on the nature of the chemical, the result of a release or spill can include death, serious injury, long-lasting health effects, and damage to buildings, homes, and other property.

While hazardous materials spills occur most commonly in homes, the quantities released are almost always too small to cause more than a highly localized hazard. It is the transportation or industrial use of such products that leads to major disaster events upon release. At present, hazardous materials are manufactured, used, or stored at an estimated 4.5 million facilities in the United States—from major industrial plants to local dry cleaning establishments or gardening supply stores.

Nuclear Accidents

Radioactive materials have provided significant benefits since their discovery, including the generation of power, scientific treatments and experiments, new detection, and imaging technologies, among many others. However, because the radiation emitted from these materials can cause immediate and lasting tissue damage to humans and animals upon exposure, these materials must be handled and contained using specialized techniques, materials, and facilities. National and international law strictly dictates who may possess these materials, how they can be used, and how and where they must be disposed of.

Exposure to radiation can be the result of an accidental or intentionally caused spill, breach of the containment vessel, escape of gasses, or an explosion. Nuclear material remains radioactive until it has shed all of its ionizing particles, called radio nuclides. This process, called radioactive decay, is the primary source of health risk to life. When released quickly, dust or gasses may rise into the atmosphere in a characteristic "plume," which carries the contaminants far from the point of origin with atmospheric currents, depositing it as radioactive fallout along its course.

In the United States, the greatest threat of exposure to radioactive materials comes from an accident or sabotage at one of the nation's many nuclear power plants. As the distance to a nuclear power plant decreases, the risk of exposure increases, and the likelihood of surviving in the event of a large-scale release of materials decreases. Since 1980, utilities operating commercial nuclear power plants in the United States have been required to maintain on- and off-site emergency response plans as a condition of maintaining their operating licenses. On-site emergency response plans are approved by the Nuclear Regulatory Commission (NRC). Off-site plans (which are closely coordinated with the utility's on-site emergency response plan) are evaluated by FEMA and provided to the NRC, who must consider the FEMA findings when issuing or maintaining a license.

A catastrophic failure of a nuclear reactor is called a meltdown, indicative of the failure of the reactor's containment due to the incredibly high heat caused by a runaway nuclear reaction. The worst nuclear accident to date was the result of a reactor core meltdown that occurred in at the Chernobyl Nuclear Power Plant in the Ukraine on April 26, 1986. So great was the radioactive plume and resultant fallout, which traveled as far as and landed primarily in neighboring Belarus, that over 336,000 people had to be evacuated and permanently resettled. Over 20 years later, the area is still uninhabitable.

In the United States, the most dangerous radioactive event, which was ultimately contained (thereby preventing any realized threat to human life), was the partial core meltdown at the Three Mile Island Nuclear Generating Station in Pennsylvania on March 28, 1979. The accident happened when a system that cooled the nuclear reaction, and therefore controlled the temperature of the reactor core, failed to operate correctly. While some nuclear material was released, the effect on people exposed was similar to that of receiving one or two medical x-rays. The public reaction to this event, however, significantly changed the course of the nuclear power industry in the United States, as expansion abruptly ended.

ADDITIONAL RESEARCH

The Nuclear Regulatory Commission released a report on the Three Mile Island nuclear accident. This report provides a summary of the events that occurred on March 29, 1979, and describes the health effects of the resulting release. Most significantly, it provides insight into the changes that the event ultimately had on the industry and on society's perception of the safety of nuclear power. This report site may be accessed at *http://www.nrc.gov/reading-rm/doc-collections/fact-sheets/3mile-isle.html*.

Terrorism

Terrorism is defined as the use of force or violence against individuals (civilians) or property for purposes of intimidation, coercion, or spreading fear in order to attain political, religious, or ideological goals. Radical or militant political and religious groups, which include or have included (for example) al Qaeda, the Khmer Rouge, the Revolutionary Armed Forces of Colombia (FARC), and Sendero Luminoso, typically lack the military means or public support to bring about societal change in favor of their representative views. These groups turn to the use of terrorism as a low-cost way to raise awareness of their message and influence the attitudes and actions of those presumably at risk from subsequent attacks. Terrorism, like war, is an influential tool that has been used by civilizations since the dawn of recorded history, and it will likewise always exist as a threat that must be mitigated and likewise managed.

Terrorism has been prevalent in the United States since long before the September 11, 2001 attacks on New York and the Pentagon, but the vast majority of these events originated from individuals or domestic organizations, used simple explosives, and were small in scale and effect. Some of the most notorious terrorists and groups that were labeled as "terrorist organizations" are the McNamara Brothers (bombed the *LA Times* building in 1910), the so-called "Unibomber" (Theodore Kaczynski), Eric Rudolph (the "Centennial Olympic Park bomber"), Timothy McVeigh (the mastermind behind the Oklahoma City bombing), the Animal Liberation Front, the Ku Klux Klan, and the Army of God.

The al Qaeda terrorists who performed the simultaneous terrorist attacks in Arlington, Virginia; New York City; and Shankville, Pennsylvania, elevated the perception of terrorism as a hazard risk and placed terrorism as a topic high on the public, policy, and media agendas due to the highly graphic, violent, and devastating impact of the attacks (which killed almost 3,000 people, caused billions of dollars in damages, and had immeasurable effects on the national and world economies). However, it is important that communities and governments remember the persistent threat that remains from domestic terrorist organizations and individuals, which have been successful in bringing about several attacks since 9/11, including the 2001 anthrax attacks, the Washington, D.C. sniper attacks in 2002, and many bombings and shootings at courthouses, abortion clinics, research centers, military recruitment centers, and others.

The primary method by which governments manage the terrorist threat is through both covert and overt intelligence gathering. Monitoring methods have expanded greatly with the advent of surveillance technologies, and statutory authorities have been expanded to allow for monitoring of phone calls, bank transactions, and other activities (to the dismay of civil rights groups who oppose such controls). Clearly, the ability of a government to monitor the terrorist risk is a delicate balance between knowing what its citizens are doing and allowing citizens the freedom of personal privacy.

Containment of the terrorist threat is another method of control, exhibited in the form of checkpoints (like in commercial airports worldwide), barriers at public and secure buildings, and security cameras and personnel placed in strategic locations. The U.S. government has developed agreements with many other national governments to coordinate transnational terrorism through the use of ports safety initiatives, traveler tracking, and monitoring of groups known to harbor terrorist intentions against the United States.

The Federal Bureau of Investigations (FBI) is the government agency in charge of tracking and preventing terrorist activities in the United States. The FBI categorizes terrorism according to two subgroups: (1) domestic terrorism, which involves groups or individuals whose terrorism activities are directed at elements of government or population without foreign direction; and (2) international terrorism, which involves groups or individuals whose terrorist activities are foreign-based and/or directed by countries or groups outside the United States or whose activities transcend national boundaries.

CBRN Incidents

One class of weapons has the potential to bring about an extraordinary degree of deaths, injuries, and property destruction. Several names have been given to this group of weapons, including weapons of mass destruction, NBC (nuclear, biological, and chemical) weapons, and ABC (atomic, biological, and chemical) weapons, but the conventional acronym used in contemporary practice is CBRN (pronounced "see-burn"), representing the acronym formed by the first letters of the chemical, biological, radiological, and nuclear devices that the category includes. Although these weapons are considered weapons of mass destruction because of their potential for creating such widespread destruction, it should be noted that they can also be distributed in such a way as to harm or kill only one or a very few individuals.

CBRN weapons may be possessed and used by both terrorists and foreign national governments. The processes by which control and containment are conducted, however, differ greatly between the two. In the case of official governments, mitigation is generally performed through the use of diplomacy, international agreements, and sanctions. With terrorist groups such measures have little or no effect, so control must be performed through the use of raw materials regulation and monitoring, surveillance and other intelligence gathering, and, at times, military action (usually not until all other options have failed).

Chemical

Chemical weapons are naturally occurring or man-made liquids, gasses, or solids (typically in the form of dust) that exhibit toxic effects on humans, animals, plants, or property upon exposure. Chemical agents are most commonly created for the sole purpose of killing, injuring, or incapacitating people. Chemical agents must be delivered onto or around intended victims to be effective, and there are a number of ways to do this. For instance, chemical agents may be aerosolized, dropped, splashed, poured into water supplies or foods, released by bombs, or sprayed from containers or vehicles (including aircraft, boats, or vehicles).

One of the greatest challenges facing emergency management and response officials is the detection of chemical agents that have been delivered via covert means. Chemical weapons can be invisible, odorless, and tasteless, and they may have an immediate identifiable effect (a few seconds to a few minutes) or have a delayed effect. The presence of a chemical agent is often easy to detect because of several telltale signs, including a sudden difficulty breathing; nausea; a burning sensation in the skin, eyes, or lungs; disorientation or loss of consciousness; or seizures.

In the case of common chemicals, such as chlorine gas, personnel familiar with the chemical's characteristics can often identify what chemical was released by smell or sight and the presence of certain effects as just listed (as well as the presence of specific containers or delivery mechanisms). However, with most chemical agents, identification of the specific chemical once detection has occurred is only possible using advanced technology. Because different chemicals have unique processes by which they are neutralized or their effects treated, identification is key to response and remediation.

These are the six primary categories of chemical agents, distinguished by their effect on humans:

- Pulmonary, or "choking," agents
- Blood agents
- Vesicants or blister agents
- Nerve agents
- Incapacitating agents
- Irritants (typically used for riot control but capable of spreading panic when used by terrorists)

Biological

Biological agents are either live organisms or the toxins produced by live organisms, either naturally occurring or genetically engineered, that can kill or incapacitate people, livestock, and crops. Biological agents are grouped into three primary categories: bacteria, viruses, and toxins.

As with chemical agents, biological agents can be delivered covertly or overtly. However, most biological agents do not have immediate effects, and it may be days or weeks before the presence of an attack involving a biological agent is recognized. This is especially true with bacteria and viruses, which have an initial period of incubation following infection where no symptoms are present in victims. Toxins, on the other hand, typically exhibit the same rate of effect as seen with chemical agents.

Recognition of a biological attack is typically made by the public health service, which monitors illnesses and deaths nationwide, and which would likely catch a rapid upsurge in strange or unidentifiable sources of similar illnesses and deaths. Other methods of detection include threat identification, the discovery of the agent or delivery and production materials, and intelligence gathering.

Biological agents are difficult to grow and maintain. Although many of these agents decay rapidly when exposed to sunlight and other environmental factors, others (such as anthrax spores) are resilient and can survive for decades or longer even in harsh conditions. Biological agents are particularly dangerous when they involve transmissible illnesses, such as smallpox, because the effect can quickly spread beyond the initial group of people exposed by contagion between affected and unaffected individuals.

Human-to-human transmission has been the primary source of infection in past epidemics that involved pathogens capable of use as a biological weapon, including smallpox, plague, and the Lassa virus. When biological agents target plants or animals, they can devastate economic sectors (including agriculture and livestock) and instill fear equal to that of agents that affect humans and can have crossover effects on humans. For instance, in 1918, the German army spread anthrax and other diseases by distributing infected livestock and animal feed.

As with chemical weapons, the primary defense lies with rapid and accurate recognition and identification. Each agent has a highly specific treatment and decontamination method associated with it. Biological agents are grouped into three categories: category A agents are those that have great potential for causing a public health catastrophe and are capable of being disseminated over a large geographic area. Examples of category A agents are anthrax, smallpox, plague, botulism, tularemia, and viral hemorrhagic fevers. Category B agents are those that have low mortality rates but may be disseminated over a large geographic area with relative ease. Category B agents include salmonella, ricin, Q fever, typhus, and glanders. Category C agents are common pathogens that have the potential for being engineered for terrorism or weapon purposes. Examples of category C agents are hantavirus and tuberculosis.

Radiological

Radiological agents are those that cause harm by exposing victims to the damaging energy emitted by unstable radioactive materials. Radiological agents require very little technological innovation to use, since the materials dispersed are naturally hazardous. However, the materials are rare in nature and highly controlled and are therefore difficult to obtain. The most common sources of radiological materials are research laboratories, medical institutions, and hazardous waste containment facilities.

The greatest threat from a radiological agent would occur if a terrorist group dispersed radiological material using either an explosive device (commonly called a "dirty bomb") or another nonexplosive method, including spraying or aerosolization, which is called a "radiological dispersion device," or RDD. It is well known that the greatest physical risk from a dirty bomb would be from the blast rather than the radiological materials themselves. However, the fear and panic that would result from the detection of radioactive materials on the victims and in the debris generated could have far-reaching economic impacts in the immediate area of the attack and throughout the country—or even the world.

An alternative to a dirty bomb or RDD that is of great concern to the U.S. government is the possibility that terrorists may attack a nuclear facility for the purpose of dispersing radiological materials and likewise instilling mass hysteria. While most nuclear facilities were designed to withstand great impacts and large explosions (including several constructed to withstand a direct hit by a commercial airliner), the possibility of sabotage on safety and cooling systems or the use of an explosive strong enough to breach containment exists. Additionally, the radioactive waste produced at these facilities is usually stored on-site. While this material is of little use for power generation, it would be extremely valuable to a terrorist who wanted to cause harm.

Nuclear

Nuclear agents are those that cause great harm through the activation of a fission or fusion chain reaction that is possible only through the most advanced weapons technology and using only the most refined nuclear materials (and in quantities necessary to sustain a blast effect). A nuclear blast is an explosion that emits intense light, heat, and damaging pressure and disperses radioactive debris over a widespread area, leading to the contamination of air, water, and ground surfaces for miles around. While the likelihood of a terrorist organization developing an operational nuclear weapon is almost nil, there is always the possibility that rogue states known to support terrorist organizations or states unable to monitor and protect their nuclear weapons caches could become a source of such weaponry for terrorist groups with great financial means.

The effect of successful terrorist use of a nuclear weapon would surely be the death of thousands and the destruction of billions of dollars in property, especially if it was detonated in a major urban center. The detonation of atomic weapons in Hiroshima and

---

CRITICAL THINKING

- What technological hazards affect your community? What are the sources of those hazards?
- Society accepts certain technological hazards because they enjoy the benefits associated with the action or process that causes the hazard. For instance, nuclear power plants produce inexpensive electricity with very little emissions. However, in the event of an accident, a major disaster could result. What benefits does your community enjoy despite the existence of associated technological hazards, and what are those hazards?

Nagasaki give insight into the power of a nuclear weapon, given that those two relatively small bombs resulted in the death of over 220,000 people and almost total destruction of the city centers in these two metropolises (see *www.ready.gov, www.dhs.gov*).

Hazards Risk Management

The process by which individuals, communities, and countries deal with the hazard risks they face is known as hazards risk management. Risk management is a primary function of government, and many different methodologies have been developed in the United States and throughout the world to manage hazards risk. Even within the United States, different government agencies may perform hazards risk management using different methods, as is the case with FEMA and the Department of Defense, for instance. However, almost all hazards risk management methodologies operate according to a four-step process:

1. Identify the hazards.
2. Assess the risks for each hazard identified.
3. Analyze the hazards risks in relation to one another.
4. Treat the hazards risk according to prioritization.

It is the differences in terminology, technologies, application of stakeholder input, and other issues that differentiate these various methods that have emerged.

Hazard identification, as the name suggests, is the process through which all hazards that have or could affect an area of focus are identified and described. This is done through a number of methods, including historical study, brainstorming, scientific analysis, and subject matter expertise. For more common hazards, such as snowstorms or tornadoes, the presence of the hazard will be obvious. However, for new or changing hazards, such as many technological hazards and intentional hazards (including terrorism), only the knowledge or opinion of experts can provide insight into the presence and range of these rare, yet real, hazards. Hazard identification results in a list of hazards that is exhaustive if done properly, irrespective of known likelihood or severity. To be comprehensive, a hazards risk management effort must look not at each hazard individually and irrespective of the others but rather at the entire hazards portfolio as interconnected and as each hazard having an influence on the effects and risks of the others.

Hazard description, or profiling as it is also called, is a component of hazard identification wherein the particular way each hazard exists within the studied area is defined. To describe a hazard, the following characteristics are often investigated:

• General description of the hazard
• The location of the hazard and spatial extent of its effects
• The duration of an event caused by the hazard
• Seasonal or other time-based patterns followed by the hazard
• Speed of onset of an actual hazard event
• Availability of warnings for the hazard

Hazard risk assessment is the process through which the threat posed by each identified hazard is investigated. Risk is calculated according to two equal factors: hazard likelihood and hazard consequence. Together, these factors inform us of how concerned we should be about the existence of a hazard and what we can do to prevent or treat the hazard. Generally, high-likelihood/high-consequence hazards are of greatest concern, while low-likelihood/low-consequence hazards are of least concern, and all of the others fall in between. However, the relationships between hazards and their associated risks are incorporated into the risk assessment and analysis processes in order to allow communities or countries to employ a comprehensive risk management program that results in the greatest reduction in lives lost and property damaged.

There are various approaches to developing a risk assessment methodology, ranging from qualitative to quantitative, as well as several computer-based models for natural hazard risk assessment that have been developed for individual hazards such as earthquakes, floods, hurricanes, and landslides. The validity and utility of any risk assessment outcome is defined by the quality and availability of data. Emergency managers must rely on a range of sources to develop accurate determinations of likelihood and consequence, despite the fact that these factors are constantly changing as a result of increased development, access to new information, changes in climates and community characteristics, and many other factors that can complicate the equations. Furthermore, it can be impossible to extrapolate exact numerical values that are representative of these two factors for each, or even any, of the hazards that have been identified.

As mentioned previously, there are many different methodologies that have been developed to overcome the difficulties that exist in the assessment of hazards risk. In the United States, Australia, and New Zealand, for instance, various qualitative assessment systems have been developed to measure likelihood and consequence values. Rather than relying on specific mathematical calculations to determine exact values, qualitative systems limit the possible values to a smaller defined range (typically five to seven values) into which each hazard is more easily placed. For example, it may be difficult to calculate the rate of return for an ice storm to the specific year (e.g., one event every 35 years), but it is much more possible to determine whether that storm will occur once or more every year or once every two to ten years. Qualitative systems are not exact, but they facilitate a process that might otherwise be too difficult or time-consuming and therefore disregarded.

Another risk assessment method is the Composite Exposure Indicator (CEI) approach, which is based on the effects of a single or multiple hazards on a series of indicator variables focused primarily on infrastructure, such as roads, pipelines, hospitals, public water supply, and so on. This system, which relies on databases maintained by FEMA and other sources, is a measure of exposure of 14 variables that produces a number that is then correlated to the population affected.

Hazard risk analysis is performed in order to determine the relative seriousness of hazard risks that have been identified and assessed. Using the processes just listed to identify the hazards that threaten the community or country, to characterize them, and to determine their likelihoods and consequences, emergency managers will have gathered all of the information necessary to determine how these risks compare to one another. For this reason, by the time the risk evaluation process begins, each hazard must have been identified, described, mapped, and analyzed according to its likelihood of occurrence and its consequences should a disaster occur.

Hazard risk analysis is so important because while all communities face a range of natural, technological, and intentional hazards—each of which requires a different degree of mitigation and risk reduction—most communities have a range of competing budgetary pressures and are therefore unable to fully mitigate all hazard risks. The goal, as a result, is to lower the number of deaths, injuries, and damage to property and the environment associated with hazards to an acceptable degree, so they must ensure that their time and other resources are dedicated to the actions and activities that give them the greatest results overall.

Risk analysis is most commonly conducted through the use of a risk matrix. To create a risk matrix, emergency managers create a graph that represents risk likelihood and consequence on the x- and y-axes, with the highest of both falling in the upper right quadrant and the lowest in the bottom left. If a quantitative system has been used, the defined values selected for each of the two risk factors are transferred onto this matrix. Otherwise, if quantitative representations of likelihood and consequences have been used, the minimum and maximum of all hazards analyzed represent the high and low limits of the two graph axes. Then, all of the hazards are plotted onto this matrix together, thereby providing a visual illustration of a community or country's hazard risks in relation to one another. Using the results of the risk matrix, a prioritized ranking of risks is created. This list becomes the basis of the final step, which is the treatment of identified hazard risks.

The value of the risk analysis process in prioritizing risks is significantly improved when performed in conjunction with supplemental methodologies. For instance, a vulnerability analysis can help to determine what is causing risks, why certain risks rank above others, and what can be done to increase resilience or decrease vulnerability through the various risk treatments identified in the fourth and final step.

Risk vulnerability looks at four factors, including social vulnerability, environmental vulnerability, physical vulnerability, and economic vulnerability. Risks can also be prioritized according to the acceptability of the population at risk. For instance, despite the fact that more people are exposed to a particular risk or that it causes more fatalities or damages each year, it might still be more palatable to the exposed population than another much less dangerous or damaging risk due to the benefits that would be lost if the risk was partially or fully mitigated. For example, transportation accidents have caused more fatalities in the United States and worldwide than nuclear power accidents. Yet, most people are much more willing to accept the risk of transportation accidents than nuclear accidents because the loss of automobiles would have a much more personal and profound impact.

The SMAUG methodology is only one of the systems developed to gauge these issues. SMAUG is an acronym that stands for the five factors according to which hazard risks are analyzed by risk managers using the system: seriousness, manageability, acceptability, urgency, and growth.

Hazard risk treatment is the process by which either the likelihood of a disaster risk is reduced or eliminated or measures are taken to reduce the impacts of those hazard events that do actually occur. Hazard risks are treated through hazard mitigation and disaster preparedness (the topics of Chapters 3 and 4, respectively). The selection of risk treatment options takes the risk assessment methodology beyond process to decision making and action. At this point, risk reduction options have been analyzed not only for their cost effectiveness but also for their acceptability by society and their long-term positive and negative impacts. The treatment process then becomes a technical and political one by which funds are finally dedicated, laws are changed or enacted and likewise enforced, and solutions are implemented.

Risk Management Technology

The nation's ability to manage and reduce hazards risk has significantly improved in the last 15 years. Through vast technological advancement, emergency managers are better able to perform all four of the previous steps. Imaging and sensing technology, including satellite imagery and aircraft-based systems (such as radar, LIDAR, and FLIR), allow for much better identification and spatial mapping of hazards risk across risk zones.

Risk modeling, including software such as the FEMA-developed HAZUS-MH (Hazards United States—MultiHazard) program, allows not only predisaster estimation of impacts and response requirements but also early disaster estimation of likely damages and needs (before actual assessment data can be collected). The connectivity of the Internet has allowed greater sharing of information and ideas across regions where similar problems are encountered and mitigated.

GIS mapping software enables the plotting of risks and resources using layers of information that would have required much more difficult resources to obtain only decades ago. Even commonly used web-based programs such as Google Earth have increased the ability of emergency managers with few resources to better understand the nature of the risk their communities face, including the plotting of floodplains and the proximity of various structures to known hazards. The research and scientific agencies of the federal government and the university community continue to develop new approaches to measuring, mapping, and predicting natural hazards. Since the September 11, 2001, attacks, federal and university-based funding dedicated to the advancement of emergency management technology has reached into the billions and is helping to develop even more methods to detect, understand, and treat natural, technological, and, most notably, terrorist hazards.

Social and Economic Risk Factors

It has long been recognized that a strong correlation exists between disasters and poverty. Because of several factors, including the inability to afford preparedness and mitigation measures, the lower rental and purchase costs associated with high-risk land and a general lack of knowledge concerning risk and its sources, the poor are more vulnerable to disasters and therefore find themselves repeatedly subject to them. While this is much more apparent in the developing countries, where the bulk of annual disaster deaths occur, risk factors based on poverty and social conditions also exist within countries.

In the United States, little has been done to address the social and economic factors of risk that make one group more vulnerable than another. Risk assessments have generally considered populations to be homogeneous for risk-planning purposes, thereby neglecting to address individual problems of certain social and economic groups that may not benefit as much, or at all, from the plans and capacities that are developed. Social advocacy groups have been working for years to raise awareness of the increased disaster vulnerability of "special populations" (which include, among others, the disabled, the elderly, the poor, children, and immigrants) with mixed success. However, Hurricane Katrina brought the reality of the socioeconomic vulnerability divide into every living room in the country via the mass media. Numerous social and political groups contend that it was poverty that caused Katrina's high number of victims and that the poor shouldered an undue portion of the region's risk, while the wealthy escaped relatively unharmed (a claim that was later refuted). Others called it a race disaster, claiming that the government neglected to bring about a more significant immediate response because a majority of the victims were African American. Regardless of the validity of these claims, it is clear that the majority of the people who failed to leave New Orleans did so because they had no access to transportation, they were afraid to leave their meager possessions behind, or they had no resources with which to shelter themselves away from the risk zone. And in the aftermath of this disaster, it has become painfully apparent that these same social and economic risk factors further hamper the poorer victims as they attempt recovery.

ADDITIONAL RESEARCH

A study conducted by Columbia University one year after the hurricane found that the poorest victims continued to suffer from significant income loss, higher than normal incidence of chronic illnesses, and a proportionally higher rate of mental health problems in children. This report, "The Recovery Divide: Poverty and the Widening Income Gap Among Mississippi Children and Families Affected by Hurricane Katrina," can be accessed at *http://www.ncdp .mailman.columbia.edu/files/recovery_divide.pdf*.

The social makeup of a population is based on a diverse set of factors that include education, culture, local government, social interaction, values, laws, beliefs, and other aspects of society. Within most communities, the hazard vulnerability of different groups varies due to a range of sociocultural factors that help or prevent individuals in those groups from taking mitigative or preparative actions to protect themselves. The behavior of epidemics among different groups, and the people of different countries, can be heavily influenced by social factors specific to each group or country that result in much closer interactions or greater "social distancing." Certain religious, cultural, or traditional practices and beliefs can also help or hinder disaster management practices.

Religious beliefs that label disasters the "will of God" are less likely to influence posi-tive mitigation and preparedness behavior than those that promote the responsibility of individuals and governments to protect life from dangers that exist in the environment. And though it may not be evident to the people practicing such behaviors, their mitiga-tive or preparatory actions may be the product of a previous social adjustment to a haz-ard. Disaster managers must be able to recognize when social interactions are either helping or hindering people in reducing their vulnerability to hazards, and they must rec-ognize what aspect of that social process is causing the alteration.

Financial status also deeply affects a population's and individuals' abilities to protect themselves from the consequences of disaster. Financial well-being, however, does not indicate that an individual or society *will* protect themselves; rather, it is just a measure of their ability to do so. Other factors may be learned from this economic profile. Trends and tendencies associated with wealth, or the lack thereof, can be deduced. For instance, the poor are often marginalized and forced to live on more dangerous land. Their housing is more likely to be constructed of materials that are unable to withstand environmental pressures. They are more likely to have zero tolerance to delays in basic necessities that often follow disasters.

When considering the definition of a disaster and the concept of vulnerability, it is easy to understand why the poor are more vulnerable. Because an event only becomes a disaster when the capacity to respond to the event is exceeded, requiring external assis-tance to manage the consequences, the poor—who survive on the brink of disaster each day—are much quicker to exhaust their resources when unforeseen events arise.

CRITICAL THINKING

- Select a hazard that affects you or your community. Describe the characteristics of the hazard (how it would affect you or the community, including strong winds, ground shaking, etc.). Assess the risk associated with this hazard for you or your community, including the frequency of the hazard affecting you and the consequences if a disaster were to occur.
- What aspects of a community's geographic profile influence the hazards they face (e.g., proximity to a coast, slope of terrain)? What human practices influence these hazards (e.g., damming of rivers, filling in wetlands)? What natural processes influence these hazards (e.g., annual rainfall, temperature)?

Conclusion

In the process by which hazard risks are managed, often called hazards risk management, the identification of hazards is the key factor that determines what preparative and pre-ventive measures will be taken by the community. In other words, a community needs to know their risks to manage them.

Through the monitoring of hazards, emergencies, and disaster throughout the world, and research conducted into the mechanism by which natural, technological, and intentional hazards operate, a greater understanding of risk is being achieved. Without this collection of valuable information, societies would be much less able to manage the consequences of the low-incidence, high-catastrophe events, such as tsunamis or weapons of mass destruction, that have traditionally gone unaddressed or have been handled in a haphazard manner. In sum, information is power, and with information about hazards, societies will have the power to act effectively to reduce or eliminate their risk.

Of course, with increased knowledge comes increased responsibility. The provision of hazard information and management tools to states and communities is but one necessary step in the risk-reduction process. Success of these efforts requires that they assume responsibility and take appropriate action. Emergency management provides the impetus for incorporating these considerations into the planning and governing of our communities.

Hazards will persist. Some, particularly technological hazards, may be reduced by our efforts, but our ability to control or eliminate natural hazards is questionable. Recent efforts to undo some of the former channelization and flood control projects undertaken by the U.S. Army Corps of Engineers, once thought to be an effective measure to eliminate flood risk, are vivid examples of our inability to control nature. However, there is still a strong argument for an increased emphasis on improved science in hazard identification and increased financial support for hazards mapping, both of which have been effective components in community hazards risk management efforts.

As our knowledge about hazards continues to expand, the economic and social logic of applying long-term solutions for reducing the risks posed by these hazards through mitigation and preparedness will gain momentum. The cost-to-benefit ratios of mitigation and preparedness efforts will become more attractive to local political bodies, and, eventually, disaster losses will begin to fall substantially. However, each and all of these local successes will be wholly dependent on the leadership potential and motivational abilities of an emergency management professional, who will be the driving force behind any such positive momentum that exists.

Important Terms

Avalanche
Blizzard
CBRN weapons
Coastal erosion
Dam failure
Disaster
Earthquake
Expansive soil
Extreme cold
Extreme heat
Flood

Hail
Hazard
Hazardous materials
Hazards risk management
Hurricane
Landslide
Lateral spread
Mass movement
Mudflow (or debris flow)
Natural hazard
Risk
Rockfall
Safe room
Severe winter storm
Storm surge
Technological hazard
Terrorism
Thunderstorm
Tornado
Tropical cyclone
Tropical storm
Tsunami
Volcano
Wildland fire (or wildfire)

Self-Check Questions

1. How is a hazard different from a disaster?
2. What is the most frequent and widespread disaster-causing hazard?
3. What scale is commonly used to describe the effects of earthquakes?
4. How are earthquakes measured?
5. Describe the process by which hurricanes form.
6. What scale is used to describe the intensity of hurricanes?
7. What are the various ways that hurricanes cause damages to a community?
8. What is a SLOSH model used to measure?
9. Why was the Fujita-Pearson Tornado Scale updated in 2006, and what changes were made?
10. What are the three categories of wildland fires?
11. How are severe weather storms measured?
12. What single disaster type caused nine of the top ten natural disasters ranked by FEMA relief costs?
13. What is the source of most hazardous materials incidents?

14. List and describe four categories of weapons of mass destruction.
15. What six steps are common to most risk assessment methodologies?
16. Name several of the social factors emergency managers must consider when assessing a community's risk.
17. What are some of the factors that make up a community's economic profile? How do these factors influence that community's disaster risk?

Out-of-Class Exercises

Visit FEMA's disaster declaration archive at *http://www.fema.gov/news/disaster_totals_ annual.fema*. View the disaster declarations for your state. Beginning with 1998 and moving forward to the present time, view the disaster declarations to determine what disasters affected your county. What hazards affected your county during this time? How many times did each occur? If possible, determine what assistance the federal government provided in response to the disaster.

3

The Disciplines of Emergency Management: Mitigation

What You'll Learn

- The variety of mitigation tools available to planners
- Impediments to mitigation and other associated problems
- Federal and nonfederal mitigation programs
- Mitigation methods in practice through specific case studies

Introduction

Disasters are a reality of living in the natural world. Despite humans' attempts to control nature that began with the early Egyptians and continue to today's massive flood-control efforts, natural hazards are something we constantly face. Over the last decade, the social and economic costs of disasters to the United States and throughout the world have grown significantly. From 2000 to 2008, the costs of disasters in the United States are estimated to be over $355 billion. Deaths and economic losses from natural disasters worldwide jumped significantly in 2008 compared to the previous seven years. In 2008 the UN estimated that 235,816 people were killed in natural disasters, 211 million were impacted, and the cost was over US$181 billion. Costs from dealing with disasters were 50 percent higher than the average costs per year from 2000 to 2007. The causes of this growth are myriad. Climatological changes such as El Niño, global warming, and a rise in sea level are some of the factors. When you add the effects of societal actions, such as increased development, deforestation and clear-cutting, the migration of populations to coastal areas, and the filling in of floodplains, you have total calamity.

Mitigation, the means for reducing these impacts, is defined as a sustained action to reduce or eliminate the risks to people and property from such hazards and their effects. In our discussion of mitigation, we focus on natural hazards mitigation efforts and programs in the United States. We will examine some of the techniques for mitigation of technological hazards, but the body of knowledge and applications in this area are still evolving. Many of the successful natural hazards techniques such as building codes, however, can be applied to technological hazards.

The function of mitigation differs from the other emergency management disciplines because it looks at long-term solutions to reducing risk as opposed to preparedness for hazards, the immediate response to a hazard, or the short-term recovery from a hazard event. Mitigation is usually not considered part of the emergency phase of a disaster as in response or as part of emergency planning as in preparedness. The definition lines do get a little blurred regarding recovery. Applying mitigation strategies should be a part of the recovery from disaster (see Chapter 7), but even in this context, these are actions that will reduce the impacts, or risks, over time.

The recovery function of emergency management still represents one of the best opportunities for mitigation, and until recently, this phase in a disaster plan provided the most substantial funding for mitigation activities. Recently, however, the trend has shifted toward greater federal spending on predisaster mitigation, which is discussed later in this chapter.

Another thing that sets mitigation apart from the other disciplines of emergency management is the participation and support of a broad spectrum of players outside of the traditional emergency management circle. Mitigation involves land-use planners; construction and building officials, both public and private; business owners; insurance companies; community leaders; and politicians. The skills and tools for accomplishing mitigation (i.e., planning expertise, political acumen, marketing and public relations, and consensus building) are different from the operational, first-responder skills that more often characterize emergency management professionals. In fact, historically, emergency management professionals have been reluctant to take a lead role in promoting mitigation. To paraphrase a state director of emergency management, "I will never lose my job for failing to do mitigation, but I could lose my job if I mess up a response."

With the exception of the fire community, whose members were early leaders in the effort to mitigate fire risks through support for building codes, code enforcement, and public education, the emergency management community has remained focused on their preparedness planning and response obligations. Throughout the decade of 2000, leadership at the federal level has supported these priorities through their funding, especially after the events of September 11, where terrorism planning and preparedness were top priorities. Even in the aftermath of Hurricane Katrina, mitigation was not viewed as a programmatic imperative. Some exceptions, such as new federal mitigation programs supported to reduce exposure under the NFIP and more interest at the local level to apply mitigation postdisaster, were evidenced. The rise in local initiatives is important because that is where mitigation can be the most effective in reducing future losses (Figure 3-1). However, the lack of leadership at the federal level is troubling, since state and local emergency managers traditionally reflect federal priorities in their actions.

This chapter discusses the tools of mitigation, the impediments to mitigation, federal programs that support mitigation, and several case studies that demonstrate how these tools have been applied to successfully reduce various risks.

Mitigation Tools

Over the years, the United States has made great strides in reducing the number of deaths that occur in natural disasters. Through building codes, warning systems, and public

FIGURE 3-1 Pascagoula, Mississippi, November 29, 2005, and August 8, 2006. Before (top) and after (bottom) photos of the elevation of a house flooded by the storm surge of Hurricane Katrina. Elevating a house is an excellent way to protect it against flooding.
Mark Wolfe/FEMA.

education, the number of deaths and casualties from natural disasters in the last century has significantly declined. Economic effects and property damages, however, have escalated. Many people believe that these costs are preventable and that the tools required to dramatically reduce these costs are now available (Figure 3-2).

Technological disasters such as the Oklahoma City bombing and the terrorist attacks of September 11, 2001, are not as easy to analyze. There is much speculation about how improved intelligence and security could reduce the human effects of these disasters. From a property perspective, many people believe that some reduction in impacts could be achieved through application of traditional mitigation techniques such as improved building construction for blast effects. Other technological disasters such as the Valdez oil spill, the Three Mile Island emergency, and so on could have been prevented through better inspections, training, education, and exercises. These measures reflect good preparedness activities more than mitigation. In any case, further research and analyses are needed to answer the questions posed by the effects of terrorist events and similar technological hazards.

Most practitioners agree that the primary intent of mitigation is to ensure that fewer communities and individuals become victims of disasters. The goal of mitigation is to create economically secure, socially stable, better built, and more environmentally sound communities that are out of harm's way (Figure 3-3).

FIGURE 3-2 Pass Christian, Mississippi, October 4, 2005. Aerial photo of the only surviving home in the area that was completely destroyed by Hurricane Katrina. Foundations are all that remain of most of the neighboring homes. The surviving home was built using many FEMA standards.
John Fleck/FEMA.

FIGURE 3-3 Malibu, California, November 16, 2007. The irrigation sprinkler system at Pepperdine University Campus is an example of how fire prevention and mitigation practices can save homes and vegetation.
Susie Shapira/FEMA.

The following mitigation tools are known to reduce risk:

- Hazard identification and mapping
- Design and construction applications
- Land-use planning
- Financial incentives
- Insurance
- Structural controls

Hazard Identification and Mapping

The hazard identification mitigation tool is fairly obvious. You can't mitigate a hazard if you don't know what it is or whom it affects. The most essential part of any mitigation strategy or plan is an analysis of what the hazards are in a particular area. The resources for hazard identification are numerous. The federal government has extensive programs that map virtually every hazard, and these products are available to communities. FEMA's National Flood Insurance Program (NFIP) provides detailed flood maps and studies, and the U.S. Geological Survey (USGS) provides extensive earthquake and landslide studies and maps. Many state agencies have refined the products for hazard identification. For example, special soil stability studies and geological investigations, which are required in some parts of California, further refine this analysis.

Geographic information systems (GIS) have become ubiquitous and are staples for all local planning organizations. What is often missing from the available tools is the ability to superimpose the human and built environment onto the hazards, thereby providing a quantified level of risk. FEMA's HAZUS methodology, which was developed in the 1990s, has become a user-oriented tool for both state and local emergency managers to assess potential losses from floods, hurricanes, and earthquakes. Potential losses estimated in HAZUS include physical damage, economic loss, and societal impacts. This tool is also available to the private sector.

The newest addition to the mapping tool kit is a program called RiskMAP that aims to reduce the losses of life and property through effective local mitigation activities driven by quality flood hazard data, risk assessments, and mitigation planning. On March 16, 2009, the U.S. Congress approved FEMA's Risk Mapping, Assessment, and Planning (RiskMAP) Multi-Year Plan for Fiscal Years 2011–2014.

ADDITIONAL RESEARCH

FEMA's Multi-Year Plan outlines the goals, objectives, and strategies for RiskMAP and identifies the roles and responsibilities of stakeholders. It is available at *http:www.fema.gov/plan/prevent/flhm*.

Design and Construction Applications

The design and construction process provides one of the most cost-effective means of addressing risk. This process is governed by building codes, architecture and design criteria, and soils and landscaping considerations. Code criteria that support risk reduction usually apply only to new construction, substantial renovation, or renovation to change the type or use of the building. Enactment of building codes is the responsibility of the states, and most state codes are derivatives of one of the three model codes, which reflect geographical differences across the United States. Some states delegate code adoption responsibility to more local governmental authorities. Because of the cost, codes that require rehabilitation of existing potentially hazardous structures have been rarely implemented.

The Los Angeles seismic retrofit ordinance is a rare example. The case study of the new design codes to decrease the impacts of wildfires in California, which have become an increasing threat, illustrates the importance of building codes to mitigation.

CASE STUDY: NEW DEVELOPMENTS' CONSTRUCTION STANDARDS REQUIRE WILDFIRE MITIGATION

Rancho Santa Fe, California. More than 2,460 multimillion-dollar houses that were constructed with the strictest construction standards possible, including expansive defensible space around and within the home development areas, survived extremely well when the Witch Fire stormed through the area in October 2007.

The blaze burned up to plants on defensible spaces and stopped. Embers blown into areas of the estates bounced off tile roofs with boxed-in eaves, stucco walls, patios, and other areas and then died out without leaving more than incidental damage, mostly scorched plants. Although a half-dozen charred embers the size of footballs were found in the Cielo estates, according to Ken Crosby, one of the realtors for the estate areas, "Nothing was burned."

Five Rancho Santa Fe developments, completed just three-plus years before the Witch Fire, basically set construction standards on the "shelter-in-place" concept developed in Australia. The standards for construction and mitigation, including mandated interior fire sprinklers, extensive defensible space, and use of fire-resistant vegetation, are the "toughest in the country," according to Cliff Hunter, fire marshal for the Rancho Santa Fe Fire Protection District, which provides fire protection for the five developments.

The strict development standards also make these homes in the shelter-in-place communities safer places to stay if the residents are unable to evacuate. Fire officials, however, advise people to evacuate rather than stay and try to fight the fires and to not get a false sense of security because their homes are considered to be a safe refuge.

The estate homes were constructed with materials and techniques intended to make the structures as resistant as possible to the effects of wildland fires. Only slow-to-ignite plants are planted near the homes. The standards are strictly maintained by the Rancho Santa Fe Fire Protection District's fire marshal.

The Sargentis' home is on the eastern edge of The Crosby, with a wide swath of defensible space adjoining the backyard. During the fire, smoke and ash entered their home through the drier vent, and the garage filled with smoke. The Sargentis explained that they had attended a program that explained how the shelter-in-place program worked. They learned that the concept had not been tested in the United States and that they should "get out early" if they chose to evacuate, as well as what to do if they stayed in their home.

When they learned that the fire was headed their way, they immediately left—well before the automatic alert that was sent to their house at 9 a.m. that Monday morning. Steve Sargenti said he "knew the house was intact," and when the family returned, they found their house untouched, other than the smoke inside. Embers that had landed on the concrete tile roof had burned out, and the courtyard in front of the house "was a repository" for spent embers, said Steve.

Source: FEMA.gov. *http://www.fema.gov/mitigationbp/bestPracticeDetailPDF.do?mitssId=5368*

Performance-based design and construction are becoming more critical, especially when building in earthquake-prone areas. This concept incorporates not just life safety requirements but continued use of the building in the aftermath of any disaster. In lieu of updated building codes, performance-based design can play a significant role in ensuring the viability of our built environment in the aftermath of a disaster.

The federal government has made a significant investment in developing technical guidance for improving the building and construction of structures in hazard areas, particularly earthquake-, wind-, and flood-prone areas. The International Code Council's (ICC) attempts to establish a single building code that would be adopted by local and state jurisdictions are moving forward and have experienced some success. The ICC is not promoting a National Code, as such, but there has been some discussion of developing a National Code to support mitigation efforts. Because the constitutional responsibility for public health and safety resides with the states, a National Code developed by the federal government is not politically feasible or practical.

Land-Use Planning

Mitigation programs are most successful when they are undertaken at the local level, where most decisions about development are made. The strategies for land-use planning offer many options for effecting mitigation, including acquisition, easements, storm water management, annexation, environmental review, and floodplain management plans. It also encompasses a myriad of zoning options such as density controls, special uses permits, historic preservation, coastal zone management, and subdivision controls.

Land-use planning was one of the earliest tools used to encourage mitigation. In 1968, Congress passed the National Flood Insurance Act that established the NFIP. This act required local governments to pass a floodplain management ordinance in return for federally backed, low-cost flood insurance being made available to the community. This act started one of the largest federal mapping efforts because the government promised local governments that they would provide them with the technical tools to determine where the floodplains were in their communities so they could steer development away from these areas. A more complete discussion of the NFIP can be found later in this chapter.

Moving structures out of harm's way through property acquisition is clearly the most effective land-use planning tool, but it is also the most costly. Following the Midwest floods of 1993, FEMA worked with Congress to make property acquisition more feasible by providing a substantial increase in funding for acquisition after a disaster. This is one of the mitigation programs that has flourished, with numerous communities working with their citizens to voluntarily agree to be moved out of harm's way in light of significant or repetitive flooding.

Land-use planning and ordinances can promote risk reduction in many other ways. The North Carolina coastal setback ordinance seeks to preserve the fragile and eroding coastlines of its barrier islands. The Alquist-Priola Act in California limits development near known earthquake faults.

CASE STUDY: A SMALL VILLAGE WITH BIG CONCERNS

Riverton, Illinois. The Sangamon River forms the west boundary of the Village of Riverton, a quaint community that 2,997 residents call home. But the Village of Riverton has had a long flood history. To lessen the impact of floods on its residents, the village joined forces with other communities in Sangamon County to devise a plan. Acquisition was definitely the mitigation measure of choice, and council members have encouraged the creation of green space in the floodplain area. According to Linda Viola, office manager and grant administrator for the Village of Riverton, "This was the second time these homes were hit. The first time was in 1994. We knew that something needed to be done."

Riverton is 550 feet above sea level. The village has a total area of 2.1 square miles: 2 square miles of land and 0.04 square miles of water (1.93 percent). Heavy rainfall causes the creek, which runs through the middle of Riverton, to frequently overtop its banks.

The Acquisition Project was initiated in July 2002 and completed in August 2006. Riverton received a grant totaling $272,867.66 from FEMA through its Hazard Mitigation Grant Program (HMGP). HMGP pays 75 percent of approved projects that will prevent or reduce damage from storms and other natural hazards. These grants are made available for both public and private projects.

"We filled out all the grant information, and we notified the homeowners. They also knew that they had a choice," said Viola. "They could choose to participate or not. Participation is voluntary. We completed the project without any major problems. When you buy someone's home, they always think that it's worth more. There were some who disagreed with the appraisal. The properties were appraised a second time. The homeowner has a right to request a second appraisal."

Buyouts of flood-prone homes located near the Sangamon River began in July 2004. The average value was $75,000, and the total project cost was $376,048.66. The village acquired six homes that were then demolished, resulting in open space within the floodplain.

A June 2008 flood event tested the success of the acquisition project as waters from the Sangamon River crept upon the 140,506-acre tract of land. If those six homes had not been removed, they would have been flooded with two to three feet of water.

A local alderman contacted Ron Davis, the state hazard mitigation officer, who acknowledged, "It was great this year when the waters came up, [and we were] able to sit back and relax and not have to mobilize our forces to fight the flood." Said Viola, "Those [acquired] homes were in the floodplain. Flooding would continue to occur. I don't know how the people could have lived with the flood and continued to rebuild in the same area knowing that it would happen again. We found a way to help them."

Source: FEMA. _http://www.fema.gov/mitigationbp/bestPracticeDetailPDF.do?mitssId=6057_

Financial Incentives

The financial incentives tool is an emerging area for promoting mitigation. Among the approaches being used by localities to reduce risks are creating special tax assessments, passing tax increases or bonds to pay for mitigation, offering relocation assistance, and targeting federal community development or renewal grant funds for mitigation.

The economic effects of repetitive flooding led the citizens of Napa, California, and Tulsa, Oklahoma, to pass small tax increases to pay for flood-mitigation activities. In both cases, the tax had a minimal effect on the community citizens but had a major effect in reducing the potential economic losses from future floods. Berkeley, California, has passed more than ten different bond issues to support seismic retrofit of public buildings, schools, and private residences.

Funding from the Community Development Block Grant (CDBG), a HUD program, has been used extensively to support local efforts at property acquisition and relocation. These funds have been used to meet the nonfederal match on other federal funding, which has often been a stumbling block to local mitigation. Other federal programs of the Small Business Administration (SBA) and the Economic Development Administration provide financial incentives for mitigation.

Other emerging areas of financial tools include special assessment districts, impact fees, and transfer of development rights. All of these tools provide either incentives or penalties to developers as a means of promoting good risk-reduction development practices.

CASE STUDY: NAPA RIVER FLOOD PROTECTION PROJECT

Napa, California. In the flood-prone valley of the Napa River lies the world-class traveler's destination of Napa, California. Over the span of 36 years (1961–1997), a total of 19 floods caused more than $542 million in residential property damage alone. That total does not include economic losses in the tourism industry, environmental damage, or the loss of human lives. During a 1986 flood, 20 inches of rain fell in a 48-hour period, resulting in 3 deaths, the destruction of 250 homes, damage to 2,500 homes, and the evacuation of 5,000 residents. Flood events in March 1995 and January 1997 were similarly destructive. The City of Napa subsequently embarked on an ambitious effort to mitigate flood losses in the community. The Napa River – Napa Creek Flood Protection Project was voted into reality by the passage of Napa County Measure A in March 1998. This half-cent local sales tax levy passed by the citizens of Napa County provided a funding mechanism for the local share of the project cost and helped solidify the partnership between the Napa County Flood Control and Water Conservation District (NCFCWCD) and the U.S. Army Corps of Engineers. Measure A funds flood protection, drainage improvements, dam safety, and watershed management projects for each community in Napa County and in the unincorporated area of the county. The project was still ongoing in 2006 and components include the following: the acquisition and removal of more than 50 mobile homes, 16 residences, and 28 commercial buildings from flood-prone areas; the creation of over 400 acres of emergent marsh and 150 acres of seasonal wetlands; the removal, reconstruction, and elevation of several bridges; the elevation of railroad tracks; home and utilities elevations; the creation of structural flood control elements such as widened stream beds, flood walls, levees, and culverts; and the construction of three detention basins with accompanying pump stations. According to NCFCWCD, "When all these project components are in place, the City of Napa will have a system to keep homes and businesses dry in the future." December 2005 was the first test of Napa County's new flood mitigation efforts when nearly 10 inches fell in a 24-hour period. Local officials were ready for the flood and had already placed sandbags and warned residents. Within four days of the flood the City had placed debris containers around town which greatly facilitated cleanup and repair. At the time of the December 2005 floods, officials estimated that the project was only 40% completed. Nevertheless, significant economic losses were avoided. A sense of confidence in the economic vitality of the City of Napa is evidenced by an all-time high in construction activity for both the residential and commercial sectors, the opening of four new downtown restaurants, the proposal for three new hotels, and an increase in commercial assessment in the downtown area. In addition to mitigating flood losses, the community has placed a revitalized, healthy river as the centerpiece of Napa. Many people now take advantage of the resources the river has to offer, including fishing, boating, walking along river trails, bird watching, and scenic dining. For up-to-date information on flood mitigation activities in Napa County, please visit the Napa County Flood Control and Water Conservation District website.

Source: FEMA. *http://www.fema.gov/mitigationbp/bestPracticeDetailPDF.do?mitssId=3045*

Insurance

Some people would argue with the inclusion of insurance as a mitigation tool. Their reasoning is that insurance by itself really only provides for a transfer of the risk from the individual or community to the insurance company. Although this is true, the NFIP is the prime example of how, if properly designed, the insurance mechanism can be a tool for mitigation. The NFIP is considered to be one of the most successful mitigation programs ever created.

The NFIP was created by Congress in response to the damages from multiple severe hurricanes and inland flooding and the rising costs of disaster assistance after these floods. At that time, flood insurance was not readily available or affordable through the private insurance market. Because many of the people being affected by this flooding were low-income residents, Congress agreed to subsidize the cost of the insurance so the premiums would be affordable. The idea was to reduce the costs to the government of disaster assistance through insurance. The designers of this program, with great insight, thought the government should get something for their subsidy. So in exchange for the low-cost insurance, they required that communities pass an ordinance directing future development away from the floodplain.

The NFIP was designed as a voluntary program and, as such, did not prosper during its early years, even though flooding disaster continued. Then in 1973, after Hurricane Agnes, the legislation was modified significantly. The purchase of federal flood insurance became mandatory on all federally backed loans. In other words, anyone buying a property with a Veterans Administration (VA) or Federal Housing Administration (FHA) loan had to purchase the insurance. Citizen pressure to buy the insurance caused communities to pass ordinances and join the NFIP. The NFIP helped the communities by providing them with a variety of flood hazard maps to define their flood boundaries and set insurance rates.

The 1993 Midwest floods triggered another major reform to the NFIP. This act strengthened the compliance procedures. It told communities that if they didn't join the program, they would be eligible for disaster assistance only one time. Any further request would be denied. As a positive incentive, the act established a Flood Mitigation Assistance (FMA) fund for flood planning, flood mitigation grants, and additional policy coverage for meeting the tougher compliance requirements such as building elevation.

Over the years, the NFIP has created other incentive programs such as the Community Rating System. This program offers reduced insurance premiums to communities that go beyond the minimum floodplain ordinance requirements. The NFIP represents one of the best public/private partnerships. Through the Write Your Own program, private insurers are given incentives to market and sell flood insurance.

Today more than 20,000 communities in the NFIP have mitigation programs in place. Other attempts have been made to duplicate this program for wind and earthquake hazards, but these have not received the support necessary to pass in Congress. If another major earthquake occurs, the issue of creating a federally supported earthquake or all-hazards insurance will resurface.

Major disasters commonly instigate changes within the national and international private insurance industries, as firms attempt to adjust operations such that they are able to continue profitable operations according to newly acquired hazard information. Industry changes resulting from the 9/11 terrorist events, which focused solely on damages caused by a perceived "long-shot" subsequent terrorism incident, focused on the availability of specialized terrorism insurance (and affected mainly a business clientele). However, Hurricane Katrina, which ranked as the costliest U.S. disaster, with between $40 to $55 billion in insured losses, has resulted in new changes whose impacts are just beginning to be understood and that are expected to profoundly affect the ever-growing coastal populations who depend on insurance coverage for financial security.

The insurance industry was lambasted during the recovery from Hurricane Katrina when it was reported that victims often faced long delays in receiving their insurance checks or, even worse, were informed that their insurance coverage did not apply to the type of damage that was caused by the hurricane (many victims found themselves without coverage when it was determined that their damages were not caused by wind, which was covered in their policies, but rather by the excluded storm surge hazard). Class action lawsuits gave many of these Gulf Coast victims some recourse, but they have in turn caused the insurance industry to reconsider whether risk assessments of coastal areas are still valid if insurers are being mandated to pay damages on events their original calculations did not consider. As a result, the insurance industry has steadily withdrawn their coverage from many of these Gulf Coast areas and in coastal areas as far away as Connecticut, Rhode Island, and Massachusetts, claiming that new conditions brought about by the lawsuits would require them to raise premiums to unaffordable levels. State Farm Insurance, the nation's largest residential insurer and one of the largest companies operating on the Gulf Coast (which paid over $1 billion in claims in Mississippi alone following Katrina), has refused to renew policies that cover homes within 1,000 feet of the water. Allstate Insurance Company has canceled or refused renewed coverage in a dozen coastal states.

However, residents in coastal areas are not the only people who will feel the ramifications from such costly megaevents. Industry experts predict that policy premiums will rise, even if slightly, in all "catastrophe-prone" areas regardless of risk level to ensure ample backing of all policies within the risk pool. In Louisiana, the state Insurance Rating Commission has approved premium rate increases of over 23 percent in some cases. Many may even find it difficult to acquire insurance as companies pull out of these areas in favor of low-risk, "safe" markets (where policies may even decrease due to competition for low-risk policies). Those living in areas where no company will provide coverage have traditionally been able to find policies under state-provided "pools" like the Mississippi Wind Pool. However, even those resources are experiencing rate hikes over 250 percent. With no insurance options, many people in these affected areas are choosing to rebuild elsewhere in places where they are able to better protect themselves.

Some states are considering state-run hurricane insurance programs. Florida was the first to approve a measure that would lower insurance premiums by pledging up to $32 billion of state money to back insurers of homeowners whose houses have been damaged or destroyed by a hurricane. The money for this "state catastrophic fund" will come from increased taxes on houses and automobiles and on other types of insurance policies that are sold in Florida. Florida state officials, recognizing that, unlike floods, not all states are affected by hurricanes, have appealed to their neighbor states that share similar risks to join the program and make it more effective in the event of a future hurricane as destructive as Katrina.

Structural Controls

Structural controls are controversial as a mitigation tool. Structural controls usually have been used to protect existing development. In doing so, they can have both positive and negative effects on the areas they are not protecting. In addition, as the name implies, they are used to control the hazard, not reduce it. Invariably, as was seen so graphically in the Midwest floods, the structures lose control and nature wins; however, in some circumstances, structural controls are the only alternative.

The most common form of structural control is the levee (Figure 3-4). The U.S. Army Corps of Engineers has designed and built levees as flood-control structures across the United States. Levees are part of the aging infrastructure of America. As mitigation tools, they have obvious limitations. They can be overtopped or breached, as in the 1993 Midwest floods; they can give residents a false sense of safety that often promotes increased development; and they can exacerbate the hazard in other locations. After the 1993 floods, a major rethinking of dependency on levees has occurred. Efforts are being made to acquire structures built behind the levees, new design criteria are being considered, and other more wetland-friendly policies are being adopted. For a city like New Orleans, however, which is built below sea level and where relocation is impractical, levees can be used effectively to protect flood-prone areas.

Other structural controls are intended to protect coastal areas. Seawalls, bulkheads, breakwaters, groins, and jetties are intended to stabilize the beach or reduce the

FIGURE 3-4 Valley City, North Dakota, April 13, 2009. Members of the U.S. Army Corps of Engineers inspect the site of a levee where severe seepage threatens the integrity of the levee in downtown Valley City, North Dakota. The Corps is working with city officials and the National Guard to ensure the safety of the levees in the town.
Photo by Patsy Lynch/FEMA.

FIGURE 3-5 Sargent County, North Dakota, May 4, 2009. Rocks and an angled culvert help prevent bank erosion on drain 11 in Sargent County. Many areas of North Dakota were covered with floodwater weeks after the storms and floods occurred in March.
Eliud Echevarria/FEMA.

impacts of wave action. These structures are equally controversial because they protect in one place and increase the damage in another. New Jersey's shoreline is a prime example of the failure of seawalls as a solution to shoreline erosion problems. Cape May, New Jersey, where cars used to be raced on the beach, lost all of its beachfront. An ongoing beach replenishment project is the only thing that has brought some of it back. Figure 3-5 shows another example of erosion mitigation.

CASE STUDY: MITIGATION MEASURES ALLEVIATE DRAINAGE PROBLEM

Grapevine, Texas. Oak Grove Park's ball field complex, located in Grapevine, Texas, was built in the 1960s and is home to local baseball and soccer teams. Over the years, surface water resulting from inadequate drainage, along with additions to the park, caused flood and maintenance issues and posed problems for pedestrians.

Acting upon requests and recommendations for new fields, the city of Grapevine came up with a master plan that involved creating berms, drainage ditches and retention walls, installing storm water drainage pipes, uprooting and replanting trees, and elevating the land in targeted areas to prevent future flooding of the park. Kevin Mitchell, Assistant Director of Parks and project manager, explained, "During the design and development stage, I along with several staff members toured many, many complexes. We wanted to look at the good as well as the bad. And we tried not to make the same mistakes that we noted."

The first obstacle was the temporary removal of hundreds of oak trees. Grapevine, Texas, is a member of "Tree City USA," a tree planting and tree care program sponsored by the National Arbor Day Foundation for cities and towns in the United States. A temporary tree farm and irrigation system were created to house and nourish the relocated trees during construction. Construction occurred around groups of trees that could not be uprooted. "We spent just shy of one-fourth of a million dollars digging up trees, moving them, and then moving them back," said Mitchell.

By nature, storm water collects debris, chemicals, dirt, and other pollutants before flowing into a storm sewer system or directly into a lake, stream, river, or wetland. Hence, the planners used storm water management as a tool to prevent this debris from entering the water system. "We used storm scepters, something new to the project, to separate the sand, silt, and clay and keep debris from going back into the lake," said Mitchell. The scepters allow water to enter into a swirl chamber, where it is filtered before moving into a "floatable" chamber. There, general debris is collected before the water is sent to the outlet chamber for disbursement into Lake Grapevine. Berms, raised mounds of soil, were created as an additional filtering system, allowing water to flow through grassy areas that serve as a biofiltering system before it reaches the lake. Design and development also included land elevation at varying heights. For example, the area where the newly constructed concession building and public restrooms are located was elevated above nine feet. Retention walls were strategically placed to stabilize the soil from runoff and erosion, especially since tiered landscaping was utilized throughout the park. It also created useable land. Stone pavers created a solid surface for sidewalks but water was still able to drain into the ground through the spaces between the pavers.

The Oak Grove ball field complex now backs to Lake Grapevine. Part of the project was to irrigate the athletic field with water from Lake Grapevine. An irrigation pond that holds approximately 3.5 million gallons of water was created, and a pumping station was built. Water is purchased from Dallas, which is a savings for the park.

According to Mitchell, transformation of the 33-acre park into a sports haven cost approximately $13 million, and construction was completed within ten months. "The good thing about this is that we paid cash for the project," said Mitchell. "We used tax money spent by people coming into our town to shop."

The design development stage took nearly a year to complete, but it was time well spent. Visiting Oak Grove Park's ball field complex after a heavy rain is no longer a problem thanks to the steps taken to reduce or eliminate long-term risks to both people and property. Good mitigation planning and cooperation with local authorities worked together to create a paradise for Little Leaguers that will be enjoyed for years to come.

Source: FEMA. *http://www.fema.gov/mitigationbp/bestPracticeDetail.do;jsessionid=4F92446D3E1C2D38CA1BA 62E7EBACCD4.WorkerTheCage?mitssId=7032*

CRITICAL THINKING

- What mitigation measures are best suited to address the hazards you face as an individual?
- What mitigation measures are best suited to address the hazards faced by your community?
- Do you feel that more should be done to address your community's hazards? If so, what could or should be done?

Impediments to Mitigation

If so many tools can be applied, why haven't risk-reduction and risk-mitigation programs been more widely applied? Some of the reasons are denial of the risk, political will, costs and a lack of funding, and taking on the issue. Despite the best technical knowledge, historic occurrence, public education, and media attention, many individuals don't want to recognize that they or their communities are vulnerable. Recognition requires action, and it could have economic consequences as businesses decide to locate elsewhere if they find the community is at risk. Some people are willing to try to beat the odds, but if a disaster strikes, they know the government will help them out. Gradually, however, such attitudes are changing. Potential liability issues are making communities more aware, media attention to disasters has brought public pressure, and the government has provided both incentives for, and penalties for not, taking action.

As previously mentioned, mitigation provides a long-term benefit. The U.S. political system tends to focus on short-term rewards. Developers are large players in the political process and often are concerned that mitigation means additional costs. Mitigation strategies and actions require political vision and will. When Tip O'Neill was Speaker of the U.S. House of Representatives, he said, "All politics is local." Well, so is mitigation. Local elected officials are the individuals who have to promote, market, and endorse adopting risk reduction as a goal. For many elected officials, the development pressures are too much, funding is lacking, and other priorities dominate their agendas; however, with the increasing attention to the economic, social, and political costs of *not* dealing with their risks, more elected officials are recognizing that they can't afford to not take action.

Mitigation costs money. Most mitigation of new structures or development can be passed on to the builder or buyer without much notice. Programs to retrofit existing structures or acquisition and relocation projects are expensive and almost always beyond the capacity of the local government. Funding for mitigation comes primarily from federal programs that need to be matched with state or local dollars. As state and local budgets constrict, their ability to match is reduced. Strong arguments can be made that it is in the best financial interest of the federal government to support mitigation. These arguments and a series of large disasters resulted in substantial increases in federal funding, including new monies for predisaster mitigation, but the fact remains that mitigation needs far outweigh mitigation funding.

Many mitigation actions involve privately owned property. A major legal issue surrounding this is the "taking" issue. The Fifth Amendment to the U.S. Constitution prohibits the taking of property without just compensation. What constitutes a taking, under what circumstances, and what is just compensation have been the focus of numerous legal cases. Several have dealt with the use of property in the floodplain and the use of oceanfront property on a barrier island. The decisions have been mixed, and taking will continue to be an issue in implementing mitigation programs and policies. In 2009, the U.S. Supreme Court agreed to hear a case brought by homeowners in Florida dealing with property lines and ownership on properties where beach replenishment was undertaken with public funds. As of the writing of this text, no decision on the case had been issued by the Court.

ADDITIONAL RESEARCH

"No Adverse Impact and the Courts: Protecting the Property Rights of All" is a report issued in November 2007 by the Association of State Flood Plain Managers (ASFPM). It discusses the general law of the nation and selected legal issues associated with a "no adverse impact" floodplain management approach.

Source: www.floods.org.

Federal Mitigation Programs

FEMA is responsible for most of the programs of the federal government that support mitigation, and in this section we examine some of them. As noted earlier, the SBA, Economic Development Administration (EDA), and HUD have policies that support mitigation. The PATH program at HUD supports incorporating mitigation into public housing. The Environmental Protection Agency (EPA) has several programs in floodplain management, and in 2002 it initiated a new pilot program for national watersheds. The National Earthquake Hazards Reduction Program includes several other federal agencies, but the predominant federal agency involved in disaster mitigation is FEMA. FEMA's programs include the NFIP, the Hazard Mitigation Grant Program (HMGP) (Figure 3-6), the Pre-Disaster Mitigation Program (PDM), the Flood Mitigation Assistance Program (FMA),

FIGURE 3-6 Albany, New York. This church is being moved half a mile to higher ground as part of the Stryker Road relocation project in Schoharie County, New York. The Hazard Mitigation Grant and Public Assistance Programs helped fund the project.
Schoharie County Planning and Development Agency photos.

the Repetitive Flood Claims Program (RFC), the Severe Repetitive Loss (SRL) National Earthquake Hazard Reduction Program (NEHRP), the National Hurricane Program, and the Fire Prevention and Assistance Grant Program.

In 2000, Congress passed the Disaster Mitigation Act of 2000 (DMA2000), which amended the Robert T. Stafford Disaster Relief and Emergency Assistance Act in an effort to encourage mitigation planning at the state and local levels, requiring that states maintain mitigation plans as a prerequisite for certain federal mitigation funding and disaster assistance programs. The program also provided incentives to states that could show increased coordination and integration of mitigation activities by establishing two different levels of state plan certification: standard and enhanced. States that demonstrated what was considered "an increased commitment to comprehensive mitigation planning" through the development of an approved Enhanced State Plan could increase the amount of funding they received through the Hazard Mitigation Grant Program (HMGP). DMA2000 also established a new requirement for local mitigation plans and authorized up to 7 percent of HMGP funds available to a state to be used for development of state, tribal, and local mitigation plans.

The Hazard Mitigation Grant Program

The HMGP is the largest source of funding for state and local mitigation activities. This program provides grants to state and local governments to implement long-term hazard mitigation programs after a major disaster has been declared by the president. HMGP projects must reduce the risks, and the benefits of the project must exceed the costs. Here are some examples of activities supported by the HMGP:

- Acquisition of property on a voluntary basis and commitment to open use of the property
- Retrofitting of structures and lifelines
- Elevation of structures
- Vegetation management programs
- Building code enforcement
- Localized flood-control projects
- Public education and awareness

This program was enacted by Congress in 1988 as part of the Robert T. Stafford Act, which was a major reworking of federal disaster policy. Besides creating the HMGP, it established a cost sharing of disaster assistance by the states. At the time, the formula for state HMGP funding was 15 percent of the public assistance costs, and it had a 50 percent federal/50 percent state cost share.

From 1988 to 1993, many states did not take advantage of the HMGP funding because it was difficult to meet the matching requirements, even though the 15 percent cap was often not very much. After the devastation of the 1993 Midwest floods, Representative Volkmer from Missouri championed a change to the legislation that would significantly increase the states' ability to mitigate. Congress amended the legislation to allow for a 75 percent federal/25 percent state match and dramatically increased the amount of funding to 15 percent of the total disaster costs. The rationale for these changes was to work aggressively to move people and structures out of the floodplain. The HMGP has allowed states to hire staff to work on mitigation and requires development of a State Hazard Mitigation Plan as a condition of funding. This program brought about a change in the emergency management community at the state and local levels. With adequate funding, states and localities began to hire staff designated to work on mitigation.

The HMGP has its detractors, and in 2002, the Office of Management and Budget (OMB) proposed that this program be eliminated in favor of a new predisaster competitive grant program. However, Congress did not agree, and the HMGP program remains intact and provides the most significant funding for mitigation at the federal level.

The Pre-Disaster Mitigation Program (PDM)

Through the Disaster Mitigation Act of 2000, Congress approved the creation of a national Pre-Disaster Mitigation Program (PDM) to provide mitigation funding not dependent on a disaster declaration. The genesis of PDM was an initiative of the Clinton administration called Project Impact: Building Disaster-Resistant Communities. Project Impact grew out of the devastating disasters of the 1990s. Many of the communities hit by these disasters took months and even years to recover emotionally and financially. James Lee Witt, then director of FEMA, questioned the wisdom of spending more than $2.5 billion per year on disaster relief and not a penny to reduce disasters *before* they happen. The mitigation tools and techniques were available, so why not work to prevent individuals and communities from becoming victims of disasters? With a small amount of seed money, FEMA launched Project Impact in 1997 in seven pilot communities.

The concept behind the initiative was simple: The mitigation activities had to be designed and tailored to the hazards in that community, and all sectors of the community had to become involved in order for it to be effective and sustainable. Project Impact brought the business community into the emergency management umbrella. Communities were asked to achieve the following four goals:

- Build a community partnership
- Assess the risks
- Prioritize risk-reduction actions
- Build support by communicating your actions

By 2001, more than 200 communities were participating in Project Impact, and Congress had appropriated $25 million to the initiative. Seattle, Washington, was one of the original pilot communities. In 2002, when a 6.8 earthquake struck Seattle, the mayor attributed the success of their Project Impact activities for the minimal damages and prompt recovery.

CASE STUDY: PROJECT IMPACT AND THE NISQUALLY EARTHQUAKE

On February 28, 2001, a magnitude 6.8 earthquake occurred 32 miles below the Nisqually wetland north of Olympia, the Washington state capital. Ironically, the quake occurred as the Seattle Project Impact Steering Committee was preparing to celebrate the initiative's third anniversary with several hundred of its partners. Had the quake occurred one hour later, all of the region's emergency managers would have been gathered at the Phinney Ridge Neighborhood Center in Seattle. Instead, committee members and a few early birds guided children from the center's two daycare programs to safety.

Members of the response and recovery community were not fully tested by the earthquake, largely because it was deep, and drought conditions in the Puget Sound region reduced the number of landslides and amount of liquefaction that would normally be caused by a quake of that magnitude. There was only one significant aftershock and a few secondary impacts (one fire and several major landslides). However, the quake did interrupt business operations and damaged numerous building components, such as chimneys, facades, water pipes, and equipment.

Many historic, commercial, and manufacturing facilities were damaged, including key government structures such as the state legislative building and the regional airport control tower. Additional damage was uncovered while engineering teams performed inspections, although structural losses (i.e., damage to components essential to a building's structural integrity) will undoubtedly be a fraction of nonstructural losses (i.e., damage to nonessential building structural elements, such as architectural features and heating and electrical systems, and losses due to lost productivity, etc.).

What effect did FEMA's Project Impact have, if any, in reducing the damage from this earthquake? In short, the program transformed the way residents deal with disasters and established an organizational structure that takes advantage of this change.

Project Impact has the broad goal of reducing risks by changing the way communities think about and deal with disasters. More importantly, it asks communities to be farsighted, to assess hazards rather than just respond to them, to protect themselves, and to become disaster-resistant. The program is based on three simple principles:

- Preventive actions must be decided at the local level and must be responsive to local hazards.
- Private sector participation is vital.
- Long-term efforts and investments in prevention are essential.

The Seattle/Tacoma metropolitan area, which includes King, Pierce, and Kitsap counties, has been heavily involved in Project Impact, and Seattle was a pilot participant in the program. It is useful to examine Project Impact's effectiveness by assessing how well its goals were met in the context of the Nisqually earthquake.

Change the way we think about and deal with disasters.

Perhaps the most significant (and most difficult to measure) effect the initiative had is in demystifying and personalizing earthquake risk reduction for thousands of individuals, small businesses, and corporate partners.

Preventive actions must be decided at the local level.

The Seattle and King, Pierce, and Kitsap County Project Impact programs were essentially collective actions taken by hundreds of partners. Seven programs can be linked directly to Project Impact, including efforts in home and school retrofitting, hazard mapping, transportation corridor vulnerability mitigation, office and home nonstructural retrofitting, and small business resumption planning. It is too early to assess the full impact of these programs, but here are some early conclusions. (For a description of individual programs, see the FEMA website: *http://www.fema.gov/impact.*)

- The most significant benefit of Project Impact might be the reduction (or minimalization) of structural damage in retrofitted buildings.
- Project Impact decommissioned very heavy and hazardous water tanks located in the attics of seven Seattle schools, and one of these schools was damaged significantly by the quake. Had the water tank been in use, the building would have suffered even more damage, and the ceilings above several classrooms most likely would have failed. The school program also included extensive nonstructural retrofitting. No losses were reported in participating schools, and, even more important, evacuation was not impeded. Other schools were not so fortunate.
- Over 1,000 homeowners attended home retrofitting workshops, and over 300 had retrofitted their homes before the quake. None of these retrofitted residences were damaged.
- Each of the four Project Impact jurisdictions had implemented long-range transportation corridor and hazard mapping programs. Information generated through these programs is greatly aiding the inspection process and helping to jump-start discussion on mitigation alternatives. In addition, these projects brought together public road managers who created "tool kits" for contingency routing that will be useful in other kinds of disasters. The quake elevated the priority of these initiatives, and funding is expected.

Private sector participation is vital.

- All four Project Impact jurisdictions and their private sector partners had developed aggressive business resumption programs. Over 100 large businesses and more than 500 small businesses were involved in Project Impact, and tens of thousands of earthquake safety products were in their offices. Business hazard reduction programs had been created by partners such as Washington Mutual, Bank of America, PEMCO, SAFECO, the Boeing Company, Bartell, the Russell Corporation, the King County Labor Council, and Home Depot, and many of the employees of these partners had implemented earthquake safety measures in their own homes as well.
- Project Impact communities and their partners ambitiously pursued risk-reduction outreach prior to the earthquake. Home Depot stores displayed home retrofitting techniques. Grocery and drug stores displayed earthquake safety products. Informational flyers accompanied utility bills, paychecks, and insurance renewal forms. A computer tie-down campaign attracted funding partners and garnered donations of computer tie-downs for area schools. The Project Impact logo was prominently displayed along with the message "Creating Disaster-Resistant Communities" during hundreds of newscasts.

Effects that were not directly related to specific programs.

- During and immediately following the earthquake, participating news organizations provided a consistent message about the earthquake hazard and described methods for preventing damage. Since its inception, Project Impact has worked regularly with the press, and the ABC and CBS local affiliates are formal Project Impact partners.
- Shortly after the quake, homeowners were able to obtain lists of area contractors trained in seismic retrofitting. This information is particularly useful immediately after a disaster, when unscrupulous contractors can prey on disaster victims.

Long-term efforts and investments in prevention are essential.
Research is currently under way to assess the more indirect long-term impacts of the Nisqually quake. FEMA and the University of Washington have established a clearinghouse to facilitate research, but an examination of efforts that are directly attributable to Project Impact indicated that Puget Sound residents accepted the responsibility for their hazard vulnerability and focused on protecting themselves. Here are three examples:

- "SecureIt" was a Pierce and King County Project Impact program, but all four project participant areas noted increased availability of computer tie-downs and other office-related items that were difficult to obtain when the programs began. After the earthquake, many vendors saw a dramatic increase in orders for these products.
- Home retrofitting activities increased substantially. Roger Faris of the Phinney Ridge Neighborhood Center Home Improvement program indicated at the time that the program could not keep up with the demand for the Project Impact home retrofitting course. Before the quake, he scheduled one course per month with 20 to 30 attendees. After the quake, he held four per month and had 60 participants per class. Private contractors could not keep up with the substantially increased demand for retrofitting services. Homeowners had difficulty hiring the 60 contractors who had taken the University of Washington (a Project Impact

partner) earthquake retrofitting course. Due to the increased interest among contractors, additional courses were scheduled.

- The Project Impact coordinator for the Seattle school district received the following letter from a school principal:

> *Just wanted to let you know the good news on how well the building did during the earthquake—and a big thanks for the retrofitting. We did not even have a single light cover come down, a computer fall over, a book come off a shelf. Now, . . . how do we get more straps to do the new things we have installed since retrofitting was done here? Thank you. You made believers out of us!*

PERFORMANCE MEASURES

Were there fewer property losses, lower costs for repairs, and less time lost from productive activity as a result of Project Impact? It depends on how one measures the costs of repairing a school that did not decommission a water tank to prevent damage, the injuries or deaths of children in classrooms directly under such a tank, the loss of homes that were not retrofitted, and the closure of firms that had not implemented business resumption measures. Whatever the savings, it looks like we will be even better prepared when the next quake occurs, and isn't that, after all, the goal of Project Impact?

Robert Freitag, Director, Institute for Hazard Mitigation Planning and Research,
University of Washington

Source: Natural Hazards Observer, University of Colorado
For more information on the earthquake in Seattle, view the Clearinghouse on the Nisqually Earthquake website: *http://maximus.ce.washington.edu/~nisqually.*

In 2002, the Bush administration decided to drop the Project Impact name and concept in exchange for a competitive grant program as their approach to predisaster mitigation through the PDM program. The program's original budget request was $300 million, and it was proposed that PDM replace both Project Impact and the HMGP. Although Congress did not agree with combining the programs, it did agree to the PDM. As designed, PDM is designed to provide "funds to states, territories, Indian tribal governments, communities, and universities for hazard mitigation planning and the implementation of mitigation projects prior to a disaster event." The program requires jurisdictions to submit applicants for a competitive grant selection.

In 2007, some changes were made to the program, including a significant eligibility requirement that local applicant communities maintain an approved FEMA Hazard Mitigation Plan in place as required by the Disaster Mitigation Act of 2000 (DMA2000). Many of the original mechanisms remain the same, however, such as the 25 percent commitment that must be covered by the local applicant and the fact that the state office of emergency management serves as grantee, while local agencies apply to the state. A subgrantee category was created for small, impoverished communities. Under this category the cost share is 90 percent federal and 10 percent local.

The Flood Mitigation Assistance (FMA) program provides annual funding for communities to take action to reduce or eliminate the risk of flood damage to buildings insured under the NFIP. The Repetitive Flood Claims (RFC) program provides funding to reduce the risk of flood damages to individual properties insured under the NFIP that have had one or more claim payments for flood damages. This program can provide up to 100 percent federal funding for eligible properties.

The Severe Repetitive Loss (SRL) program provides annual funding to reduce the risk of flood damage to individual residential properties insured through the NFIP. To qualify, the structure must be designated a severe repetitive loss structure, in which case the federal share can be as high as 90 percent.

The National Earthquake Hazard Reduction Program

The National Earthquake Hazard Reduction Program (NEHRP) is a federal government effort established by Congress in 1977 (Public Law 95-124) as a long-term, nationwide program to reduce the risks to life and property in the United States resulting from earthquakes. This is accomplished through the establishment and maintenance of an effective earthquake hazards reduction program.

The NEHRP is a multiagency effort that works to improve understanding, characterization, and prediction of hazards and vulnerabilities; improve model building codes and land-use practices; reduce risk through postearthquake investigations and education; develop and improve design and construction techniques; improve mitigation capacity; and accelerate application of research results. The NEHRP provides funding to states to establish programs that promote public education and awareness, planning, loss estimation studies, and some minimal mitigation activities.

The specific roles of each of the agencies within NEHRP are as follows:

- FEMA is responsible for emergency response and management, estimation of loss potential, and implementation of mitigation actions.
- NIST conducts applied earthquake engineering research to provide the technical basis for building codes, standards, and practices, and provides the NEHRP lead agency function.
- NSF conducts basic research in seismology, earthquake engineering, and social, behavioral, and economic sciences, and it operates the Network for Earthquake Engineering Simulation (which includes the tsunami wave basin research facility and supporting tsunami research).
- USGS operates the seismic networks, develops seismic hazard maps, coordinates postearthquake investigations, and conducts applied earth sciences research (which includes tsunami research and risk assessment).
- NSF and USGS jointly support the Global Seismographic Network (GSN), the main facility for pinpointing earthquakes in real time.

Since its inception, NEHRP has been reviewed and reauthorized by Congress every two or three years. Congress recently completed a thorough two-year review of NEHRP, resulting in enactment of the NEHRP Reauthorization Act of 2004 (P.L. 108-360), which President Bush signed into law on October 25, 2004. Public Law 108-360 designates NIST as the lead agency for NEHRP, transferring that responsibility from FEMA, which had filled that role since the program's inception.

The NEHRP Reauthorization act of 2004 authorized $900 million to be spent during the period from 2004 to 2009. The law also authorized the spending of $72.5 million over a three-year period for the creation of a National Windstorm Impact Reduction Program modeled according to NEHRP. Funds have never been appropriated for this new program, but supporters introduced the concept again in 2009 as part of the NEHRP reauthorization.

The National Hurricane Program

This FEMA program supports activities at the federal, state, and local levels that focus on the physical effects of hurricanes, improved response capabilities, and new mitigation techniques for the built environment. The program has done significant work in storm surge modeling and evacuation planning, design and construction of properties in hurricane-prone areas, and public education and awareness programs for schools and communities. The amount of funding that FEMA receives for this program is in the range of $3 million annually, which is clearly not commensurate with the risk.

The Fire Prevention and Assistance Act

This program was created in 2001 to address the needs of the nation's paid and volunteer fire departments and to support prevention activities. Congress had long-standing concerns about the status of this first-responder community. New threats from potential biochemical terrorism, increasing wildfire requirements, and a stagnant search-and-rescue capability provided the rationale for funding this program. This multimillion-dollar grant program provides competitive grants to fire companies throughout the United States. In the wake of 9/11, the appropriations for this program tripled in 2002 and have continued at around the $600 million level.

Other federal agencies such as the previously mentioned HUD, the U.S. Army Corps of Engineers (COE), the Small Business Administration (SBA), the Department of Agriculture (DOA), and the Economic Development Administration (EDA) will provide in the aftermath of a disaster varying levels of support for local mitigation projects.

CRITICAL THINKING

- Should mitigation funding from the federal government be tied to individual disasters like it is with the Hazard Mitigation Grant Program, or should it be independent of disasters altogether like with the Pre-Disaster Mitigation Program? Explain your answer.
- What are the advantages of having a hazard-specific grant program such as the National Earthquake Hazard Reduction Program (NEHRP)? Are there any disadvantages?

Nonfederal Mitigation Grant Programs

The most significant mitigation funding in the United States comes from federally funded grant programs. However, all states have established State Hazard Mitigation Officers (SHMOs) to manage the programmatic and financial matching requirements of the federal programs. SHMOs are responsible for producing a statewide hazard mitigation plan, which is a requirement for receiving HMGP funding postdisaster, and the quality of the plan can become a factor in altering the cost share formula after an event. Increasingly, states are playing a more active role in historic preservation and mitigation of historic, cultural, and environmentally sensitive areas.

Regional programs such as Rebuild Northwest Florida, administered by a public-private partnership in Florida, provide grant money to homeowners who wish to structurally mitigate their homes from storm damage. Rebuild approves grants from qualified homeowners that help them improve the strength of their houses through such mitigation measures as creating secondary water barriers, improving roofing and roof decks, bracing gable ends, applying tie-down ("hurricane") straps, reinforcing wall-to-wall connections, and much more. Some nongovernmental programs, whether private, nonprofit, or public, provide the monetary, material, and technical assistance that individuals, businesses, and communities require to mitigate their hazard risks. The Institute for Business and Home Safety (IBHS), for example, creates guidance documents that illustrate various structural and nonstructural mitigation techniques. IBHS employees work with various entities, such as daycare centers, to help them reduce hazard vulnerabilities.

Two other entities are focusing on mitigation and related issues. The Association of State Flood Plain Managers (ASFPM) is a strong proponent of mitigation at all levels and has successfully lobbied Congress for increases in federal mitigation dollars. A goal of the National Hazard Mitigation Association (NHMA) is to promote mitigation nationwide and within the international community. The International Association of Emergency Managers (IAEM), which represents local emergency managers worldwide, has recently become more engaged in promoting mitigation among its membership.

Conclusion

Disasters occur in every state. The direct costs of these events are staggering, but the indirect effect to the economy and the social fabric of communities is even worse. A study done for FEMA by the Multi-Hazard Mitigation Council (MMC) of the National Institute for Building Sciences (NIBS) found that for every $1 invested in mitigation, $4 would be saved in future losses. Depending on the type of disaster and locale, this number was as high as $8. Mitigation works. The case studies included in this chapter are just a few examples of successful, sustained programs that are reducing risk and making communities safer. Mitigation programs exist at all levels of government, and there is a growing interest in the private sector for taking mitigation actions to reduce their risk exposure. To many people, even in a time when terrorism preoccupies the emergency management psyche, mitigation is—and should be—the future direction of emergency management.

Important Terms

Building codes
Hazard identification
Land-use planning
Mitigation
Structural controls

Self-Check Questions

1. How does the function of mitigation differ from other emergency management disciplines?
2. Which other emergency management function offers the best opportunities for mitigation?
3. Why is it more difficult to analyze, and therefore mitigate, the effects of terrorism?
4. How have geographic information systems (GIS) aided the practice of mitigation?
5. Why have building codes that require rehabilitation of existing potentially hazardous structures rarely been implemented?
6. At what government level are mitigation programs most effective, and why?
7. What is the most effective as well as the most expensive land-use planning tool? Why is it so effective?
8. How has the Community Development Block Grant served to help communities perform local mitigation?
9. Why do some people consider insurance to not be a proper mitigation method?
10. Why are structural controls a controversial mitigation tool? How can structural mitigation negatively affect the areas they are presumably protecting?
11. What are some impediments faced by communities wishing to perform hazard mitigation?
12. Name the primary federal mitigation programs, and explain how they serve to reduce hazard risk.
13. Do nonfederal mitigation programs exist?

Out-of-Class Exercises

Get a copy of your community's hazard mitigation plan from your local office of emergency management. Create a mitigation plan for yourself that addresses the hazards identified in the community plan as they affect you on a personal level. Determine if there are any hazards that you face as an individual that are not covered by the plan, and describe what mitigation measures you can take or have taken to address those hazards.

- Contact your state's office of emergency management, and find out what mitigation programs are currently offered. Are they all federally funded, or are there any programs funded by the state or another entity? Find out if your local government participates in any of these programs or if they offer any additional programs funded by other sources. Do you believe that your community is taking advantage of every mitigation program that it can, or do you feel more could be done with what is currently offered?
- The Institute for Business and Home Safety (IBHS) has developed a mitigation guide for daycare centers (*http://www.ibhs.org/docs/childcare.pdf*). Using this guide, assist a daycare center in your community to perform the mitigation techniques suggested in the guide.

4

The Disciplines of Emergency Management: Preparedness

What You'll Learn

- Why preparedness is considered the building block of emergency management
- The difference between mitigation and preparedness
- How FEMA's Community and Family Preparedness Program educates the public about disasters
- Why evacuation planning is important
- Why special consideration must be made for certain populations when planning for emergencies and disasters
- How the Emergency Management Institute promotes community-level disaster preparedness
- The types of exercises and what each involves
- How training and equipment help first responders to prepare
- How businesses and nongovernmental organizations prepare for emergencies

Introduction

Preparedness in the field of emergency management can best be defined as a state of readiness to respond to a disaster, crisis, or any other type of emergency situation. Preparedness is not only a state of readiness, but it is also a theme throughout most aspects of emergency management. If you look back in U.S. history, you will see that our forebearers practiced the preparedness that emergency managers use today. The fallout shelters of the 1950s and the air raid wardens were promoting preparedness for a potential nuclear attack from the Soviet Union. An early 1970s study prepared by the National Governors Association talked about the importance of preparedness as the first step in emergency management. Since then, preparedness has advanced significantly and continues to do so even today. The federal government dedicates billions of dollars each year to emergency preparedness, and no emergency management organization can function without a strong preparedness capability. The capacity to respond and recover from emergency and disaster events is only developed through planning, training, and exercising—the heart of preparedness. It is the expansion of preparedness activities, including a movement into the areas of higher education, that has led to an increased professionalism within the discipline. And as the role of all sectors of society in the management of emergencies and disasters has come to light, preparedness activities have gradually expanded to include the private sector, NGOs, individuals, and others.

Today we recognize that all organizations, whether they are private, nongovernmental, or governmental, are susceptible to the consequences of disasters and must therefore ensure their preparedness. We also know that preparedness must focus not only on the protection of citizens, property, and essential government services in the aftermath of a disaster event but also on ensuring that the viability of the community—including its businesses and markets, social services, and character—can be sustained despite the hazard risks that exist. Emergency management agencies alone cannot ensure this, which is why the practice continues to expand.

This chapter discusses the preparedness cycle from a systems approach, preparedness programs, hazard preparedness, training programs, and exercise programs. The focus is on federal efforts—predominantly FEMA—and best practices are highlighted through several case studies.

A Systems Approach: The Preparedness Cycle

As an academic field as well as an applied practice in the public and private sector, emergency management is still in the early stages of its establishment. As such, it has thus far drawn heavily on existing external fields, including emergency medicine, fire suppression, public health, business risk management, and law enforcement, for many of its foundational elements and core competencies. However, these disciplines are steeped in their own traditions, methods, and cultures, and they were not developed with the same goals as those in the emergency management field. Without its own foundation joining academia and structured analytic methodologies with the practices and competencies required of emergency management professionals in all sectors, advancement outside of the government sector will fall behind. The management of major emergency events and disasters requires navigation through extreme complexity and often requires coordination among hundreds to thousands of individuals and dozens of agencies and organizations. It is out of this need that a systematic approach for the preparedness function of emergency management must take such a prominent position today, not only for emergency managers and the traditional emergency services but for all emergency management stakeholders (including individual private citizens).

Figure 4-1, which was developed by the FEMA National Preparedness Directorate, shows the planning process, beginning with planning for the range of hazards that exist and working in a systematic approach toward a cyclical process to establish and improve preparedness. This cycle recognizes the importance of the four major components of any preparedness effort: planning, equipment, training, and exercise. This cycle also represents preparedness not only for government jurisdictions at all levels but also the preparedness actions taken by individuals, businesses, nongovernmental organizations, and other entities.

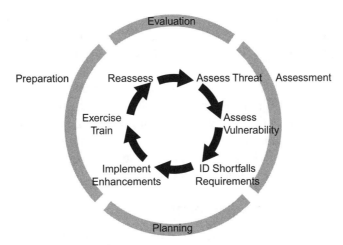

FIGURE 4-1 The preparedness planning cycle.

Step 1: Planning

In Figure 4-1, the preparedness cycle begins with the creation of various plans through which disaster response and recovery become possible. Planning is an ambitious effort in and of itself, and it requires significant effort to achieve the many tasks involved. Planning most often begins with the hazards risk assessment process described in Chapter 2, wherein all applicable hazards are identified and assessed for prioritization. While it is true that modern emergency management philosophy proclaims plans are most effective when they address all hazards risks, it is important to be aware that all-hazards preparedness is most effective when it takes into account, and therefore places a general focus on, those hazards that are actually likely to occur. Each community makes the best of the limited funds they have, so their full spectrum of equipment, resources, and trained staff need to focus on what actually might happen. This is why, for instance, communities in North Dakota might dedicate significant funds for the capabilities and resources to manage snow removal equipment, while communities in Florida spend the same effort and funding on conducting evacuation plans, even though both involve an "all-hazards" focus.

Planning also involves a scooping of community vulnerability. In the planning phase, vulnerability helps planners to understand why disasters occur, where they are most likely to have the greatest impact, and, thus, what the appropriate response should be. Vulnerability assessment for a jurisdiction, business, organization, or individual also includes an assessment of current preparedness levels to determine the capabilities and resources that may be counted on and therefore planned for. This always includes the outside resources that may be called upon in times of need, such as mutual aid partners (e.g., town to town, business to business), emergency management assistance compacts (e.g., state to state assistance), interjurisdictional assistance (e.g., federal assistance, state to local assistance), contracts with private businesses and resource suppliers (e.g., debris removal companies, hazmat remediation businesses), and others. Statutory authorities—the foundation of emergency management actions—must be understood, since government practice and authority is always dictated by law, even (or especially) in times of emergency.

Emergency planning is what often fills the majority of time spent by emergency management officials and those individuals tasked with the management of emergencies at businesses or in organizations. Luckily, as stated in Chapter 2, most events that occur on a daily basis fall within what is considered "normal" and are therefore managed with little or no problem. The product of planning is, of course, the plan, which is often called the emergency operations plan or the emergency plan.

Step 2: Organization and Equipment

Preparedness is limited by several factors, two of which include actual possession or access to the equipment needed to manage response requirements and the organization of people and agencies through which the necessary response and recovery tasks will take place. Emergency management is technical in practice, and its various functions rely more and more on the use of equipment. There are several categories of equipment in the emergency management profession, including (for example) personnel protective equipment (PPE), which protects responders from the effects of the hazards; communications equipment, which allows responders to talk to one another both within and between different organizations; and special search and rescue equipment, which allows responders to enter compromised buildings, navigate hazardous waters, or detect signs of life.

Equipment is primarily dictated by the hazards that exist and the functions laid out in the emergency operations plan. The purchase and maintenance of emergency management equipment have always been a challenge for communities because of limited funds available. Clearly (though to a limited degree), the more equipment a jurisdiction can acquire in order to manage the consequences likely to befall that jurisdiction, the more prepared they will be to meet the needs of people and property when the time comes. However, as that ideal will likely never be reached, and so many competing demands exist in the community for those same funds, difficult decisions must be made. In recent years, however, a few solutions have emerged that help communities to better meet their equipment needs. These include a great expansion of federal funding for which equipment is eligible, expansion in mutual assistance practices wherein equipment that is rarely used is shared among several communities, and the development of cheaper and more effective technologies, wherein equipment that was once considered "out of reach" is now more realistically accessible.

Step 3: Training

Training of emergency response officials is paramount to their ability to conduct the tasks required of them. Contemporary practice recognizes that it is not only the officials involved with the traditional emergency services who must participate in emergency management training but also the elected officials responsible for key disaster-specific decisions, the businesses and nongovernmental organizations operating in the community that will be called upon to provide products or services, and the individuals whose responsibility it is to decrease their own vulnerability and assist in the overall community response. This is a lofty goal but one that has expanded at a rate that rivals most other disciplines. Training is conducted both at technical institutes, such as fire and police academies at the national, state, and local levels, and at the various universities, colleges, and community colleges around the country and the world. Training is also conducted by nongovernmental organizations, like the American Red Cross, by private companies that specialize in training for profit, and in the communities themselves, as is the case with the ever-popular Community Emergency Response Team (CERT) courses that are offered in all U.S. states and territories. And finally, the goal of enabling a trained public is one that continues to grow in importance in the writings and words of practitioners and scholars alike.

Step 4: Exercise

The adage that "practice makes perfect" is certainly true with emergency management. Training is even more so a critical component of preparedness efforts because the rare nature of emergency events means that few officials have experienced them firsthand and thus have little applicable experience to rely on when these events do occur. Through a regimen of training, including drills, tabletop exercises, functional exercises, and full-scale exercises, a much better understanding of the realities of response is achieved, as well as the identification of shortfalls or failures in planning, training, organization, or equipment.

Step 5: Evaluation and Improvement

The final step in the preparedness cycle takes the lessons learned and applies them to future iterations. Evaluation and improvement are generally the product of two sources. The first is that of exercise. By examining how the plans, equipment, and trained staff respond to imagined scenarios, it is possible to identify where changes in planning, purchases of more or better equipment, and more comprehensive training should be applied. Evaluation and improvement are also the result of actual disaster experience. Disasters show us in bold fashion the full limits of an emergency management organization's capabilities and identify the highest benefit to cost ratio for future spending and dedication of time and staff resources. Through the use of after action reporting (AAR), disaster experiences become lessons learned and the foundation of future planning cycles.

Many of the topics described here are expanded upon in the remainder of this chapter. The cycle of preparedness is one that, as its cyclical nature dictates, is ongoing. Moreover, all steps are occurring at all times, in a constant state of evolution and improvement as information, budgets, staff, political will, and perceptions change.

Mitigation versus Preparedness

Despite their unique definitions and both being distinct emergency management functions, significant confusion often arises over what constitutes *mitigation* and *preparedness* (and to what extent these two functions overlap). At the federal level, mitigation and preparedness are highly defined, with FEMA maintaining two completely distinct directorates (mitigation and national preparedness) to manage these functions. However, at the state, local, organizational, and private levels, there is much less of a defined boundary between the two. The major distinction between these two functions at every level is best characterized by the mission of the actions themselves, which calls into play the definitions that have been provided for mitigation and preparedness. In most simple terms, *mitigation* attempts to eliminate hazard risk by reducing either the likelihood or the consequences of the risk associated with the particular hazard. Associated activities, devices, or actions try to prevent a hazard from ever manifesting into a disaster in the first place, or they try to make the disaster much less damaging to humans, property, or the environment if an emergency or disaster situation arises. Typically, these actions are taken prior to the instance of an emergency event. *Preparedness*, on the other hand, seeks to improve the abilities of agencies and individuals to respond to the consequences of a disaster event *once the disaster event has occurred*. Preparedness assumes the occurrence of an event, whereas mitigation attempts to prevent the event altogether.

Preparedness: The Emergency Operations Plan

The emergency operations plan (EOP) is the playbook by which emergency management response operations are conducted. However, the development of an EOP is not just a documentation of what will be done and by whom, but rather it is the process by which these factors are determined. The planning process, like the preparedness process, is a cyclical one that is dependent on each of the subsequent steps on the preparedness cycle, and each determines how the other changes periodically. Planning must be dynamic to be effective to meet the changing character and needs of the jurisdiction or organization for which it is conducted.

The National Response Framework (which is discussed in Chapter 6) is but one example of an emergency plan. Emergency plans literally come in all shapes and sizes and in all manner of quality. These plans, however, are designed by a standard paradigm. Through an evolutionary process of lesson sharing, doctrine, and guidance, select components now appear in almost all emergency plans. These components have formed because they are the most logical presentation through which the response and recovery needs of jurisdictions and agencies may be represented and therefore relied upon in times of need. These components include the following:

- *The Base Plan:* Contains the most comprehensive information about the community, its risks, its statutory authorities, and the general concept by which emergency operations are conducted (including the officials responsible and the tasks they will be held accountable for). This section also includes the assumptions according to which the plans were created and the process by which the plans are updated and distributed.

- *Functional Annexes:* Describe in more detail the different types of assistance that the responsible agencies and officials will provide, assigning responsibility for more task-oriented information. The functional annexes tend to be more operational in nature than what is found in the base plan.
- *Hazard or Situational Annexes:* Hazard annexes recognize that despite the all-hazards nature of base plans, some of the factors are unique to specific hazards that must be described in detail and communicated to emergency management and related officials when the need arises. Using hazard annexes keeps situation-specific information out of the base plan, which can make the base plan more concise and more effective in the time-constrained period of disaster response.

The planning process and the emergency operations plan both depend heavily on all of the steps in the preparedness cycle. Planning both dictates and accounts for the equipment that must be purchased to treat the disaster consequences that are planned for and to carry out the tasks assigned. Planning also becomes the basis of training and exercise, and responders train to the capabilities laid out in the plan and rely upon the assumptions captured by the plan to determine those core competencies that are sought. The exercises that are conducted test the jurisdiction's or organization's ability to carry out what is prescribed in the plan.

Nationwide planning efforts are currently guided by the FEMA-produced *Comprehensive Planning Guide-101 (CPG-101)*. This federal document was created to provide general yet standardized guidelines on developing emergency operations plans (EOPs) and the terminology used in planning efforts and emergency management in general. The purpose of this guide was to promote a common understanding of the fundamentals of planning and decision making, which in turn would foster a more coordinated response when multiple agencies responded in concert to large-scale, multijurisdictional events. Given the pressures on communities to adopt the National Incident Management System and the contingencies placed on federal grant programs, it is understandable that communities would require such guidance. CPG-101 is not the first instance of the federal government providing guidelines. In fact, as long as 50 years ago, the *Federal Civil Defense Guide* was released for the same purpose. The *Civil Preparedness Guide 1-8, Guide for the Development of State and Local Emergency Operations Plans,* and *State and Local Guide (SLG) 101, Guide for All-Hazards Emergency Operations Planning* followed, and they were influential predecessors to *CPG-101*. *CPG-101* can be accessed at *http://www.fema .gov/pdf/about/divisions/npd/cpg_101_layout.pdf.*

Many states guide EOP planning efforts through the release of standard planning guidelines. Some states even provide templates for EOP development, which allow for standardization of not only content but of structure as well. From a state-level coordination perspective this makes perfect sense because a unified command response will call upon some form of synchronization from the various agencies involved. Such templates ensure that responders are referring to the same functions and using the same terminology, among other needs. Virginia is one state that has such guidelines, which can be accessed at *http://www.vaemergency.com/library/plans/local_eop.cfm*.

Evacuation Planning

For many communities, one of their most important planning considerations is how they will evacuate citizens in the event of a major disaster. For disasters where advanced notice of a hazard event is possible (e.g., hurricanes or tsunamis) or for situations where it is essential that all citizens be removed from the affected area as soon as possible after an event has occurred (e.g., terrorist attacks involving weapons of mass destruction), advanced planning is required in order to determine, among other things, activation procedures, the determination of adequate and effective routes, methods of transportation, destinations for those evacuated, security precautions for homes and belongings, adherence by citizens to evacuation orders, and facilitation of the evacuation itself.

While many communities have conducted some form of evacuation planning as part of the basic emergency operations plan, few have been able to conduct a full-scale test that gives them an accurate idea of how the plan will work in a real-life situation. The difficulties that were experienced by local emergency managers in the evacuations from Hurricanes Katrina and Rita in 2005 highlight both the need for evacuation planning and the shortfalls of existing plans. In the Katrina evacuation—the largest in U.S. history, resulting in the displacement of over 1.3 million people—failure to consider how the evacuation would affect people of lower economic standing resulted in thousands refusing to or being unable to leave. In Hurricane Rita, as determined by a University of Texas study, a strong majority of the deaths (90 of the 113) associated with that storm were a result of the poorly planned evacuation itself.

After these events, the U.S. Department of Transportation conducted a study of the evacuation plans in the Gulf Coast region, where hurricanes are most likely to strike. The study looked at each of the five Gulf Coast states (Alabama, Florida, Mississippi, Louisiana, and Texas) and 58 of the counties and parishes in them to determine where the weaknesses lay in their evacuation plans and to learn from any best practices that existed. According to this study, seven key elements can be used to measure the comprehensive nature of a plan:

- Decision making and management
- Planning
- Public communication and preparedness
- Evacuation of people with special needs
- Operations
- Sheltering considerations
- Mass evacuation training and exercises

The study found that while most of the plans were effective in terms of creating standard operating procedures, conducting exercises and drafting after-action reports, updating plans, and defining evacuation direction and control, they were often weak in the following areas:

* Keeping evacuees informed during the evacuation
* Providing for evacuating individuals with various special needs
* Returning evacuees to their homes
* Using contraflow (reversed lane) operations
* Providing for the care and protection of animals

ADDITIONAL RESEARCH

Evacuation planning research has come to the forefront since the experiences in Texas and Louisiana exposed the challenges posed in any evacuation effort. Although many lessons were learned from the botched evacuation after Hurricane Katrina, it was obvious that little progress had been made before the evacuations during the lead-up to Hurricane Rita occurred. The following reports provide insight into the issues involved in evacuation planning and the difficulties in bringing about progress.

The Texas House Research Organization. *Evacuation Planning in Texas: Before and After Hurricane Rita. http://www.hro.house.state.tx.us/interim/int79-2.pdf*

U.S. Department of Transportation. *Report to Congress on Catastrophic Hurricane Plan Evaluation. http://www.fhwa.dot.gov/reports/hurricanevacuation/*

Emergency Planning for Special Needs Populations

Traditionally, emergency planning has looked at a homogenous population thought of collectively as the "community." However, communities are made up of distinct individuals and groups, each with unique conditions that define their lives, their interactions, and their abilities. Several of these individuals have special needs that emergency planners must consider when drafting emergency operations plans and other emergency procedures in the community. In the absence of such consideration, any plans are likely to fail these individuals, as their provisions will be irrelevant or inappropriate.

There is no set criteria that categorizes an individual as "special needs." Likewise, there is no standard set of special needs populations that exist in all communities. Each community must assess its own population to determine what special needs exist and how those needs must be addressed in the emergency plan if it is to adequately protect all of the community's citizens equally.

In considering special needs populations, planners must work with representatives from each group (or, in the case of children, the mentally ill, and other groups, they must work with experts who deal with those types of individuals). By including these key stakeholders, the planners are better able to adjust existing policies or to create new policies that allow for the safety and security of these groups before, during, and after emergency events. Consideration of special needs groups is something that must be addressed in all four phases of emergency management. The following are examples of considerations that must be made:

- Foreign language training and materials
- Registry of special needs individuals' locations and emergency requirements
- Special emergency equipment and forms of transportation
- Special communications equipment or methods
- Alternate (nontraditional) warning media and procedures
- Special protection measures at shelters and during evacuations
- Inclusion of certain prescription drugs and physical support devices in shelters and other emergency facilities
- Special education measures targeting newcomers and transient populations
- Special transportation and holding facilities for incarcerated evacuees or victims
- Training for emergency responders in special needs care

During many, if not all, of the recent U.S. disasters, it was apparent that certain special needs populations exhibited a greater degree of vulnerability and, as a result, experienced a proportionally greater impact than other groups affected by the same event. Two specific examples include the 1995 heat wave in Chicago, in which almost all of the 600 victims were elderly poor, and Hurricane Katrina, where most of the residents who failed to evacuate (and died as a result) were the urban poor. In the recovery phase of Katrina (as well as many other recent major disasters), it was the illegal immigrant population, who had never registered for services out of fear of deportation, who suffered to a greater degree. To an increasing degree, however, campaigns advocating for increased consideration of special needs populations in emergency planning, initiated primarily by activist groups representing the individual groups, have accelerated the acceptance by emergency planners of the planning need throughout the United States.

CRITICAL THINKING

Why is evacuation planning so difficult? What kinds of things can go wrong during an actual evacuation? What do you think can be done to minimize these potential setbacks?

Preparedness Equipment

Emergency management organizations rely upon an incredibly diverse range of equipment categories with which they perform the response roles assigned to them. These categories of equipment, which include (among many others) personal protective equipment (PPE), firefighting apparatus, and communications systems, are described in detail throughout this book. Equipment is very important in the preparedness phase because it is during this phase that equipment needs are identified, equipment is purchased, and staff are trained in the use of the equipment.

The federal government, through FEMA, facilitates the acquisition of significant amounts of emergency management equipment at the state and local levels through a number of emergency management grant vehicles with an equipment focus. In order to inform communities about the specific categories and specifications of equipment that are eligible under these grants, FEMA created the authorized equipment list (AEL). The AEL is a virtual catalog of the many different types of equipment that responders are likely to require in the course of their response and recovery efforts. This list indicates a continued federal focus on the terrorism hazard, even though most of these grant programs maintain all-hazards eligibility.

Education and Training Programs

Education and training have always been integral to the emergency services. Firefighters receive their education at the fire academy, police officers get theirs at the police academy, and EMS officials get medical and emergency first aid training from both public and private sources. However, a revolution of sorts has occurred in the provision of education and training in the emergency management profession. Only a few decades ago, emergency management was an outgrowth of the emergency services and a position for which little or no training was provided (nor was it felt that additional training was needed).

The advent of emergency management training and education coincided with the creation of the Federal Emergency Management Agency in 1979, which touched off the development of the practice as a profession. At that time, few officials (both within and outside the traditional emergency services) had any background in emergency management, and few people were dedicated to the function even within major city governments. At the nation's universities, few programs provided even minor degrees or certificates in the field, and only a handful of colleges offered such courses.

At first, it was FEMA that defined the profession as one that required specific academic courses and training. FEMA's Emergency Management Institute became the focus of these efforts. Working with practitioners at select colleges and universities that offered similar programs, FEMA defined the core competencies of emergency management professionals and developed a definition for an "emergency management curriculum."

It was the events of September 11, 2001, however, that truly transformed emergency management training and education. Since then, primarily due to an explosion in funding available and jobs created in the growing emergency management marketplace (both public and private), scores of colleges and universities have begun to offer traditional emergency management degrees, and hundreds of schools offer emergency management classes. Many private training facilities have opened to meet the expanding training needs of the profession, and traditional emergency services academies have expanded their curriculums to accommodate the growing number of courses required by full-time emergency management professionals.

The FEMA Emergency Management Institute (EMI) and National Fire Academy (NFA)

Since its inception in 1979, FEMA has emerged as a leader in providing direction for the education and training of emergency management professionals through both the development and provision of actual training courses and the development of higher education courses and materials. The Emergency Management Institute (EMI) and the National Fire Academy (NFA), both in Emmitsburg, Maryland, serve the training and educational needs of hundreds of thousands of firefighters, fire officers, emergency managers, and others. These institutions offer training program courses whose primary objective is to enhance emergency management practice in the United States. At present, approximately 10,000 students are enrolled in EMI's resident courses. Nonresident courses, which are administered by the states through their emergency management agencies (under a cooperative agreement with FEMA), accommodate an additional 100,000 students each year. Emergency management exercises that are supported by EMI draw over 150,000 participants annually, and through the range of independent study program courses administered through the Institute's website, several hundred thousand other individuals receive training.

Three EMI programs of note are the Integrated Emergency Management Course (IEMC) curriculum, the Disaster-Resistant Jobs courses, and several Train-the-Trainer courses that are available in many different subject areas. The IEMC is a set of courses for public officials that cover all aspects of the community emergency management function. Community officials from Oklahoma City participated in the IEMC program just months before the Alfred P. Murrah building terrorist bombing in 1995, and they credit the lessons they learned through the program with helping them to respond quickly and effectively in the aftermath of that event. The Disaster-Resistant Jobs course was developed in cooperation with the Economic Development Administration (EDA) of the U.S. Department of Commerce and is designed to "help small and medium-sized communities protect the economy from the effects of catastrophic events." This course was developed in response to the devastating impact the 1997 floods had on the city of Grand Forks, North Dakota. The EDA and FEMA recognized that more economic development planning could be done to reduce the impacts of future disasters on local economies.

FEMA's EMI Higher Education Project works to establish and support emergency management curriculum in junior colleges, colleges, and universities. The project has developed a prototype curriculum for associate degrees in emergency management. Currently, for emergency management, FEMA lists 9 doctoral programs, 61 masters degree programs, 23 bachelors degree programs, 28 bachelors-level emergency management concentrations and minors, 38 associates-level programs, 63 standalone certificate programs, and 45 additional programs offering one or more courses. For homeland security, EMI lists 3 doctoral programs, 29 masters programs, 14 bachelors programs, 14 bachelors-level homeland security concentrations and minors, 14 associates degree programs, and 57 certificate programs.

The NFA proclaims that "through its courses and programs, the National Fire Academy works to enhance the ability of fire and emergency services and allied professionals to deal more effectively with fire and related emergencies." The NFA was first created in 1975 to serve as the primary delivery mechanism for the fire training efforts of the congressionally mandated U.S. Fire Administration (USFA). Since that time, the NFA estimates it has trained more than 1.4 million students. Like EMI, the NFA delivers many of its courses in Emmitsburg, Maryland, and across the country in cooperation with state and local fire training organizations and local colleges and universities.

The NFA's on-campus programs target middle- and top-level fire officers, fire service instructors, technical professionals, and representatives from allied professions. Any person with substantial involvement in fire prevention and control, emergency medical services, or fire-related emergency management activities is eligible to apply for NFA courses. The NFA also delivers courses using CD-ROMs, their simulation laboratory, and the Internet.

Public Preparedness Education

Perhaps the most difficult component of emergency management preparedness training is the one that focuses on the general public. Public preparedness education, also called risk communication, is a field that has seen vastly mixed success. One of the greatest emergency management public education efforts came out of the civil protection era when the government sought to protect its citizens from the assumed risk of aerial bombing from enemy governments. This campaign focused on the notorious "air raid drills" that instructed children on how to protect themselves by crouching under their desks. Since that time, there has been a flurry of mass communication in the emergency management and preparedness spectra, but very little has come close to achieving such widespread behavioral change. Public education efforts are not very successful for two reasons: First, most campaigns are conducted by emergency managers with understandably little training in the highly complex social marketing and public education disciplines. The field is just learning the value of a systematic or academic approach to the task, and improvements in efficacy can be expected as a result. Second, it is common knowledge that the public faces myriad risks on a daily basis beyond what is being communicated, and many of those daily hazards, as they are often called, take precedence over any major disaster that has little likelihood of ever occurring (as well as many other risk perception factors that prevented widespread success) to individuals. There are, of course, individual success stories, including the stop, cover, and roll fire safety drills and the stop, drop, and cover earthquake drills, but research has shown that most families still fail to take even the most basic preparations to protect themselves from major disasters even though a highly visible succession of disasters has befallen the nation.

FEMA has expended much effort over the years to manage the public education reform. Before 9/11, FEMA's training efforts consisted primarily of publishing educational materials for teachers, community centers, and other organizations. After the terrorist attacks, however, these efforts expanded greatly through the establishment of a well-publicized preparedness website developed by FEMA called Ready.gov. This website provided preparedness information on what FEMA considered the three important preparedness responsibilities of all citizens and businesses: get a kit, make a plan, and stay informed. Unfortunately, the site never caught on, and few people even looked at it.

FEMA also published the preparedness guide *Are You Ready?* This is a downloadable and printable step-by-step guide that discusses the risks people face today and how they can mitigate them. FEMA also published an instructor's guide so the book can be used for a class instead of just being read (which can be much less effective). A video titled *Getting Ready for Disaster* also accompanies the guide, providing another alternative channel for preparedness learning. Each of these resources can be found and accessed on the FEMA Are You Ready website at *http://www.fema.gov/areyouready/.*

Today, one of the greatest success stories in the public education domain is the growing network of Community Emergency Response Team (CERT) programs operating around the country. CERT was developed with the belief that after a major disaster, first responders are likely to be quickly overwhelmed and therefore unable to meet the demand for certain services. Factors such as the presence of mass numbers of casualties, failures in infrastructure (such as communication systems), and other confounding variables like road blockages will prevent equitable access to emergency assistance. In these situations, people will have to rely on one another for help to meet their immediate lifesaving and life-sustaining needs. By training members of the general public to perform many of these functions that are normally assumed by the emergency services, the scope of preparedness within the community increases greatly, and vulnerability to hazard risk is reduced. Therefore, CERT's goals are as follows:

1. Present citizens with the facts about what to expect following a major disaster in terms of immediate services.
2. Give the message about their responsibility for mitigation and preparedness.

3. Train them in needed lifesaving skills, with an emphasis on decision-making skills, rescuer safety, and doing the greatest good for the greatest number.
4. Organize teams so they are an extension of first-responder services, offering immediate help to victims until professional services arrive.

The Community Emergency Response Team (CERT) concept was developed and implemented by the Los Angeles City Fire Department (LAFD) in 1985. The Whittier Narrows earthquake in 1987 underscored the areawide threat of a major disaster in California. Further, it confirmed the need for training civilians to meet their immediate needs. As a result, the LAFD created the Disaster Preparedness Division to train citizens and private and government employees.

The training program that the LAFD initiated was recognized for its ability to further the process through which citizens understand their responsibility in preparing for disaster. It also increased their ability to safely help themselves, their family, and their neighbors. FEMA recognizes the value of this program and helped to expand its reach nationwide. The EMI and the National Fire Academy adopted and expanded the CERT materials, believing them to be applicable to all hazards. Today, CERT training is conducted within easy reach of almost every community in the country.

CERT prepares unaffiliated citizens to respond to and cope with the aftermath of a disaster. CERT groups are provided with the skills and knowledge to provide immediate assistance to victims in their area, organize spontaneous volunteers who have not had any training, and collect disaster intelligence that will assist professional responders with prioritizing and allocating resources following a disaster. Since 1993, when FEMA made this training available nationally, communities in almost all states and territories have conducted CERT training. The CERT course is delivered in the community by a team of first responders who have the requisite knowledge and skills to instruct the sessions. The CERT training for community groups usually is delivered in two-and-a-half-hour sessions, one evening per week, over a seven-week period. CERT is maintained by the FEMA Community Preparedness Division, which also runs the Citizen Corps Program that oversees CERT.

Emergency Management Exercises

Once a plan has been developed, equipment has been purchased, and personnel have been trained in the plan and the use of equipment, it is time to make sure that a critical level of preparedness has been achieved. In actuality, the only true validation of preparedness efforts comes as the result of a response to an actual disaster event. However, it serves little good to wait until such an event occurs because at that point it is too late to identify weaknesses and make changes as necessary. In order to substitute for "battlefield experience," emergency management agencies use programs of disaster exercises to simulate many of the situations that may arise.

Exercises provide an opportunity to evaluate the efficiency and effectiveness of the plan and its components and to test the systems, facilities, and personnel involved in

FIGURE 4-2 Salinas, Puerto Rico, March 25, 2009. To test a swift response to an unexpected disaster in Salinas, FEMA joined the PR State Emergency Management Agency, the National Guard Bureau, the U.S. Department of Defense Northern Command, and other federal, state, and local emergency managers in the "Vigilant Guard exercise." The Vigilant Guard aims to assess the response capabilities of all of the participating agencies and organizations to a simulated 7.0 earthquake scenario in the southern region of the island. Ashley Andujar/FEMA.

implementing the plan. Exercises are conducted at all levels of government, in the private sector, at educational facilities, and more. FEMA defines an exercise as "a controlled, scenario-driven, simulated experience designed to demonstrate and evaluate an organization's capability to execute one or more assigned or implicit operational tasks or procedures as outlined in its contingency plan." These are the common categories of emergency management exercises (Coppola, 2006):

- *Drill.* A controlled, supervised method by which a single disaster management operation or function is practiced or tested.
- *Tabletop exercise.* Designed to allow officials to practice components of or the full activation of the emergency response plan within the confines of a controlled, low-stress discussion scenario.
- *Functional exercise.* Tests and practices response capabilities by simulating an event to which responsible officials must respond. Unlike a drill, which tests one function or activity, the functional exercise tests a full range of associated activities that together fulfill a greater overall response purpose.
- *Full-scale exercise.* A scenario-based event that seeks to create an atmosphere closely mimicking an actual disaster. All players required to act during a real event, as outlined in the EOP, are involved in the full-scale exercise, working in real time and using all of the required equipment and procedures (Figures 4-2 and 4-3).

FEMA supports exercises at all jurisdictional levels through the Homeland Security Exercise and Evaluation Program (HSEEP; pronounced "hee-sep"). HSEEP was created to provide guidance and standardization to the exercise efforts of emergency management

FIGURE 4-3 Salinas, Puerto Rico, March 25, 2009. Alejandro De La Campa, the Caribbean area division director, at a press conference after the Salinas exercise.
Ashley Andujar/FEMA.

organizations and to develop a framework for evaluation. HSEEP has met both praise and complaint, since it is the most comprehensive tool of its kind, but many jurisdictions feel that it is just another way the federal government is trying to dictate actions at the local level. This, in part, is due to the fact that federally funded exercises must comply with HSEEP regulations and standards to be covered under emergency management grant programs, which are the only option for funding such exercises for the majority of departments. HSEEP also ties together other emergency management doctrines that have not met uniform acceptance across all jurisdictions, including that of NIMS and the NRF, which must be tested in the course of exercise conduct.

FEMA requires HSEEP compliance for grant eligibility. *Compliance* is defined as adherence to specific processes and practices for exercise program management and exercise design, development, conduct, evaluation, and improvement planning. Four specific performance requirements are established in the HSEEP policy and guidance documentation:

1. Conduct an annual training and exercise planning workshop, and maintain a multiyear training and exercise plan (TEP).
2. Plan and conduct exercises in accordance with the guidelines set forth in the HSEEP policy.
3. Develop and submit a properly formatted after-action report/improvement plan.
4. Track and implement corrective actions identified in the AAR/IP.

The penultimate emergency management exercise series is the DHS-supported National Level Exercise (NLE) program. The NLE program, formerly called TOPOFF (for Top Officials), is a full-scale exercise held once a year that tests the response to major disaster events spanning states, regions, and across international borders. Traditionally, NLE exercises have focused on terrorism hazards. However, in 2011, NLE will for the first time focus on a natural hazard: a major earthquake on the New Madrid Fault Zone in central United States. NLE is maintained by the DHS National Exercise Program, which provides the coordination and planning for federal, regional, and state exercise activities beyond what the states conduct themselves. NLE predates DHS because the first TOPOFF exercise was held in May 2000 to test a simultaneous biological attack in Colorado and a chemical attack in New Hampshire. Since that time, the following exercises have been conducted:

- TOPOFF 2: Conducted in May 2003, tested a simultaneous radiological attack in Washington State and a biological attack in Illinois.
- TOPOFF 3: Conducted in April 2005, tested a simultaneous chemical attack in Connecticut and a biological attack in New Jersey.
- TOPOFF 4: Conducted in October 2007, tested simultaneous radiological attacks in Oregon, Arizona, Guam, and Washington, D.C.
- NLE 2009: Conducted in July and August 2009, this exercise focused exclusively on the prevention of a terrorist attack around the country (but focused on Washington, D.C., Arkansas, Louisiana, New Mexico, Oklahoma, and Kansas).
- NLE 2010: Conducted in May 2010, focused on the detonation of a nuclear device.

Evaluation and Improvement

It is through evaluation and assessment that those responsible for response and recovery are best able to refine preparedness capabilities. While this chapter so far has discussed the processes by which preparedness capabilities are built up, including the drafting of plans, equipment acquisitions, and the conduct of exercises, it is through the evaluation process that capabilities are kept on track and improved over time. There are several programs by which emergency management evaluation may be conducted. Here are a few of the more common ones:

- *EMAP:* Probably the most recognizable organizational preparedness evaluation effort, the Emergency Management Accreditation Program (EMAP) evaluates state, territorial, and local emergency management agencies according to the peer-reviewed Emergency Management Standard. EMAP is funded by FEMA but maintained by an independent nonprofit organization. Agencies that are interested in accreditation pay a fee for evaluation by independent reviewers.
- *SPR:* The State Preparedness Report (SPR) was developed to satisfy the requirements for state-level emergency management disaster preparedness defined by the Post-Katrina Emergency Management Reform Act (PKEMRA). Under this initiative, states and territories submit an annual SPR as a means to report on the progress, capabilities, and accomplishments of their all-hazards preparedness program. This report is designed to enable states to communicate to Congress current accomplishments in meeting the preparedness priorities and capabilities defined by DHS and how they will continue to increase statewide preparedness. States develop

their individual SPRs using a standard template, wherein they address the actions they have taken to address the eight National Priorities (as identified in the National Preparedness Guidelines):

a. Implement the NIMS and the NRF
b. Expand regional collaboration
c. Implement the National Infrastructure Protection Plan (NIPP)
d. Strengthen information sharing and collaboration capabilities
e. Strengthen interoperable and operable communications capabilities
f. Strengthen CBRNE detection, response, and decontamination capabilities
g. Strengthen medical surge and mass prophylaxis capabilities
h. Strengthen planning and citizen capabilities

- *TCL:* The Target Capabilities List (TCL) is a FEMA-administered program that identifies and defines capabilities that may be needed to respond to the various hazard risks facing the country. Under TCL, capabilities need not be maintained by each individual agency but rather must be something that the agency is able to draw upon from within its own ranks or from any mutual aid, EMAC, or other partners. Under TCL, jurisdictions are expected to develop and maintain capability at levels that reflect the differing risk and needs throughout the country. The TCL identifies 37 distinct capabilities developed in consultation with representatives from all levels of government, the private sector, and nongovernmental organizations. Users refer to the TCL to design plans, procedures, training, exercises, and evaluations that develop and assess capacity and proficiency to perform their assigned missions and tasks in major events. The TCL is intended to serve as foundational reference document and planning guide to achieve national preparedness.

- *NIMSCAST:* The NIMS Compliance Assistance Support Tool (NIMSCAST), maintained by the FEMA National Preparedness Directorate, is a system that allows organizations in the emergency management community to self-report on their progress in implementing the National Incident Management System (NIMS).

- *DEC Communications Project:* The Disaster Emergency Communications (DEC) Communications Project is a FEMA-administered 28-state initiative that analyzes emergency communications. DEC's mission focus is the provision of communications capabilities when landlines and cellular networks are damaged or congested, particularly during the first 96 hours of a disaster, for situational awareness and command and control, state and local first responders, and emergency responders performing disaster missions. At the conclusion of scheduled state assessments, an assessment team drafts a detailed report that encompasses communications requirements, proposed mitigation strategies, negotiated mission assignments, and acquisition strategies. The team also writes regional emergency communications plans and equipment specifications.

- *CAS:* The Comprehensive Assessment System (CAS) is a FEMA-administered emergency management assessment system that identifies issues and shortfalls across the spectrum of homeland security operations with respect to resource allocation and the performance of specific all-hazards capabilities at the federal, state, tribal, and local jurisdictional levels. Mandated by PKEMRA, CAS assesses compliance with the National Preparedness System, the National Incident Management System (NIMS), and other related plans; assesses resource needs; and assesses the performance of training, exercises, and operations. FEMA hopes that CAS will one day function as a central repository for national preparedness data.

- *CEM:* Individual emergency management preparedness capabilities may be evaluated through the Certified Emergency Manager (CEM) program maintained by the International Association of Emergency Managers (IAEM). This fee-based program ensures that individuals have received a requisite array of courses and experience that prepare them for the demands of an actual disaster response. Those passing certification are permitted to use the acronym *CEM* in their professional title.

Preparedness: A National Effort

Emergency and disaster preparedness is conducted at all levels of government, but it is through the FEMA National Preparedness (NP) Directorate that a national-level strategy for preparedness is developed, communicated, and supported. Following the failed response to Hurricane Katrina, Congress determined, through the Post-Katrina Emergency Management Report Act of 2006, that there was a dire need for a national direction on emergency preparedness to ensure that the national government, states, counties, parishes, cities, towns, and communities were equipped with the knowledge, funding, and guidance to ensure proper response and recovery from major disaster events at all government and organizational levels. As a result, the National Preparedness Directorate (NPD) was established on April 1, 2007, in order to oversee coordination and development of the strategies necessary to achieve these goals. NPD was established to provide preparedness policy and planning guidance and to help build disaster response capabilities. As a FEMA directorate, NPD has wide leverage to develop and institute preparedness programs that include training courses, national policy development and state/local policy guidance, and the planning and conduct of exercises, including the National Level Exercises (NLEs) described previously.

The requirements of a national-level preparedness effort are guided by the National Response Framework (NRF), which superseded the National Response Plan (NRP) in January 2008. The NRF was released to establish a comprehensive, national, all-hazards approach to domestic incident response and to provide clear guidance over the integration of community, state, tribal, and federal response efforts. In order to achieve the capability to conduct the necessary actions prescribed within this framework, FEMA has released a series of doctrines guiding preparedness at a strategic level. Homeland Security Presidential Directive-8 (HSPD-8) directed the secretary of Homeland Security to develop a national domestic all-hazards preparedness goal. As part of that effort, in March 2005, DHS released the Interim National Preparedness Goal. This goal was later adapted into what is now the National Preparedness Guidelines. These guidelines have the following four elements:

1. The *National Preparedness Vision,* which provides a concise statement of the core preparedness goal for the nation.
2. The *National Planning Scenarios,* which depict 15 high-consequence threat scenarios involving natural and (yet primarily) terrorist hazards according to which preparedness may be based. These scenarios have come under considerable scrutiny since their release, and their use has been extensively limited as a result.
3. The *Universal Task List (UTL),* which includes approximately 1,600 unique tasks identified as being key to preventing, protecting against, responding to, and recovering from the major events represented by the national planning scenarios.
4. The *Target Capabilities List (TCL),* which was just described and that defines 37 specific capabilities that FEMA has determined to be essential to communities, the private sector, and all levels of government in order to respond effectively to disasters.

These two FEMA programs also help to guide national-level preparedness:

• The Radiological Emergency Preparedness Program (REPP): *http://www.fema.gov/about/divisions/thd_repp.shtm*
• The Chemical Stockpile Emergency Preparedness Program (CSEPP): *http://www.fema.gov/about/divisions/thd_csepp.shtm*

These two programs provide preparedness guidance that is highly specific to two hazard threats (radiological and chemical hazards) for which significant understanding is beyond what is typically possessed by state and local emergency management officials. They also provide standards for the private, governmental, and military facilities that are the source of such hazards to ensure that these hazards are adequately contained and that the capabilities to respond to accidents or incidents that involve the release of chemicals are in place.

The National Preparedness Directorate is comprised of several individual divisions that address different aspects of preparedness. In addition to EMI, these include the following:

• *Preparedness Policy, Planning, and Analysis (PPPA):* PPPA strengthens national preparedness through the development of national-level preparedness policy, including (for instance) maintenance of the Target Capabilities List and National Preparedness Guidelines; establishment and support of national planning systems (such as a catastrophic planning program targeting the nation's major urban areas); and the development of assessment methodologies to analyze preparedness benchmarks (such as the Comprehensive Assessment System and the National Preparedness Report).
• *Technological Hazards Division (THP):* THP coordinates national efforts to enhance preparedness in communities around nuclear power plants and military chemical

weapons sites. The two programs just described, including the Radiological Emergency Preparedness Program (REPP) and the Chemical Stockpile Emergency Preparedness Program (CSEPP), are part of this division's efforts.

- *National Integration Center (NIC):* The NIC is responsible for developing, managing, and coordinating all national-level programs focused on training, education, exercise, and lessons learned. The NIC also maintains the Lessons Learned Information System (LLIS; pronounced "ellis"), which is an online-accessible database of best practices designed to enhance preparedness efforts of local, state, and federal emergency management agencies, and the Responder Knowledge Base (RKB), a website designed to provide emergency managers with easy access to the preparedness background data they might need (and accessed at *www.rkb.us*).

- *The Community Preparedness Division:* This division works to enhance public disaster preparedness, mainly by administering the Citizen Corps program. Community Preparedness also develops policies targeting public preparedness efforts and designs materials that may be accessed by those who provide disaster preparedness education to various stakeholder groups outside of the emergency services.

- *The Preparedness Coordination Division:* PCD provides support to federal, state, and local agencies through field-based methods, primarily under the management federal preparedness coordinators, who work out of the 10 FEMA regional offices.

Preparedness Grant Programs

The FEMA National Preparedness Directorate currently administers a wide range of grant programs that target preparedness efforts at all government levels, though primarily those of states, territories, tribes, and local jurisdictions. These programs differ according to their goals, the agencies eligible to apply for them, and the activities and equipment eligible to be funded. Some of the grant programs that received funding in 2010 include the following.

Emergency Management Performance Grant Program (EMPG): $329.9 million available in 2010

The EMPG was created to assist state and local governments in enhancing and sustaining all-hazards emergency management capabilities. Eligible applicants include the states and territories. State administrative agencies or state emergency management agencies (EMAs) are eligible to apply directly to FEMA for EMPG funds on behalf of state and local emergency management agencies. This grant has a 50 percent federal and 50 percent state cost share, cash or in-kind match requirement. Grant information can be found at *http://www.fema.gov/pdf/government/grant/2010/fy10_empg_kit.pdf*.

Emergency Operations Center (EOC) Grant Program: $57.6 million available in 2010

The EOC Grant Program is created to improve emergency management and preparedness capabilities by supporting flexible, sustainable, secure, and interoperable emergency operations centers (EOCs), with a focus on addressing identified deficiencies and needs. This program provides funding for construction or renovation of a state, local, or tribal government's principal EOC. Only the state can apply for this grant, though much of the funding is then passed to the local government. Grant information can be found at *http://www.fema.gov/pdf/government/grant/2010/fy10_eoc_kit.pdf.*

The Homeland Security Grant Program (HSGP)

The HSGP is comprised of seven separate grant programs, each described here.

State Homeland Security Program (SHSP): $842 million available in 2010
The HSGP provides funds to build response capabilities at the state and local levels and to implement the goals and objectives included in state homeland security strategies and initiatives in each state preparedness report (see SPR earlier in this chapter). States are required to ensure that at least 25 percent of SHSP-appropriated funds are dedicated toward law enforcement terrorism prevention–oriented planning, organization, training, exercise, and equipment activities, including those activities that support the development and operation of fusion centers. Only the state government can apply to FEMA for SHSP funds. Each state will receive a minimum 0.36 percent of the total funds, and the remainder is based on several risk factors (four territories—American Samoa, Guam, the Northern Mariana Islands, and the U.S. Virgin Islands—receive a minimum allocation of 0.08 percent of the total funds).

Urban Area Security Initiative (UASI): $832.5 million available in 2010
The UASI program focuses on enhancing regional preparedness in major metropolitan areas in support of the National Preparedness Guidelines. The program assists selected jurisdictions in developing integrated regional systems for disaster mitigation, preparedness, response, and recovery. States are required to ensure that at least 25 percent of UASI-appropriated funds are dedicated toward law enforcement terrorism prevention–oriented planning, organization, training, exercise, and equipment activities, including those activities that support the development and operation of fusion centers. Only the state governments may apply for the UASI grant programs, though most of the money is passed directly to the urban areas.

The Metropolitan Medical Response System (MMRS) Program: $39.36 million available in 2010
The MMRS program supports the integration of emergency management, health, and medical systems into a coordinated response to mass-casualty incidents. The grant program seeks to augment existing local operational response systems in the preparedness phase. Only state governments may apply to FEMA for MMRS funds, but most of the funding is passed through to 124 MMRS jurisdictions. Each jurisdiction receives $317,419 to establish or sustain local capabilities.

Citizen Corps Program (CCP): $12.48 million available in 2010

The Citizen Corps mission is to bring community and government leaders together to coordinate community involvement in emergency preparedness, planning, mitigation, response, and recovery. Again, only the state and territorial governments can apply to FEMA for CCP funds. CCP allocations are distributed according to risk-based formulas that specify that all 50 states, the District of Columbia, and the Commonwealth of Puerto Rico receive a minimum of 0.75 percent of the total available grant funding and that four territories (American Samoa, Guam, the Northern Mariana Islands, and the U.S. Virgin Islands) receive a minimum of 0.25 percent of total funding. The remainder is distributed on a population-share basis.

Operation Stonegarden (OPSG): $60 million available in 2010

OPSG was created to enhance cooperation and coordination among local, state, and federal law enforcement agencies to secure international borders with Mexico and Canada, as well as states and territories with international water borders. Prospective recipients for OPSG include local units of government at the county level and federally recognized tribal governments in the states bordering Canada (including Alaska), southern states bordering Mexico, and states and territories with international water borders. Grant information can be found at *http://www.fema.gov/pdf/government/grant/2010/fy10_hsgp_kit.pdf.*

FY 2010 Port Security Grant Program (PSGP): $288 million available in 2010

The PSGP seeks to protect critical port infrastructures from terrorism, particularly attacks using explosives and nonconventional threats that could cause major disruptions to commerce. PSGP funds are used to increase port preparedness, primarily to assist ports in enhancing maritime domain awareness; enhancing risk management capabilities to prevent, detect, respond to, and recover from attacks involving improvised explosive devices (IEDs), chemical, biological, radiological, nuclear, explosive (CBRNE), and other nonconventional weapons; as well as training and exercises and transportation worker identification credential (TWIC) implementation. Seven port areas have been selected as Group I (highest risk), and 48 port areas have been selected as Group II. Ports not identified in Group I or II are eligible to apply as a Group III or "all other port areas" applicant. Grant information can be found at *http://www.fema.gov/pdf/government/grant/2010/fy10_psgp_guidance.pdf.*

Regional Catastrophic Preparedness Grant Program (RCPGP): $33.6 million available in 2010

RCPGP enhances catastrophic incident preparedness in selected high-risk, high-consequence urban areas and their surrounding regions. RCPGP is intended to support coordination of regional all-hazards planning for catastrophic events, including the development of integrated planning communities, plans, protocols, and procedures to manage a catastrophic disaster. Eligible applicants include 11 predesignated high-risk, high-consequence urban areas. Grant information can be found at *http://www.fema.gov/ pdf/government/grant/2010/fy10_rcp_kit.pdf.*

CRITICAL THINKING

Why do you think the ODP focuses its preparedness efforts on terrorism? Should preparedness activities funded by ODP be all-hazards? Why or why not?

Business Continuity Planning and Emergency Management

Business continuity planning (BCP) is the process by which businesses prepare for disasters by identifying the risks to their business processes, their facilities, their employees, and their information, and then take action to reduce that risk. BCP also includes identification and enactment of the processes by which businesses are able to continue to function (even if at a reduced capacity) during periods of disaster such that they are able to remain viable for the long term and so the products and services they provide to the community and country remain available. BCP is the most effective way for businesses to prepare for emergencies because the process initiates a much greater understanding of how community risk affects the businesses and what will be required of the business (rather than being provided by traditional emergency responders or other entities). BCP, like all preparedness efforts, increases community-wide resilience, since the sooner the business sector is able to get back up and running, the sooner the community is able to recover.

Business disaster planning first began with the information age, and preparedness focused primarily on information storage and retrieval. Since that time, the concept of continuity has evolved in response to a changing environment. Major events have demanded that BCP encompass a growing number of concerns. The terrorist attacks of September 11 showed almost all businesses how a disaster can impact a country at a national level through the ripples of economic and psychological effects. Since 9/11, the following changes have occurred in the BCP sector:

1. Terrorism is given greater consideration as a threat by many businesses, regardless of the business focus or location.
2. BCP has expanded to include concern for the physical safety of employees.
3. BCP may involve the decentralization of business operations.
4. BCP may have to expand its sphere of concern to include the regional impacts of a disaster (including economic) to the area where a business is located.
5. The human relationships that a business depends on for its survival has become a more significant concern.
6. Businesses are striving for zero downtime during disasters by incorporating off-site operations capabilities.
7. Novel approaches are being taken with regards to critical data backup and retrieval.
8. Physical security has become a BCP concern.
9. There is an increased professionalization of the BCP industry, and more and more businesses are employing full-time emergency management and BCP staff.

The events of September 11 raised awareness of the fact that the survival of business depends on many external factors, such as critical infrastructure and transportation systems. The federal government also recognized the importance of BCP because so much of the nation's public infrastructure was privately owned and therefore independent of most government preparedness efforts. FEMA has begun to work more closely with businesses to bring about preparedness, since businesses are not only the recipients of disaster assistance but are also the providers of many of the products and services needed in the lead-up to and aftermath of disaster events and therefore must be brought into the preparedness and planning process.

The FEMA Private Sector Division in the Office of External Affairs leads up the development of this partnership and initiates various working groups that aim to bring about business sector preparedness and recovery planning activities. For instance, in the 2009 H1N1 pandemic influenza outbreak, the Private Sector Division developed an H1N1 preparedness guide for small businesses, which were particularly susceptible to business closure from the flu outbreak because they depend on such a limited workforce.

In November 2009, FEMA announced the Voluntary Private Sector Preparedness Accreditation and Certification Program (PS-Prep). This program was mandated by legislation that followed 9/11. The PS-Prep Program was created to enhance private sector preparedness by providing a mechanism by which private sector entities could become certified as adequately prepared for disasters. This process involves the development of preparedness standards, of course, that did not exist previously. Participation in the program is completely voluntary, and the government maintains no authority to require businesses to comply with any standard adopted under the program. The following standards were developed and/or adopted:

- ASIS International SPC.1-2009. *Organizational Resilience: Security Preparedness, and Continuity Management System*
- British Standards Institution 25999. *Business Continuity Management: Part 1 (2006) and Part 2 (2007)*
- National Fire Protection Association 1600: 2007. *Standard on Disaster/Emergency Management and Business Continuity Program*

The ANSI-ASQ National Accreditation Board (ANAB) was selected to develop and oversee the certification process, manage the accreditation, and accredit qualified third parties to carry out the certification in accordance with the accepted procedures of the program. Private sector organizations, including businesses and critical infrastructure and key resource entities, may apply for certification to the applicable requirements of preparedness standards that have been developed or adopted. Certification, in the context of this program, is confirmation that an accredited third-party certification organization has validated a private sector entity's preparedness to a standard. DHS will then maintain and make public a listing of any private sector entity certified as being in compliance with PS-Prep if that private sector entity consents to such a listing, which would presumably instill greater public confidence in that company.

Business continuity planning, however, is chiefly driven by the private sector itself. For instance, DRI International (DRII), a business continuity planning institute, provides significant guidance on higher education programs on BCP, supports BCP research, and maintains a capacity to enable businesses to self-assess their preparedness capabilities. DRII, like FEMA, has a certification process through which businesses can prove that they have met a minimum level of preparedness for various hazard risks, thereby instilling confidence among investors and/or shareholders. Other organizations that provide a similar service include Disaster Recovery World, Nonprofit Risk, Business Continuity World, and the Public Entity Risk Institute.

Conclusion

Preparedness consists of four basic elements: preparing a plan, acquiring equipment, training to the plan, and exercising the plan. Preparedness planning at the community level is critical to reducing the effects of disaster events. FEMA sponsors numerous planning, training, and education activities designed to assist communities and states in developing effective preparedness plans and training personnel to implement these plans. Through its National Preparedness Directorate, FEMA helps provide national-level preparedness guidance and significant funding to support preparedness efforts.

Business continuity planning is a significant growth area for the emergency management community. The devastating impacts of September 11 have resulted in increased coordination and cooperation between business and emergency managers. The emergency management community has just begun to exploit this opportunity and more than ever before is encouraging businesses to become more active in supporting all phases of emergency management.

CASE STUDY: THE TSUNAMIREADY PROGRAM

TsunamiReady is an initiative that promotes tsunami hazard preparedness as an active collaboration among federal, state, and local emergency management agencies, the public, and the NWS tsunami warning system. This collaboration is dedicated to promoting better and more consistent tsunami awareness and mitigation efforts among communities at risk. Through the TsunamiReady program, NOAA's National Weather Service gives communities the skills and education needed to survive a tsunami before, during, and after the event. TsunamiReady was designed to help community leaders and emergency managers strengthen their local tsunami operations (NOAA, N/D).

The TsunamiReady program is based on the NWS StormReady model (which can be viewed at *http://www.stormready.noaa.gov/*). The primary goal of TsunamiReady is the improvement of public safety during tsunami emergencies. As just stated, TsunamiReady is designed for those coastal communities that are at known risk of the tsunami hazard (tsunami hazard risk maps can be seen at *http://www.pmel.noaa.gov/tsunami/time/*).

Traditionally, tsunami hazard planning along the U.S. West Coast and Alaska has been widely neglected because of the statistically low incidence of tsunamis. As result of that perceived rarity, many individuals and communities have not worked to become as "tsunami-aware" as they could and should be. Among those communities that are considered to be prepared, that level of exhibited preparedness varies significantly (NWS, N/D).

However, as is true with the earthquakes and other rare events that generate tsunamis, avoidable casualties and property damage will only continue to rise unless these at-risk communities become better prepared for tsunamis. As previously mentioned, readiness involves two key components: awareness and mitigation. *Awareness* involves educating key decision makers, emergency managers, and the public about the nature (physical processes) and threat (frequency of occurrence, impact) of the tsunami hazard; *mitigation* involves taking steps *before* the tsunami occurs to lessen the impact (loss of life and property) of that event. As is true with earthquakes, there is no question that tsunamis will strike again.

The National Weather Service (NWS) TsunamiReady program was designed to meet both of the recognized elements of a useful readiness effort. It was designed to educate local emergency management officials and their public and to promote a well-designed tsunami emergency response plan for each community.

PROGRAM OBJECTIVES

TsunamiReady promotes tsunami hazard readiness as an active collaboration among federal, state, and local emergency management agencies; the public; and the NWS tsunami warning system. This collaboration supports better and more consistent tsunami awareness and mitigation efforts among communities at risk. The main goal is improvement of public safety during tsunami emergencies. To meet this goal, the following objectives must be met by the community:

- Create minimum standard guidelines for a community to follow for adequate tsunami readiness.
- Encourage consistency in educational materials and response among communities and states.
- Recognize communities that have adopted TsunamiReady guidelines.
- Increase public awareness and understanding of the tsunami hazard.
- Improve community preplanning for tsunami disasters.

Program Methodology

The processes and guidelines used in the TsunamiReady program were modeled to resemble those of the National Weather Service "StormReady" program. TsunamiReady established minimum guidelines for a community to be awarded the TsunamiReady recognition, thus promoting minimum standards based on expert knowledge rather than subjective considerations. Communities that accept the challenge to become TsunamiReady and are deemed to have met these requirements set by the NWS TsunamiReady program are designated as "TsunamiReady Communities." Guidelines to achieve TsunamiReady recognition are given in Table B-1 and discussed in detail in the sections that follow. Four community categories (based on the population of the community and provided in the table's headings) are used to measure tsunami readiness.

Table B-1   Guidelines to Becoming a TsunamiReady Community

Guidelines	Population			
	<2,500	2,500–14,999	15,000–40,000	>40,000
1: Communications and Coordination				
24-hour warning point (WP)	X	X	X	X
Emergency Operations Center		X	X	X
2: Tsunami Warning Reception				
Number of ways for EOC/WP to receive NWS tsunami messages (if in range, one must be NWR with tone-alert; NWR-SAME is preferred)	3	4	4	4
3: Warning Dissemination				
Number of ways for EOC/WP to disseminate warnings to public	1	2	3	4
NWR tone-alert receivers in public facilities (where available)	X	X	X	X
For county/borough warning points, county/borough communication network ensuring information flow between communities	X	X	X	X
4: Community Preparedness				
Number of annual tsunami awareness programs	1	2	3	4
Designate/establish tsunami shelter/area in safe zone	X	X	X	X
Designate tsunami evacuation areas and evacuation routes, and install evacuation route signs	X	X	X	X
Provide written, locality-specific, tsunami hazard response material to public	X	X	X	X
In schools, encourage tsunami hazard curriculum, practice evacuations, and provide safety material to staff and students	X	X	X	X
5: Administrative				
Develop formal tsunami hazard operations plan	X	X	X	X
Yearly meeting/discussion by emergency manager with NWS	X	X	X	X
Visits by NWS official to community at least every other year	X	X	X	X

Note that Guideline 3 has been skipped because it refers exclusively to the StormReady program, which shares these guidelines with the TsunamiReady program. This is a key factor to consider, since it ensures by default that all communities that are StormReady will also be TsunamiReady (as of 2002). As such, all communities being certified for TsunamiReady also must pass all StormReady criteria. StormReady requires access to local weather monitoring equipment (Guideline 2) and some further administrative requirements (Guideline 6). Other than that, the requirements are identical.

Guideline 1: Communications and Coordination Center

It is well known that the key to any effective hazards management program is effective communication. This could not be more valid when considering tsunami-related emergencies, since the arrival of the giant waves can occur within minutes of the initial precipitating event. These so-called "short-fused" events, therefore, require an immediate but careful, systematic, and appropriate response. To ensure such a proper response, TsunamiReady requires that communities establish the following:

24-Hour Warning Point It is the NWS and not the community that determines a tsunami threat exists. Therefore, in order to receive recognition under the TsunamiReady program, an applying agency needs to establish a 24-hour warning point (WP) that can receive NWS tsunami information in addition to providing local reports and advice to constituents. Typically, the functions of this type of facility merely are incorporated into the existing daily operation of a law enforcement or fire department dispatching (ECC) point.

For cities or towns without a local dispatching point, a county agency could act in that capacity for them. In Alaska, where there may be communities that have populations of fewer than 2,500 residents and no county agency to act as a 24-hour warning point, the community is required to designate responsible members of the community who are able to receive warnings 24 hours per day and who have the authority to activate local warning systems. Specifically, the warning point is required to have the following:

- 24-hour operations
- Warning reception capability
- Warning dissemination capability
- Ability and authority to activate local warning system(s)

Emergency Operations Center Agencies serving jurisdictions larger than 2,500 people are required to have the ability to activate an emergency operations center (EOC). It must be staffed during tsunami events to execute the warning point's tsunami warning functions. The following list summarizes the tsunami-related roles required of the EOC:

- Activate, based on predetermined guidelines related to NWS tsunami information and/or tsunami events.
- Staff with emergency management director or designee.
- Establish warning reception/dissemination capabilities equal to or better than the warning point.
- Maintain the ability to communicate with adjacent EOCs/warning points.
- Maintain the ability to communicate with local NWS office or Tsunami Warning Center.

Guideline 2: Tsunami Warning Reception

Warning points and EOCs each need multiple ways to receive NWS tsunami warnings. TsunamiReady guidelines to receive NWS warnings in an EOC/WP require a combination of the following, based on population:

- NOAA Weather Radio (NWR) receiver with tone alert. Specific Area Message Encoding (SAME) is preferred. Required for recognition only if within range of transmitter.
- NOAA Weather Wire drop: satellite downlink data feed from NWS
- Emergency Managers Weather Information Network (EMWIN) receiver: satellite feed and/or VHF radio transmission of NWS products
- Statewide telecommunications system: automatic relay of NWS products on statewide emergency management or law enforcement system
- Statewide warning fan-out system: state-authorized system of passing messages throughout the warning area
- NOAA weather wire via Internet NOAAport Lite: provides alarmed warning messages through a dedicated Internet connection
- Direct link to NWS office, such as amateur or VHF radio
- E-mail from Tsunami Warning Center: direct e-mail from Warning Center to emergency manager
- Pager message from Tsunami Warning Center: page issued from Warning Center directly to EOC/WP
- Radio/TV via emergency alert system: local radio/TV or cable TV
- U.S. Coast Guard broadcasts: WP/EOC monitoring of USCG marine channels
- National Warning System (NAWAS) drop: FEMA-controlled civil defense hotline

Guideline 3: Warning Dissemination

Upon receipt of NWS warnings or other reliable information suggesting that a tsunami is imminent, local emergency officials must be able to communicate this threat information with as much of the population as possible. This is fundamental to making the preparedness program effective. As such, receiving TsunamiReady recognition requires that communities have one or more of the following means of ensuring timely warning dissemination to their citizens (based upon population, as described in Table B-1):

- A community program that subsidizes the purchase of NWR. (NWR receiver with tone alert. SAME is preferred. Required for recognition only if within range of transmitter.)
- Outdoor warning sirens
- Television audio/video overrides
- Other locally controlled methods, such as local broadcast system or emergency vehicles
- Phone messaging (dial-down) systems

It is required that at least one NWR that is equipped with a tone alert receiver be located in each critical public access and government-owned building and must include a 24-hour warning point, EOC, the school superintendent's office, or equivalent. Critical public access buildings are defined by each community's tsunami warning plan. Locations that are recommended for inclusion by the NWS include all schools, public libraries, hospitals, fairgrounds, parks and recreational areas, public utilities, sports arenas, departments of transportation, and designated shelter areas. (SAME is preferred. This is required for recognition only if the community exists within range of a transmitter.)

For counties and boroughs only, a communications network that conveys information to all cities and towns within those administrative borders must be in place. This would include provision of a warning point for the smaller towns and fanning out of the message as required by state policy.

Guideline 4: Community Preparedness

Public education is vital in preparing citizens to respond properly to tsunami threats. An educated public is more likely to take the steps required to receive tsunami warnings, recognize potentially threatening tsunami events when they exist, and respond appropriately to those events. Therefore, communities that are seeking recognition in the TsunamiReady program must be able to do the following:

- Conduct or sponsor tsunami awareness programs in schools, hospitals, fairs, workshops, and community meetings (the actual number of talks that must be given each year is based on the community's population).
- Define tsunami evacuation areas and evacuation routes and install evacuation route signs.
- Designate a tsunami shelter/area outside the hazard zone.
- Provide written tsunami hazard information to the populace, including the following:
  - Hazard zone maps
  - Evacuation routes
  - Basic tsunami information
- These instructions can be distributed through mailings (utility bills, for example), in phone books, and posted at common meeting points located throughout the community, such as libraries, supermarkets, and public buildings.
- Local schools must meet the following guidelines:
  - Encourage the inclusion of tsunami information in primary and secondary school curriculums. NWS will help to identify curriculum support material.
  - Provide an opportunity biennially for a tsunami awareness presentation.
  - Schools within the defined hazard zone must have tsunami evacuation drills at least biannually.
  - Provide written safety material to all staff and students.
  - Have an earthquake plan.

Guideline 5: Administrative

No program can be successful without formal planning and a proactive administration. The following administrative requirements are necessary for a community to be recognized in the TsunamiReady program:

- A tsunami warning plan must be in place and approved by the local governing body. This plan must address the following:
  - Warning point procedures
  - EOC activation guidelines and procedures

- Warning point and EOC personnel specification
- Hazard zone map with evacuation routes
- Procedures for canceling an emergency for those less-than-destructive tsunamis
- Guidelines and procedures for activation of sirens, cable TV override, and/or local system activation in accordance with state Emergency Alert System (EAS) plans, and warning fan-out procedures, if necessary
- Annual exercises

- Yearly visits or discussions with local NWS forecast office warning coordination meteorologist or Tsunami Warning Center personnel must be conducted. This can include a visit to the NWS office, a phone discussion, or e-mail communication.
- NWS officials will commit to visit accredited communities, at least every other year, to tour EOCs/warning points and meet with key officials.

Benefits of the TsunamiReady Program

The benefits of participating in the TsunamiReady community program include the following:

- The community is more prepared for the tsunami hazard.
- Regularly scheduled education forums increase public awareness of existing dangers.
- Contact with experts (emergency managers, researchers, NWS personnel) is increased and enhanced.
- Community readiness resource needs are identified.
- Positioning to receive state and federal funds is improved.
- Core infrastructure to support other community concerns is enhanced.
- The public is allowed the opportunity to see firsthand how their tax money is being spent in hazard programs.

Conclusion

Through the TsunamiReady program, NOAA's National Weather Service gives communities the skills and education needed to survive a tsunami before, during, and after the event. TsunamiReady helps community leaders and emergency managers strengthen their local tsunami operations. Tsunami
Ready communities are better prepared to save lives from the onslaught of a tsunami through better planning, education, and awareness. Communities have fewer fatalities and property damage if they plan *before* a tsunami arrives. No community is tsunami-proof, but TsunamiReady can help communities save lives.

Sources: FEMA. 2004. Fact Sheet: Tsunamis. *http://www.govexec.com/dailyfed/1104/111804h1.htm.*
Folger, Tim. 1994. "Waves of Destruction," *Discover Magazine*, May, 69–70.
NOAA (National Oceanic & Atmospheric Administration). N/D. The National Tsunami Hazard Mitigation Program Brochure. *http://wcatwc.arh.noaa.gov/tsunamiready/trbrochure.pdf.*
NTHMP (National Tsunami Hazard Mitigation Program). 2003. Frequently Asked Questions. *http://www .pmel.noaa.gov/tsunami-hazard/tsunami_faqs.htm.*
NWS. N/D. TsunamiReady; The Readiness Challenge. *http://www.prh.noaa.gov/ptwc/tsunamiready/ tsunami_ready_full_document.pdf.*

Important Terms

Business continuity planning
Continuity of Operations Plan (COOP)
Drill
Full-scale exercise
Functional exercise
Preparedness
Tabletop exercise

Self-Check Questions

1. What kinds of organizations must consider disaster preparedness?
2. What is the difference between mitigation and preparedness?
3. What are the steps involved in the preparedness cycle?
4. According to Ready.Gov, what are the three basic steps people can take to prepare for any type of disaster?
5. What are the seven key elements that can be used to measure the comprehensive nature of an evacuation plan?
6. Name five special needs populations, and describe what makes their disaster planning needs unique.
7. Why is it important to involve representatives from all stakeholders in the disaster planning process?
8. What kinds of training opportunities are provided by the federal government? What agencies provide these courses, workshops, and other programs?
9. What are the four types of disaster exercises? What does each involve?
10. Name the ways that the National Preparedness Directorate guides national preparedness efforts.

Out-of-Class Exercises

1. Create an individual or family plan using the guidance provided in FEMA's *Are You Ready* publication (*http://www.fema.gov/areyouready/*). Did you find any shortfalls in this program? What did you learn by using the publication?
2. Contact your local office of emergency management and find out if there is an evacuation plan for your local community. What must occur for an evacuation to be ordered? Who has the authority to issue that order?
3. Determine what special needs populations exist in your community. Select one, and find out whether special preparedness and emergency planning considerations have been made to accommodate their unique needs.

4. Assist a local small business or nonprofit organization in identifying their hazards and mitigating their risks (often called a Business Continuity Plan, or Continuity of Operations Plan). Several resources are available to help you carry out this exercise, including the following:

Ready.Gov Business: *http://www.ready.gov/business/*
Institute for Business and Home Safety "Open for Business" guide: *http://www.ibhs.org/publications/view.asp?cat=84&id=556*
Volunteer Florida Continuity of Operations Planning Guide: *http://www.floridadisaster.org/documents/COOP/COOP%20Implementation %20Guidance.pdf*

The Disciplines of Emergency Management: Communications

What You'll Learn

- The mission and five assumptions of an effective disaster communications strategy
- Which audiences, or customers, receive disaster communications
- Communicating in the homeland security era
- Disaster communications in a changing media world
- Building an effective disaster communications capability

Introduction

Communications has become an increasingly critical function in emergency management. The dissemination of timely and accurate information to the general public, elected and community officials, and the media plays a major role in the effective management of disaster response and recovery activities. Communicating preparedness, prevention, and mitigation information promotes actions that reduce the risk of future disasters. Communicating policies, goals, and priorities to staff, partners, and participants enhances support and promotes a more efficient disaster management operation.

Communications failures by government responders in Hurricane Katrina were noted in a report prepared by the House of Representatives that stated, "The lack of a government public communications strategy and media hype of violence exacerbated public concerns and further delayed relief." The House report also asked "why coordination and information sharing between local, state, and federal governments was so dismal, ... why situational awareness was so foggy, for so long, ... why unsubstantiated rumors and uncritically repeated press reports—at times fueled by top officials—were able to delay, disrupt, and diminish the response" (Select Bipartisan Committee to Investigate the Preparation for and Response to Hurricane Katrina, 2006). This chapter does the following:

- Defines the mission of an effective disaster communications strategy
- Examines communication in the era of homeland security
- Examines the various forms of media that emergency managers have historically relied on and the new forms of media that are changing how disaster news and information are shared with the public
- Details the seven elements that comprise an effective disaster communications capability in the future

The Mission

The mission of an effective disaster communications strategy is to provide timely and accurate information to the public in all four phases of emergency management:

- *Mitigation*—to promote implementation of strategies, technologies, and actions that will reduce the loss of lives and property in future disasters
- *Preparedness*—to communicate preparedness messages that encourage and educate the public in anticipation of disaster events
- *Response*—to provide to the public notification, warning, evacuation, and situation reports on an ongoing disaster
- *Recovery*—to provide individuals and communities affected by a disaster with information on how to register for and receive disaster relief

The foundation of an effective disaster communications strategy is built on five critical assumptions:

- Customer focus
- Leadership commitment
- Inclusion of communications in planning and operations
- Good information
- Media partnership

THE FIVE CRITICAL ASSUMPTIONS FOR A SUCCESSFUL COMMUNICATIONS STRATEGY

1. *Customer focus:* Understand what information your customers and your partners need, and build communications mechanisms that deliver this information in a timely and accurate fashion.
2. *Leadership commitment:* The leader of the emergency operations must be committed to effective communications and must participate fully in the communications process.
3. *Inclusion of communications in planning and operations:* Communications specialists must be involved in all emergency planning and operations to ensure that communicating timely and accurate information is considered when action decisions are being considered.
4. *Situational awareness:* Effective communications is based on the timely collection, analysis, and dissemination of information from the disaster area in accordance with basic principles of effective communications such as transparency and truthfulness.
5. *Media partnership:* The media (i.e., television, radio, Internet, newspapers, etc.) are the most effective means for communicating timely and accurate information to the public. A partnership with the media involves understanding the needs of the media and including trained staff who work directly with the media to get information to the public. And now that citizen journalists and new media technologies (cell phones, laptops, digital cameras) have become more vital and accepted sources of information and imaging from the front lines of a disaster, methods for incorporating this data and information must also be implemented.

Customer Focus

An essential element of any effective emergency management system is a focus on customers and customer service. This philosophy should guide communications with the public and with all partners in emergency management. A customer service approach includes placing the needs and interests of individuals and communities first, being responsive and informative, and managing expectations.

The customers for emergency management are diverse. They include internal customers, such as staff, other federal agencies, states, and other disaster partners. External customers include the general public, elected officials at all levels of government, community and business leaders, and the media. Each of these customers has specific information needs, and a good communications strategy considers and reflects their requirements.

Leadership Commitment

Good communications starts with a commitment by the leadership of the emergency management organization to sharing and disseminating information both internally and externally. One of the lessons learned from Hurricane Katrina was "We need public officials to lead. Communicating confidence to citizens and delivering on promises are both critical in crises" (Kettl, 2005).

The leader of any disaster response and recovery effort must openly endorse and promote open lines of communications among the organization's staff, partners, and public in order to effectively communicate. This leader must model this behavior to clearly illustrate that communications is a valued function of the organization.

LEADERSHIP MODELING GOOD COMMUNICATIONS

In the 1990s, FEMA director James Lee Witt was a strong advocate for keeping FEMA staff informed of agency plans, priorities, and operations. Witt characterized a proactive approach in communicating with FEMA's constituents. His accessibility to the media was a significant departure from previous FEMA leadership. Witt exhibited his commitment to effective communications in many ways:

- He held weekly staff meetings with FEMA's senior managers and required that his senior managers hold regular staff meetings with their employees.
- He published an internal newsletter to employees entitled "Director's Weekly Update" that was distributed to all FEMA employees in hard copy and on the agency electronic bulletin board that updated employees on agency activities.
- He made himself and his senior staff available to the media on a regular basis, especially during a disaster response, to answer questions and to provide information.
- During a disaster response, he held media briefings daily and sometimes two to three times a day.
- He held special meetings with victims and their families.

- He led the daily briefings among FEMA partners during a disaster response.
- He devoted considerable time to communicating with members of Congress, governors, mayors, and other elected officials during both disaster and nondisaster times, at times holding joint press briefings with these officials.
- He met four to five times per year with the State Emergency Management Directors, FEMA's principal emergency management partners.
- He gave speeches all over this country and around the world to promote better understanding of emergency management and disaster mitigation.

Including Communications in Planning and Operations

The most important part of leadership's commitment to communications is including communications in all planning and operations. This means that a communications specialist is included in the senior management team of any emergency management organization and operation. It means that communications issues are considered in the decision-making processes and that a communications element is included in all organizational activities, plans, and operations.

In the past, communicating with external customers, and in many cases internal customers, was not valued or considered critical to a successful emergency management operation. Technology has changed that equation. In today's world of 24-hour television and radio news and the Internet, the demand for information is never-ending, especially in an emergency response situation. Emergency managers must be able to communicate critical information in a timely manner to their staff, partners, the public, and the media.

To do so, the information needs of the various customers and how best to communicate with these customers must be considered at the same time that planning and operational decisions are being made. For example, a decision process on how to remove debris from a disaster area must include discussion of how to communicate information on the debris removal operation to community officials, the public, and the media.

Again the response to Hurricane Katrina clearly illustrates the downside of failing to include consideration of communications issues in conducting a response operation. The "Lessons Learned" report prepared by White House Homeland Security Advisor Francis Townsend noted, "The lack of communications and situational awareness had a debilitating effect on the federal response. The Department of Homeland Security should develop an integrated public communications plan to better inform, guide, and reassure the American public before, during, and after a catastrophe. The Department of Homeland Security should enable this plan with operational capabilities to deploy coordinated public affairs teams during a crisis" (Townsend, 2006).

Situational Awareness

Situational awareness is key to an effective disaster response. Knowing the number of people killed and injured, the level of damage at the disaster site, the condition of homes and community infrastructure, and current response efforts provide decision makers with the situational awareness needed to identify need and appropriately apply available resources. The collection, analysis, and dissemination of information from the disaster site are the basis for an effective communications operation in a disaster response.

This is also true during the disaster recovery phase, especially early in the recovery phase when the demand for information from the public, and therefore the media, is at its highest. Developing effective communications strategies to promote community preparedness and/or mitigation programs requires detailed information about the nature of the risk that impacts the community and how the planned preparedness programs will help individuals and communities to be ready for the next disaster, and the mitigation programs will reduce the impacts of future disasters. A glaring lack of situational awareness was identified as a severe hindrance to the government response to Hurricane Katrina.

SITUATIONAL AWARENESS AND MEDIA STORIES

"Without sufficient working communications capability to get better situational awareness, the local, state, and federal officials directing the response in New Orleans had too little factual information to address—and, if need be, rebut—what the media were reporting. This allowed terrible situations—the evacuees' fear and anxiety in the Superdome and Convention Center—to continue longer than they should have and, as noted, delayed response efforts by, for example, causing the National Guard to wait to assemble enough force to deal with security problems at the Convention Center that turned out to be overstated."

Source: Select Bipartisan Committee to Investigate the Preparation for and Response to Hurricane Katrina, 2006, "A Failure of Initiative: Final Report of the Special Bipartisan Committee to Investigate the Preparation for and Response to Hurricane Katrina," Government Printing Office, February 15, 2006, *http://www .gpoacess.gov/congress/index.hmtl.*

CRITICAL THINKING

Why is the commitment of the executive and senior managers so important to having an effective communications capability? What parties must be involved in providing timely and accurate information to decision makers as they shape their communications priorities in a disaster?

FEMA's National Incident Management System (NIMS) includes a section on public information in its Incident Command System (ICS) component. One of the three top command staff reporting to the incident commander in ICS is the public information officer (Figure 5-1). FEMA's NIMS document (2007) states, "Public Information consists of the processes, procedures, and systems to communicate timely, accurate, and accessible information on the incident's cause, size, and current situation to the public, responders, and additional stakeholders (both directly affected and indirectly affected).

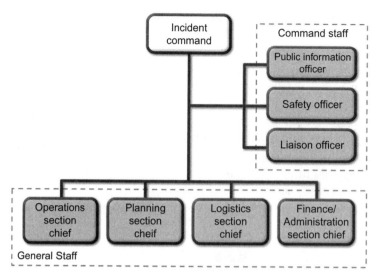

FIGURE 5-1 Incident Command System: the command staff and the general staff.
FEMA. National Incident Command System: FEMA 501/Draft August 2007.

Public information must be coordinated and integrated across jurisdictions and across agencies/organizations; among federal, state, tribal, and local governments; and with the private sector and NGOs. Well-developed public information, education strategies, and communications plans help to ensure that lifesaving measures, evacuation routes, threat and alert systems, and other public safety information is coordinated and communicated to numerous audiences in a timely, consistent manner. Public Information includes processes, procedures, and organizational structures required to gather, verify, coordinate, and disseminate information."

Media Partnership

The media plays a primary role in communicating with the public. No government emergency management organization could ever hope to develop a communications network comparable to those networks already established and maintained by television, radio, newspapers, and online news outlets across the country. To effectively provide timely disaster information to the public, emergency managers must establish a partnership with their local media outlets.

The goal of a media partnership is to provide accurate and timely information to the public in both disaster and nondisaster situations. The partnership requires a commitment by both the emergency manager and the media to work together, and it requires a level of trust between both parties. Traditionally, the relationship between emergency managers and the media has been strained. There is often a conflict between the need of the emergency manager to respond quickly and the need of the media to obtain information on the response so it can report it just as quickly. This conflict sometimes results in inaccurate reporting and tension between the emergency manager and the media. The loser in this conflict is always the public, which relies on the media for its information.

It is important for emergency managers to understand the needs of the media and the value they bring to facilitating response operations. An effective media partnership provides the emergency manager with a communications network to reach the public with vital information and provides the media with access to the disaster site, access to emergency managers and their staff, and access to critical information for the public that informs and ensures the accuracy of their reporting.

CRITICAL THINKING

- As a private, nongovernmental organization, is the primary concern of the media their publicity ratings, or helping the public with disasters?
- Does the media have a responsibility to warn the public about disasters?
- Should members of the media be required to have training in emergency management? Why or why not?

Audiences/Customers

In order to effectively communicate disaster information, emergency managers must clearly identify their various audiences and customers. Included in many of these audiences are both partners and stakeholders. Basic emergency management audiences include the following:

- *General public.* The largest audience, of which there are many subgroups, such as the elderly, those with disabilities, minorities, low income, youths, and so on, and all are potential customers
- *Disaster victims.* Those individuals affected by a specific disaster event
- *Business community.* Often ignored by emergency managers but critical to disaster recovery, preparedness, and mitigation activities
- *Media.* An audience and a partner critical to effectively communicating with the public
- *Elected officials.* Governors, mayors, county executives, state legislators, and members of Congress
- *Community officials.* City/county managers, public works, department heads
- *First responders.* Police, fire, and emergency medical services
- *Volunteer groups.* American Red Cross, Salvation Army, the NVOADs, and so on, which are critical to first response to an event

Communications with some of these customers, such as the first responders, is accomplished principally through radio and phone communications (see Chapter 6). Communicating with most of these other audiences is accomplished through briefings, meetings, provision of background materials, and, in some instances, one-on-one interviews. Communications strategies, plans, and operations should be developed to meet the information needs of each of these customers and staffed and funded accordingly.

Communicating in the Era of Homeland Security

Communicating with the public is an area that needs to be improved if the nation is going to have a truly effective homeland security system. To date, the Department of Homeland Security (DHS) has shown little interest in communicating with the public, and when it has, the results have not always been positive—the "duct tape and plastic" fiasco and recent reports of former DHS Secretary Ridge questioning terror alert warnings are some classic examples. DHS and its state and local partners need to address three factors to improve its communications with the American people. First, there must be a commitment from the leadership, not only at DHS and its state and local partners but at all levels of government, including the executive level, to communicate timely and accurate information to the public. This is especially important in the response and recovery phases to a terrorist incident.

In a disaster scenario, the conventional wisdom that information is power and that hoarding information helps to retain such power is almost categorically reversed. Withholding information during disaster events generally has an overall negative impact on the well-being of the public, as well as on the impression the public forms about involved authorities. In practice, sharing information is what generates authority and power when that information is useful and relates to the hazard at hand. A good example of this is former New York City Mayor Rudy Giuliani's actions after 9/11. Giuliani went to great lengths to get accurate and timely information to the public in a time of crisis, and his efforts both inspired the public and greatly enhanced the effectiveness of the response and recovery efforts he guided.

To date, DHS leadership and the political leadership have been reluctant to make this commitment to share information with the public. This is something that must change if they expect the American people to fully comprehend the homeland security threat and to become actively engaged in homeland security efforts. Few citizens have any idea of what actual terrorism risks they face, and fewer can actually relate those risks in any comparable fashion to the risks they face every day.

Second, homeland security officials at all levels must resolve the conflict between sharing information with the public in advance and in the aftermath of a terrorist incident that has value for intelligence or criminal prosecution purposes. This is directly linked to the commitment issue discussed in the previous paragraphs and has been repeatedly cited by homeland security officials as reasons for not sharing more specific information with the public.

Also at issue is the question of when to release relevant information to the public without compromising intelligence sources and/or ongoing criminal investigations. This is an issue that rarely if ever confronts emergency management officials dealing with natural and unintentional man-made disasters. Therefore, there is little precedent or experience for current homeland security officials to work with in crafting a communications strategy that balances the competing need for the public to have timely and accurate information with the need to protect intelligence sources and ongoing criminal investigations. To date, the needs of the intelligence and justice communities have clearly been judged to outweigh those of the public—but at a cost.

Withholding information leaves the public vulnerable and suspicious of the government. The Aspen Institute report, *First Informers in the Disaster Zone: The Lessons of Katrina*, noted that the task of journalists was to convince government officials that over the long run, transparency can build trust and save lives: "The same information that a terrorist can use to do great damage can possibly give families information about which escape route to use to get away from a nuclear power plant. I think we're going to find that if we have a flu pandemic, the information that can be used to terrorize and scare people can also be used to save their lives. I think what we have to do is work very hard at convincing people that access to information is ultimately going to be our friend" (May, 2006).

The recent announcement by the Obama administration that the DHS had created a task force of outside experts to redesign the much maligned Homeland Security Advisory System (HSAS) is a critical first step in reestablishing trust with the public for the warning system ("Secretary Napolitano Announces 60-Day Review of Homeland Security Advisory System," *http://www.dhs.gov/ynews/releases/pr_1247586668272.shtm*). From this starting point, additional communications mechanisms can be developed to ensure that the public gets timely and accurate information both in advance of any terrorist incident and during the response and recovery phases in the aftermath of the next terrorist attack.

Third, more effort must be invested by federal departments and agencies to better understand the principal terrorist threats that our nation faces (i.e., biological, chemical, radiological, nuclear, and explosives) and to develop communications strategies that educate and inform the public about these threats with more useful information. The 2001 Washington, D.C., anthrax incident is a perfect example of uninformed or misinformed public officials sharing what is often conflicting and, in too many instances, just plain wrong information with the public.

The nation's public officials must become better informed about these principal risks and be ready to explain complicated information to the public. As the anthrax incident made clear, this is not a luxury but a necessity if the response to similar incidents in the future is to be successful.

Decades of research and a new generation of technologies now inform emergency managers as they provide information about hurricanes, tornadoes, earthquakes, and hazardous materials incidents to the public. A similar research effort must be undertaken for these five new terrorist risks and communications strategies that will ensure that homeland security officials at all levels are capable of clearly explaining to the public the hazards posed by these threats. These communications strategies must consider how to communicate to the public when incomplete information is all that is available to homeland security officials. In the vast majority of cases, this partiality of information is probable.

A public health crisis will not wait for all the data to be collected and analyzed, nor will the public. Homeland security officials must develop strategies for informing the public effectively, as the crisis develops, by forming effective messages that are able to explain to the public how what is being said is the most accurate information available based on the information that, likewise, is available—despite its incomplete nature. Clearly, this is not an easy task, but it is not impossible. The public will increasingly expect such communications efforts, so the sooner such a system is in place, the better the next incident will be managed.

Disaster Communications in a Changing Media World

Working with the media before, during, and after a disaster is a fact of life for an emergency management official. The media remains the single most effective means for communicating timely and accurate information to the public. Historically, emergency managers have shied away from talking to the media, especially during a disaster response. That day is over. As we noted earlier, emergency managers or other government officials involved in disaster response can no longer ignore the media. Developing a partnership with the media should now be standard operating procedure for any and all emergency management operations in this country and around the world.

However, the media is constantly changing, and emergency managers must keep up with these changes to have an effective communications operation. Disaster preparedness information used to be exclusively published in brochures and pamphlets that were distributed in post offices and courthouses around the country. In the 1950s, Civil Defense workers went directly to communities to dispense information on nuclear preparedness in town hall meetings. Years later, representatives from the National Flood Insurance Program (NFIP) held similar meetings in communities around the country to inform residents about flood mapping and flood insurance.

Over time, the radio has become an integral part of communicating warning messages to the public before the next tornado or hurricane strikes. In turn, radio has often been the sole source of information in the immediate aftermath of a massive disaster that cuts off electricity to the disaster area for days at a time because of the availability of transistor and crank radios that do not require electricity. Television has become a big part of disasters in the past 50 years. The pictures and stories that are generated by disaster events are a natural fit for television. It was the size of the satellite photo of Hurricane Floyd on television coupled with evacuation warnings from local, state, and federal officials transmitted by television that prompted 3 million residents in Florida, Georgia, and South Carolina to evacuate their homes as the storm threatened the Eastern Seaboard. It is also television that graphically communicated the sorry events that occurred in New Orleans after Hurricane Katrina.

Over time television has changed considerably. The three national networks and usually three or four local stations in any given community have given way to hundreds of channels available nationwide along with 24/7 news channels and the Weather Channel, and they are available across the country.

The rise of the Internet as a source for disaster and emergency-related information and news has been spectacular. A survey conducted in April 2008 by the Canadian Centre for Emergency Preparedness (CCEP) found that the Internet has surpassed newspapers on the list of emergency information sources used by the Canadian public. Television and radio are ranked number one and number two on this list, but it may not be long before the Internet grabs even more of the public's attention, especially as older and low- to moderate-income individuals and families gain access to the Internet.

The media continues to change with the advent of "first informers"—ordinary citizens armed with a cell phone who can take pictures and/or video at the disaster site and add commentary and post their submissions on the Internet or provide them to CNN or MSNBC or other outlets. Some of the first photos and commentaries coming out of the Asian Tsunami disaster in 2004 were filed by these "first informers," who were there when the tsunami struck and survived to provide information and images of the damage and destruction.

The Evolution of New Media Use in Disasters

The magnitude and frequency of natural disasters are increasing. According to the Center for Research on the Epidemiology of Disasters, there were four times as many weather-related disasters in the last 20 years than in the previous 75 years. With this new "Age of Extreme Weather" has come the evolution and maturation of new media tools and technologies, a dramatic rise in the number of citizen journalists, and an almost annual increase in their contribution to the flow of new information during disasters. "Disasters have provided a unique trigger that has consolidated technological advances in concert with democratizing influences operating outside the traditional brokers of information and aid" (Laituri and Kodrich, 2008).

Even though the 1990s was a time of transformation in communications technology, with the emergence of the World Wide Web, 24/7 cable television, and an array of digital tools from affordable and widely available wireless mobile devices to high-resolution satellite maps, new media were not a factor in natural disaster coverage or recovery until 2001.

UNITED NATIONS REPORT: NEW TECHNOLOGIES IN EMERGENCIES AND CONFLICTS—THE ROLE OF INFORMATION AND SOCIAL NETWORKS

There have been some dramatic advances in communications technology—in the number of new technologies, the mobility and range of functions available, and the spread of these technologies. Growth has been particularly strong in the penetration of mobile phones and more recently the uptake of social networking websites, including Facebook and Twitter. One important change is a shift from one-to-many forms of communication, such as television and radio, to many-to-many forms of communication, such as social networking and crowdsourcing websites, that is changing the way in which information is delivered and exchanged.

Communications advances present an opportunity for humanitarian organizations to harness modern technology to communicate more effectively with communities affected by disasters and to allow members of those communities to communicate with one another and with the outside world. People in affected communities can recover faster if they can access and use information. A look at the use of communications technology during disasters in recent years shows that while it has played a positive role, its full potential has not yet been realized. Moreover, governments, humanitarian agencies, and local communities face challenges and risks associated with modern technological innovation, including the following:

- Information flows must be two-way to be effective—from the external world to the affected community but also from those affected to the agencies seeking to help them in useful ways.
- Information will not be used unless it is trusted. The utility of any technologies will depend on the social context. People are a vital part of the communication system.
- Information will be helpful only if it is accurate. There are risks in unregulated information flows, especially when these are spread rapidly online, and these risks need to be managed. Authentication is a key challenge.

This tension between the potential benefit to humanitarian efforts from harnessing these technologies and the risks they pose is a key theme of this report. The report examines how authorities and humanitarian and aid organizations can best balance the opportunities and challenges of exploiting different technologies at the key stages on the timeline of crisis—early warning and preparedness, immediate humanitarian relief, and reconstruction and long-term development.

Source: United Nations, 2009. *New Technologies in Emergencies and Conflicts: The Role of Information and Social Networks. http://www.unfoundation.org/press-center/publications/new-technologies-emergencies-conflicts.html*

In the aftermath of the September 11, 2001, terrorist attacks, citizen-shot videos of the attacks on the Twin Towers dominated news coverage, and Americans turned to the Internet for information. But the sharp spike in traffic froze and crashed websites. In many ways, 9/11 was the last disaster covered under the old model of crisis communications: Newspapers printed "Extra" editions, people turned to television for news, and "the familiar anchors of the broadcast networks—Tom Brokaw, Peter Jennings, and Dan Rather—took on their avuncular roles of the past for a nation looking for comfort and reassurance" (May, 2006).

Every disaster since 9/11 has involved more citizen journalists and expanded the use and utility of the new media tools and technologies. In 2003, during China's SARs epidemic, people used text messaging to exchange information that the government tried to suppress (Hattotuwa, 2007). Three major disasters within nine months—the Asian tsunami (2004), the London transit bombings (2005), and Hurricane Katrina (2005)—marked the coming of age of participatory media.

The December 26, 2004, Asian tsunami has been defined as "the turning point—a before-and-after moment for citizen journalism." Blogs, websites, and message boards provided news and aid in real time. One blog, "waveofdestruction.org," logged 682,366 unique visitors in four days (Cooper, 2007). Wikipedia—a group-created website that can be edited by any user—became the site for basic information, particularly for hot-lines that allowed people to search for missing loved ones and find housing, medical, and other assistance.

Minutes after four bombs rocked London's transportation system, a definitive web page, "July 7, 2005, London Bombings," was started with five sentences on Wikipedia. The page "received more than a thousand edits in its first four hours of existence as additional news came in." Users added links to traditional news sources, and information was posted about what public transportation was shut down, listing contacts to help track a missing person and offering directions to commuters trying to get home. "What was conceived as an open encyclopedia in 2001 [became] a general purpose tool for gathering and distributing information quickly" (Shirky, 2008).

A cell phone photo taken by a commuter in a smoked-clogged tunnel in the Tube became the iconic image of the disaster. Londoners pooled their digital photos on Flickr—a photo-sharing site and service that allows people to tag pictures with comments and labels. "The photos that showed up after the bombings weren't just amateur replacements for traditional photojournalism; people did more than provide evidence of the destruction and its aftermath. They photographed official notices ("All Underground services are suspended"), notes posted in schools ("Please do not inform children of the explosions"), messages of support from the rest of the world ("We love you, London"), and within a day of the bombings, expressions of defiance addressed to the terrorists ("We are not afraid" and "You will fail"). Not only did Flickr host all of these images, but they made them available for reuse, and bloggers writing about the bombings were able to use the Flickr images almost immediately, creating a kind of symbiotic relationship among various social tools"(Shirky, 2008). Police asked people to turn in cell phone photos or videos because they might contain clues about the terrorists (Shirky, 2008).

In August 2005, Hurricane Katrina, a Category 3 hurricane, tore through New Orleans, Louisiana; Mobile, Alabama; and Gulfport, Mississippi. Over 1,500 people were killed, and tens of thousands were left homeless. Blogs became the primary information-providing tool used by both traditional media and citizen journalists. Staff reporters for New Orleans's daily newspaper, the *Times-Picayune*, created a blog that for a time became the front page of their news operation. It enabled members of the community isolated by floodwaters and debris to show and tell one another what they were experiencing (Gillmor, 2006).

Message boards provided critical information about shelter locations, family tracing, and missing persons. Internet expert Barbara Palser counted 60 separate online bulletin boards that were created to locate missing people within two weeks of the storm. "These sites included major portals such as Yahoo! and Craigslist, an array of newspaper and television sites, websites hosted by government and relief organizations, and individual technologists, including a group of programmers who enlisted about 2,000 volunteers to create a database called the Katrina PeopleFinder Project." PeopleFinder was established "to create a consolidated database of missing people built outside the traditional, centralized institutions (i.e., FEMA, Red Cross)" (May, 2006). Google Earth and Google Maps, which provide and use online satellite imagery, were used to illustrate damage assessments—particularly to the Gulf Coast and barrier islands (Laituri, 2005).

After the Java earthquake in 2006, mobile phones became mobile news services. Internews, an international media support group, worked with 180 Indonesian journalists to set up a text messaging service that helped local radio stations to report on the recovery (Hattotuwa, 2007). In October 2007, wildfires in Southern California resulted in the loss of nearly 2,200 homes and over $1 billion in damages and marked a major step forward in the integration of mainstream media and citizen journalists. "Local media has been highlighting user-submitted photos and videos and embedding new technology in their prime coverage. San Diego's public television station, KPBS, used Twitter to give its audience updates when its website went down, and the Twitter updates now have a prominent place on their home page" (Glaser, 2007).

San Diego TV station News 8 responded to the crisis by taking down its entire regular website and replacing it with a rolling news blog, linking to YouTube videos of its key reports, plus Google Maps showing the location of the fire (Stabe, 2007). Also on the site were links to practical information that viewers needed, including how to contact insurance companies, how to volunteer or donate to the relief efforts, evacuation information, and shelter locations. "It's an exemplary case study in how a local news operation can respond to a major rolling disaster story by using all the reporting tools available on the Internet" (Catone, 2007).

Local and national television stations asked for submissions from wildfire witnesses and victims. The NBC affiliate in San Diego received over 2,000 submissions of pictures and video related to the wildfires. CNN's I-Reports section reportedly received about the same number of fire-related submissions (Catone, 2007). The Google Maps (Internet GIS) tool was used to develop maps of shelter locations and fire updates (Wagner, 2007). Clearly, a symbiotic relationship is emerging between citizen journalists and the mainstream news media. With every new major disaster, the mainstream media's use of Internet-facilitated reporting increases. Government, however, has been slow to appreciate the power or potential of the new media tools and Internet culture.

New Media: New World

When disasters happened in the past, we learned about them after the fact. That is no longer the case. New technologies—laptops, cell phones, text messaging systems, digital cameras, the Internet—have changed the way news is gathered and distributed. These technologies have also profoundly altered the flow of information, undermining the traditional gatekeepers and replacing the centralized, top-down model used by the government and professional media with a more dynamic flow of information that empowered citizens and created ad hoc distributive information networks. In their essay "Citizen Journalism and Humanitarian Aid: Boon or Bust?" Dan Gillmor and Sanjana Hattotuwa (2007) explained, "These technologies create new ways for citizens to be heard, governments to be held accountable and the state to answer to failures of governance. Ordinary citizens … are increasingly using technology, through devices such as mobile phones, to support powerful frameworks of transparency and accountability that citizens can use to hold decision makers responsible for the action, and indeed, inaction." According to Gillmor (2006), the days of news as a "lecture"—when traditional media told the audience what was considered news—are done. Now news is more of a conversation, and the lines have blurred between producers and consumers: "The communications network itself will be a medium for everyone's voice, not just the few who can buy multimillion-dollar printing presses, launch satellites, or win the government's permission to squat on the public's airwaves." In their article "We Media: How Audiences Are Shaping the Future of News and Information," Bowman and Willis (2003) state, "The venerable profession of journalism finds itself at a rare moment in history where, for the first time, its hegemony as gatekeeper of the news is threatened by not just new technology and competitors but, potentially, by the audience it serves." The once passive audience has become an active participant in the creation and dissemination of news, and the flow of information is no longer controlled by journalists and government agencies.

The increasing participation and power of ordinary citizens in emergency communications are starting to have more observable consequences. The Aspen Institute report, *First Informers in the Disaster Zone: The Lessons of Katrina,* noted in its conclusion, "There was a difference in how the online environment changed the media mix and altered the flow of information during and after the disaster … At times the traditional flow of information from government to media to public reversed course. … As one pair of new media experts put it, Katrina '"revealed extraordinary changes taking place within a society increasingly connected by digital networks, a society at the cusp of a new era in human history in which individuals possess an unprecedented capacity to access, share, create, and apply information'" (May, 2006).

One participant in the Aspen Institute's assessment of lessons learned from Katrina was Jon Donley, the editor of NOLA.com—the *Times-Picayune's* online companion and the primary source of news when the daily could not print in the weeks following the hurricane. Donley explained that the new media had fostered a two-way flow of information, in contrast to the old paradigm in which information flows down from government and media to a passive audience. "I would really encourage everybody to think about this new media age that we're in, where the audience isn't playing that game anymore. We have had a revolution" (May, 2006).

In addition to forcing the traditional media to reconsider and redefine its role in disaster communications, the new participatory media enhanced the amount of information and number of sources and added to the problems that were endemic in times of disaster: the need to sort truth from rumor and the tension between media demanding transparency and accessibility and government officials charged with managing information during a disaster. The information available to citizens at times of crises is often inadequate, incorrect, or dated. According to Gillmor and Hattotuwa, "Studies show that the problem lies not with the technologies (or lack thereof) but with the culture of information sharing. The access, dissemination, and archiving of information is often controlled by government's agencies, institutions who have a parochial interest in controlling its flow—what gets out where, to whom, how, and when" (Gillmor, 2006).

"If we waited for the government to release information during a disaster, it would be days before the public would know anything," complained one participant in the Aspen Katrina assessment. Chet Lunner, acting director of state and local government coordination in DHS and a former national reporter for the Gannett News Service, spoke from the government's perspective in the Aspen session. He disagreed with a comment from CNN's David Borhman that the government instinct in a crisis was to hide. "They are not hiding. They are sort of defensive, in a crouch ... because [they] don't trust the media" (May, 2006).

Katrina, the Aspen report concludes, exacerbated the already burgeoning distrust between media and government. "As rival proxies for the public, the two institutions clashed openly during and after the storm. ... The first failure was caused by lack of good situational awareness by federal officials themselves, who painted a rosy scenario that clashed with the pictures and reports from the scene from journalists. 'Don't you guys watch television? Don't you guys listen to the radio?' ABC's Ted Koppel famously asked Michael Brown, then FEMA director. Federal, state, and local officials gave contradictory messages to the public, creating confusion and feeding the perception that government sources lacked credibility, the White House report concluded" (May, 2006).

The emergence and proliferation of citizen media complicated the information mix and increased the tension between the government and traditional media. Explained Sanjana Hattotuwa (2007) in "Who is Afraid of Citizen Journalists?" "Information in the hands of citizens continues to instill fear and loathing in the minds of those who wish to manufacture public opinion to their benefit by the careful selection and publication of information."

Government official Chet Lunner explained his unease in the Aspen report: "I get concerned when I see the term 'citizen journalists' and 'blogs' lumped in with everything else, as if that were journalism in the way that it is practiced by professionals. That is often the problem we have, which is that something that starts out as a blog does not necessarily meet the standards of most source-tested journalism that has been in practice for all these years. ... We have enough trouble with things that do go through the [mainstream media] filter. The amount of time and energy and social unrest by readers and/or the people trying to practice in the field dealing with these things that are exaggerated rumors, etc., is a problem, particularly in the framework of these disaster times when people are depending upon or relying on that" (May, 2006).

"On the other hand," the editor of NOLA.com explained, "the very first reports [that] we had of life-threatening flooding in New Orleans came from citizens typing it into cell phones. The very first news we had of clear levee breaks, of looting, of a shooting death, or a suicide in the Superdome—every one of those things we heard first from citizens whom we were encouraging to have a two-way dialogue with us" (May, 2006).

Participatory journalism and the generation of news and information from "first informers"—citizens on the scene when disaster happens—are not trends that are going to go away. In fact, as noted previously, the 2008 disasters in Burma and China may mark the coming of age of text messaging, blogging, and video sharing as tools that can bring faster coverage of a news event than traditional media. The challenge now for traditional news sources and cautious governmental hierarchies is to plan for and maximize the use of an increased and accelerated flow of information, to seize the opportunity to share information and build community that online media creates.

User-generated content is here to stay, according the Lou Ferrara of the Associated Press. "The landscape has changed, but we're all about getting this information. What's the best way to do it? Do we outsource, partner, do it ourselves?" (Ferrara, 2007). Yahoo!'s Bill Gannon reflected on the Katrina communications experience: "What we realized is that users wanted not just to read information, but they wanted to be empowered. What they wanted to do was get personally involved either through a message board or simply by making a donation" (May, 2006). How to channel and sustain that empowerment is the challenge of the next crisis. All types of organizations and groups are getting involved with new media, as evidenced in the U.S. Pacific Command's January 2010 blog entry, which appears in the box on page 150.

CASE STUDY IN NEW MEDIA: CYCLONE NARGIS, MYANMAR

On May 2, 2008, Cyclone Nargis struck the Irrawaddy Delta region of Myanmar (Burma). The cyclone, with winds of 120 mph, made landfall at the mouth of the Irrawaddy River—a low-lying, densely populated region—and pushed a 12-foot wall of water 25 miles inland, killing at least 80,000 people and leaving as many as 2.5 million homeless. Ten days later, on May 12, 2008, a 7.9 earthquake devastated China's Sichuan province, toppling buildings, collapsing schools, killing more than 69,000, injuring over 367,000, and displacing between 5 and 11 million people.

Two disasters, one common link. These incidents demonstrated that new technologies— the Internet, text messaging systems, camera phones, Google Map mash-ups—and citizen journalists, especially bloggers, have irrevocably altered the nature of disaster reporting and replaced the top-down flow of information from the government and the traditional media in times of crisis with a dynamic and democratic two-way exchange.

In Myanmar, where Internet and cell phone access is limited, the military government refused to allow aid workers or journalists to reach disaster areas and moved fast to restrict communications. Ironically, it was a local online news source, the Burma News, that reported on the "guidelines" the junta had laid out for journalists' coverage, specifically prohibiting showing dead bodies or reporting about insufficient aid for victims (Burma News, 2008).

In spite of these restrictions, Burmese blogs and news sites were quick to react by posting eyewitness accounts of the disaster and mobilizing fundraising efforts. According to BBC News, "People inside Burma have been giving their updates from the disaster zone. Burmese blogger Nyi Lynn Seck has a section of his blog devoted to daily updates from the Delta region. 'They are seeing dead bodies,' he writes. 'Nobody has cremated or buried these dead bodies.' He also carries a report of how one private donor in Bogalay was forced to give his donation to the local authorities rather than people in need" (BBC News, 2008).

The BBC also noted that the Mizzima news site, based in India and run by Burmese exiles, used long-standing personal networks to gather compelling accounts of loss and survival. Other exile Burmese news sites such as Yoma3 reported on the spread of disease among the cyclone victims in Bogalay. Stories of monks and local residents pulling together and co-coordinating local cleanups and sharing water could be found on the Democratic Voice of Burma and other sites such as The Irrawaddy. The Rule of Lords blog reported that people were been turned away from hospitals because of the lack of electricity and water.

In addition to the news gathering done by citizen journalists online (bloggers), other new media technologies helped tell the story of the Burmese disaster and recovery:

- Twitter—a short messaging service (SMS) that uses cell phones and 140-character messages that are also posted online—emerged quickly as an important medium for coverage of the crisis. Aid agencies working in Burma, including AmeriCares and the Salvation Army, are also using Twitter to disseminate information and coordinate activities (Washkuch, May 20, 2008).
- YouTube hosted scores of videos recording the devastation and feeble response. User AfterNargisYgn uploaded a multipart series of videos featuring images of the effects of the cyclone in Yangon, Myanmar's largest city, previously known as Rangoon. His series also documents the growing anger and desperation of the storm victims. Burma4u uploaded a video of the aftermath in Latbutta, with Cyclone Nargis's victims crowded in refugee shelters, trying to sleep. Videos depicting dozens of people who died in the cyclone, which are banned by the junta, are also posted on YouTube (Rincon, May 16, 2008, YouTube).
- Google Earth and the Associated Press produced interactive maps that tracked the cyclone's passage through the country and illustrated the extent of the storm damage—especially the dramatic erosion of the shoreline and the degree of inundation.
- Global Voices Online and traditional media like the *New York Times,* BBC, and CNN featured, linked to, or aggregated coverage by bloggers and linked to videos and photos recorded by eyewitnesses.

U.S. PACIFIC COMMAND (PACOM) AND SOCIAL MEDIA

This past year, a lot of things have happened within PACOM's Area of Responsibility (AOR). In the last three months alone, we've seen the value of social media in connecting us with people around the world as we carry out our mission in the Asia-Pacific region. We are thankful for those who have helped us spread the word via retweeting/reposting our messages, primarily via Twitter and Facebook, most especially during our Humanitarian Assistance/Disaster Relief operations in the Philippines, Indonesia, and American Samoa this past October. While it was good to see how much our daily Disaster Relief Fact sheets and Flickr photos were used and shared online, it was even more amazing to see how people came together in a time of crisis to help each other out. A picture is truly worth a thousand words, and it's a great way to show the various activities of our Air Force, Army, Marine Corps, and Navy service members around the AOR, such as participating in local community projects and outreach programs, leading or participating in joint military exercises, building relationships, and collaborating with other countries to prepare for large-scale natural disasters, sharing best practices with local authorities to promote peace and security, and, more recently, spreading the holiday cheer. We are always moved by the comments that we receive, and we would like to thank our social media friends for amplifying our messages through the "likes" and reposts on Facebook, as well as via the mentions and retweets on Twitter, especially during #militarymonday and #followfriday. We get to hear of your support for our troops (#SOT on Twitter) not just on special occasions but every day! Social media has definitely helped PACOM in telling stories that are often untold via traditional sources, but more importantly, it has helped us in connecting with you. We have certainly learned a lot, and we are looking forward to learning how we can further develop our social media efforts in 2010. What are ways in which we can better connect with you this New Year? What's on your mind? We'd love to hear your thoughts!

Source: U.S. Pacific Command. *http://us-pacific-command.blogspot.com/2009/01/how-social-media-helped-pacom-in-2009.html*

CRITICAL THINKING

How has social media changed reporting by the media on disasters? How has social media changed the way information has been collected and analyzed by the government, the private sector, and voluntary agency responders? Will social media continue to change they way people receive information about a disaster and how to secure disaster assistance in the future?

Building an Effective Disaster Communications Capability in a Changing Media World

The world of emergency management is changing rapidly. The onslaught of major catastrophic disasters around the world and the projected impact of global climate change have forced the emergency management community to reexamine all of its processes, including communications. Managing information before, during, and after a disaster has changed significantly in recent years, and emergency operations at all levels—local, state, and national—must recognize and acknowledge this change and adapt accordingly.

As we have noted throughout this chapter, the biggest change in disaster communications has come with the emergence of the "first informers"—citizen journalists—and their use of new, widely available online and digital technologies to gather and share information and images. No organization working in the emergency management field— government, nongovernmental groups, voluntary agency, or private sector—can ignore the role these "first informers" and their information networks will play in future disasters. In the future, emergency management organizations must establish partnerships with both the traditional media outlets and the new media in order to meet their primary communications mission of providing the public with timely and accurate information before, during, and after a disaster.

Creating Effective Disaster Communications

Seven elements will be necessary in the future to comprise an effective disaster communications capability:

- A communications plan
- Information coming in
- Information going out
- Messengers

- Staffing
- Training and exercises
- Monitor, update, and adapt

A Communications Plan

Disaster communication plans can take several forms. Planning for communicating in disaster response focuses on collecting, analyzing, and disseminating timely and accurate information to the public. A disaster response communications plan will include protocols for collecting information from a variety of sources, including citizen journalists, analyzing this data in order to identify resource needs and to match available resources to these needs, and then disseminating information concerning current conditions and actions to the public through both traditional and new media outlets. The plan will identify trusted messengers who will deliver disaster response information to the public. The plan will identify how disaster communications will be delivered to special needs and non-English-speaking populations.

The disaster response communications plan will include a roster of local, state, and national media outlets; reporters; and first informers. This roster will be contacted to solicit information and to disseminate information back out to the public. Finally, the plan should include protocols for monitoring the media, identifying new sources of information collection or dissemination, and evaluating the effectiveness of the disaster communications. This information would be used to update the plan.

A communications plan for the recovery phase will look very similar. The recovery phase plan must also include protocols for collecting, analyzing, and disseminating timely and accurate information. During the recovery phase, much of the information to be disseminated to the public will come from government and other relief agencies and focus on available resources to help individuals and communities to rebuild.

The communications plan must place a premium on delivering this information to the targeted audiences and must identify the appropriate communications mechanisms to communicate these messages. Information collection from the field from a wide variety of sources must be a priority in the communications plan for the recovery phase. Community relations staff, community leaders, and first informers are all good sources of information on the progress of recovery activities and can provide valuable perspectives of the mood of the individuals and communities impacted by the disaster. These sources are also effective in identifying communities, groups, and individuals who have been passed over by recovery programs. It is in the recovery phase that consensus is sought, since crucial long-term decisions have to be made at the state and community levels.

Information Coming In

Information is the basis of effective disaster communications. In disaster response, receiving and processing regular information concerning conditions at a disaster site and what is being done by agencies responding to the disaster help disaster communicators to provide timely and accurate information to the public. In collecting this information, no potential source should be ignored, and all possible sources should be encouraged to forward relevant information. To be successful in this task, you should identify all potential sources of information and develop working relationships with these various sources *before* the next disaster strikes. You must also be prepared to identify and partner with new sources of information as they come on the scene in the aftermath of a disaster.

Potential disaster information sources include the following:

- *Government damage assessment teams:* Government disaster agencies at every level have staff responsible for assessing damages in the aftermath of a disaster. For a major disaster, a damage assessment team may include representatives from local, state, and federal response agencies. The information collected will include deaths and injuries and any damages to homes, infrastructure, and the environment.
- *First responders:* Among the first on the scene at any disaster, they are equipped with the necessary communications devices and trained to be observant.
- *Voluntary agencies:* These groups often have members or volunteers who are trained in damage assessment and can make first and ongoing assessments. For example, the Red Cross has extensive experience in reporting damage to homes and numbers of people evacuated and in shelters.
- *Community leaders:* Trusted leaders who have their own neighborhood network or work with community-based organizations with networks into the community can be a valuable source of on-the-ground information.
- *First informers:* These are the individuals in the disaster site with the wherewithal to collect information and images and to communicate that information and those images by cell phone, handheld device, or laptop.
- *New media:* These include blogs (weblogs), Google Earth, Google Maps, wikis (Wikipedia), SMS (text messaging postings like Twitter), Flickr, Picasa (photo survey sites), and YouTube (video sharing sites).
- *Online news sites:* These are aggregates of community news, information, and opinions.
- *Traditional media:* Television, radio, and newspaper reporters, editors, and news producers can be good sources of information, especially if they have deployed news crews to the disaster area before or just after a disaster strikes.

Having identified the potential information sources in your area, you must reach out to these sources to develop a working partnership and to put in place whatever protocols and technologies are needed to accept information from these sources. It is important that all potential sources of information understand what types of information you need from any situation so they are looking for the specific information you need to make decisions. Government response agencies and voluntary agencies practicing NIMS and ICS will know what information to collect. You must reach out to the nongovernmental, nontraditional information sources before the next disaster to let them know what information you need and how to communicate that information to you.

Here are some ideas for developing these working partnerships with nongovernmental, nontraditional information sources:

- Build neighborhood communications networks. Partner with community-based organizations, churches, and neighborhood associations to build neighborhood communications networks. Local residents can be trained in information collection, maybe as part of Community Emergency Response Team (CERT) training, and local community leaders can be entrusted to collect this information and forward it to emergency officials. These networks could also be used to send messages from emergency officials to neighborhood residents through trusted community leaders.
- Create and distribute a disaster information protocol for first informers. List what information you will be seeking over the course of a disaster response, and get this list out to the public. Make sure they know where to e-mail or post the information and images they collect.
- Establish a point of contact within your organization for information sources. Designate staff who will work with information sources during a disaster and are accessible.
- Create an electronic portal for information from the field. Wikis and weblogs (blogs) can accept and aggregate comments from users; set up a Twitter website that can be updated via text messages, and create a homepage on YouTube and Flickr.
- Include first informers and traditional and new media outlets in disaster response training and exercises. Incorporate these information sources into your disaster exercises to identify issues and gaps and to update plans accordingly. Media are not always included in exercises, and neither are first informers, but by including these groups in your exercises, you make the exercise more authentic and you create an opportunity to identify difficult issues prior to facing them in the next disasters so you can make appropriate adjustments. It is also a chance to get to know one another.
- Meet with traditional and new media types on a regular basis, which is another way to create personal relationships with these critical partners in any disaster response.
- Include information sources in your after-action debriefs. Their perspectives and experiences can be used to update plans and operations.

Many of these information sources can be identified as part of hazard mitigation and preparedness campaigns. Working relationships can be developed during these nondisaster periods that will facilitate information collection and flow in disaster response.

Information Going Out

If information coming in is the basis for disaster communication, then information going out is the goal. Timely and accurate information can save lives in disaster response and in hazard mitigation and preparedness programs. In getting information to the public, you must use all available communications mechanisms, including the following:

- *Traditional media:* television, radio, newspapers, and the Internet
- *New media:* post new information on community websites, blogs, wikis, and bulletin boards; share timely photos and video online, and tell traditional media that online outlets are being updated routinely
- *Neighborhood communications networks:* trusted community leaders who go door to door

Historically, emergency officials have disseminated disaster information to the traditional media by means of press conferences, briefings, tours of the disaster site, one-on-one interviews with disaster officials, press releases, situation reports, and postings on the Internet. Radio actualities, photographs, and videotapes have also been provided to traditional media. In major disasters, emergency management agencies have used satellite uplinks and video and audio press conferences to reach traditional media outlets across large sections of the country.

Disseminating information through new media outlets is something new for emergency officials and will require patience and understanding of how these new media function with their audiences. Most of this work can occur during nondisaster periods. This is the time to learn more about Wikipedia, Twitter, blogs, Flickr, Facebook, YouTube, and social networking sites and to discover how you as an emergency manager can best use these new media to deliver preparedness and hazard mitigation messages as well as communicate with their target audiences in the disaster response and recovery phases.

Prior to the next disaster you might consider the following:

- Start a blog. Get your message out there about the risks your community faces; how community members can take action to reduce those risks and protect their families, homes, and businesses; how to prepare for the next disaster; when to evacuate and how; what will happen when your organization responds; and how members of your community can become first informers.
- Create a bulletin board. This could serve as a link to community leaders involved in hazard mitigation and preparedness programs in the neighborhoods and could be accessed by all community members before, during, and after a disaster.
- Get on Wikipedia. Load preparedness and hazard mitigation information and links for more information on the site. Understand that this site will grow with information added by readers.
- Start a YouTube site. Include "how-to" videos on how to disaster-proof your home, office, and business. Post videos that explain how to survive the next disaster (how much water and food to have on hand, where to go for information).
- Create a Google Map. Include the locations of designated shelters and evacuation routes.

In August 2009, FEMA announced that its Public Affairs Office would be aggressively engaging in the use of new media in its response and recovery communications. See the FEMA press release at *http://www.fema.gov/news/newsrelease.fema?id=49302.*

USE OF SOCIAL MEDIA TOOLS AT FEMA

Social media tools are increasingly more engaged and important in crisis management informatics. These Internet and mobile-based tools offer like-minded (and mutually interested) social communities a locality-based, sector-based, incident-based platform for exchange of potentially lifesaving information.

WHY FEMA IS INVOLVED IN SOCIAL MEDIA

FEMA is engaged in the expanding world of Web 2.0 communications specifically through its use of existing social media tools and through incorporating compatibility into its website and communications strategies. These tools provide opportunities to communicate directly with stakeholders, partners, the general public, and the media officially and rapidly as part of the next generation of online communications. FEMA's venture into social media is being coordinated through its office of External Affairs and provides supplemental products to enhance current outreach objectives.

FEMA's goals with social media are to provide timely and accurate information related to disaster preparedness response and recovery; to present a human, public face to the agency; to provide the public with transparency into the agency's operations; and to engage in a public dialogue that provides the appropriate forum for internal and external voices. External Affairs' social media ventures function as a supplemental outreach and appropriate channels for unofficial input.

FEMA External Affairs has been pragmatically adapting its communications efforts to include social media since June 2008. FEMA External Affairs, in coordination with the FEMA Office of Chief Counsel, was one of the first federal agencies to achieve a modified user agreement with Google in May 2008, providing a working example for other federal agencies. It also broke new ground for a federal agency through its use of Twitter to host the first all-access "press conference" through the tool. For the Twitter event, FEMA set new ground rules for federal engagement and provided its results online in a move to usher in full transparency (*http://www.fema.gov/media/2009/010909.shtm*) behind federal social media exchanges.

HOW FEMA IS INVOLVED

FEMA is expanding its use of Web 2.0 tools to distribute external products by adapting existing information to current standards and applications. This includes direct text-based communications as well as broad-scope visual products that can be shared across platforms.

All off-network accounts (outside of the FEMA.gov domain) for FEMA social media carry the *femainfocus* look and feel. This provides consistency and accountability for nonnetwork content in that the public and our partners can rest assured it is the authorized FEMA account and that the information is accurate.

Starting with YouTube as a platform to host and share videos, FEMA began capturing stories from disaster response and recovery efforts to explain the scope of its mission. Videos have ranged in subject from preparedness, response, and recovery to mitigation and explanations of how specific federal aid programs operate. The subjects, or voices, have been FEMA staff, state and local authorities, and individuals who have been affected by disasters. The approach to these Web videos is to capture the voice and perspective of the community involved in a disaster and present it as an opportunity to help educate others on FEMA's mission and programs.

FEMA has been using Twitter (*www.twitter.com/femainfocus*) since October 2008 as a means of providing information about the agency's mission, efforts, and perspective. The agency also launched its YouTube page (*www.youtube.com/fema*) in October 2008 to provide stories about how its programs work in communities nationwide as they prepare for, respond to, and recover from disasters.

SPECIFIC SOCIAL MEDIA TOOLS

Apart from efforts on third-party social networking sites, FEMA continues to grow its use of Web 2.0 tools to improve content on the agency's website. The official FEMA website (*www .FEMA.gov*) is currently undergoing a redesign of its multimedia site to enable better graphic display and end-user functionality. The new multimedia site replaces the agency's online "Radio Network" with Podcast capabilities, video sharing, and other standard social media functions being integrated as part of this redesign. This builds on the mission to provide timely and accurate information in a format that can be easily transferred among public and private networks. By doing so, FEMA will have a greater opportunity to prepare the nation for disasters and provide information during disaster response and recoveries.

FEMA also promotes transparent communication and collaboration using e-mail and Web 2.0 technologies that allow any visitor to the FEMA website to register to receive updates across 86 important topic areas. Sign-up options are promoted on the homepage and across the website with "subscribe" links functioning like "add to cart" links might in the private sector. The site also provides robust collaboration with 15-plus other agencies using a Web 2.0 mash-up.

FEMA has also engaged in *beta-tests*, monitored, developed, and activated multiple third-party tools, including the following:

- *YouTube:* This is a video service that gives FEMA the opportunity to tell timely and accurate stories about its mission. Recently, the FEMA channel (*www.youtube.com/fema*) was used to help state partners host and share public service announcements and explain federal reimbursement processes and mitigation efforts local to specific communities. These short videos provide access to the overall operation and offer an opportunity for the voices within the community to explain how programs affect, or don't affect, their lives.
- *Twitter:* This microblog gives FEMA the opportunity to direct followers and users of the tool to specific information in a timely manner, such as during emergencies and disasters. Current followers of FEMA's account (*www.twitter.com/femainfocus*) are from the emergency management community, the media, and the general public. Twitter provides SMS capability for instant texting during disasters, and FEMA also uses Twitter to supplement the efforts of state and local responders by rebroadcasting, or "retweeting," posts from these partners. FEMA uses Twitter to engage the general public in discussions on disaster preparedness, recovery processes, and mitigation tools.
- *Widgets:* Widgets provide data feeds through transportable well-defined Web-based graphical interfaces. This is akin to a "box score" anyone can put on a website they use that

is fed data from sources we define. Earlier this year, DHS launched a widget on its site that provided a feed of FEMA's response and recovery information related to Hurricane Gustav (*http://www.dhs.gov/xprepresp/programs/gc_1220128923561.shtm*). FEMA External Affairs has developed widgets for similar data. Current widgets can be found at *http://www .fema.gov/help/widgets/ike_index.shtm*. The real value of a widget is to provide specific, localized data in a specific reporting cycle for non-FEMA.gov sites to incorporate into their informational products. One example would be a "box score" of public assistance applicants for infrastructure projects and money disbursed related to a specific disaster that is updated automatically through validated internal sources and presented through a widget on a local newspaper or TV station's website.

*   *RSS:* FEMA currently offers national-level RSS feeds that provide subscribers with automated updated information (*http://www.fema.gov/help/rss.shtm*). Apart from press release and disaster declaration information, subscribers can receive notifications on the issuance of new situation reports and photographs added to the official FEMA photolibrary.
*   *Google Books:* FEMA has been working with Google Books to provide its published content in a free, easy-to-access format online. FEMA currently offers publications on preparedness, mitigation, and its recovery programs in hard copy through its distribution warehouse. FEMA will be able to provide this content and future content on a broader scale by leveraging the technology and networking platform that Google provides.

RECENT EXAMPLES

FEMA has recently been using its social media tools to tell the complex story of its mission and to personalize the delivery of aid it provides to American communities. One topic of focus has been the debris removal issue along the Texas Gulf Coast following Hurricane Ike. Media reports slammed the agency for a perceived sluggish response. In truth, debris removal can be a fairly complex issue involving many factors and levels of government and private sector involvement, which means it takes time, money, and a lot of planning.

FEMA External Affairs captured some of these stories on video and played the vignettes online to help demystify the process. One vignette, "Working Dog Searches for Missing in Bolivar Debris," focused on the Texas-based fire and rescue team performing searches for human remains among the debris. Told honestly and with dignity by the local team lead, the short video achieved several important goals: It explained FEMA's commitment to the families affected by the storm, depicted how we work with state and local partners, and showed the complexity of debris removal following major disasters.

Since its upload to the FEMA YouTube channel on December 19, more than 879 individuals have watched the "Working Dog" video. Overall, FEMA's YouTube site counts new subscribers every day, and currently 17,644 individuals have logged on to view the 60 videos currently playing. These individuals can further play the videos by embedding them on their websites.

On Twitter, another social media tool that we use, comments have been positive to the videos in general. In fact, other users are promoting their presence from time to time as the subject matter relates to their interest. In regards to the specific video, one user not affiliated with the agency promoted it among his own network, saying, "A grave and serious video about missing people from Hurricane Ike: *http://is.gd/cOrC*. FEMA is important."

THE WAY AHEAD

More collaborative tools and deeper integration of social networking practices into FEMA's communications plan will help it achieve its mission to help the nation prepare for, respond to, and recover from disasters. FEMA is also looking toward integrating new media or Web 2.0 practices into its public communications through such functions as online GIS data and automated feeds for disaster-specific information.

Concurrently, FEMA is working to implement social media tools to enhance internal collaboration. Organizational plans for internal communications focus on awareness and education for employees as well as facilitating dialogue. As FEMA continues to develop its capabilities to communicate in new methods that leverage social networks, the focus of these messages will continue to be in line with the agency's mission of preparedness, response, recovery, and mitigation for all hazards.

Source: FEMA social media Fact Sheet, *http://www.fema.gov/pdf/hazard/hurricane/2009/social_media_factsheet.pdf*

When the next disaster strikes, consider the following:

- *Regular updates on your blog* give you the opportunity to provide a direct link to members of your community. Include time in your schedule to get interactive and answer questions and inquiries.
- *Regular updates on your bulletin board* also give you the opportunity to talk directly to members of the community and another chance to get interactive.
- *Review and update Wikipedia.* Place your information in the Wikipedia file on the disaster, and keep it regularly updated. Update disaster aid and shelter information, links to missing persons sites, correct inaccurate information, and confront rumors.
- *Post on YouTube* videos from informational briefings from affected neighborhoods and appeals for help.
- *Update Google Maps* to show locations of open shelters and hospitals.
- *Display on Google Earth* the locations of affected areas.

Maintain and regularly update all of these sites during the recovery phase.

Messengers

The person who delivers the messages plays a critical role in disaster communications. The messenger puts a human face on disaster response and is critical to building confidence in the public that people will be helped and their community will recover. Public information officers (PIOs) regularly deliver information and messages to the media and the public. However, the primary face of the disaster response should be an elected or appointed official (i.e., mayor, governor, county administrator, city manager) or the director of the emergency management agency or both. These individuals bring a measure of authority to their role as messenger and, in the case of the emergency management director, someone who is in charge of response and recovery operations.

The public wants to hear from an authority figure, and the media wants to know that the person they are talking to is the one making the decisions. Elected officials who served as successful messengers in recent disasters include California Governor Arnold Schwarzenegger during the 2007 Southern California wildfires, New York City mayor Rudy Giuliani during the September 11 attacks, Florida governor Jeb Bush during the four hurricanes that struck Florida in 2004, and Oklahoma governor Frank Keating during the 1995 Oklahoma City bombing.

Successful emergency managers who served as messengers include former FEMA director James Lee Witt and California Office of Emergency Services director Dick Andrews in the 1994 Northridge Earthquake and Craig Fugate with the Florida Division of Emergency Management during recent hurricanes, tornadoes, and wildfires in Florida. Witt and former president Clinton worked very well together in delivering messages concerning federal relief programs in numerous disasters in the 1990s.

Prior to the next disaster, each emergency management agency should determine if an elected or appointed official will serve as the primary messenger alone or in tandem with the emergency agency director. It is best to work out in advance what types of information will be delivered by which messenger. Protocols for briefing books and situational updates should be developed. A determination should be made as to who will lead press briefings and news conferences, who will be available to the media for one-on-one interviews, and who will be involved in communicating with the new media outlets. Again, all of these activities can be shared by the elected/appointed official and the emergency agency director.

Emergency management agencies should also designate appropriate senior managers who will be made available to both the traditional and new media to provide specific information on their activities and perspective. This is helpful in even the smallest disaster when persons with expertise in specific facets of the response can be very helpful in delivering disaster response information and messages.

Staffing

Not many emergency management agencies have a single communications specialist, much less a communications staff. Federal agencies such as FEMA, DHS, HHS, and others involved in disasters have extensive communications staff. Most state emergency management operations have at least a communications director. The depth of staff support for communications varies widely. Emergency management agencies in major cities in the United States often have communications directors and in some cases extensive communications staff. Small to midsize cities and communities are unlikely to have a communications director or staff.

The time has come for all organizations involved in emergency management to establish an ongoing communications staff capability. For agencies in small to midsized communities, this may require enlisting help from the local government's communications staff. One way to do this is to provide funding for a percentage of this individual's time each month. In this way communications activities required during nondisaster periods could be acquired on a consistent basis. This will also allow for the local government communications staff and director to become better informed of the emergency management agency's activities and be better prepared to work with the emergency agency director during disaster response and recovery.

For large cities and federal and voluntary agencies with existing communications staff, it is now a matter of reordering priorities to meet the demands of working with the new media. Staff will be required to establish and maintain working relationships with new media outlets and to interact with the various blogs, bulletin boards, social networking sites, and other new media outlets that serve their community. At a minimum, there should be one designated staff person on the communications staff who is responsible for the day-to-day interactions with new media. Additional staff should be made available in a major disaster to work with these groups.

The new media designated staff would also work with new media outlets in promoting hazard mitigation and preparedness campaigns in the community and serve as the staff support for the establishment and maintenance of neighborhood communications networks working with trusted leaders in the community.

Training and Exercises

An effective disaster communications operation requires well-trained messengers and staff and should be a vital part of all disaster exercises. Elected/appointed officials, agency directors, and public information officers should all receive formal media training in order to become comfortable working with the media to communicate disaster messages to the public. Media training provides methods for communicating a message effectively, techniques for fielding difficult questions, and the opportunity to practice delivery outside the crucible of a crisis. If possible, media training should be provided to senior staff who may appear in the media.

Staff training should come in several forms, including the following:

- Media relations—learning how to work with traditional and new media, including meeting deadlines, responding to inquiries, scheduling interviews, understanding what types of information each media outlet requires, and learning how a news operation works.
- New media—learning what a blog is, how social networking works, and how to establish and maintain a neighborhood communications network.
- Marketing—learning how to pitch a story idea for a preparedness program or hazard mitigation project to all forms of media, how to develop supporting materials for preparedness and hazard mitigation campaigns, and how to evaluate the effectiveness of such efforts.

Communications operations must always be included in future disaster exercises. It is highly recommended that these exercises include reporters from traditional media outlets and representatives from the new media, including bloggers and online news sites. Working with new media and online news sites should be included in the exercise, such as updating and correcting a Wikipedia site and posting information on a community bulletin board. Community leaders involved in neighborhood communications networks should also be included in the exercise.

Monitor, Update, and Adapt

Staff should be assigned to regularly monitor all media outlets. Summaries of news stories in the traditional media should be compiled regularly. Staff should routinely monitor new media outlets and provide regular summaries of news on these sites. This activity is especially important during a disaster response. Through monitoring, the media staff is capable of identifying problems and issues early in the process and can shape communications strategies to address these issues before they become big problems. This is also an opportunity to identify trends in how information flows through the media to the public and to identify areas for improvement in message development and delivery. Regular monitoring will identify rumors and misinformation and speed corrections.

The information collected as part of monitoring activities can be used to update communications plans, strategies, and tactics. This data can be used to determine how to allocate staff resources and to update training and exercise programs. Emergency management agencies must be constantly on the lookout for emerging communications technologies and opportunities.

Conclusion

Whether dealing with the media, the public, or partners, effective communication is a critical element of emergency management. Media relations should be open and cooperative; the information stream must be managed to provide a consistent, accurate message; and officials need to be proactive about telling their own story before it is done for them.

A customer service approach is essential to communicating with the public, a collaborative approach should be taken to promoting programs, and great care should be given as to how and when risk is communicated to citizens. Multiple agencies and unclear lines of responsibility make communications among partners a challenge; political skill and acumen are needed to overcome such hurdles.

The changing shape of emergency management in the coming years will demand that communications take a larger role in all emergency operations and programming. Incorporating new media forms and functions into communications plans and strategies and adapting to new technologies will be the order of the day for all emergency management agencies. Emergency officials can no longer avoid communicating with the media and the public. Emergency agencies must accept the expanded role of communications in all four phases of emergency management and embrace it as a valuable tool in meeting the needs of the public.

Important Terms

Disaster communications strategy
Joint Information Center
New media
Situation report

Self-Check Questions

1. What is the mission of an effective disaster communications strategy?
2. What are the five critical assumptions of an effective disaster communications strategy?
3. What are some of the ways FEMA director James Lee Witt exhibited his commitment to effective communications?
4. What is the goal of a media partnership?
5. Name and describe six basic emergency management audiences.
6. What three factors do DHS and its state and local partners need to address to improve its communications with the American people?
7. What communications media have traditionally been used to communicate disaster information?
8. Name several types of new media, and describe how they have been used in recent years in communicating disaster information.
9. What role have "first informers" come to play in disaster communications?
10. List and summarize the seven elements of an effective disaster communications capability.

Out-of-Class Exercises

1. Using the Internet, the library, or another information source, print out three different articles that describe the same disaster event. Compare the three articles to determine which provides the most useful information to the reader in terms of immediate response and recovery information.
2. Go to your state office of emergency management's website. Print out disaster preparedness and mitigation guidance provided on that site. Critique this information with regards to how useful it is to you personally and to the members of your community.

The Disciplines of Emergency Management: Response

What You'll Learn

- The roles and responsibilities of local first responders and emergency managers
- How states are involved in emergency management
- The contribution of volunteer organizations to disaster response efforts
- What the Incident Command System (ICS) is, and how it functions
- The presidential disaster declaration process
- How the federal government provides assistance in the aftermath of a declared disaster
- The National Response Framework, its affiliated agencies, and how it functions

Introduction

When a disaster event such as a flood, earthquake, or hurricane occurs, the first responders to this event are always local police, fire, and emergency medical personnel. Their job is to rescue and attend to those injured, suppress fires, secure and police the disaster area, and begin the process of restoring order. They are supported in this effort by local emergency management personnel and community government officials.

If the size of the disaster event is so large that the capabilities of local responders are overwhelmed and the costs of the damage inflicted exceeds the capacity of the local government, the mayor or county executive will turn to the governor and state government for assistance in responding to the event and in helping the community to recover. The governor will turn to the state's emergency management agency and possibly the state National Guard and other state resources to provide this assistance to the stricken community.

If the governor decides that, based on information generated by community and state officials, the size of the disaster event exceeds the state's capacity to respond, the governor will make a formal request to the president for a presidential major disaster declaration. This request is prepared by state officials in cooperation with regional staff from FEMA. The governor's request is analyzed first by the FEMA regional office and then forwarded to FEMA headquarters in Washington, D.C. FEMA headquarters staff review and evaluate the governor's request and forward their analysis and recommendation to the president. The president considers FEMA's recommendation and then makes a decision to grant the declaration or turn it down.

In January 2008, FEMA introduced the National Response Framework (NRF) "to ensure that government executives, private sector and nongovernmental organization (NGO) leaders, and emergency management practitioners across the nation understand the domestic incident response roles, responsibilities and relationships in order to respond more effectively to any type of incident" (FEMA, 2008). The NRF superseded the National Response Plan that had been adopted by FEMA in December 2004 and amended in May 2006. The National Response Plan (NRP) was developed in the aftermath of the September 11, 2001, terrorists attacks and superseded the Federal Response Plan (FRP) that had guided the federal government's response to disaster since the early 1990s.

If the president grants a major disaster declaration, federal government departments and agencies involved in the response effort would follow the guidance provided in the National Response Framework in working with state and local officials, emergency managers, nongovernmental groups, and the private sector. The presidential declaration also makes available several disaster assistance programs through FEMA and other federal agencies designed to assist individuals and communities to begin the process of rebuilding their homes, their community infrastructure, and their lives (see the *Columbia* Space Shuttle case study).

CASE STUDY: THE SPACE SHUTTLE *COLUMBIA* DISASTER

On February 1, 2003, as the space shuttle *Columbia* reentered the earth's atmosphere following a successful space mission, it suddenly began to break apart, showering debris over an area of hundreds of square miles in east Texas and western Louisiana. President Bush issued emergency declarations for Texas and Louisiana in the absence of requests for assistance from either governor, as the shuttle craft was considered federal property. Within hours, federal and state agencies had deployed teams to the disaster area to assist local fire, law enforcement, and emergency management authorities already on-site. More than 60 agencies, including public and private groups, responded with personnel, supplies, and equipment. Disaster field offices (DFOs) were opened at Barksdale Air Force Base in Los Angeles, California, and in Lufkin, Texas, and a satellite DFO was established in Fort Worth, Texas. The Lufkin DFO was the regional center of all search-related operations. This was the first major response performed by the newly created Department of Homeland Security.

As this was a federally declared disaster, FEMA was in charge of FRP coordination, and it also coordinated the response and recovery operations. NASA, with the assistance of the Texas Forest Service (TFS), the U.S. Forest Service (USFS), the Environmental Protection Agency (EPA), and many other groups, supervised the search for shuttle material. The EPA's role was to assist FEMA and NASA by conducting environmental monitoring and assisting in the cleanup of hazardous materials from *Columbia*. EPA experts from across the country were mobilized to help local, county, and state officials protect public health and the environment, as well as to assist officials in recovering materials from communities and providing for safe transport of these materials to secure locations.

From the onset, the agencies' priorities were threefold: ensure public safety, retrieve evidence—pieces of the shuttle that ultimately could determine the cause of the tragedy—

and reimburse expenses of state and local governments and private citizens who may have sustained property damage as a result of the accident and search. NASA quickly identified potential hazardous materials, such as tanks containing toxic substances or unexploded pyrotechnic devices, and once found, the material was secured by the EPA. The EPA also worked with state and local authorities to clear school campuses and public access areas, and it tested air and water samples taken along the flight path for shuttle contaminates. Using the resources of the Emergency Response and Removal Service (ERRS) contractors and the U.S. Coast Guard (USCG) Gulf Strike Team, the EPA found no evidence of hazardous material in the atmosphere or drinking water supplies. Early in the recovery effort, teams from NASA, the FBI, the National Guard, Urban Search and Rescue (US&R) organizations, the Department of Public Safety, and others conducted a successful search in Texas to recover and bring home the bodies of *Columbia*'s crew.

Three days after the accident, local fire and police departments, volunteers, Texas Department of Public Safety officers (DPS), Louisiana State Police, and EPA, USFS, TFS, and National Guard units from Texas, Louisiana, Oklahoma, and New Mexico began clearing shuttle debris in high-traffic areas. A one-page set of guidelines prepared by the state of Texas, NASA, and the EPA enabled the teams to collect, document, tag, and transport nonhazardous debris without prior EPA or NASA clearance. These initial teams ended their search operations on February 17. The TFS, under the direction of NASA, now assumed responsibility for search activities in the field, which involved extensive air and ground searches in a 10-mile by 240-mile corridor along the projected shuttle flight path. The TFS—through the Texas Interagency Coordination Center—called upon experienced management and firefighting crews from across the nation and Puerto Rico. The air operations, managed by TFS, included up to 36 helicopters and 10 fixed-wing aircraft. Also involved in the air search but not managed by TFS were motorized paragliders, an ER-2 (similar to the U-2), a specially equipped DC-3, and the Civil Air Patrol (CAP), among others. Volunteers put in more than 800 search-days of flying in the weeks just after the accident and covered the flight corridor area west of Fort Worth to the New Mexico border. The USFS, Bureau of Indian Affairs, Bureau of Land Management, National Park Service, U.S. Fish and Wildlife Service, along with state forestry organizations and contractors, provided the greatest number of crews, drawing from their expertise in wildland firefighting. More than 4,000 people at a time searched 12 hours a day, seven days a week. Camp crews were stationed at sites near Hemphill, Nacogdoches, Palestine, and Corsicana, with a goal of finding as much material as possible before spring vegetation growth made the search more difficult.

The U.S. Navy supervised the water search activities in Lake Nacogdoches and Toledo Bend Reservoir, located at the eastern end of the 2,400-square-mile search area. Beginning on February 22, 60 divers from the Navy, USCG, EPA, DPS, Houston and Galveston police and fire departments, and Jasper County Sheriff's department combed the lakes using sophisticated sonar-equipped boats to help identify shuttle material. As in any operation of this magnitude, the hazards for all the searchers were challenging. Ground crews slogged through mud, dense vegetation, and rocky areas; faced wild hogs, snakes, and other wild animals; and dealt with the ever-changing weather. Divers reckoned with the murky waters of the Texas lakes, along with underwater forests and various submerged hazards.

Ground and air operations covered over 1.5 million acres, mostly in Texas, with searches also conducted in Louisiana, California, Utah, Nevada, and New Mexico. Over 82,500 shuttle items were recovered and processed by the Kennedy Space Center in Florida, weighing 84,800 pounds and amounting almost 40 percent of the total weight of *Columbia*. The total cost of the search and recovery operation amounted to $161,945,000. These funds include costs associated with the ground, air, and water search operations; equipment; and personnel. FEMA Public Assistance, working through Texas and Louisiana, reimbursed the two states approximately $4.5 million for their efforts. FEMA turned over control of the recovery operation to NASA on April 30. The same day, NASA opened the *Columbia* Recovery Operation (CRO) office at the Johnson Space Center in Houston. FEMA closed the Disaster Field Office in Lufkin, Texas, on May 10.

Source: *www.fema.gov.*

In the 1990s, the emergency management system in the United States was tested repeatedly by major disaster events such as the 1993 Midwest floods; the 1994 Northridge, California, earthquake; and a series of devastating hurricanes and tornadoes. In each instance, the system worked to bring the full resources of the federal, state, and local governments to produce the most comprehensive and effective response possible. The system also leveraged the capabilities and resources of America's cadre of volunteer organizations to provide immediate food and shelter. In recent years, government officials and agencies at all levels have begun to reach out to the business community to both leverage their response capabilities and to work closer with them in the recovery effort (Figure 6-1).

The September 11 terrorist attacks have caused all levels of government to reevaluate response procedures and protocols. The unusual loss of so many first responders to this disaster event has resulted in numerous after-action evaluations that have led to

FIGURE 6-1 Eagle, Alaska, July 27, 2009. Don and Judy Mann's house in Eagle, Alaska, was pushed 300 feet off its foundation by ice and floodwaters this past spring. They are rebuilding through the assistance of FEMA and volunteers.
Ben Brennan/FEMA.

changes in the procedures and protocols for first responders in the future. Additionally, the possibility of future terrorist attacks has focused attention on how best to protect first responders from harm in future attacks. These issues are discussed in detail in Chapter 9.

The botched response to Hurricane Katrina in 2005 resulted in a reexamination of how all parties should work together when responding to a catastrophic disaster. Numerous after-action reports were prepared by the U.S. Senate, the U.S. House of Representatives, and the White House, resulting in FEMA and the Department of Homeland Security crafting the National Response Framework and embracing the national Incident Management System (NIMS) as the backbone for coordinating the response to major disasters by federal, state, and local government;, voluntary and nongovernmental organizations; and the private sector.

CASE STUDY: THE RESPONSE TO HURRICANE KATRINA

By all accounts, the response to Hurricane Katrina was a failure on all levels. According to the White House Report, "The response to Hurricane Katrina fell far short of the seamless, coordinated effort that had been envisioned by President Bush when he ordered the creation of the National Response Plan in February 2003" (Townsend, 2006). The Senate report found that "the suffering … continued longer than it should have because of—and in some cases exacerbated by—the failure of government at all levels to plan, prepare for, and respond aggressively to the storm. These failures were not just conspicuous; they were pervasive" (Senate Committee on Homeland Security and Governmental Affairs, 2006). The report concludes that "among the many factors that contributed to these failures, the Committee found that there were four overarching ones:

1. Long-term warnings went unheeded, and government officials neglected their duties to prepare for a forewarned catastrophe.
2. Government officials took insufficient actions or made poor decisions in the days immediately before and after landfall.
3. Systems on which officials relied on to support their response efforts failed.
4. Government officials at all levels failed to provide effective leadership" (Senate Committee on Homeland Security and Governmental Affairs, 2006).

The report prepared by the House of Representatives crafted 13 findings based on their review of the response:

-   "The accuracy and timeliness of National Weather Service and National Hurricane Center forecasts prevented further loss of life.
-   The Hurricane Pam exercise reflected recognition by all levels of government of the dangers of a Category 4 or 5 hurricane striking New Orleans.
-   Levees protecting New Orleans were not built for the most severe hurricanes.
-   The failure of complete evacuations led to preventable deaths, great suffering, and further delays in relief.
-   Critical elements of the National Response Plan were executed late, ineffectively, or not at all.
-   DHS and the states were not prepared for this catastrophic event.
-   Massive communications damage and a failure to adequately plan for alternatives impaired response efforts, command and control, and situational awareness.

- Command and control was impaired at all levels, delaying relief.
- The military played an invaluable role, but coordination was lacking.
- The collapse of local law enforcement and lack of effective public communications led to civil unrest and further delayed relief.
- Medical care and evacuations suffered from a lack of advance preparations, inadequate communications, and difficulties coordinating efforts.
- Long-standing weaknesses and the magnitude of the disaster overwhelmed FEMA's ability to provide emergency shelter and temporary housing.
- FEMA logistics and contracting systems did not support a targeted, massive, and sustained provision of commodities.
- Contributions by charitable organizations assisted many in need, but the American Red Cross and others faced challenges due to the size of the mission, inadequate logistics capacity, and a disorganized shelter process" (Select Bipartisan Committee to Investigate the Preparation for and Response to Hurricane Katrina, 2006).

In summary, these reports found that the government response lacked leadership at the top, was unprepared, operated on poor information and situational awareness, was poorly coordinated, and was incapable of communicating among the various responding agencies and with the general public. All of these factors added up to the confusion, violence, and suffering documented in the first weeks by the media and witnessed by billions across the globe.

FIGURE 6-2 New Orleans, LA, February 24, 2006. FEMA contractors remove debris created by Hurricane Katrina from the lower 9th ward. Crews continue collecting wreckage throughout the neighborhood as more people return to rebuild New Orleans.
Robert Kaufmann/FEMA.

This chapter describes how local, state, and federal government officials and their partners respond to disasters in this country. The chapter includes sections discussing local response, state response, volunteer group response, the Incident Command System and the National Incident Management System (NIMS), the National Response Framework, and communications among responding agencies.

Local Response

Minor disasters occur daily in communities around the United States. Local fire, police, and emergency medical personnel respond to these events usually in a systematic and well-planned course of action. Firefighters, police officers, and emergency medical technicians respond to the scene. Their job is to secure the scene and maintain order, rescue and treat the injured, contain and suppress fire or hazardous conditions, and retrieve the dead.

The types of minor disasters responded to at the community level include hazardous materials transportation and storage incidents, fires, and localized flooding. Local officials are also the first responders to major disaster events such as large floods, hurricanes, and major earthquakes, but in these instances, their efforts are supported, upon request by community leaders, by state government and, by request of the governor and approval of the president, by the federal government.

The actions of local first responders are driven by procedures and protocols developed by the responding agency (i.e., fire, police, and emergency medical). Most communities in the United States have developed communitywide emergency plans that incorporate these procedures and protocols. These community emergency plans also identify roles and responsibilities for all responding agencies and personnel for a wide range of disaster scenarios. The plans include copies of the statutory authorities that provide the legal backing for emergency operations in the community.

In the aftermath of 9/11, many communities reviewed and reworked their community emergency plans to include procedures and protocols for responding to all forms of terrorist attacks, including bioterrorism and weapons of mass destruction. In the aftermath of Hurricane Katrina, FEMA has required that all state and local emergency responders be trained in the Incident Command System (ICS) and become NIMS compliant. In March 2009, FEMA published "Developing and Maintaining State, Territorial, Tribal, and Local Government Emergency Operations Plans" (*Comprehensive Preparedness Guide (CPG) 101*). This is the latest in a series of preparedness guides authored by the federal government in the past 50 years. According to FEMA, "The FEMA *Comprehensive Preparedness Guide, CPG 101,* provides general guidelines on developing emergency operations plans (EOPs). It promotes a common understanding of the fundamentals of planning and decision making to help emergency planners examine a hazard and produce integrated, coordinated, and synchronized plans. This guide helps emergency managers in state, territorial, local, and tribal governments in their efforts to develop and maintain a viable all-hazard EOP" (FEMA, 2009).

Local Emergency Managers

It is usually the responsibility of the designated local emergency manager to develop and maintain the community emergency plans. This individual often holds one or more other positions in local government, such as fire or police chief, and serves only part-time as the community's emergency manager. The profession of local emergency management has been maturing since the 1980s. There are now more opportunities for individuals to receive formal training in emergency management in the United States. Currently, more than 170 junior college, undergraduate, and graduate programs offer courses and degrees in emergency management and related fields. Additionally, FEMA's Emergency Management Institute (EMI) located in Emmitsburg, Maryland, offers emergency management courses on campus and through distance learning programs. EMI has also worked closely with junior colleges, colleges and universities, and graduate schools to develop coursework and curriculums in emergency management. More information on EMI and other emergency management education programs can be found in Chapter 4.

More and more communities have designated emergency managers responsible for guiding response and recovery operations. Training and education programs in emergency management are expanding dramatically, resulting in a growing number of professionally trained and certified local emergency managers. The maturing of this profession can only lead to more effective and efficient local responses to future disaster events.

State Response

Each of the 50 states and six territories that constitute the United States maintains a state government office of emergency management. Funding for state emergency management offices comes principally from FEMA and state budgets. For years, FEMA has provided up to $175 million annually to states to fund state and local government emergency management activities. This money is used by state emergency management agencies to hire staff, conduct training and exercises, and purchase equipment. A segment of this funding is targeted for local emergency management operations as designated by the state. State budgets also provide funding for emergency management operations, but this funding historically has been inconsistent, especially in those states with minimal annual disaster activity.

The principal resource available to governors in responding to a disaster event in their state is the National Guard. The resources of the National Guard that can be used in disaster response include personnel, communications systems and equipment, air and road transport, heavy construction and earth-moving equipment, mass care and feeding equipment, and emergency supplies such as beds, blankets, and medical supplies.

In early 2007, with the passing of the John Warner National Defense Reauthorization Act (PL 109-364), the authority of governors to deploy the National Guard was severely eroded. In section 1076 of this Act, the president was given the authority to effectively commandeer total control of this invaluable response resource. It is believed that the provision was a reaction to sentiments that the federal government should have taken over the response to the Katrina disaster and that the military would have been best suited to manage in that case. The NGA, an organization representing the interests of the leadership of all 50 states, immediately voiced their opposition to the inclusion of such a provision in the legislation, as they felt it undermined their authority over the National Guard and therefore further limited their ability to ensure the safety of their constituents. The governors wrote, "By granting the president specific authority to usurp the Guard during a natural disaster or emergency without the consent of a governor, Section 1076 could result in confusion and an inability to respond to residents' needs because it calls into question whether a governor or the president has primary responsibility during a domestic emergency" (NGA, 2007).

Response capabilities and capacities are strongest in those states and territories that experience high levels of annual disaster activity. North Carolina is one of those states with high risk of hurricanes and floods. How the North Carolina Department of Emergency Management describes its response process on its website provides an example of state response functions.

Volunteer Group Response

Volunteer groups are on the front line of any disaster response. National groups such as the American Red Cross and the Salvation Army roster and maintain local chapters of volunteers who are trained in emergency response. These organizations work with local, state, and federal authorities to address the immediate needs of disaster victims. These organizations provide shelter, food, and clothing to disaster victims who have lost their homes to disasters large and small.

In addition to the Red Cross and the Salvation Army, numerous volunteer groups across the country provide aid and comfort to disaster victims. The National Volunteer Organizations Against Disasters (NVOAD) consists of 49 national member organizations, 52 state and territorial VOADs, and a growing number of local VOADs involved in disaster response and recovery operations around the country and abroad. Formed in 1970, NVOAD helps member groups at a disaster location to coordinate and communicate in order to provide the most efficient and effective response. A list of the NVOAD member organizations is provided.

Hurricane Katrina has changed the landscape in terms of the involvement of voluntary agencies, nongovernmental organizations (NGOs), and the private sector in disaster response. The size of Katrina required resources and capabilities beyond the usual government programs. The massive evacuation in advance of the hurricane created an extraordinary demand for shelters, medicine, food, and temporary housing (Figure 6-3). NGOs and the private sector provided many of the support services to help Katrina victims to get back on their feet. Over 5,000 children were separated from their parents in the evacuations, and the NGO National Center for Missing and Exploited Children helped to successfully reunite every one of them. The private sector helped to raise over $1 billion for the response and supported a number of activities not covered by government relief programs. For example, Chevron worked with the Early Childhood Institute at Mississippi State University and Save the Children to rebuild and resupply child care centers across the three Mississippi coastal counties.

Here is a list of NVOAD member organizations:

- Adventist Community Services
- American Baptist Men USA

FIGURE 6-3 New Orleans, LA, Sunday, August 28, 2005. People inside the Superdome, which is being used as a shelter during Hurricane Katrina.
Marty Bahamonde/FEMA.

- American Disaster Reserve
- American Radio Relay League
- American Red Cross
- America's Second Harvest
- Ananda Marga Universal Relief Team
- Catholic Charities USA
- Center for International Disaster Information
- Christian Disaster Response
- Christian Reformed World Relief Committee
- Church of the Brethren Emergency Response
- Church World Service
- Churches of Scientology Disaster Response
- Convoy of Hope
- Disaster Psychiatry Outreach
- Episcopal Relief and Development
- Feed the Children
- Friends Disaster Service
- Hope Coalition America (Operation Hope)
- Humane Society of the United States
- International Aid
- International Critical Incident Stress Foundation (ICISF)
- International Relief and Development, Inc. (IRD)
- International Relief Friendship Foundation

- Lutheran Disaster Response
- Mennonite Disaster Services
- Mercy Medical Airlift
- National Association of Jewish Chaplains (NAJC)
- National Emergency Response Team
- National Organization for Victim Assistance
- Nazarene Disaster Response
- Northwest Medical Teams International Operation Blessing
- Operation Blessing
- The Phoenix Society for Burn Survivors
- Points of Light Foundation & National Volunteer Center Network
- The Presbyterian Church (USA)
- REACT International
- Salvation Army
- Samaritan's Purse
- Save the Children
- Society of St. Vincent De Paul
- Southern Baptist Convention
- Tzu Chi Foundation
- United Church of Christ
- United Jewish Communities
- United Methodist Committee on Relief
- United Way of America
- Volunteers of America
- World Vision

Incident Command System

A difficult issue in any response operation is determining who is in charge of the overall response effort. The Incident Command System (ICS) was developed after the 1970 fires in Southern California. Duplication of efforts, lack of coordination, and communication problems hindered all agencies responding to the expanding fires. The main function of ICS is to establish a set of planning and management systems that would help the agencies responding to a disaster to work together in a coordinated and systematic approach. The step-by-step process enables the numerous responding agencies to effectively use resources and personnel to respond to those in need (Figure 6-4).

There are multiple functions in the ICS system. They include common use of terminology, integrated communications, a unified command structure, resource management, and action planning. A planned set of directives includes assigning one coordinator to manage the infrastructure of the response, assigning personnel, deploying equipment, obtaining resources, and working with the numerous agencies that respond to the disaster scene. In most instances the local fire chief or fire commissioner is the Incident Commander.

FIGURE 6-4 Warren Grove, New Jersey, May 16, 2007. Firefighters being briefed at the Warren Park Incident Command Post. A fire management assistance declaration from FEMA was granted for the Warren Grove Fire burning in Burlington and Ocean Counties. The declaration triggers a way for federal funding to reimburse state and locals for firefighting efforts. It will allow firefighters to do what they need to do to protect people and property, and FEMA will help to cover the costs.
Andrea Booher/FEMA.

For the ICS to be effective, it must provide for effective operations at three levels of incident character: (1) single jurisdiction and/or single agency, (2) single jurisdiction with multiple agency support, and (3) multijurisdictional and/or multiagency support. The organizational structure must be adaptable to a wide variety of emergencies (i.e., fire, flood, earthquake, and rescue). The ICS includes agency autonomy, management by objectives, unity integrity, functional clarity, and effective span of control. The logistics, coordination, and ability of the multiple agencies to work together must adhere to the ICS so efficient leadership is maintained during the disaster. One of the most significant problems before the ICS was that agencies who would respond to major disasters would assign their own commander and there would be power struggles, miscommunication, and duplication of efforts (Irwin, 1980).

There are five major management systems within the ICS: command, operations, planning, logistics, and finance.

- The *command* section includes developing, directing, and maintaining communication and collaboration with the multiple agencies on site, working with the local officials, the public, and the media to provide up-to-date information regarding the disaster.
- The *operations* section handles the tactical operations, coordinates the command objectives, and organizes and directs all resources to the disaster site.
- The *planning* section provides the necessary information to the command center to develop the action plan to accomplish the objectives. This section also collects and evaluates information as it is made available.
- The *logistics* section provides personnel, equipment, and support for the Command Center. They handle the coordination of all services that are involved in the response,

FIGURE 6-5 Greensburg, Kansas, May 19, 2007. Twice-daily incident command briefings in the FEMA Emergency Operations Center keep relief organizations and government officials updated on progress. Representatives of 16 agencies are cooperating in the recovery effort from the May 4 tornado.
Photo by Greg Henshall/FEMA.

from locating rescue equipment to coordinating the response for volunteer organizations such as the Salvation Army and the Red Cross.
- The *finance* section is responsible for accounting for funds used during the response and recovery aspect of the disaster. This section monitors costs related to the incident and provides accounting procurement time recording cost analyses.

In today's world, the public, private, and political values at risk in major emergencies demand the most efficient methods of response and management. Meeting this demand when multiple and diverse agencies are involved becomes a difficult task. The Unified Command concept of ICS offers a process that all participating agencies can use to improve overall management, whether their jurisdiction is of a geographical or functional nature (Irwin, 1980).

The Unified Command is best used when there is a multiagency response. Because of the nature of the disaster, multiple government agencies need to work together to monitor the response and manage the large number of personnel who respond to the scene (Figure 6-5). It allows for the integration of the agencies to operate under one overall response management system.

PROCEDURES FOR AN INCIDENT COMMAND SYSTEM

For an ICS to be effective, these procedures must be followed closely:

- A command post needs to be established.
- Proper equipment, such as computers, radios, and telephone lines, need to be installed and in working order.

- A media/press area needs to be established.
- Topographic maps need to be located and posted. After tornados, street signs or other identifying landmarks are destroyed, and rescue personnel are unable to use traditional road maps.
- Locate/prepare a missing persons list.
- Monitor the movement and location of triage areas and transportation of victims.
- Have the ability to maintain continuous communication with local hospitals to monitor the number of victims received.
- Establish and grid the search area.
- Based on the type of disaster, such as flooding, responders may have to use boats to search for and rescue victims.
- Determine what resources are available within the local area and what resources are being deployed.
- As the response system expands, reevaluate tasks that need to be performed and develop new tasks.

Source: Irwin, 2002.

The Incident Commander (IC) prepares to delegate responsibilities as needed, to maintain focus on the overall situation. The IC needs to assign positions, such as debriefers, coordinators, and unit leaders, to manage the command center. As the response and recovery process proceeds, the IC needs to have an ongoing dialogue with staff and officials to monitor and manage the response. The IC needs to evaluate the continuing needs of the responders and determine if additional resources are needed. In the after-action reports, discussion and evaluation of the disaster determines the success based on the initial competence and effectiveness of the Incident Commander and the Center.

The Federal Response

Once the governor has determined that a disaster event has overwhelmed the capacity of state and local governments to effectively respond and to subsequently fund the recovery effort, the governor forwards a letter to the president requesting a presidential disaster declaration. This is the first step toward involving federal officials, agencies and departments, and resources in a disaster event. If the president declares a major disaster, 32 federal departments and agencies, including the American Red Cross, work together to support the efforts of state and local officials.

The Department of Homeland Security, through FEMA, is responsible for coordinating all federal activities in support of state and local response and recovery efforts in a presidentially declared disaster. In such an instance, FEMA activates the National Response Plan (NRP) (Figure 6-6). FEMA also manages several programs that provide disaster assistance to individuals and affected communities. These programs are discussed in detail in Chapter 7.

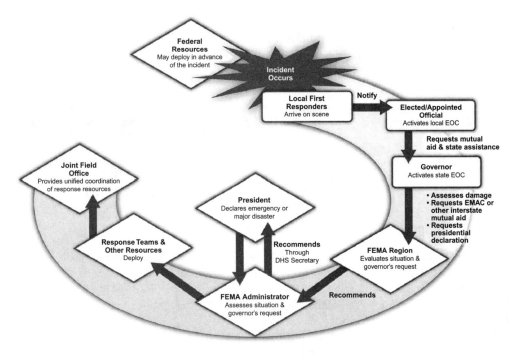

FIGURE 6-6 The National Response Plan.

Presidential Disaster Declaration Process

The presidential disaster declaration makes available the resources of the federal government to the disaster area. Although a formal declaration does not have to be signed for the federal government to respond, the governor must make a formal request for assistance and specify in the request the specific needs of the disaster area. In the presidential major disaster declaration process, federal, state, local, tribal, private sector, and nongovernmental organizations report threats, incidents, and potential incidents, using established communications and reporting channels. The HSOC receives threat and operational information regarding incidents or potential incidents and makes an initial determination to initiate the coordination of federal information-sharing and incident management activities. The decision to make a disaster declaration is completely at the discretion of the president. There are no set criteria to follow and no government regulations to guide which events are declared by the president and which events are not. FEMA has developed several factors it considers in making its recommendation to the president, including individual property losses per capita, level of damage to existing community infrastructures, and insurance coverage. In the end, however, the decision to make the declaration is the president's alone.

A presidential disaster declaration can be made in as short a time as a few hours, as was the case in the 1994 Northridge earthquake and the 1995 Oklahoma City bombing.

Sometimes, however, it takes weeks for damages to be assessed and the capability of state and local jurisdictions to fund response and recovery efforts to be evaluated. If the president turns down the governor's request, the governor has the right to appeal and can be successful, especially if new damage data become available and are included in the appeal.

CASE STUDY: THE OKLAHOMA CITY BOMBING

On April 19, 1995, an explosion rocked the federal plaza in Oklahoma City. Within 45 minutes after notification from the Oklahoma Department of Civil Emergency Management, FEMA deployed staff to Oklahoma City. FEMA coordinated the federal response to the Oklahoma City bombing and later worked closely with state and local officials on recovery efforts. The president signed an Emergency Declaration within eight hours of the occurrence. This was the first time that section 501(b) of the Stafford Act, granting FEMA the primary federal responsibility for responding to a domestic consequence management incident, was ever used. The president subsequently declared a major disaster on April 26, 1995. Because the disaster site was also a federal crime scene, FEMA appointed a liaison to the FBI to coordinate site access, support requirements, control public information, and other issues. The coordinated work among federal agencies in Oklahoma City led to the further clarification of agency and department roles in crisis and consequence management.

Harsh lessons were learned in Oklahoma City. A situation arose when local radio stations requested that all medical personnel should respond to the disaster area. A nurse who answered the call was killed by falling debris while trying to rescue victims in the building. A term constantly used after the bombing was the *Oklahoma Standard*. Oklahoma had personnel on the scene within 30 minutes. Federal officials were notified within minutes of the disaster. Volunteer services were immediate, and because this was a local disaster, everyone took responsibility to do whatever they could to help. Hospital personnel established an effective and efficient triage system. Phone numbers, Internet sites, and briefings were launched within hours of the disaster. The American Red Cross, as in all disasters, was quick to respond with personnel and supplies to help family members of those who were injured or killed in the bombing. The Salvation Army responded within hours with food and supplies. By the end of the day, the Salvation Army had deployed seven units to provide services to the workers and the victims. Law enforcement and EMS personnel had up-to-date training. Oklahoma had excellent coordination with the Public Works Department, the National Weather Service, and the National Guard. The Department of Public Safety also had a predetermined disaster plan in place.

Presidential declarations are routinely sought for such events as large floods, hurricanes, earthquakes, and big tornadoes. In recent years, governors have become more inventive and have requested presidential disaster declarations for snow removal, drought, the West Nile virus, and economic losses caused by failing industries such as the Northwest salmon spawning decline. Since 1979, there have been 1,292 presidential major disaster declarations, averaging 42 declarations per year. As an example of disaster declaration activity in a single year, in 2009 there were 52 major disaster declarations in 29 states and American Samoa.

DECLARATION PROCESS FACT SHEET

THE EMERGENCY RESPONSE PROCESS

Local emergency and public works personnel, volunteers, humanitarian organizations, and other private interest groups provide emergency assistance required to protect the public's health and safety and to meet immediate human needs. If necessary, a governor can declare a state of emergency and invoke the state's emergency plan to augment individual and public resources as required.

A governor may determine, after consulting with local government officials, that the recovery appears to be beyond the combined resources of both the state and local governments and that federal assistance may be needed. In requesting supplemental federal assistance, under the Robert T. Stafford Disaster Relief and Emergency Assistance Act, 42 U.S.C. §§ 5121-5206 (Stafford Act), the governor must certify that the severity and magnitude of the disaster exceed state and local capabilities; certify that federal assistance is necessary to supplement the efforts and available resources of the state and local governments, disaster relief organizations, and compensation by insurance for disaster-related losses; confirm execution of the state's emergency plan; and certify adherence to cost-sharing requirements.

Under the declaration process and to assist a governor to determine if a request for assistance should be made, a preliminary damage assessment is conducted. These assessments are conducted in counties affected by the disaster event. FEMA works with the state's emergency management agency to accomplish these assessments.

THE PRELIMINARY DAMAGE ASSESSMENT

This preliminary damage assessment team is comprised of personnel from FEMA, the state's emergency management agency, county and local officials and the U.S. Small Business Administration. The team's work begins with reviewing the types of damage or emergency costs incurred by the units of government and the impact to critical facilities, such as public utilities, hospitals, schools, and fire and police departments. They will also look at the effect on individuals and businesses, including the number damaged, the number of people displaced, and the threat to health and safety caused by the storm event. Additional data from the Red Cross or other local voluntary agencies may also be reviewed. During the assessment, the team will collect estimates of the expenses and damages.

The governor can then use this information to support a declaration request—showing that the cost of response efforts, such as emergency personnel overtime, other emergency services, and damage to citizens, is beyond state and local recovery capabilities. The information gathered during the assessment will help the governor certify that the damage exceeds state and local resources.

THE DECLARATION PROCESS

As set forth in the Stafford Act, a governor seeks a presidential declaration by submitting a written request to the president through the FEMA regional office. In this request the governor certifies that the combined local, county, and state resources are insufficient and that the situation is beyond their recovery capabilities. Following a FEMA regional and national office review of the request and the findings of the preliminary damage assessment, FEMA provides the president with an analysis of the situation and a recommended course of action.

CRITERIA USED BY FEMA

The federal disaster law restricts the use of arithmetical formulas or other objective standards as the sole basis for determining the need for federal supplemental aid. As a result, FEMA assesses a number of factors to determine the severity, magnitude, and impact of a disaster event. In evaluating a governor's request for a major disaster declaration, a number of primary factors, along with other relevant information, are considered in developing a recommendation to the president for supplemental disaster assistance:

- Amount and type of damage (number of homes destroyed or with major damage)
- Impact on the infrastructure of affected areas or critical facilities
- Imminent threats to public health and safety
- Impacts to essential government services and functions
- Unique capability of the federal government
- Dispersion or concentration of damage
- Level of insurance coverage in place for homeowners and public facilities
- Assistance available from other sources (federal, state, local, voluntary organizations)
- State and local resource commitments from previous, undeclared events
- Frequency of disaster events over recent time period

The very nature of disasters—their unique circumstances, the unexpected timing, and varied impacts—precludes a complete listing of factors considered when evaluating disaster declaration requests, but the preceding list covers many of them.

Source: FEMA. *http://www.fema.gov/media/fact_sheets/declaration_process.shtm.*

CRITICAL THINKING

Should there be more strict guidelines about what events the president can declare a disaster? Why or why not?

The Federal Response Plan (FRP), the National Response Plan (NRP), and the National Response Framework (NRF)

In 1992 FEMA created the Federal Response Plan (FRP). FEMA defined the FRP as a signed agreement among 27 federal departments and agencies, including the American Red Cross that does the following: provides the mechanism for coordinating delivery of federal assistance and resources to augment efforts of state and local governments overwhelmed by a major disaster or emergency, supports implementation of the Robert T. Stafford Disaster Relief and Emergency Assistance Act, as amended (42 U.S.C. 5121, et seq.), as well as individual agency statutory authorities, and supplements other federal emergency operations plans developed to address specific hazards.

The fundamental goal of the FRP was to maximize available federal resources in support of response and recovery actions taken by state and local emergency officials.

Following the absorption of FEMA into the Department of Homeland Security on February 18, 2003, President Bush signed Presidential Directive 5 (HSPD-5) "to enhance the ability of the United States to manage domestic incidents by establishing a single, comprehensive national incident management system." This action authorized the design and development of a National Response Plan (NRP) to "align federal coordination structures, capabilities, and resources into a unified, all-discipline, and all-hazards approach to domestic incident management."

The NRP was designed according to the template of the National Incident Management System (NIMS; released March 1, 2004) to ensure that a consistent doctrinal framework existed for the management of incidents at all jurisdictional levels, regardless of the incident cause, size, or complexity. NIMS was created to integrate effective practices in emergency preparedness and response into a comprehensive national framework for incident management. NIMS enables responders at all levels to work together more effectively and efficiently to manage domestic incidents no matter what the cause, size, or complexity, including catastrophic acts of terrorism and disasters.

In January 2008, DHS published the National Response Framework (NRF) that replaced the National Response Plan (NRP) and currently serves as the guide for response to major disaster events in the United States. According to FEMA:

> *The National Response Framework (NRF) presents the guiding principles that enable all response partners to prepare for and provide a unified national response to disasters and emergencies—from the smallest incident to the largest catastrophe. The Framework defines the key principles, roles, and structures that organize the way we respond as a nation. It describes how communities, tribes, states, the federal government, and private sector and nongovernmental partners apply these principles for a coordinated, effective national response. The national response framework is always in effect, and elements can be implemented at any level at any time. (FEMA, http:// www.fema.gov/pdf/emergency/nrf/nrf-overview.pdf)*

According to FEMA, the NRF is based on the following five key principles that are the basis of the NRF's response doctrine:

- Engaged partnership
- Tiered response
- Scalable, flexible, and adaptable operational capabilities
- Unity of effort through unified command
- Readiness to act

The NRF is comprised of the following five components:

- Roles and responsibilities
- Response actions
- Response organization

- Planning
- Additional resources

The NRF identifies the key players and their roles in the NRF.

KEY PLAYERS—THE NATIONAL RESPONSE FRAMEWORK

LOCAL GOVERNMENTS

Local governments (counties, cities, or towns) respond to emergencies daily using their own resources. They also rely on mutual aid and assistance agreements with neighboring jurisdictions when they need additional resources. The National Incident Management System (NIMS) provides information on mutual aid and assistance agreements. When local jurisdictions cannot meet incident response resource needs with their own resources or with help available from other local jurisdictions, they may ask the state for assistance.

TRIBAL GOVERNMENTS

Tribal governments respond to the same range of emergencies and disasters that other jurisdictions face. They may require assistance from neighboring jurisdictions under mutual aid and assistance agreements and may provide assistance as well. The United States has a trust relationship with American Indian tribes and recognizes their right to self-government. As such, tribal governments are responsible for coordinating resources to address actual or potential incidents. When local resources are not adequate, tribal leaders seek assistance from states or the federal government.

For certain types of federal assistance, tribal governments work with the state, but as sovereign entities, they can also elect to deal directly with the federal government for other types of assistance. To obtain federal assistance via the Robert T. Stafford Disaster Relief and Emergency Assistance Act (Stafford Act), the state governor must request a presidential declaration on behalf of a tribe.

STATE GOVERNMENTS

The state helps local governments if they need assistance. States have significant resources of their own, including emergency management and homeland security agencies, state police, health agencies, transportation agencies, incident management teams, specialized teams, and the National Guard.

If additional resources are required, the state may request assistance from other states through interstate mutual aid and assistance agreements such as the Emergency Management Assistance Compact (EMAC). Administered by the National Emergency Management Association, EMAC is a congressionally ratified organization that provides form and structure to the interstate mutual aid and assistance process.

If an incident is beyond the local and state capabilities, the governor can seek federal assistance. The state will collaborate with the impacted communities and the federal government to provide the help needed.

FEDERAL GOVERNMENT

The federal government maintains a wide array of capabilities and resources that can assist state governments in responding to incidents. Federal departments and agencies provide this assistance using processes outlined later in this document. In addition, federal departments and agencies may also request and receive help from other federal departments and agencies.

NONGOVERNMENTAL ORGANIZATIONS

Nongovernmental and voluntary organizations are essential partners in responding to incidents. Working through emergency operations centers and other structures, nongovernmental and voluntary organizations assist local, tribal, state, and federal governments in providing sheltering, emergency food supplies, counseling services, and other vital support services to support response and promote the recovery of disaster victims. These groups often provide specialized services that help individuals with special needs, including those with disabilities.

To engage these key partners most effectively, local, tribal, state, and federal governments coordinate with voluntary agencies, existing Voluntary Organizations Active in Disaster (VOADs), community and faith-based organizations, and other entities to develop plans to manage volunteer services and donated goods, establish appropriate roles and responsibilities, and train and exercise plans and procedures before an incident occurs.

PRIVATE SECTOR

Forming the foundation for the health of the nation's economy, the private sector is a key partner in local, tribal, state, and federal incident management activities. The private sector is responsible for most of the critical infrastructure and key resources in the nation and thus may require assistance in the wake of a disaster or emergency. They also provide goods and services critical to the response and recovery process, either on a paid basis or through donations.

Source: FEMA. *http://www.fema.gov/pdf/emergency/nrf/nrf-overview.pdf*

Federal Assistance

According to FEMA, "Federal disaster assistance is often thought of as synonymous with presidential declarations and the Stafford Act. The fact is that federal assistance can be provided to state, tribal, and local jurisdictions, and to other federal departments and agencies, in a number of different ways through various mechanisms and authorities. Federal assistance does not always require coordination by the Department of Homeland Security (DHS) and may be provided without a presidential major disaster or emergency declaration. Federal assistance for incidents that do not require DHS coordination may be led by other federal departments and agencies consistent with their authorities. The secretary of Homeland Security may monitor such incidents and may activate Framework mechanisms to provide support to departments and agencies without assuming overall leadership for the federal response to the incident" (FEMA, *http://www.fema.gov/pdf/emergency/nrf/nrf-overview.pdf*).

FEMA's description of how the federal government supports states during a major disaster is included in the NRF and in the box on page 186.

STAFFORD ACT

Federal support to states and local jurisdictions takes many forms. The most widely known authority under which assistance is provided for major incidents is the Stafford Act. When an incident occurs that exceeds or is anticipated to exceed local, tribal, or state resources, the governor can request federal assistance under the Stafford Act. The Stafford Act authorizes the president to provide financial and other assistance to state and local governments, certain private nonprofit organizations, and individuals to support response, recovery, and mitigation efforts following presidential emergency or major disaster declarations.

Most incidents are not of sufficient magnitude to warrant a presidential declaration. However, if state and local resources are insufficient, a governor may ask the president to make such a declaration. Before making a declaration request, the governor must activate the state's emergency plan and ensure that all appropriate state and local actions have been taken or initiated, including but not limited to:

- Surveying the affected areas to determine the extent of private and public damage.
- Conducting joint preliminary damage assessments with Federal Emergency Management Agency officials to estimate the types and extent of federal disaster assistance required.

Ordinarily, only the governor can initiate a request for a presidential emergency or major disaster declaration. In extraordinary circumstances, the president may unilaterally make such a declaration. The governor's request is made through the FEMA regional administrator and based on a finding that the disaster is of such severity and magnitude that effective response is beyond the capabilities of the state and affected local governments and that federal assistance is necessary.

The governor's request includes the following:

- Information on the extent and nature of state resources that have been or will be used to address the consequences of the disaster.
- A certification by the governor that state and local governments will assume all applicable nonfederal costs required by the Stafford Act.
- An estimate of the types and amounts of supplementary federal assistance required.
- Designation of the state coordinating officer.

The FEMA regional administrator evaluates the damage and requirements for federal assistance and makes a recommendation to the FEMA administrator, who, acting through the secretary of Homeland Security, then recommends a course of action to the president. The governor, appropriate members of Congress, and federal departments and agencies are immediately notified of a presidential declaration.

NON–STAFFORD ACT FEDERAL SUPPORT TO STATE AND LOCAL JURISDICTIONS

While the Stafford Act is the most familiar mechanism by which the federal government may provide support to state, tribal, and local governments, it is not the only one. Often, federal assistance does not require coordination by DHS and can be provided without a presidential major disaster or emergency declaration.

In these instances, federal departments and agencies provide assistance to states, as well as directly to tribes and local jurisdictions, consistent with their own authorities. For example, under the Comprehensive Environmental Response, Compensation, and Liability Act, local and tribal governments can request assistance directly from the Environmental Protection Agency and/or the U.S. Coast Guard.

This support is typically coordinated by the federal agency that has primary jurisdiction rather than DHS. The secretary of Homeland Security may monitor such incidents and may, as requested, activate Framework mechanisms to support federal departments and agencies without assuming overall leadership for the incident.

Source: FEMA. *http://www.fema.gov/pdf/emergency/nrf/nrf-overview.pdf*

The NRF includes 15 emergency support functions (ESFs) that provide an organizing function for response activities by federal departments and agencies, state and local governments, tribal organizations, voluntary agencies, and the private sector. The function of the ESFs and the roles and responsibilities of each stakeholder are presented in the box below.

EMERGENCY SUPPORT FUNCTION ANNEXES: INTRODUCTION

The federal government and many state governments organize much of their resources and capabilities—as well as those of certain private sector and nongovernmental organizations—under 15 emergency support functions (ESFs). ESFs align categories of resources and provide strategic objectives for their use.

During a response, ESFs are a critical mechanism to coordinate functional capabilities and resources provided by federal departments and agencies, along with certain private sector and nongovernmental organizations. ESFs may be selectively activated for both Stafford Act and non–Stafford Act incidents where federal departments or agencies request DHS assistance or under other circumstances as defined in Homeland Security Presidential Directive 5 (HSPD-5). Not all incidents result in the activation of ESFs.

ESFs may be activated to support headquarters, regional, and/or field activities (Figure 6-7). The Incident Command System provides for the flexibility to assign ESF and other stakeholder resources according to their capabilities, tasking, and requirements to augment and support the other sections of the Joint Field Office (JFO)/Regional Response Coordination Center (RRCC) or National Response Coordination Center (NRCC) in order to respond to incidents in a more collaborative and crosscutting manner.

While ESFs are typically assigned to a specific section at the NRCC or in the JFO/RRCC for management purposes, resources may be assigned anywhere within the unified coordination structure. Regardless of the section in which an ESF may reside, that entity works in conjunction with other JFO sections to ensure that appropriate planning and execution of missions occur. For example, if a state requests assistance with a mass evacuation, the JFO would request personnel from ESF #1 (transportation), ESF #6 (mass care, emergency

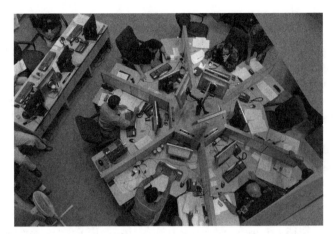

FIGURE 6-7 Clanton, Alabama, August 29, 2005. The Alabama Emergency Response Team work at the Alabama Emergency Operations Center (EOC). FEMA and the state of Alabama are monitoring Hurricane Katrina as it makes landfall on the Gulf Coast.
FEMA/Mark Wolfe.

assistance, housing, and human services), and ESF #8 (public health and medical services). These would then be integrated into a single branch or group within the operations section to ensure effective coordination of evacuation services.

ESF MEMBER ROLES AND RESPONSIBILITIES
Each ESF Annex identifies the coordinator and the primary and support agencies pertinent to the ESF. Several ESFs incorporate multiple components, with primary agencies designated for each component to ensure seamless integration of and transition between preparedness, response, and recovery activities.

- **ESF Coordinator.** The ESF coordinator is the entity with management oversight for that particular ESF. The coordinator has ongoing responsibilities throughout the preparedness, response, and recovery phases of incident management. The role of the ESF coordinator is carried out through a "unified command" approach as agreed upon collectively by the designated primary agencies and, as appropriate, support agencies.
- **ESF Primary Agency(ies).** An ESF primary agency is a federal agency with significant authorities, roles, resources, or capabilities for a particular function within an ESF. ESFs may have multiple primary agencies, and the specific responsibilities of those agencies are articulated within the relevant ESF Annex. A federal agency designated as an ESF primary agency serves as a federal executive agent under the federal coordinating officer (or federal resource coordinator for non–Stafford Act incidents) to accomplish the ESF mission.
- **ESF Support Agencies.** Support agencies are those entities with specific capabilities or resources that support the primary agency(ies) in executing the mission of the ESF.

Source: FEMA, *http://www.fema.gov/pdf/emergency/nrf/nrf-overview.pdf.*

A typical ESF Annex in the National Response Framework (NRF) includes a purpose statement, a description of capabilities, an overview of the concept of operations within the ESF, and the designation of ESF members identifying the ESF coordinator and primary and support agencies.

ESF #5—EMERGENCY MANAGEMENT

PURPOSE
Emergency Support Function (ESF) #5—Emergency Management is responsible for supporting the overall activities of the federal government for domestic incident management. ESF #5 provides the core management and administrative functions in support of the National Response Coordination Center (NRCC), the Regional Response Coordination Center (RRCC), and Joint Field Office (JFO) operations.

CAPABILITIES
ESF #5 serves as the coordination ESF for all federal departments and agencies across the spectrum of domestic incident management from hazard mitigation and preparedness to response and recovery. ESF #5 preparedness activities include the following:

- Identifying resources for alert, activation, and subsequent deployment
- Ensuring that there are trained and experienced staff to fill appropriate positions in the NRCC, RRCC, Initial Operating Facility, and JFO, when activated or established

During the postincident response phase, ESF #5 is responsible for support and planning functions. ESF #5 activities include those functions that are critical to support and facilitate multiagency planning and coordination, including the following:

- Alerts and notifications
- Staffing and deploying of Department of Homeland Security (DHS) and DHS/FEMA response teams, as well as response teams from other federal departments and agencies
- Incident action planning
- Coordination of operations, direction, and control
- Logistics management
- Information collection, analysis, and management
- Facilitation of requests for federal assistance
- Resource acquisition and management
- Federal worker safety and health
- Facilities management
- Financial management

CONCEPT OF OPERATIONS OVERVIEW
The National Response Coordination Center (NRCC), staffed by ESF #5 and other ESFs when activated, monitors potential or developing incidents and supports the efforts of regional and field operations. In the event of a no-notice event, the secretary of Homeland Security or his or her designee may direct execution of the Catastrophic Incident Supplement, depending on the size of the incident.

The Regional Response Coordination Center (RRCC), staffed by ESF #5 and other ESFs as required, coordinates operations and situational reporting to the NRCC until the Joint Field Office (JFO) is operational. Once the JFO is operational, the RRCC assumes a monitoring role. ESF #5 operations transition from the RRCC to the JFO when the JFO is established. When the JFO begins to stand-down operations, ESF #5 operations transition back to the RRCC, as required. To see the complete annex, as well as other pertinent information, refer to the NRF Resource Center at *www.fema.gov/NRF*.

Source: FEMA, *http://www.fema.gov/pdf/emergency/nrf/nrf-overview.pdf.*

The NRF currently has 15 ESFs:

ESF #1—Transportation
ESF #2—Communications
ESF #3—Public Works and Engineering
ESF #4—Firefighting
ESF #5—Emergency Management
ESF #6—Mass Care, Emergency Assistance, Housing, and Human Services
ESF #7—Logistics Management and Resource Support
ESF #8—Public Health and Medical Services
ESF #9—Search and Rescue
ESF #10—Oil and Hazardous Materials Response
ESF #11—Agriculture and Natural Resources
ESF #12—Energy
ESF #13—Public Safety and Security
ESF #14—Long-Term Community Recovery
ESF #15—External Affairs

The NRF also includes the following support annexes that "describe how federal departments and agencies; state, tribal, and local entities; the private sector; volunteer organizations; and nongovernmental organizations coordinate and execute the common functional processes and administrative requirements necessary to ensure efficient and effective incident management. During an incident, numerous procedures and administrative functions are required to support incident management" (NRF, *http://www.fema.gov/emergency/nrf/ index.htm#*):

- Critical Infrastructure and Key Resources
- Financial Management
- International Coordination
- Private Sector Coordination
- Public Affairs
- Tribal Relations

- Volunteer and Donations Management
- Worker Safety and Health

Roles and Responsibilities

The NRF defines the roles and responsibilities of public, private, and nonprofit parties involved in incident management at the local, state, and national levels.

Governor

As a state's chief executive, the governor is responsible for the public safety and welfare of the people of that state or territory and does the following:

- Is responsible for coordinating state resources to address the full spectrum of actions to prevent, prepare for, respond to, and recover from incidents in an all-hazards context to include terrorism, natural disasters, accidents, and other contingencies.
- Under certain emergency conditions, typically has police powers to make, amend, and rescind orders and regulations.
- Provides leadership and plays a key role in communicating to the public and in helping people, businesses, and organizations cope with the consequences of any type of declared emergency within state jurisdiction.
- Encourages participation in mutual aid and implements authorities for the state to enter into mutual aid agreements with other states, tribes, and territories to facilitate resource-sharing.
- Is the commander in chief of state military forces (National Guard when in state active duty or Title 32 status and the authorized state militias).
- Requests federal assistance when it becomes clear that state or tribal capabilities will be insufficient or have been exceeded or exhausted.

Local Chief Executive Officer

A mayor or city or county manager, as a jurisdiction's chief executive, is responsible for the public safety and welfare of the people of that jurisdiction. The local chief executive officer does the following:

- Is responsible for coordinating local resources to address the full spectrum of actions to prevent, prepare for, respond to, and recover from incidents involving all hazards including terrorism, natural disasters, accidents, and other contingencies.
- Dependent on state and local law, has extraordinary powers to suspend local laws and ordinances, such as to establish a curfew, direct evacuations, and, in coordination with the local health authority, to order a quarantine.
- Provides leadership and plays a key role in communicating to the public, and in helping people, businesses, and organizations cope with the consequences of any type of domestic incident within the jurisdiction.

- Negotiates and enters into mutual aid agreements with other jurisdictions to facilitate resource-sharing. Requests state and, if necessary, federal assistance through the governor of the state when the jurisdiction's capabilities have been exceeded or exhausted.

Tribal Chief Executive Officer

The tribal chief executive officer is responsible for the public safety and welfare of the people of that tribe and does the following as authorized by tribal government:

- Is responsible for coordinating tribal resources to address the full spectrum of actions to prevent, prepare for, respond to, and recover from incidents involving all hazards, including terrorism, natural disasters, accidents, and other contingencies.
- Has extraordinary powers to suspend tribal laws and ordinances, such as to establish a curfew, direct evacuations, and order a quarantine.
- Provides leadership and plays a key role in communicating to the tribal nation, and in helping people, businesses, and organizations cope with the consequences of any type of domestic incident within the jurisdiction.
- Negotiates and enters into mutual aid agreements with other tribes/jurisdictions to facilitate resource-sharing. Can request state and federal assistance through the governor of the state when the tribe's capabilities have been exceeded or exhausted.
- Can elect to deal directly with the federal government. (Although a state governor must request a presidential disaster declaration on behalf of a tribe under the Stafford Act, federal agencies can work directly with the tribe within existing authorities and resources.)

Secretary of Homeland Security

Pursuant to HSPD-5, the secretary of Homeland Security does the following:

- Is responsible for coordinating federal operations within the United States to prepare for, respond to, and recover from terrorist attacks, major disasters, and other emergencies.
- Serves as the "principal federal official" for domestic incident management. The secretary is also responsible for coordinating federal resources utilized in response to or recovery from terrorist attacks, major disasters, or other emergencies if and when any of the following four conditions applies:
  - A federal department or agency acting under its own authority has requested DHS assistance.
  - The resources of state and local authorities are overwhelmed and federal assistance has been requested.
  - More than one federal department or agency has become substantially involved in responding to the incident.
  - The secretary has been directed to assume incident management responsibilities by the president.

Attorney General

The attorney general is the chief law enforcement officer in the United States. In accordance with HSPD-5 and other relevant statutes and directives, the attorney general has lead responsibility for criminal investigations of terrorist acts or terrorist threats:

- By individuals or groups inside the United States
- Directed at U.S. citizens or institutions abroad

Generally acting through the FBI, the attorney general—in cooperation with other federal departments and agencies engaged in activities to protect national security—coordinates the activities of the other members of the law enforcement community. Nothing in the NRP derogates the attorney general's status or responsibilities.

Secretary of Defense

The DOD has significant resources that may be available to support the federal response to an Incident of National Significance. The secretary of defense authorizes Defense Support of Civil Authorities (DSCA) for domestic incidents as directed by the president or when consistent with military readiness operations and appropriate under the circumstances and the law. The secretary of defense retains command of military forces under DSCA, as with all other situations and operations. Nothing in the NRP impairs or otherwise affects the authority of the secretary of defense over the DOD.

Secretary of State

The secretary of state is responsible for coordinating international prevention, preparedness, response, and recovery activities relating to domestic incidents, and for the protection of U.S. citizens and U.S. interests overseas.

Nongovernmental Organizations (NGOs)

NGOs collaborate with first responders, governments at all levels, and other agencies and organizations providing relief services to sustain life, reduce physical and emotional distress, and promote recovery of disaster victims when assistance is not available from other sources.

Private Sector

DHS and NRP primary and support agencies coordinate with the private sector to effectively share information, form courses of action, and incorporate available resources to prevent, prepare for, respond to, and recover from Incidents of National Significance. The roles, responsibilities, and participation of the private sector during Incidents of National Significance vary based on the nature of the organization and the type and impact of the incident. Private sector organizations may be involved as:

- *An impacted organization or infrastructure.* Private sector organizations may be affected by direct or indirect consequences of the incident. Examples of privately owned infrastructure include transportation, telecommunications, private utilities, financial institutions, and hospitals.

- *A response resource.* Private sector organizations may provide response resources (donated or compensated) during an incident, including specialized teams, equipment, and advanced technologies.
- *A regulated and/or responsible party.* Owners/operators of certain regulated facilities or hazardous operations may bear responsibilities under the law for preparing for and preventing incidents from occurring, and responding to an incident once it occurs. For example, federal regulations require owners/operators of nuclear facilities that are regulated by the Nuclear Regulatory Commission to maintain emergency (incident) preparedness plans, procedures, and facilities and to perform assessments, prompt notifications, and training for a response to an incident.
- *A member of state/local emergency organizations.* Private sector organizations may serve as an active partner in local and state emergency preparedness and response organizations and activities.

Citizen Involvement

Strong partnerships with citizen groups and organizations provide support for incident management prevention, preparedness, response, recovery, and mitigation. The U.S. Citizen Corps brings these groups together and focuses efforts of individuals through education, training, and volunteer service to help make communities safer, stronger, and better prepared to address the threats of terrorism, crime, public health issues, and disasters of all kinds.

THE NATIONAL RESPONSE FRAMEWORK RESPONSE ORGANIZATIONS

Incident Command Post (ICP)
This is the field location at which the primary tactical-level, on-scene incident command functions are performed. The ICP may be collocated with the incident base or other incident facilities and is normally identified by a green rotating or flashing light.

Area Command (Unified Area Command)
This organization was established to (1) oversee the management of multiple incidents that are each being handled by an ICS organization or (2) oversee the management of large or multiple incidents to which several incident management teams have been assigned. Area Command has the responsibility to set overall strategy and priorities, allocate critical resources according to priorities, ensure that incidents are properly managed, and ensure that objectives are met and strategies followed. Area Command becomes Unified Area Command when incidents are multijurisdictional. Area Command may be established at an EOC facility or at some location other than an ICP.

Local Emergency Operations Center (EOC)

This is the physical location at which the coordination of information and resources to support local incident management activities normally takes place.

State Emergency Operations Center (EOC)

This is the physical location at which the coordination of information and resources to support state incident management activities normally takes place.

State Coordinating Officer (SCO)

The SCO plays a critical role in managing the state response and recovery operations following Stafford Act declarations. The governor of the affected state appoints the SCO, and lines of authority flow from the governor to the SCO, following the state's policies and laws. For certain anticipated events in which a Stafford Act declaration is expected, such as an approaching hurricane, the secretary of Homeland Security or the FEMA administrator may predesignate one or more federal officials to coordinate with the SCO to determine resources and actions that will likely be required and begin deployment of assets. The specific roles and responsibilities of the SCO include serving as the primary representative of the governor for the affected state or locality with the RRCC or within the JFO once it is established; working with the federal coordinating officer to formulate state requirements, including those that are beyond state capability, and set priorities for employment of federal resources provided to the state; ensuring coordination of resources provided to the state via mutual aid and assistance compacts; providing a linkage to local government; and serving in the Unified Coordination Group in the JFO.

National Operations Center (NOC)

The NOC is the primary national hub for situational awareness and operations coordination across the federal government for incident management. It provides the secretary of Homeland Security and other principals with the information necessary to make critical national-level incident management decisions. The NOC is a continuously operating multiagency operations center. The NOC's staff monitors many sources of threat and hazard information from across the United States and abroad. It is supported by a 24/7 watch officer contingent, including (1) NOC managers; (2) selected federal interagency, state, and local law enforcement representatives; (3) intelligence community liaison officers provided by the DHS chief intelligence officer; (4) analysts from the Operations Division's interagency planning element; and (5) watch standers representing dozens of organizations and disciplines from the federal government and others from the private sector. The NOC facilitates homeland security information sharing and operations coordination with other federal, state, tribal, local, and nongovernmental partners. During a response to a significant incident, the NOC meets its information-fusion and information-sharing responsibilities by providing spot reports, situation reports, and other information-sharing tools, all supported by and distributed through its common operating picture. The continued development and rapid integration at the federal, state, tribal, and local levels of electronic reporting and information-sharing tools supporting the NOC's common operating picture is a very high priority of the Framework.

National Response Coordination Center (NRCC)

The NRCC is FEMA's primary operations management center, as well as the focal point for national resource coordination. As a 24/7 operations center, the NRCC monitors potential or developing incidents and supports the efforts of regional and field components. The NRCC also has the capacity to increase staffing immediately in anticipation of or in response to an incident by activating the full range of ESFs and other personnel as needed to provide resources and policy guidance to a JFO or other local incident management structures. The NRCC provides overall emergency management coordination, conducts operational planning, deploys national-level entities, and collects and disseminates incident information as it builds and maintains a common operating picture. Representatives of nonprofit organizations within the private sector may participate in the NRCC to enhance information exchange and cooperation between these entities and the federal government.

National Infrastructure Coordinating Center (NICC)

The NICC monitors the nation's critical infrastructure and key resources on an ongoing basis. During an incident, the NICC provides a coordinating forum to share information across infrastructure and key resources sectors through appropriate information-sharing entities such as the Information Sharing and Analysis Centers and the Sector Coordinating Councils.

National Military Command Center (NMCC)

The NMCC is the nation's focal point for continuous monitoring and coordination of worldwide military operations. It directly supports combatant commanders, the chairman of the Joint Chiefs of Staff, the secretary of defense, and the president in the command of U.S. Armed Forces in peacetime contingencies and war. Structured to support the president and secretary of defense effectively and efficiently, the center participates in a wide variety of activities, ranging from missile warning and attack assessment to management of peacetime contingencies such as Defense Support of Civil Authorities (DSCA) activities. In conjunction with monitoring the current worldwide situation, the center alerts the Joint Staff and other national agencies to developing crises and will initially coordinate any military response required.

National Counterterrorism Center (NCTC)

The NCTC serves as the primary federal organization for integrating and analyzing all intelligence pertaining to terrorism and counterterrorism and for conducting strategic operational planning by integrating all instruments of national power.

Strategic Information and Operations Center (SIOC)

The FBI SIOC is the focal point and operational control center for all federal intelligence, law enforcement, and investigative law enforcement activities related to domestic terrorist incidents or credible threats, including leading attribution investigations. The SIOC serves as an information clearinghouse to help collect, process, vet, and disseminate information relevant to law enforcement and criminal investigation efforts in a timely manner. The SIOC maintains direct connectivity with the NOC. The SIOC, which is located at FBI headquarters, supports the FBI's mission in leading efforts of the law enforcement community to detect, prevent, preempt, and disrupt terrorist attacks against the United States. The SIOC maintains liaison with the National Joint Terrorism Task Force (NJTTF). The mission of the NJTTF is to enhance communications, coordination, and cooperation among federal, state, tribal, and local agencies representing the intelligence, law enforcement, defense, diplomatic, public safety, and homeland security communities by providing a point of fusion for terrorism intelligence and by supporting Joint Terrorism Task Forces throughout the United States.

Other DHS Operations Centers

Depending on the type of incident (e.g., National Special Security Events), the operations centers of other DHS operating components may serve as the primary operations management center in support of the secretary. These are the U.S. Coast Guard, the Transportation Security Administration, U.S. Secret Service, and U.S. Customs and Border Protection operations centers.

Joint Field Office (JFO)

The JFO is a temporary federal facility established locally to coordinate operational federal assistance activities to the affected jurisdiction(s) during Incidents of National Significance. The JFO is a multiagency center that provides a central location for coordination of federal, state, local, tribal, nongovernmental, and private sector organizations with primary responsibility for threat response and incident support. The JFO enables the effective and efficient coordination of federal incident-related prevention, preparedness, response, and recovery actions. The JFO utilizes the scalable organizational structure of the NIMS Incident Command System (ICS). The JFO organization adapts to the magnitude and complexity of the situation at hand and incorporates the NIMS principles regarding span of control and organizational structure: management, operations, planning, logistics, and finance/administration. Although the JFO uses an ICS structure, the JFO does not manage on-scene operations. Instead, the JFO focuses on providing support to on-scene efforts and conducting broader support operations that may extend beyond the incident site.

Joint Operations Center (JOC)

The JOC branch is established by the Senior Federal Law Enforcement Officer (SFLEO) (e.g., the FBI SAC during terrorist incidents) to coordinate and direct law enforcement and criminal investigation activities related to the incident. The JOC branch ensures management and coordination of federal, state, local, and tribal investigative/law enforcement activities. The emphasis of the JOC is on prevention as well as intelligence collection, investigation, and prosecution of a criminal act. This emphasis includes managing unique tactical issues inherent to a crisis situation (e.g., a hostage situation or terrorist threat). When this branch is included as part of the Joint Field Office (JFO), it is responsible for coordinating the intelligence and information function (as described in NIMS), which includes information and operational security, and the collection, analysis, and distribution of all incident-related intelligence. Accordingly, the Intelligence Unit within the JOC branch serves as the interagency fusion center for all intelligence related to an incident.

The Joint Information Center (JIC) is also a valuable tool for getting emergency management partners on the same page. In disasters of catastrophic or nationally significant proportions, a JIC is established to coordinate the dissemination of information about all disaster response and recovery programs. Public Affairs Officers (PAOs) who represent all of the federal, state, local, and voluntary agencies providing response or recovery services are invited to collocate and be a part of JIC operations. Interagency coordination is one of the central functions of the JIC, and teamwork is a key to implementing successful public information and media affairs programs. JICs involve coordination among the FCO, the lead state PAO, the congressional liaison, community relations and disaster assistance program managers, and other public agency PAOs.

Source: FEMA, *http://www.fema.gov/pdf/emergency/nrf/nrf-core.pdf*.

FIELD-LEVEL ORGANIZATIONAL STRUCTURES: JFO SECTIONS

The role of each JFO section is as follows:

Operations Section. The Operations Section coordinates operational support to on-scene incident management efforts. Branches may be added or deleted as required, depending on the nature of the incident. The Operations Section also is responsible for coordination with other federal command posts that may be established to support incident management activities. The Operations Section may include the following elements:

- The **Response and Recovery Operations Branch** coordinates the request and delivery of federal assistance and support from various special teams. This branch is composed of four groups: Emergency Services, Human Services, Infrastructure Support, and Community Recovery and Mitigation.
- The **Law Enforcement Investigative Operations Branch/Joint Operations Center (JOC)** is established by the Senior Federal Law Enforcement Official (SFLEO) (e.g., the FBI SAC during terrorist incidents) to coordinate and direct law enforcement and criminal investigation activities related to a terrorist incident. The JOC branch ensures management and coordination of federal, state, local, and tribal investigative/law enforcement activities. The emphasis of the JOC is on prevention as well as intelligence collection, investigation, and prosecution of a criminal act. This emphasis includes managing unique tactical issues inherent to a crisis situation (e.g., a hostage situation or terrorist threat).
- For National Special Security Events (NSSEs), a third branch, the **Security Operations Branch, or Multi-agency Command Center (MACC)**, may be added to coordinate protection and site security efforts. In these situations, the Operations Section Chief is designated by mutual agreement of the JFO Coordination Group based on the agency with greatest jurisdictional involvement and statutory authority for the current incident priorities. The agency providing the Operations Section Chief may change over time as incident priorities change.

Planning Section. The Planning Section provides current information to the JFO Coordination Group to ensure situational awareness, determine cascading effects, identify national implications, and determine specific areas of interest requiring long-term attention. The Planning Section also provides technical and scientific expertise. The Planning Section is composed of the following units: Situation, Resources, Documentation, Technical Specialists, and Demobilization. The Planning Section may also include an Information and Intelligence Unit (if not assigned elsewhere) and an HSOC representative who aids in the development of reports for the HSOC and IIMG.

Logistics Section. The Logistics Section coordinates logistics support that includes the following:

- Control and accountability for federal supplies and equipment
- Resource ordering
- Delivery of equipment, supplies, and services to the JFO and other field locations
- Facility location, setup, space management, building services, and general facility operations
- Transportation coordination and fleet management services
- Information and technology systems services, administrative services such as mail management and reproduction, and customer assistance

The Logistics Section may include Coordination and Planning, Resource Management, Supply, and Information Services Branches.

Finance and Administration Section (Comptroller). The Finance and Administration Section is responsible for the financial management, monitoring, and tracking of all federal costs relating to the incident and the functioning of the JFO while adhering to all federal laws, acts, and regulations. The position of the financial and administration chief will be held exclusively by a comptroller who serves as the senior financial advisor to the team leader (e.g., FCO) and represents the coordinating agency's chief financial officer (CFO) as prescribed by the CFO Act of 1990.

Source: FEMA, *http://www.fema.gov/pdf/emergency/nrf/nrf-core.pdf*

FEMA maintains several response teams that can be deployed to assist in response to major disasters including the Emergency Response Team National (ERT-N), the Regional Emergency Response Team (ERT-A), and Incident Management Assistance Teams (IMATs). Brief descriptions of each of these teams are presented in the box below.

FINAL RESPONSE TEAMS

The ERT-N is composed of a small number of highly qualified and experienced professionals who serve as the initial disaster management team providing assistance to an impacted region to coordinate the full range of federal response and recovery operations in large, complex events, WMD/terrorist events, or incidents of national significance. Currently there are two ERT-Ns that are deployed at the discretion of the response division director in coordination with the regional director of the impacted region. Each ERT-N team consists of 32 members.

The ERT-N establishes operations at the Joint Field Office (JFO). Regional personnel are integrated with the ERT-N to form one unified ERT. ERT-As are disaster response teams located in each of FEMA's ten regions that can be deployed in the early phases of an incident to work directly with states to assess disaster impact, gain situational awareness, help coordinate the disaster response, and respond to specific requests for state and local assistance. The ERT-As consist of approximately 25 individuals from the FEMA regions who also have day-to-day responsibilities beyond their team assignments and representatives from the Emergency Support Function departments and agencies. The ERT-A initially establishes its presence in a state Emergency Operations Center and later helps to staff the Joint Field Office (JFO) to support the disaster response. The ERT-As deploy with basic communications capabilities, including cell phones, wireless laptop computers, and a limited number of satellite cell phones. As needed, they can also be supported by FEMA's Mobile Emergency Response Support (MERS) detachments and their emergency communications capabilities.

FEMA has also developed a next generation of rapidly deployable emergency response teams called Incident Management Assistance Teams (IMATs). The IMATs are full-time, rapid-response teams with dedicated staff able to deploy within two hours and arrive at an incident within 12 hours to support the local incident commander. The teams support the initial establishment of a unified command and provide situational awareness for federal and state decision makers crucial to determining the level and type of immediate federal support that may be required.

IMATs were developed from an expanded concept of the former Emergency Response Teams (ERTs) at the national and regional levels (see the Hurricane Floyd case study for an understanding of how the former ERTs were utilized). The plan is to eventually have three National IMATs with 26 full-time staff each, and 10 regional IMATs staffed with 15 full-time personnel each. Currently two national IMATs and three regional IMATs are operational; a fourth, the region VII IMAT, will be operational later this year.

IMATs provide a forward federal presence to facilitate the management of the national response to catastrophic incidents. The primary mission of a FEMA IMAT is to rapidly deploy to an incident or incident-threatened venue, provide leadership in the identification and provision of federal assistance, and coordinate and integrate interjurisdictional response in support of an affected state or territory.

IMATs are led by experienced, senior-level emergency managers and staffed with a core of permanent full-time employees, unlike FEMA's Emergency Response Teams (ERTs), which were staffed on a collateral duty basis. When not deployed, the teams are responsible for building and maintaining a close working relationship with regional, state, tribal, and local emergency management officials, federal partners, and the private sector to support planning, training, exercising, and other activities in preparation for disaster response.

Source: FEMA, *http://www.fema.gov/pdf/hazard/hurricane/2008/gustav/regional_ert_factsheet2008.pdf*; *http://www.fema.gov/media/fact_sheets/ert-n.shtm*; *http://www.fema.gov/pdf/hazard/hurricane/2009/imat_ factsheet.pdf*.

CASE STUDY: HURRICANE FLOYD

On September 14, 1999, FEMA began mobilizing federal resources in preparation for possible landfall by Hurricane Floyd. Although, in previous years, states had to wait for the disaster to strike before obtaining FEMA assistance, in the case of Hurricane Floyd, FEMA took a proactive stance by activating Emergency Response Teams, allocating funds to local communities for law enforcement, and working with the Tropical Predication Center to monitor Hurricane Floyd's track. The ROC was put into action three days before the actual landfall of Hurricane Floyd.

On September 16, 1999, Hurricane Floyd made landfall near Cape Fear, North Carolina. The Category 2 hurricane had sustained winds of 110 miles per hour, but unlike Hurricane Andrew, the local first responders in coordination with FEMA were better prepared to handle this disaster. Emergency materials, generators, sheeting, tarps, bottled water, blankets, and clothing were identified and available for immediate delivery. Disaster Medical Assistance Teams (DMATs) had been placed on alert to provide medical services. Public works, including engineers, electricians, phone company employees, and public work personnel also were prepared for deployment to the area. Although forecasters thought that Floyd would hit Florida or Georgia, FEMA officials were mobile as the hurricane continued to track farther north. On September 15, 1999, President Clinton signed emergency declarations for North and South Carolina to fund law enforcement officials to help evacuate the areas. More than 2,100 employees were prepared to respond to the disaster. FEMA Urban Search and Rescue Teams from Indiana, Maryland, and Pennsylvania were activated. Upon the hurricane reaching land, FEMA's Mobile Emergency Response System (MERS) provided communication support to the affected communities.

FEMA's proactive response before landfall ensured that those affected by the hurricane would have the needed materials and services to help in the recovery phase. While the rain was still falling, FEMA established their toll-free service line. Within days, people were receiving financial aid to help them through the disaster. Although FEMA took some flack from certain areas of North Carolina and Virginia because of the long-lasting flooding, lives were saved and damage was reduced because of FEMA's and the 27 agencies' responses to the hurricane.

INCIDENT MANAGEMENT ACTIONS

NOTIFICATION AND ASSESSMENT
Federal, state, local, tribal, private sector, and nongovernmental organizations report threats, incidents, and potential incidents using established communications and reporting channels. The Homeland Security Operations Center (HSOC) receives threat and operational information regarding incidents or potential incidents and makes an initial determination to initiate the coordination of federal information-sharing and incident management activities. When notified of a threat or an incident with possible national-level implications, the HSOC assesses the situation and notifies the secretary of Homeland Security accordingly.

REPORTING
Federal, state, tribal, private sector, and nongovernmental Emergency Operations Centers (EOCs) report incident information to the HSOC. In most situations, incident information will be reported using existing mechanisms to state or federal operations centers, which in turn will report the information to the HSOC. Information regarding potential terrorist threats normally is reported initially to a local or regional Joint Terrorism Task Force (JTTF) and, subsequently, from the FBI Strategic Information and Operations Center (SIOC) to the HSOC if the FBI deems the threat to be credible.

ACTIVATION

For actual or potential Incidents of National Significance, the HSOC reports the situation to the secretary of Homeland Security and/or senior staff as delegated by the secretary, who then determines the need to activate components of the NRP to conduct further assessment of the situation, initiate interagency coordination, share information with affected jurisdictions, and/or initiate deployment of resources. Concurrently, the secretary also makes a determination of whether or not an event meets the criteria established for a potential or actual Incident of National Significance as defined in the NRP. When the secretary declares an Incident of National Significance, federal departments and agencies are notified by the HSOC (as operational security considerations permit) and may be called upon to staff the Interagency Incident Management Group (IIMG) and National Response Coordination Center (NRCC). The affected state(s) and tribes also are notified by the HSOC using appropriate operational security protocols. In the preincident mode, such notification may be conducted discreetly, on a need-to-know basis, to preserve the operational security and confidentiality of certain law enforcement and investigative operations. The NRCC and RRCC deploy, track, and provide incident-related information until the JFO is established.

RESPONSE

Once an incident occurs, the priority shifts to immediate and short-term response activities to preserve life, property, the environment, and the social, economic, and political structure of the community. Actions also are taken to prevent and protect against other potential threats. Examples of response actions include immediate law enforcement, fire, and emergency medical service actions; mass care, public health, and medical services; emergency restoration of critical infrastructure; control of environmental contamination; and responder health and safety protection. During the response to a terrorist event, law enforcement actions to collect and preserve evidence and to apprehend perpetrators are critical. These actions take place simultaneously with the response operations necessary to save lives and protect property.

RECOVERY

Recovery involves actions needed to help individuals and communities return to normal when feasible. The JFO is the central coordination point among federal, state, local, and tribal agencies and voluntary organizations for delivering recovery assistance programs. Long-term environmental recovery may include cleanup and restoration of public facilities, businesses, and residences; reestablishment of habitats and prevention of subsequent damage to natural resources; protection of cultural or archeological sites; and protection of natural, cultural, and historical resources from intentional damage during other recovery operations.

MITIGATION

Hazard mitigation involves reducing or eliminating long-term risk to people and property from hazards and their side effects. The JFO's Community Recovery and Mitigation Branch is responsible for coordinating the delivery of all mitigation programs within the affected area, including hazard mitigation for:

- Grant programs for loss reduction measures (if available)
- Delivery of loss-reduction building-science expertise

- Coordination of federal flood insurance operations
- Community education and outreach necessary to foster loss reduction

DEMOBILIZATION

When a centralized federal coordination presence is no longer required in the affected area, the JFO Coordination Group implements the demobilization plan to transfer responsibilities and close out the JFO. After the JFO closes, long-term recovery program management and monitoring transition to individual agencies' regional offices and/or headquarters, as appropriate.

REMEDIAL ACTIONS AND AFTER-ACTION REPORTS

DHS formally convenes interagency meetings called *hotwashes* to identify critical issues requiring headquarters-level attention, lessons learned, and best practices associated with the federal response to Incidents of National Significance. Hotwashes typically are conducted at major transition points over the course of incident management operations and should include state, local, and tribal participation. Identified issues are validated and promptly assigned to appropriate organizations for remediation. Following an incident, the JFO Coordination Group submits an after-action report to DHS headquarters detailing operational successes, problems, and key issues affecting incident management. The report includes appropriate feedback from all federal, state, local, tribal, nongovernmental, and private sector partners participating in the incident.

Source: FEMA Emergency Management Institute.

Key Federal Response Officials

Key senior federal officials that typically may be deployed with a federal incident management team include the following.

Principal Federal Official (PFO)

By law and by presidential directive, the secretary of Homeland Security is the principal federal official responsible for coordination of all domestic incidents requiring multiagency federal response. The secretary may elect to designate a single individual to serve as his or her primary representative to ensure consistency of federal support as well as the overall effectiveness of the Federal incident management. When appointed, such an individual serves in the field as the PFO for the incident. Congress has provided that, notwithstanding the general prohibition on appointing a PFO for Stafford Act incidents, "there may be instances in which FEMA should not be the lead agency in charge of the response, such as a pandemic outbreak or an Olympic event." In such cases, the secretary may assign a PFO. Congress also recognized that there may be "major non–Stafford Act responses that may include a Stafford Act component." In such cases, also, the secretary may assign a PFO. The secretary will only appoint a PFO for catastrophic or unusually complex incidents that require extraordinary coordination. When appointed, the PFO interfaces with federal, state, tribal, and local jurisdictional officials regarding the overall federal incident management strategy and acts as the primary federal spokesperson for coordinated media and public communications. The PFO serves as a member of the Unified Coordination Group and provides a primary point of contact and situational awareness locally for the secretary of Homeland Security. A PFO is a senior federal official with proven management experience and strong leadership capabilities. The PFO deploys with a small, highly trained mobile support staff. Both the PFO and support staff undergo specific training prior to appointment to their respective positions. Once formally designated for an ongoing incident, a PFO relinquishes the conduct of all previous duties to focus exclusively on his or her incident management responsibilities. The same individual will *not* serve as the principal federal official and the federal coordinating officer (see following) at the same time for the same incident. When both positions are assigned, the FCO will have responsibility for administering Stafford Act authorities, as described below. The secretary is not restricted to DHS officials when selecting a PFO.

The PFO does not direct or replace the incident command structure established at the incident, nor does the PFO have directive authority over a federal coordinating officer, a senior federal law enforcement official, a DOD Joint Task Force commander, or any other federal or state official. Other federal incident management officials retain their authorities as defined in existing statutes and directives. Rather, the PFO promotes collaboration and, as possible, resolves any federal interagency conflict that may arise. The PFO identifies and presents to the secretary of Homeland Security any policy issues that require resolution.

Federal Coordinating Officer (FCO)

For Stafford Act incidents (i.e., emergencies or major disasters), upon the recommendation of the FEMA administrator and the secretary of Homeland Security, the president appoints an FCO. The FCO is a senior FEMA official trained, certified, and well experienced in emergency management, and specifically appointed to coordinate federal support in the response to and recovery from emergencies and major disasters. The FCO executes Stafford Act authorities, including commitment of FEMA resources and the mission assignment of other federal departments or agencies. If a major disaster or emergency declaration covers a geographic area that spans all or parts of more than one state, the president may decide to appoint a single FCO for the entire incident, with other individuals as needed serving as deputy FCOs.

In all cases, the FCO represents the FEMA administrator in the field to discharge all FEMA responsibilities for the response and recovery efforts under way. For Stafford Act events, the FCO is the primary federal representative with whom the SCO and other state, tribal, and local response officials interface to determine the most urgent needs and set objectives for an effective response in collaboration with the Unified Coordination Group.

In Stafford Act incidents, the FCO is the focal point of coordination within the Unified Coordination Group, ensuring overall integration of federal emergency management, resource allocation, and seamless integration of federal activities in support of, and in coordination with, state, tribal, and local requirements. Some FCOs are given additional, specialized training regarding unusually complex incidents. For example, one may be further trained for catastrophic earthquake response, whereas another might cultivate unique skills for response related to weapons of mass destruction or pandemic influenza.

Predesignated PFOs and FCOs

In certain scenarios, the secretary of Homeland Security may predesignate a PFO and/or an FCO. Such predesignation can focus on specified geographic areas or be based on specific potential threats, or a combination of both. For example, beginning in 2007, the secretary predesignated a national PFO and five regional PFOs together with a national FCO and regional FCOs, who will serve in the event of a nationwide outbreak of pandemic influenza or other similar nationwide biological event. Predesignation of these leadership teams is allowing for sustained advance planning conducted with state, tribal, and local leaders.

Federal Resource Coordinator (FRC)

In non–Stafford Act situations, when a federal department or agency acting under its own authority has requested the assistance of the secretary of Homeland Security to obtain support from other federal departments and agencies, DHS may designate an FRC. In these situations, the FRC coordinates support through interagency agreements and memorandums of understanding. Relying on the same skill set, DHS may select the FRC from the FCO cadre or other personnel with equivalent knowledge, skills, and abilities. The FRC is responsible for coordinating timely delivery of resources to the requesting agency.

Defense Coordinating Officer (DCO)

The DOD has appointed ten DCOs and assigned one to each FEMA region. If requested and approved, the DCO serves as the DOD's single point of contact at the JFO for requesting assistance from the DOD. With few exceptions, requests for Defense Support of Civil Authorities (DSCA) originating at the JFO are coordinated with and processed through the DCO. The DCO may have a Defense Coordinating Element consisting of a staff and military liaison officers to facilitate coordination and support to activated ESFs.

Specific responsibilities of the DCO (subject to modification based on the situation) include processing requirements for military support, forwarding mission assignments to the appropriate military organizations through DOD-designated channels, and assigning military liaisons, as appropriate, to activated ESFs.

Senior Federal Law Enforcement Official (SFLEO)

The SFLEO is an official appointed by the attorney general during an incident requiring a coordinated federal response to coordinate all law enforcement, public safety, and security operations with intelligence or investigative law enforcement operations directly related to the incident. The SFLEO is a member of the Unified Coordination Group and, as such, is responsible to ensure that allocation of law enforcement requirements and resource allocations are coordinated as appropriate with all other members of the Group. In the event of a terrorist incident, the SFLEO will normally be a senior FBI official who has coordinating authority over all law enforcement activities related to the incident, both those falling within the attorney general's explicit authority as recognized in HSPD-5 and those otherwise directly related to the incident itself.

Joint Task Force (JTF) Commander

Based on the complexity and type of incident, and the anticipated level of DOD resource involvement, the DOD may elect to designate a JTF to command federal (Title 10) military activities in support of the incident objectives. If a JTF is established, consistent with operational requirements, its command and control element will be colocated with the senior on-scene leadership at the JFO to ensure coordination and unity of effort. The colocation of the JTF command and control element does not replace the requirement for a DCO/Defense Coordinating Element as part of the JFO Unified Coordination staff. The DCO remains the DOD single point of contact in the JFO for requesting assistance from the DOD. The JTF commander exercises operational control of federal military personnel and most defense resources in a federal response. Some DOD entities, such as the U.S. Army Corps of Engineers, may respond under separate established authorities and do not provide support under the operational control of a JTF commander. Unless federalized, National Guard forces remain under the control of a state governor. Close coordination among federal military, other DOD entities, and National Guard forces in a response is critical.

Other Senior Officials

Based on the scope and nature of an incident, senior officials from other federal departments and agencies, state, tribal, or local governments, and the private sector or NGOs may participate in a Unified Coordination Group. Usually, the larger and more complex the incident, the greater the number of entities represented.

Other FEMA Response Resources

FEMA manages a cadre of nearly 4,000 temporary Disaster Assistance Employees (DAEs), who support FEMA response and recovery activities in the field in areas such as logistics, facility management, public affairs, community relations, and customer service (Figures 6-8 and 6-9). FEMA manages a mobile operations capability that provides communications and logistical support to state and local emergency officials.

FIGURE 6-8 San Diego, California, October 26, 2007. Northern California fire crews set fire backburn to stop the Poomacha fire from advancing westward. Currently the fires in Southern California have burned more than 355,000 acres.
FEMA photo/Andrea Booher.

FIGURE 6-9 Baytown, Texas, September 28, 2008. Members of the American Red Cross working side by side with the North Carolina Baptist Men Convention (in yellow shirts) to distribute meals to local residents recovering from Hurricane Ike. These mobile kitchens are capable of serving 70,000 meals per day.
Mike Moore/FEMA.

CRITICAL THINKING

- What are the strengths and weaknesses of the National Response Plan?
- Would disaster response be more efficient if the federal government had the authority to assume power over any disaster response, regardless of the ability of local response agencies? Why or why not?

FEMA'S MOBILE OPERATIONS CAPABILITY

Disasters may require resources beyond the capabilities of the local or state authorities. In response to regional requests for support, FEMA provides mobile telecommunications, operational support, life support, and power generation assets for the on-site management of disaster and all-hazard activities. This support is managed by the Response and Recovery Directorate's Mobile Operations Division (RR-MO).

The Mobile Operations Division has a small headquarters staff and five geographically dispersed Mobile Emergency Response Support (MERS) Detachments and the Mobile Air Transportable Telecommunications System (MATTS) to:

- Meet the needs of the government emergency managers in their efforts to save lives, protect property, and coordinate disaster and all-hazard operations.
- Provide prompt and rapid multimedia communications, information processing, logistics, and operational support to federal, state, and local agencies during catastrophic emergencies and disasters for government response and recovery operations.

The MERS and MATTS support the Disaster Field Facilities. They support the federal, state, and local responders—not the disaster victims.

AVAILABLE SUPPORT

Each of the MERS Detachments can concurrently support a large Disaster Field Office and multiple field operating sites within the disaster area. MERS is equipped with self-sustaining telecommunications, logistics, and operations support elements that can be driven or airlifted to the disaster location. MATTS and some of the MERS assets can be airlifted by C-130 military cargo aircraft.

The MERS and MATTS are available for immediate deployment. As required, equipment and personnel will deploy promptly and provide:

- Multimedia communications and information processing support, especially for the Communications Section, Emergency Support Function (ESF) #2 of the Federal Response Plan (FRP)
- Operational support, especially for the Information and Planning Section, ESF #5 of the FRP
- Liaison to the Federal Coordinating Officer (FCO)
- Logistics and life support for emergency responders
- Automated information and decision support capability
- Security (facility, equipment, and personnel) management and consultation

Most equipment is preloaded or installed on heavy-duty, multiwheel drive trucks. Some equipment is installed in transit cases.

Source: FEMA, *www.fema.gov.*

The Emergency Management Assistance Compact (EMAC)

The Emergency Management Assistance Compact (EMAC) was established in 1996 (Figure 6-10). According to the EMAC website:

> *EMAC is the first national disaster–relief compact since the Civil Defense and Disaster Compact of 1950 to be ratified by Congress. Since its ratification and sign-ing into law in 1996 (Public Law 104-321), 50 states, the District of Columbia, Puerto Rico, Guam, and the U.S. Virgin Islands have enacted legislation to become EMAC members. The strength of EMAC and the quality that distinguishes it from other plans and compacts lie in its governance structure; its relationship with federal orga-nizations, states, counties, territories, and regions; and the ability to move just about any resource one state has to assist another state, including medical resources.*

EMAC offers the following benefits:

- EMAC assistance may be more readily available than other resources.
- EMAC allows for a quick response to disasters using the unique human resources and expertise possessed by member states.

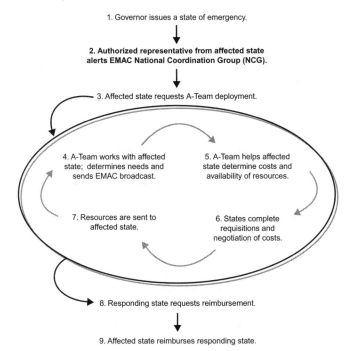

1. Governor issues a state of emergency.

2. **Authorized representative from affected state alerts EMAC National Coordination Group (NCG).**

3. Affected state requests A-Team deployment.

4. A-Team works with affected state; determines needs and sends EMAC broadcast.

5. A-Team helps affected state determine costs and availability of resources.

7. Resources are sent to affected state.

6. States complete requisitions and negotiation of costs.

8. Responding state requests reimbursement.

9. Affected state reimburses responding state.

FIGURE 6-10 The EMAC process flow. Reprinted courtesy of *www.emacweb.org*.

- EMAC offers state-to-state assistance during governor-declared states of emergency and a responsive and straightforward system for states to send personnel and equipment to help disaster relief efforts in other states. When resources are overwhelmed, EMAC helps to fill the shortfalls.
- EMAC establishes a firm legal foundation: Once the conditions for providing assistance to a requesting state have been set, the terms constitute a legally binding contractual agreement that makes affected states responsible for reimbursement. Responding states can rest assured that sending aid will not be a financial or legal burden, and personnel sent are protected under workers' compensation and liability provisions. The EMAC legislation solves the problems of liability and responsibilities of cost and allows for credentials to be honored across state lines.
- EMAC provides fast and flexible assistance: EMAC allows states to ask for whatever assistance they need for any type of emergency, from earthquakes to acts of terrorism. EMAC's simple procedures help states dispense with bureaucratic wrangling.
- EMAC can move resources such as medical provisions that other compacts cannot.

Conclusion

Responding to disaster events is the most visible activity that any federal, state, or local emergency management agency conducts. The politicians, the media, and the general public rate the success of an emergency management organization by how well it functions in the response phase of a disaster. A successful disaster response at any level of government requires a strong command and control system, clear lines of communication, and coordination of numerous agencies from multiple jurisdictions. Local first responders—fire, police, and emergency medical technicians—are on the scene first. Local and state emergency managers coordinate resources and assess the damage and the capacity of their jurisdictions to respond effectively. For major disaster events, a presidential disaster declaration activates the NRP that delivers the full resources of the federal government in support of local and state authorities.

Currently, the nation's response to major disasters is guided by the National Response Framework (NRF), which defines the roles and responsibilities of federal, state, and local government, voluntary agencies, and the private sector and provides guidance on how these groups plan and work together in a disaster response. One element that is currently missing in the nation's response capability is an agreement similar to the Federal Response Plan (FRP) and the National Response Plan (NRP) that preceded the NRF that identifies and empowers a single federal agency responsible for coordinating the efforts of federal government in responding to a major disaster in support of state and local partners. FEMA was created in 1979 in response to the demand made by state emergency management directors and their governors that the federal government establish a single agency to coordinate the federal response. The NRF does not designate a single federal agency that has the authority to coordinate the activities of all federal departments and agencies as FEMA did as part of the FRP and the NRP. This missing piece in the current federal response is of concern to its state and local partners and must be addressed if the federal response is to be timely and effective in the future.

Important Terms

Emergency management/response personnel
Emergency Operations Plan
Emergency Support Function
First responders
Incident Command System
Incident commander
National Incident Management System
National Response Framework
Unified command

Self-Check Questions

1. How is the National Guard deployed to assist in response to a disaster?
2. What is the role of first responders when a routine "minor disaster" occurs in a local community?
3. What drives the actions of local first responders?
4. Where can you find a detailed description of the roles and responsibilities of first responders in your community?
5. Who is usually in charge of developing and maintaining the community emergency plan?
6. Where does the emergency management office reside at the state level? Give three examples.
7. What is the principal source of funding for state emergency management offices?
8. What kinds of things do volunteer organizations provide for victims in the aftermath of a disaster?
9. What is the Incident Command System, and why was it originally developed?
10. What are the five major management systems within the Incident Command System?
11. What is the role of the incident commander?
12. At whose discretion is the decision to make a disaster declaration?
13. What is the National Response Framework?
14. How does the National Response Framework compare to its predecessors, the National Response Plan and the Federal Response Plan?
15. What are some of the reasons why communications among responding agencies is crucial?

Out-of-Class Exercises

1. Contact your state National Guard office. Find out what kinds of resources they can offer to assist local communities in the event of a disaster and what kind of training and exercises they conduct to prepare their members for disaster response.
2. Make a list of the primary differences between the command and control, and the coordination response models.
3. Contact your local ham radio organization and take a certification course. Use your certification to get involved in local response. You can get more information from the Amateur Radio Relay League (ARES; *http://www.arrl.org/*).
4. Take a Community Emergency Response Team (CERT) course. To find a course near you, visit the Citizen Corps CERT website at *https://www.citizencorps.gov/cert/*.

7

The Disciplines of Emergency
Management: Recovery

What You'll Learn

- The role of the federal government in disaster recovery operations
- The recovery programs administered by FEMA to fuel individual and community recovery operations
- How federal agencies other than FEMA contribute to disaster recovery
- The role of national voluntary relief organizations
- Tools that are available for community recovery planning
- The role of the National Disaster Recovery Framework
- How to develop a Community Long-Term Recovery Plan

Introduction

A theoretical debate has been raging over when the response function ends and the recovery function begins. For this book, the *response function* is classified as the immediate actions to save lives, protect property, and meet basic human needs. The recovery function is not so easily classified. This function often begins in the initial hours and days following a disaster event and can continue for months and, in some cases, years, depending on the severity of the event (Figure 7-1).

Unlike the response function, where all of the efforts have a singular focus, the recovery function or process is characterized by a complex set of issues and decisions that must be made by individuals and communities. Recovery involves decisions and actions relative to rebuilding homes, replacing property, resuming employment, restoring businesses, and permanently repairing and rebuilding infrastructure. The recovery process requires balancing the more immediate need to return the community to normalcy with the longer-term goal of reducing future vulnerability. The recovery process can provide individuals and communities with opportunities to become more economically secure and improve the overall safety and quality of life.

Because the recovery function has such long-lasting effects and usually high costs, the participants in the process are numerous. They include all levels of government, the business community, political leadership, community activists, and individuals. Each of these groups plays a role in determining how the recovery will progress. Some of these roles are regulatory, such as application of state or local building ordinances, and some, such as

FIGURE 7-1 New Orleans, Louisiana, September 18, 2005. The city skyline looks over a neighborhood south of the city still flooded after three weeks. Recovering from Hurricane Katrina would prove to be an arduous process. Win Henderson / FEMA.

the insurance industry, provide financial support. The goal of an effective recovery is to bring all the players together to plan, finance, and implement a recovery strategy that will rebuild the disaster-affected area safer and more secure as quickly as possible.

As noted in Chapter 4, the precipitating event for an area affected by a disaster is the presidential declaration of disaster under the Stafford Act. Recovery activities begin immediately after a presidential declaration as the agencies of the federal government collaborate with the state in the affected area in coordinating the implementation of recovery programs and the delivery of recovery services.

Historically, FEMA has obligated an average of $2.88 billion on public assistance projects annually for major disaster declarations, with an average of $58 million per major disaster declaration annually. In addition, FEMA has historically obligated over $153 million in public assistance for emergency declarations annually, averaging nearly $11 million per emergency declaration.

In the period from 1990 to 1999, FEMA spent more than $25.4 billion for declared disasters and emergencies compared to $3.9 billion in current dollars for 1980–1989. For the 1990–1999 period, more than $6.3 billion was provided in grants for temporary housing, home repairs, and other disaster-related needs for individuals and families. An additional $14.8 billion went to states and local governments for cleanup and restoration projects, including more than $1.37 billion for mission-assigned work undertaken by other federal agencies. In the 1990s, a total of 88 declarations were issued for hurricanes and typhoons, for which FEMA obligated more than $7.78 billion for disaster costs. The most costly to FEMA was Hurricane Georges in 1998, followed closely by Hurricane Andrew in 1992.

CASE STUDY: NEW ORLEANS FOUR YEARS AFTER HURRICANE KATRINA (BROOKINGS INSTITUTION KATRINA INDEX)

Amy Liu and Allison Plyer

The nation's deepening economic recession has produced dissolution and despair across the country as many communities grapple with the social and economic ramifications of massive layoffs, prolonged unemployment, shuttered businesses, and home foreclosures. By contrast, rebuilding from the woes caused by Hurricane Katrina has helped cushion greater New Orleans from the ravages of the downturn.

As New Orleans ends its fourth year since the hurricane and levee failures, the region has been buoyed by postdisaster recovery efforts and its fortunate industry mix. Specifically, this year's special anniversary edition of the New Orleans Index finds that:

- The New Orleans economy is weathering the recession relatively well due in part to its industry composition. The New Orleans metro area lost 0.9 percent of its jobs since last June, compared to the 4.1 percent lost nationally. The industries hardest hit—manufacturing and construction—comprise relatively small shares of the New Orleans economy and since last June have shed few jobs. The four largest sectors of the region's economy—trade and transportation, government, leisure and hospitality, and education and health services—either stagnated or added jobs. The New Orleans metro area's unemployment rate rose to 7.3 percent while it climbed to 9.5 percent for the nation.
- Ongoing rebuilding activities are attracting people, jobs, and investments, further shoring up the greater New Orleans economy. New Orleans added more than 8,500 households (actively receiving mail) in the past year, the biggest one-year expansion since 2007, reflecting a mix of new and returning residents. While home rebuilding has slowed dramatically since 2007, postdisaster infrastructure investments in the levee system, schools, police stations, and other public facilities have continued apace. Since July 2008, FEMA has paid over $800 million for infrastructure repair projects across the five-parish area. In the city of New Orleans, 94 facilities and public works projects were completed as of April 2009, and 113 more were under construction.[1]
- Yet, New Orleans is not immune from the economic crisis. Like many metropolitan areas, the housing market has stalled, with home sales down 39 percent and new construction down 48 percent. The slowdown in consumer spending has contributed to a plunge in city sales tax revenues with 21 percent fewer receipts from general sales, motel/hotel stays, and motor vehicle purchases in April and 6 percent fewer receipts in May compared to the previous year.
- Further, massive blight, affordable housing for low-income workers, and significant flood risk remain the area's major challenges. While there are fewer unoccupied residences in

---

[1]The primary for the 2010 mayoral race is on February 6, with a runoff election on April 22. Mayor Ray Nagin is not eligible due to term limits.

Orleans, St. Bernard and Jefferson parishes this year, the scale of blight remains high—65,888, 14,372, and 11,516 residences, respectively—posing significant challenges for local governments. Steep rent increases have abated, but at 40 percent higher than pre-Katrina, rents remain out of reach for many critical workers. Typical rent for an efficiency apartment is $733 per month, unaffordable for food preparation, health care support, and retail sales workers. Finally, a timeline recently released by the Army Corps of Engineers indicates that they are behind schedule in completing the Hurricane and Storm Damage Risk Reduction System by 2011. While the levee system will be improved when finished, additional protective measures and land-use provisions will be necessary to protect the city from Katrina-strength storms.[2]

Residents and leaders are eager to get beyond "disaster recovery" to implement bold plans for creating a sustainable, inclusive, and prosperous city and region. Locally, key moves are creating the foundation for transformation to meet residents' long-term aspirations. Last November, New Orleans voters approved two important amendments to the city charter. The first gave the city's master plan teeth by requiring all zoning and land-use requirements to conform, providing predictability, market confidence for development, and a more transparent and organized process for public participation. The second measure provided a dedicated revenue source to the newly created Inspector General's office, giving the office steady resources necessary for accountability in the wake of pervasive public mistrust, waste, and fraud. And recently, the City Council approved funds for a newly created, quasi-public New Orleans Economic Development Corporation to lead the city's economic growth activities and provide a measure of continuity across mayoral administrations.

The Obama administration and the next mayor of New Orleans must work together with the state to build on this current progress to help the city truly reinvent itself.[3] The administration has many opportunities to lead a robust interagency effort that applies new policy initiatives that leverage the economic assets of New Orleans—in innovation, human capital, infrastructure, and quality neighborhoods. For instance, to invest in people and innovation, the administration could help state and local leaders resolve the future of Charity Hospital and facilitate the delivery of quality, affordable health care for all residents while making a critical investment in the growth of its health care cluster. To maximize interagency efforts, the Office of Gulf Coast Rebuilding's leadership, institutional knowledge, and established partnerships must be retained and elevated within the White House.[4] In addition, state and local leaders could partner with Congress and the Obama administration to take advantage of new federal opportunities—linking school reform with neighborhood revitalization, investing in green industries (including coastal restoration and protection), and bolstering ports, major transportation, and freight corridors.

With strong partnerships, local leadership, and leveraged assets, New Orleans could emerge as a model of resilience for metro areas recovering from natural catastrophes or major economic shocks, as those triggered by this recession.

Sources: City of New Orleans: Monthly Progress Report, Recovery Projects, April 2009. Available at *http://neworleans.iprojweb.com/doc/monthlyreport_april2009.pdf.*

U.S. Army Corps of Engineers, "Hurricane & Storm Damage Risk Reduction System Contract Information." Available at *www.mvn.usace.army.mil/hps/hps_contract_info.aspx*.
National Research Council, "The New Orleans Hurricane Protection System: Assessing Pre-Katrina Vulnerability and Improving Mitigation and Preparedness." Available at *www.nap.edu/catalog .php?record_id=12647*.
Source: Brookings Institution, *https://gnocdc.s3.amazonaws.com/NOLAIndex/NOLAIndex.pdf*

CASE STUDY: LONG-TERM RECOVERY ACTION PLAN FOR HURRICANE GEORGES

On September 21, 1998, Hurricane Georges, sustaining winds as high as 150 miles per hour, struck Puerto Rico and dumped more than two feet of rain on the island. More than 100,000 residences were damaged or destroyed, and 31,500 people were forced to seek refuge in shelters. This was the worst natural disaster to hit Puerto Rico in 70 years, and a major disaster was declared for all 78 of Puerto Rico's municipalities. In response to the severity and scope of the destruction, the president activated the Long-Term Recovery Task Force composed of 15 federal departments, agencies, and offices, and headed by then FEMA director James Lee Witt. The president directed the group to develop an action plan to facilitate the coordination and delivery of federal recovery assistance to Puerto Rico.

The purpose of the Task Force is to coordinate and target the diverse disaster programs of more than a dozen federal agencies to ensure the greatest level of effective federal support. The Task Force worked in collaboration with representatives of the government of Puerto Rico to identify five long-term recovery priorities: mitigation, housing, economic revitalization and sustainability, energy, and transportation.

The government of Puerto Rico identified *mitigation* as one of the core elements of its vision for long-term recovery. Federal mitigation actions emphasized three areas: building codes, planning and coordination, and floodplain management. FEMA provided technical assistance for developing long-term strategies to reduce losses in future disasters and provided funding under the Hazard Mitigation Grant Program. The federal government also worked with Puerto Rico to acquire property and elevate structures in the floodplain. The U.S. Army Corp of Engineers worked with Puerto Rico to identify funding for and expedite construction of flood control projects.

Federal assistance for housing focused on repairing existing homes, addressing long-term shelter needs, replacing destroyed homes, restoring public housing, and providing technical assistance and training. FEMA provided funding assistance under the Disaster Housing Assistance program and the Individual and Family Grant program. Additional funding was provided through the SBA Home Disaster Loans and the USDA Rural Housing Service. HUD provided disaster funds through the Community Development Block Grant program. FEMA collaborated with Puerto Rico on improved housing design plans for low-income residents and also provided technical assistance and funding for the development of long-term sheltering options.

The federal government worked with Puerto Rico to put in place improvements to achieve the long-term benefits of economic revitalization and sustainability. In the agricultural sector this was accomplished through financial assistance for crop and physical losses, expanding agricultural insurance and coverage, and financial and technical assistance for conservation measures to reduce flooding and erosion. The USDA Risk Management Agency provided funding for crop loss insurance claims. The USDA Natural Resources Conservation Service provided financial and technical assistance to address flooding and soil erosion problems.

In the nonagricultural sector, the federal government provided community development planning assistance, supported small business recovery, encouraged new investment, proposed fiscal assistance, provided unemployment assistance, and promoted flood insurance for homeowners, renters, and businesses. HUD made available technical assistance for economic development strategies and financial packaging. The EDA provided a community planning grant to the University of Puerto Rico's Economic Development University Center and committed funds to Puerto Rico's Economic Development Bank for a revolving loan fund assistance program. The DOL provided funding to create temporary jobs to assist in the immediate and long-term cleanup and recovery efforts. The DOL also provided unemployment assistance.

Hurricane Georges caused 100 percent of the electrical service in Puerto Rico to be disrupted. Its failure crippled other basic services such as water and sewage treatment, telephone service, transportation, and local commerce. Federal assistance for the energy sector included providing resources for repairing electrical transmission and distribution lines and recommendations for design improvements, emergency generators, and assistance for developing a more reliable electrical system. The cost for repairing the island's electrical system was paid by a combination of Puerto Rico's self-insurance coverage and funding through FEMA's public assistance program. Electric utility workers, trucks, and equipment were flown to the island to assist local crews. Emergency generators were provided to keep critical facilities operational, and plans were developed to keep some of the generators in place to provide backup power during future disasters. The Department of Energy, FEMA, and Puerto Rico examined mitigation measures to improve the disaster resistance of the electrical system through enhanced generation/transmission relationships, better power line placement, and placing poles deeper in the ground.

Key transportation issues that were addressed included repairing damaged roads and bridges, developing a reliable power source for the Tren Urbano project, and dredging harbors. The Army Corps removed tons of debris from roadways, installed four temporary bridges, and provided financial assistance for critical dredging activities to maintain safe harbor channels. The FHA and FEMA provided financial assistance for rebuilding the island's damaged transportation system. Mitigation measures were incorporated into road and bridge repairs to reduce the risk of such severe damage in the future. The Federal Transit Authority and FEMA worked with the government of Puerto Rico to explore funding options to establish a reliable power source for the Tren Urbano, a San Juan metro-area mass transit system.

The governor of Puerto Rico, Pedro Rosselló, stated, "From the president on down, the federal government mobilized all of the resources at its disposal—even before the hurricane struck—and has earned the eternal gratitude of Puerto Rico's 3.9 million people for its role in helping us cope with this catastrophe. The scope of the response is illustrated by the fact that the president's Long-Term Recovery Task Force is rarely activated."

The most frequently declared disaster type is flooding resulting from severe storms, with more than $7.3 billion committed by FEMA for response and recovery costs. The most costly were the Midwest floods in 1993 and the Red River Valley floods in 1997. By December 2001, the disaster assistance provided by FEMA, the Small Business Administration (SBA), and the state of New York for the September 11, 2001, World Trade Center event had reached $700 million. Recovery costs for this disaster as of December 5, 2001, included the following:

- More than $344 million in public assistance funds to help New York City repair damaged infrastructure, restore critical services, and remove, transport, and sort debris.
- More than $196 million in individual assistance approved in the form of grants and loans. This assistance includes temporary disaster housing assistance, mortgage and rental assistance, disaster food stamps, individual and family grants, and SBA low-interest loans to homeowners and businesses.
- More than $151 million provided through other agencies, including the U.S. Army Corp of Engineers, Disaster Medical Assistance Teams from the Department of Health and Human Services, and FEMA's Urban Search-and-Rescue Task Force.

Hurricane Katrina has become the costliest disaster in U.S. history. The federal government expects to provide in excess of $100 billion in disaster relief to individuals and communities impacted by Katrina along the Gulf Coast and to communities around the country who have hosted the over 250,000 persons displaced by Katrina.

ADDITIONAL RESEARCH

The White House report on Katrina, "The Federal Response to Hurricane Katrina: Lessons Learned," estimated damage to housing at $67 billion; business property suffered $20 billion in damages, and government property an estimated $3 billion in damages (Townsend, 2006).

Without a doubt, the federal government plays the largest role in providing the technical and financial support for recovery. For that reason, this chapter focuses on the federal role in the disaster recovery function. It discusses the structure and the various programs available to assist individuals and communities in the postdisaster environment. The various national voluntary organizations that provide some assistance for recovery are briefly referenced, and several case studies (including one on Tropical Storm Allison) are included to demonstrate the different types of recovery.

CASE STUDY: TROPICAL STORM ALLISON AND UNIVERSITY OF HOUSTON O'QUINN LAW LIBRARY

Tropical Storm Allison formed on Wednesday evening, June 6, 2001, in the Gulf of Mexico, southeast of Galveston, Texas, and eventually exited the United States on Sunday night, June 17, after passing through Florida and proceeding up the East Coast. Allison proved to be the most destructive tropical storm in U.S. history, costing 43 lives and nearly $5 billion. The storm hit Houston, Texas, especially hard, dumping between 30 to 40 inches of rain and causing an estimated $1 billion in damage. On June 9, 2001, President Bush declared a major disaster for the state of Texas, with 28 counties eligible for public assistance. The University of Houston O'Quinn Law Library was flooded with 8 feet of water after the heavy rains from Tropical Storm Allison.

The lower floor of the library filled nearly to the 12-foot ceilings with a mixture of water, oil, asbestos, and other pollutants. The 35,000 square feet of space in the lower level were equal to nearly two floors of a typical downtown skyscraper. The metal shelves were destroyed, partly by the tremendous weight of waterlogged books and partly by being literally exploded as the wet books began swelling and exerting tremendous sideways pressure. The library lost between 200,000 and 500,000 books, and damages were estimated at $30 million.

Through the Public Assistance Program, FEMA approved $21.4 million for the replacement of 174,000 copies of law books and the microfiche storage collection. The funding approved by FEMA was for two separate projects: one project in the amount of $1,204,600 was for the microfiche collection, and the other project in the amount of $27,295,196 was for law book replacement. FEMA provided 75 percent of the cost, with the remaining 25 percent coming from local sources. "With the support of all our communities, and major assistance from FEMA, not only have we recovered, but we're putting in place an even stronger and more secure resource for our law center faculty and students as well as the community," said University of Houston president Arthur K. Smith.

As noted earlier, the decisions during recovery are predominantly driven by local government. At the end of the chapter is a listing of potential planning tools for the recovery process. This, along with a more encompassing discussion of the complexities of recovery, and roles and responsibilities of the various players in it, can be found in a book prepared for FEMA by the American Planning Association entitled *Planning for Post-Disaster Recovery and Reconstruction*.

The National Response Framework for Disaster Recovery Operations

Issued in 2005, the National Response Plan (NRP) outlined how the federal government implements the Robert T. Stafford Disaster Relief and Emergency Assistance Act, as amended, to assist state and local governments when a major disaster or emergency overwhelms their ability to respond effectively. The NRP describes the policies, planning assumptions, concept of operations, response and recovery actions, and responsibilities of 32 federal departments and agencies, including the American Red Cross, that guide federal operations following a presidential declaration of a major disaster or emergency.

The NRP is built on the template of the National Incident Management System (NIMS), which provides a consistent doctrinal framework for incident management at all jurisdictional levels, regardless of the cause, size, or complexity of the incident. The activation of the NRP and its coordinating structures and protocols—either partially or fully—for specific Incidents of National Significance provides mechanisms for the coordination and implementation of a wide variety of incident management and emergency assistance activities. Included in these activities are federal support to state, local, and tribal authorities; interaction with nongovernmental, private donor, and private sector organizations; and the coordinated, direct exercise of federal authorities, when appropriate.

In January 2008, the National Response Framework (NRF) was published, and it replaced the National Response Plan (NRP) as the guide for how all responding parties (government, private sector, and voluntary agencies) work together in responding to a major disaster. According to FEMA, "The National Response Framework presents the guiding principles that enable all response partners to prepare for and provide a unified national response to disasters and emergencies—from the smallest incident to the largest catastrophe. This important document establishes a comprehensive, national, all-hazards approach to domestic incident response. The Framework defines the key principles, roles, and structures that organize the way we respond as a Nation. It describes how communities, tribes, states, the federal government, and private sector and nongovernmental partners apply these principles for a coordinated, effective national response. It also identifies special circumstances where the federal government exercises a larger role, including incidents where federal interests are involved and catastrophic incidents where a state would require significant support. The Framework enables first responders, decision makers, and supporting entities to provide a unified national response." The guidance included in the NRF concerning recovery is presented in the box below.

RECOVERY

Once immediate lifesaving activities are complete, the focus shifts to assisting individuals, households, critical infrastructure, and businesses in meeting basic needs and returning to self-sufficiency. Even as the immediate imperatives for response to an incident are being addressed, the need to begin recovery operations emerges. The emphasis upon response will gradually give way to recovery operations. Within recovery, actions are taken to help individuals, communities, and the Nation return to normal. Depending on the complexity of this phase, recovery and cleanup efforts involve significant contributions from all sectors of our society.

- *Short-term recovery* is immediate and overlaps with response. It includes actions such as providing essential public health and safety services, restoring interrupted utility and other essential services, reestablishing transportation routes, and providing food and shelter for those displaced by the incident. Although called "short term," some of these activities may last for weeks.

- *Long-term recovery*, which is outside the scope of the Framework, may involve some of the same actions but may continue for a number of months or years, depending on the severity and extent of the damage sustained. For example, long-term recovery may include the complete redevelopment of damaged areas.

Recovery from an incident is unique to each community and depends on the amount and kind of damage caused by the incident and the resources that the jurisdiction has ready or can quickly obtain. In the short term, recovery is an extension of the response phase in which basic services and functions are restored. In the long term, recovery is a restoration of both the personal lives of individuals and the livelihood of the community. Recovery can include the development, coordination, and execution of service- and site-restoration plans; reconstitution of government operations and services; programs to provide housing and promote restoration; long-term care and treatment of affected persons; and additional measures for social, political, environmental, and economic restoration. Recovery programs do the following:

- Identify needs and resources.
- Provide accessible housing and promote restoration.
- Address care and treatment of affected persons.
- Inform residents and prevent unrealistic expectations.
- Implement additional measures for community restoration.
- Incorporate mitigation measures and techniques, as feasible.

The JFO remains the central *coordination* point among local, tribal, state, and federal governments, as well as private sector and nongovernmental entities that are providing recovery assistance. Here are some examples of federal and state recovery actions:

- Coordinating assistance programs to help individuals, households, and businesses meet basic needs and return to self-sufficiency. Such programs include housing assistance, other needs assistance, crisis counseling services, disaster legal services, and unemployment or reemployment programs. Other activities include coordinating with local and tribal governments the need for and locations of Disaster Recovery Centers.
- Establishing Disaster Recovery Centers. Federal, state, tribal, local, voluntary, and nongovernmental organizations determine the need for and location of Disaster Recovery Centers. Staff provide recovery and mitigation program information, advice, counseling, and related technical assistance.
- Coordinating with private sector and nongovernmental organizations involved in donations management and other recovery activities.
- Coordinating public assistance grant programs authorized by the Stafford Act. These programs aid local, tribal, and state governments and eligible private nonprofit organizations with the cost of emergency protective services, debris removal, and the repair or replacement of disaster-damaged public facilities and associated environmental restoration.
- Coordinating with the private sector on restoration and recovery of CIKR. Activities include working with owners/operators to ensure the restoration of critical services, including water, power, natural gas and petroleum, emergency communications, and health care.
- Coordinating mitigation grant programs to help communities reduce the potential impacts of future disasters. Activities include developing strategies to rebuild resilient communities.

After the JFO closes, ongoing activities transition to individual agencies with primary recovery responsibilities. Federal partners then work directly with their regional or headquarters offices to administer and monitor recovery programs, support, and technical services.

Source: National Response Framework. January 2008.
http://www.fema.gov/pdf/emergency/nrf/nrf-core.pdf.

Beginning in August 2009, FEMA initiated the process for developing a National Disaster Recovery Framework (NDRF) to help coordinate recovery functions among federal, state, and local governments; the private sector; tribal organizations; and voluntary agencies. Since 2009, FEMA has been engaged in an effort to solicit input from all stakeholders in the development of the NDRF. A description of the NDRF effort is presented in the box below.

NATIONAL DISASTER RECOVERY FRAMEWORK INITIATIVE

On August 27, 2009, FEMA administrator Craig Fugate announced the establishment of a National Disaster Recovery Framework Working Group. Elizabeth Zimmerman, assistant administrator for Disaster Assistance, was appointed to lead the effort. The goal was to engage recovery stakeholders to create a comprehensive coordinating structure that will enhance our ability to work together and effectively deliver recovery assistance.

On September 29, 2009, President Obama announced an effort to examine lessons learned during previous catastrophic disaster recovery efforts, areas for improved collaboration between federal agencies, and among the federal government and state and local governments and stakeholders. At the president's request, the secretaries of Homeland Security and Housing and Urban Development are cochairing a Long-Term Disaster Recovery Working Group composed of the secretaries and administrators of more than 20 departments, agencies, and offices. This high-level, strategic initiative will provide operational guidance for recovery organizations, as well as make suggestions for future improvement. An intensive stakeholder outreach effort during October and November 2009, involving state, local, and tribal government representatives, as well as a wide array of private organizations and private nonprofit organizations, will inform these efforts.

The National Disaster Recovery Framework Working Group is now cochaired with HUD and comes under the umbrella of the White House's Long-Term Disaster Recovery Working Group effort. It will provide one of the two main outcomes of the effort. The other outcome is a "Report to the President" that will summarize the findings of the Working Group.

The National Disaster Recovery Framework will do the following:

- Define the federal, state, local, tribal, private nonprofit, and private sector roles and individual citizen's roles in disaster recovery.
- Design and establish an effective coordinating structure for disaster recovery programs.
- Identify gaps, as well as duplications, in recovery programs and funding.
- Establish performance standards for the federal support of state and local recovery.

DESIRED OUTCOME
The desired outcome is recovery programs and capabilities at all levels of the government and in all sectors that will function together harmoniously and be supported by:

- A coordinating structure with defined roles and responsibilities.
- Clearly defined measures of success.

- A communications strategy designed to keep all stakeholders informed about the recovery arena.

Outcomes are subject to further refinement.

APPROACH

- Merging efforts with the Long-Term Recovery Working Group, the team will engage federal agency partners and state, tribal and local governments and nongovernmental organizations in a comprehensive collaborative review and shaping of the national approach to managing disaster recovery.
- Develop the Framework based on the stakeholders' perceptions of how recovery should be organized and managed.
- Include all stakeholders, particularly those representing traditionally underserved communities, such as children and adults with disabilities and low-income, multicultural, and rural communities.

TIMELINE

- Phase I—Stakeholder Engagement and Concept Design by December 31, 2009
- Phase II—Coordination and Publication by June 1, 2010

Source: FEMA. *http://www.fema.gov/recoveryframework/*.

The Response and Recovery Operations Branch coordinates the request and delivery of federal assistance and support from various special teams. This branch is composed of four groups: Emergency Services, Human Services, Infrastructure Support, and Community Recovery and Mitigation.

When established in coordination with state and local jurisdictions, a Disaster Recovery Center (DRC) is a satellite component of the Joint Field Office (JFO—includes the Federal Coordinating Officer (FCO), State Coordinating Officer (SCO), and other senior federal officials) and provides a central facility where individuals affected by a disaster can obtain information on disaster recovery assistance programs from various federal, state, local, tribal, private sector, and voluntary organizations.

The JFO is the central coordination point among federal, state, local, and tribal agencies and voluntary organizations for delivering recovery assistance programs. The JFO Operations Section includes the Human Services Branch, the Infrastructure Support Branch, and the Community Recovery and Mitigation Branch. The Human Services and Infrastructure Support Branches of the JFO Operations Section assess state and local recovery needs at the outset of an incident and develop relevant time frames for program delivery. These branches ensure that federal agencies that have relevant recovery assistance programs are notified of an incident and share relevant applicant and damage information with all involved agencies as appropriate, ensuring that the privacy of individuals is protected. Brief summaries of these branches are in the following sections.

Human Services Branch

This branch coordinates assistance programs to help individuals, families, and businesses meet basic needs and return to self-sufficiency (Figure 7-2). This branch also coordinates with volunteer organizations and is involved in donations management, and it coordinates the need for and location of DRCs with local and tribal governments. Federal, state, local, tribal, voluntary, and nongovernmental organizations staff the DRCs, as needed, with knowledgeable personnel to provide recovery and mitigation program information, advice, counseling, and related technical assistance.

Infrastructure Support Branch

This branch coordinates public assistance programs authorized by the Stafford Act to aid state and local governments and eligible private nonprofit organizations with the cost of emergency protective services and the repair or replacement of disaster-damaged public facilities and associated environmental restoration.

Community Recovery and Mitigation Branch

This branch works with the other operations branches and state and local officials to assess the long-term impacts of an Incident of National Significance, define available resources, and facilitate the development of a course of action to most efficiently apply available resources to restore and revitalize the community as well as reduce the impacts from future disasters.

FIGURE 7-2 Baker, Louisiana, September 29, 2005. A laborer walks across the end of a section of a temporary housing site, which has more than 400 of the 550 travel trailers that are to be installed. This FEMA travel trailer park, one of several to be built at selected locations, will house individuals and families left homeless by Hurricane Katrina.
Win Henderson / FEMA.

These branches coordinate with one another to identify appropriate agency assistance programs to meet applicant needs, synchronizing assistance delivery and encouraging incorporation of hazard mitigation measures where possible. Hazard mitigation measures are identified in concert with congressionally mandated, locally developed plans. Hazard mitigation risk analysis; technical assistance to state, local, and tribal governments, citizens, and businesses; and grant assistance are included within the mitigation framework.

Additionally, these branches work in tandem to track the overall progress of the recovery effort, particularly noting potential program deficiencies and problem areas. Long-term environmental recovery may include cleanup and restoration of public facilities, businesses, and residences; reestablishment of habitats and prevention of subsequent damage to natural resources; protection of cultural or archeological sites; and protection of natural, cultural, and historical resources from intentional damage during other recovery operations.

Emergency Support Function #14 (ESF #14)

Long-Term Community Recovery and Mitigation provides a framework for federal government support to state, regional, local, and tribal governments; nongovernmental organizations (NGOs); and the private sector, designed to enable community recovery from the long-term consequences of an Incident of National Significance. This support consists of available programs and resources of federal departments and agencies to enable community recovery, especially long-term community recovery, and to reduce or eliminate risk from future incidents, where feasible.

Federal disaster assistance available under a major disaster falls into three general categories: Individual Assistance, Public Assistance, and Hazard Mitigation Assistance. Individual Assistance is aid to individuals, families, and business owners. Public Assistance is aid to public and certain private nonprofit entities for emergency services and the repair or replacement of disaster-damaged public facilities (see Figure 7–3). Hazard Mitigation Assistance is funding available for measures designed to reduce future losses to public and private property. A detailed description of the first two types of assistance follows. More information on Hazard Mitigation Assistance can be found in Chapter 3.

FEMA's Individual Assistance Recovery Programs

Individual Assistance programs are oriented to individuals, families, and small businesses, and the programs include temporary housing assistance, individual and family grants, disaster unemployment assistance, legal services, and crisis counseling. The disaster victim must first register for assistance and establish eligibility. Three national centers provide centralized disaster application services for disaster victims. FEMA's National

Processing Service Centers (NPSCs) are located in Denton, Texas; Berryville, Virginia; and Hyattsville, Maryland.

Since the first national center opened in 1994, more than 4 million applications have been processed and over 4.5 million calls have been taken for more than 300 major disasters. These NPSCs house an automated teleregistration service, through which disaster victims apply for Disaster Housing and the Individual and Family Grant program and through which their applications are processed and their questions answered.

This automated system provides automatic determination of eligibility for about 90 percent of Disaster Housing cases, usually within ten days of application. The other 10 percent of cases, which may need documentation, take a little longer. Cases are also automatically referred to the state for possible grant assistance if the applicant's needs exceed the Disaster Housing program and the individual cannot qualify for a disaster loan from the Small Business Administration.

Following the September 11 events, FEMA was concerned that many individuals and businesses had not sought help in the aftermath of the attack. Working with the Advertising Council and a volunteer ad agency, Muezzin Brown & Partners, a public service advertising campaign was developed to let viewers know that assistance was available by calling FEMA's toll-free registration number. The advertisements were distributed to electronic and media outlets in New York, New Jersey, Connecticut, Pennsylvania, and Massachusetts.

Disaster Housing Program

The Disaster Housing Program ensures that people whose homes are damaged by disaster have a safe place to live until repairs can be completed. These programs are designed to provide funds for expenses that are not covered by insurance and are available to homeowners and renters who are legal residents of the United States and who were displaced by the disaster.

- *Lodging expenses reimbursement* provides a check for reimbursement for the costs of short-term lodging such as hotel rooms that were incurred because of damage to a home or an officially imposed prohibition against returning to a home.
- *Emergency minimal repair assistance* provides a check to help repair a home to a habitable condition.
- *Temporary rental assistance* provides a check to rent a place for the predisaster household to live.
- *Mortgage and rental assistance* provides a check to pay the rent or mortgage to prevent evictions or foreclosure. In order to qualify, the applicant must be living in the same house before and after the disaster and have a documented disaster-related financial hardship that can be verified by FEMA.

FIGURE 7-3 Austell, Georgia, October 19, 2009. This Cobb County elementary school's 18 temporary classrooms were immersed in 12 feet of water from Sweetwater Creek and are extensively damaged. FEMA Public Assistance funds may pay up to 75 percent of the costs to repair or replace them if an application is made and eligibility is determined.
George Armstrong/FEMA.

Individuals and Households Program (IHP)

The Individuals and Households Program (IHP), formerly called the Individual and Family Grant (IFG) Program, provides funds for the necessary expenses and serious needs of disaster victims that cannot be met through insurance or other forms of disaster assistance. The IHP is not designed to cover all of a victim's losses (home, personal property, household goods) that resulted from the disaster, nor is it intended to restore damaged property to its condition before the disaster. Also, the IHP does not cover any business-related losses that resulted from the disaster. By law, the IHP cannot provide any money for losses that are covered by insurance.

IHP provides assistance for the following:

- *Temporary housing* (a place to live for a limited period of time). Money is available to rent a different place to live or a government-provided housing unit when rental properties are not available (Figure 7-4).
- *Repairs.* Money is available to homeowners to repair damage from the disaster that is not covered by insurance. The goal is to make the damaged home safe, sanitary, and functional.
- *Replacements.* Money is available to homeowners to replace their home destroyed in the disaster that is not covered by insurance. The goal is to help the homeowner with the cost of replacing their destroyed home.
- *Permanent housing construction.* This involves either direct assistance or money for the construction of a home. This type of help occurs only in insular areas or remote

FIGURE 7-4 Hope, Arkansas, March 10, 2007. The remaining six of seven travel trailers to be delivered to the Dumas, Arkansas, area to house residents left homeless by recent tornadoes are hitched up and ready to begin their four-hour journey across the state.
FEMA Photo by Win Henderson.

locations specified by FEMA, where no other type of housing assistance is possible.

- *Other needs.* Money is available for necessary expenses and serious needs caused by the disaster. This includes medical, dental, funeral, personal property, transportation, moving and storage, and other expenses that are authorized by law.

The IHP covers only repair or replacement of items that are damaged as a direct result of the disaster that are not covered by insurance. Repairs or rebuilding may not improve a victim's home above its predisaster condition unless such improvements are required by current building codes.

Housing Needs

Money to repair a home is limited to making the home "safe and sanitary" so the victim can continue to live there. IHP will not pay to return a home to its predisaster condition. Grants may be used for housing needs to repair the following:

- Structural parts of your home (foundation, outside walls, roof)
- Windows, doors, floors, walls, ceilings, cabinetry
- Septic or sewage systems
- Wells or other water systems
- Heating, ventilating, and air conditioning system
- Utilities (electrical, plumbing, and gas systems)
- Entrance and exit ways from your home, including privately owned access roads
- Blocking, leveling, and anchoring of a mobile home and reconnecting or resetting its sewer, water, electrical, and fuel lines, and tanks

Other Needs

Money to repair damaged personal property or to pay for disaster-related necessary expenses and serious needs is limited to items or services that help prevent or overcome a disaster-related hardship, injury, or adverse condition. Grants may be used to pay for the following:

- Disaster-related medical and dental costs
- Disaster-related funeral and burial cost
- Clothing, household items (room furnishings, appliances), tools (specialized or protective clothing and equipment) required for a job, necessary educational materials (computers, school books, supplies)
- Fuels for primary heat source (heating oil, gas, firewood)
- Cleanup items (wet/dry vacuum, air purifier, dehumidifier)
- Disaster-damaged vehicle
- Moving and storage expenses related to the disaster (moving and storing property to avoid additional disaster damage while disaster-related repairs are being made to the home)
- Other necessary expenses or serious needs as determined by FEMA

Money received from IHP for "housing" and "other" needs must be used for eligible expenses only, as identified by FEMA. If a grantee does not use the money for the reasons defined in the grant application, he or she may not be eligible for any additional help and may have to return any grant money provided. Grant money has the following features:

- Is usually limited to up to 18 months from the date the president declares the disaster.
- Does not have to be repaid.
- Is tax-free.
- Is not counted as income or a resource in determining eligibility for welfare, income assistance, or income-tested benefit programs funded by the federal government.
- Is exempt from garnishment, seizure, encumbrance, levy, execution, pledge, attachment, release, or waiver.
- May not be reassigned or transferred to another person.

FEMA pays 100 percent of the "housing" portion of the grant, and 75 percent of the "other needs" portion. The state pays the remaining 25 percent of the "other needs" portion. The states may administer only the "other needs" portion of the grant. The total maximum amount of grant assistant for each family or individual in fiscal year 2005 is $25,000, and this amount is broken down further into the various types of assistance provided. For example, although up to $25,000 may be provided for home repairs, a maximum of $10,000 will be provided for replacement of "owner occupied private residences."

Although some money often is made available through the IHP, most disaster aid from the federal government is provided in the form of loans from the Small Business Administration (SBA) that must be repaid. Applicants to IHP may be required to seek help from the SBA first before being considered for certain types of IHP help. The SBA can provide three types of disaster loans to qualified homeowners and businesses to repair or replace homes, personal property, or businesses that sustained damages not covered by insurance:

- *Home disaster loans* provide funds to homeowners and renters to repair or replace disaster-related damages to home or personal property.
- *Business physical disaster loans* provide funds to business owners to repair or replace disaster-damaged property, including inventory, and supplies.
- *Economic injury loans* provide capital to small businesses and to small agricultural cooperatives to assist them through the disaster recovery period. If the SBA determines that the individual is ineligible for a loan, or if the loan amount is insufficient to meet the individual's needs, then the applicant is referred to the IFG program.

Disaster Unemployment Assistance

The Disaster Unemployment Assistance (DUA) program provides unemployment benefits and reemployment services to individuals who have become unemployed because of major disasters and who are not eligible for disaster benefits under regular unemployment insurance programs.

Legal Services

The Young Lawyers' Division of the American Bar Association, through an agreement with FEMA, provides free legal assistance to low-income disaster victims. The assistance that the participating lawyers provide is for insurance claims; counseling on landlord/tenant problems; assistance in consumer protection matters, remedies, and procedures; and replacement of wills and other important legal documents destroyed in a major disaster. This assistance is intended for individuals who are unable to secure legal services adequate to meet their needs as a consequence of a major disaster.

Special Tax Considerations

Taxpayers who have sustained a casualty loss from a declared disaster may deduct that loss on the federal income tax return for the year in which the casualty occurred or through an immediate amendment to the previous year's return. Businesses may file claims with the Bureau of Alcohol, Tobacco, and Firearms (ATF) for payment of federal excise taxes paid on alcoholic beverages or tobacco products lost, rendered unmarketable, or condemned by a duly authorized official under various circumstances, including where a major disaster has been declared by the president.

Crisis Counseling

The Crisis Counseling Assistance and Training Program is designed to provide short-term crisis counseling services to people affected by a presidentially declared disaster. The purpose of the crisis counseling is to help relieve any grieving, stress, or mental health problems caused or aggravated by the disaster or its aftermath. These short-term services are provided by FEMA as supplemental funds granted to state and local mental health agencies. The American Red Cross, the Salvation Army, and other voluntary agencies, as well as churches and synagogues, also offer crisis counseling services.

Cora Brown Fund

Cora C. Brown of Kansas City, Missouri, died in 1977 and left a portion of her estate to the United States to be used as a special fund solely for the relief of human suffering caused by natural disasters. The funds are used to assist victims/survivors of presidentially declared major disasters for disaster-related needs that have not or will not be met by government agencies or other organizations.

CRITICAL THINKING

- Do you think that FEMA's individual grant programs provide enough assistance to individuals and families that are affected by disasters?
- Should federal assistance programs be available to all disaster victims regardless of their income or net worth? Why or why not?

FEMA's Public Assistance Grant Programs

FEMA, under the authority of the Stafford Act, administers the Public Assistance Program. The Public Assistance Grant Program provides federal assistance to state and local governments and to certain private nonprofit (PNP) organizations. These grants allow them to recover from the impact of disasters and to implement mitigation measures to reduce the impacts from future disasters. The grants are aimed at governments and organizations with the final goal to help a community and its citizens recover from devastating major disasters. The federal share of assistance is not less than 75 percent of the eligible cost for emergency measures and permanent restoration. The state determines how the nonfederal share is split with the applicants.

Eligible applicants include the states, local governments, and any other political subdivision of the state, Native American tribes, Alaska Native Villages, and certain PNP organizations. Eligible PNP facilities include educational, utility, irrigation, emergency, medical, rehabilitation, temporary or permanent custodial care, and other PNP facilities that are open to the public and provide essential services of a governmental nature to the general public. The work must be required as the result of the disaster, be located within the designated disaster area, and be the legal responsibility of the applicant. PNPs that provide critical services such as power, water, sewer, wastewater treatment, communications, or emergency medical care may apply directly to FEMA for a disaster grant. All other PNPs first must apply to the SBA for a disaster loan. If the loan is declined or does not cover all eligible damages, the applicant may reapply for FEMA assistance.

Work that is eligible for supplemental federal disaster grant assistance is classified as either emergency work or permanent work:

- *Emergency work* includes debris removal from public roads and rights-of-way as well as from private property when determined to be in the public interest. This may also include protective measures performed to eliminate or reduce immediate threats to the public.
- *Permanent work* is defined as work that is required to restore an eligible damaged facility to its predisaster design. This effort can range from minor repairs to replacement. Some categories for permanent work include roads, bridges, water control facilities, buildings, utility distribution systems, public parks, and recreational facilities. With extenuating circumstances the deadlines for emergency and permanent work may be extended.

As soon as possible after the disaster declaration, the state, assisted by FEMA, conducts the applicant briefings for state, local, and PNP officials to inform them of the assistance that is available and how to apply for it (see Figure 7–5). A Request for Public Assistance must be filed with the state within 30 days after the area is designated eligible for assistance.

FIGURE 7-5 Atlanta, Georgia, October 8, 2009. At the Fulton County EMA office, FEMA Public Assistance (PA) Project officers (from left) Peter Floyd, Joe Serbia, Armand Ruocco, and Terry Willis meet with city officials. FEMA Public Assistance funds help municipalities recover from storm and flooding damage.
George Armstrong, FEMA.

A combined federal, state, and local team work together to design and deliver the appropriate recovery assistance for the communities. In determining the federal costs for the projects, private or public insurance can play a major role. For insurable buildings within special flood hazard areas (SFHAs) and damaged by floods, the disaster assistance is reduced by the amount of insurance settlement that would have been received if the building and its contents had been fully covered by a standard NFIP policy. For structures located outside of an SFHA, the amount is reduced by the actual or anticipated insurance proceeds.

In 1998, FEMA redesigned the Public Assistance program to provide money to applicants more quickly and to make the application process easier. The redesigned program was approved for implementation on disasters declared after October 1, 1998. This redesigned program placed new emphasis on people, policy, process, and performance. The focus of the program was also modified to provide a higher level of customer service for disaster recovery applicants and to change the role of FEMA from inspection and enforcement to an advisory and supportive role.

In December 2008, the U.S. General Accounting Office (GAO) released an evaluation of FEMA's Public Assistance program's activities in helping to rebuild the Gulf Coast in the aftermath of the 2005 hurricanes that devastated numerous communities along the Gulf Coast. The GAO report raised a number of issues concerning current Public Assistance program activities principally in the areas of program development, information sharing and tracking, project approval and appeals, and human capital. A summary of the GAO report's findings and recommendations is presented in the box below.

GAO REPORT ON DISASTER RECOVERY

FEMA'S PUBLIC ASSISTANCE GRANT PROGRAM EXPERIENCED CHALLENGES WITH GULF COAST REBUILDING

The devastation caused by the 2005 Gulf Coast hurricanes presented the nation with unprecedented rebuilding challenges. The Federal Emergency Management Agency's (FEMA) Public Assistance (PA) grant program is a key tool for providing funds to support recovery, including rebuilding public schools, roads, and utilities.

GAO was asked to examine the amount of PA grants FEMA has provided for rebuilding the Gulf Coast; challenges in the day-to-day operation of the PA program; and human capital challenges; as well as actions taken to address them. Toward this end, GAO reviewed relevant laws, PA regulations and procedures, and analyzed data from FEMA's National Emergency Management Information System. GAO also interviewed federal officials from FEMA and the Department of Homeland Security's (DHS) Office of the Federal Coordinator for Gulf Coast Rebuilding, as well as more than 60 officials from state government and eight localities in Louisiana and Mississippi.

WHAT GAO RECOMMENDS

GAO makes several recommendations to the secretary of Homeland Security, including to direct FEMA to improve information sharing within the PA process and to further enhance continuity and communication when staff rotate on and off PA projects. In commenting on a draft of this report DHS generally agreed with our recommendations.

Funding for PA grants related to the 2005 Gulf Coast hurricanes is already more than $11 billion, surpassing that of any previous disaster, and will likely be higher than FEMA's total cost estimate of $13.2 billion. About 90 percent of these funds have gone to the states of Louisiana and Mississippi, about half of which have passed from the states to grant applicants to date. GAO identified challenges in the following broad areas, many of which contributed to slowing down rebuilding projects.

Project Development

Challenges in the development of PA projects included difficulties (1) determining the amount of damage that was disaster-related, (2) using PA program flexibilities to rebuild in a way that meets postdisaster needs, (3) assessing project scope including whether to repair or replace damaged structures, (4) estimating project costs, and (5) having sufficient resources to initiate projects. For example, assessing the damage to New Orleans's water and sewer system was complicated by the difficulty distinguishing disaster-related from preexisting damage. Estimating the cost of PA projects presented special challenges because of unusual market conditions for labor and materials in the postdisaster economy.

Information Sharing and Tracking

GAO identified challenges in sharing information among federal, state, and local participants in the PA process as well as in tracking the status of projects. For example, in Louisiana, information sharing was made more difficult in the absence of an effective document-sharing system and because key FEMA and state officials who review PA applications are located in different cities.

Project Approvals and Appeals

FEMA's approval decisions on some projects were reversed after applicants had already moved ahead with construction. In addition, decisions on appeals were often not made within required time frames due to the large number of rebuilding projects.

Human Capital

Human capital challenges at all levels of government underlie many of the above challenges and also slowed rebuilding projects. Shortages of experienced and knowledgeable staff were particularly problematic during the initial stages of rebuilding. FEMA's early reliance on temporary rotating staff did not provide the level of continuity needed for the complex demands of Gulf Coast rebuilding.

Among the actions DHS has taken to address these challenges are the finalization of a PA catastrophic disaster recovery concept plan that recognizes the need to more easily tailor projects to meet postdisaster conditions; the development of new management information systems to better track and manage projects and increase the transparency of PA funding; and the creation of a credentialing program for employees.

Source: United States Government Accountability Office. December 2008. "Disaster Recovery: FEMA's Public Assistance Grant Program Experienced Challenges in Gulf Coast Rebuilding." *http://www.gao.gov/new.items/ d09129.pdf.*

Other Federal Agency Disaster Recovery Funding

Other federal agencies have programs that contribute to social and economic recovery. Most of these additional programs are triggered by a presidential declaration of a major disaster or emergency under the Stafford Act; however, the secretary of agriculture and the administrator of the SBA have specific authority relevant to their constituencies to declare a disaster and provide disaster recovery assistance. All the agencies are part of the structure of the NRP. This section does not provide a complete list of all disaster recovery programs available after a disaster declaration, but it provides a summary of many of the federal agencies in addition to FEMA that provide disaster recovery programs. These agencies include the following:

- U.S. Army Corps of Engineers
- Department of Housing and Urban Development
- Small Business Administration
- U.S. Department of Agriculture
- Department of Health and Human Services
- Department of Transportation
- Department of Commerce
- Department of Labor

A more comprehensive list is available in the Catalog of Federal Domestic Assistance (CFDA), which is available through the Federal Assistance Programs Retrieval System. Each automated edition is revised in June and December.

U.S. Army Corps of Engineers

In a typical year, the Corps of Engineers responds to more than 30 presidential disaster declarations, plus numerous state and local emergencies. Under the NRP, the Corps has the lead responsibility for public works and engineering missions. For example, after the events of September 11, 2001, the Corps provided technical assistance for the debris removal operation. By December 2001, more than 661,430 tons of debris had been moved to the Staten Island landfill.

Department of Housing and Urban Development

The Department of Housing and Urban Development (HUD) provides flexible grants to help cities, counties, and states to recover from presidentially declared disasters, especially in low-income areas, subject to availability of supplemental appropriations. When disasters occur, Congress may appropriate additional funding for the Community Development Block Grant (CDBG) and HOME programs to rebuild the affected areas and bring crucial seed money to start the recovery process. Because it can fund a broader range of recovery activities than most other programs, CDBG disaster recovery assistance supplements recovery assistance from FEMA and helps communities and neighborhoods that otherwise might not recover because of limited resources.

The CDBG program funds have been especially useful to communities that are interested in incorporating mitigation into their recovery process. These funds have been combined with FEMA assistance to remove or elevate structures from the flood plain and to relocate residents and businesses to safer areas.

The HOME Program helps expand the supply of decent, affordable housing for low- and very-low-income families by providing grants to states and local governments. Funds can be used for acquisition, new construction, rehabilitation, and tenant-based rental assistance. HOME disaster recovery grants are an important resource for providing affordable housing to disaster victims.

Small Business Administration

The SBA Disaster Loan Program offers low-interest loans to assist in long-term recovery efforts for those who are trying to rebuild their homes and businesses in the aftermath of a disaster. Disaster loans from the SBA help homeowners, renters, businesses of all sizes, and nonprofit organizations fund rebuilding efforts. The SBA Disaster Loan Program reduces federal disaster costs compared to other forms of assistance, such as grants, because the loans are repaid to the U.S. Treasury.

The SBA can approve loans only to applicants who have a reasonable ability to repay the loan and other obligations from earnings. The terms of each loan are established in accordance with each borrower's ability to repay. Generally, more than 90 percent of the SBA's disaster loans are made to borrowers without credit available elsewhere and have an interest rate of around 4 percent. The disaster loans require borrowers to maintain appropriate hazard and flood insurance coverage, thereby reducing the need for future disaster assistance.

The SBA is authorized by the Small Business Act to make two types of disaster loans: physical disaster loans and economic injury disaster loans. Physical disaster loans are a primary source of funding for permanent rebuilding and replacement of uninsured disaster damages to privately owned real and/or personal property. Economic injury disaster loans provide necessary working capital until normal operations resume after a physical disaster.

In Fiscal Year 2009 (October 1, 2008 to September 30, 2009), the SBA approved 21,780 disaster loans for $1,129,515,400, with the following breakdown: physical loans—21,132, totaling $1,079,642,500; and economic injury loans—648, totaling $49,872,900. Since the inception of the program in 1953, the SBA has approved more than 1.8 million disaster loans for more than $47 billion. In the aftermath of Hurricanes Katrina, Rita, and Wilma in 2005, the SBA approved 160,805 disaster loans totaling $10.9 billion. In 2001 after 9/11, the SBA approved more than $526 million in low-interest loans to more than 5,300 applicants for home repairs, business loans, and loans to assist small businesses suffering economic injury as a result of losses caused by the disaster.

U.S. Department of Agriculture

The U.S. Department of Agriculture (USDA) Farm Service Agency (FSA) provides low-interest loan assistance to eligible farmers and ranchers to help cover production and physical losses in counties declared as disaster areas by the president or designated by the secretary of agriculture. The emergency loans can be used to restore or replace essential physical property, pay all or part of production costs associated with the disaster year, pay essential family living expenses, reorganize the farming operation, and refinance debts.

Department of Health and Human Services

The Department of Health and Human Services (DHHS) is the lead federal agency responsible for implementing the health and medical portion of the NRP. Their activities provide support to individuals and communities affected by disasters, state and local mental health administrators, and other groups that respond to those affected by human-caused disasters (such as school violence). The Center for Mental Health Services (CMHS) within the DHHS works with FEMA to implement the Crisis Counseling Assistance and Training Program discussed earlier in this chapter.

The DHHS also provides disaster assistance for older Americans through its Administration on Aging (AoA). Older people often have difficulty obtaining necessary assistance because of progressive physical and mental impairments and other frailties that often accompany aging. Many older people who live on limited incomes, and are sometimes alone, find it impossible to recover from disasters without special federal assistance services. The AoA's national aging network assists older persons by providing critical support such as meals and transportation, information about temporary housing, and other important services on which older adults often rely.

Department of Transportation

Congress authorized a special program from the Highway Trust Fund for the repair or reconstruction of federal-aid highways and roads on federal lands that have suffered serious damage as a result of natural disasters or catastrophic failures from an external cause. The Department of Transportation (DOT) Federal Highway Administration (FHWA) administers the Emergency Relief Program, which supplements the commitment of resources by states, their political subdivisions, or other federal agencies to help pay for damages resulting from disasters. The applicability of the program to a natural disaster is based on the extent and intensity of the disaster.

Department of Commerce

Within the Department of Commerce, the Economic Development Administration (EDA) administers programs and provides grants for infrastructure development, business incentives, and other forms of assistance designed to help communities alleviate conditions of substantial and persistent unemployment in economically distressed areas and regions. The EDA provides postdisaster economic assistance for communities affected by declared natural disasters. Funding for this program has been a problem over the years.

Department of Labor

The Department of Labor (DOL) Disaster Unemployment Assistance (DUA) program provides financial assistance to individuals whose employment or self-employment has been lost or interrupted as a direct result of a major disaster and who are not eligible for regular state unemployment insurance. Funding for this program comes from FEMA. The DUA is administered by the state agency responsible for providing state unemployment insurance.

The Workforce Investment Act of 1998 authorizes the U.S. secretary of labor to award National Emergency Grants to assist any state that has suffered an emergency or major disaster to provide disaster relief employment. These funds can be used to finance the creation of temporary jobs for workers dislocated by disasters to clean up and recover from the disaster and to provide employment assistance to dislocated workers. Interestingly, in creating this program, Congress expanded eligibility beyond people affected by the disaster to dislocated workers and certain civilian Department of Defense employees affected by downsizing and certain recently separated members of the armed forces.

National Voluntary Relief Organizations

Many voluntary organizations and nongovernmental organizations (NGOs) are involved in disaster recovery. These organizations help individuals to get back on their feet in the immediate aftermath of a disaster event by providing food, shelter, medicine, and clothing. These groups also provide long-term assistance in many areas such as housing repair and rebuild, child care, and assistance in accessing government relief. After Hurricane Katrina, a voluntary agency provided case management services to individual Katrina victims. For the most part, voluntary agencies and NGOs address the unmet needs of individuals that government relief programs do not cover.

National Voluntary Organizations Active in Disaster (NVOAD)

National Voluntary Organizations Active in Disaster (NVOAD) coordinates planning efforts by many voluntary organizations responding to disaster in order to provide more effective service to people affected by disaster. Members include 34 national voluntary organizations that are active in disaster mitigation and response, 52 state and territorial chapters (VOADs), and dozens of local organizations. Once a disaster occurs, NVOAD or an affiliated state VOAD encourages members and other voluntary agencies to convene on site. The member organizations provide a wide variety of disaster relief services, including emergency distribution services, mass feeding, disaster child care, mass or individual shelter, comfort kits, supplementary medical care, cleaning supplies, emergency communications, stress management services, disaster assessment, advocacy for disaster victims, building or repair of homes, debris removal, mitigation, burn services, guidance in managing spontaneous volunteers, and victim and supply transportation. NVOAD maintains a close relationship with FEMA and encourages the state and local affiliates to work closely with the state and local emergency management agencies.

The American Red Cross

Although the American Red Cross is not a government agency, its authority to provide disaster relief was formalized when, in 1905, the Red Cross was chartered by Congress to "carry on a system of national and international relief in time of peace and apply the same in mitigating the sufferings caused by pestilence, famine, fire, floods, and other great national calamities, and to devise and carry on measures for preventing the same." Red Cross disaster relief focuses on meeting people's immediate emergency disaster-caused needs and provides disaster assistance to individuals to enable them to resume their normal daily activities independently. The Red Cross provides shelter, food, and health and mental health services to address basic human needs. The Red Cross also feeds emergency workers, handles inquiries from concerned family members outside the disaster area, provides blood and blood products to disaster victims, and helps those affected by disaster to access other available resources.

The Red Cross is one of the nongovernmental organizations included in the NRP and is designated a support agency for ESF #6, Mass Care, Housing, and Human Services. The Red Cross helps coordinate the use of federal mass care resources in a presidentially declared disaster or emergency, and works closely in support of state and local efforts to meet the mass care needs of victims of a disaster. This federal assistance supports the delivery of mass care services of shelter, feeding, and emergency first aid to disaster victims; the establishment of systems to provide bulk distribution of emergency relief supplies to disaster victims; and the collection of information to operate a Disaster Welfare Information system to report victim status and assist in family reunification.

Recovery Planning Tools

Despite the pressures on politicians and community leaders to return to a period of normalcy as quickly as possible and because of federal incentives, public interest, and insurance retractions, more and more communities are looking at ways to reduce their future vulnerability. As disasters repeat themselves and the public sees the emotional and financial benefits of mitigation, communities are making the long-term investment in mitigation. For example, the devastating 1993 Midwest floods that occurred again in some areas in 1995 had a minimal impact in those towns where buyout and relocation programs were undertaken after the 1993 flood. The following is a partial list of policy areas and tools that should be considered by decision makers as they develop their recovery plan:

- *Land-use planning techniques*, including acquisition, easements, annexation, stormwater management, and environmental reviews
- *Zoning*, including special-use permits, historic preservation, setbacks, density controls, wetlands protection, floodplain, and coastal zone management
- *Building codes*, including design controls, design review, height and type, and special study areas (soil stability ratings)
- *Financial*, including special districts, tax exemptions, special bonds, development rights, property transfer, or use change fees
- *Information and oversight*, including public awareness and education, regional approaches and agreements, global information systems, town hall meetings, and public hearings

Long-Term Recovery Planning Annex

Within the National Response Framework (NRF) is Emergency Support Function #14 (ESF #14)—Long-Term Community Recovery Annex. This annex outlines the roles and responsibilities of all stakeholders in helping a community to develop a long-term recovery plan. A brief description of the federal agencies involved in ESF #14 and the purpose, scope, policies, and concept of operations of ESF #14 are presented in the box below.

EMERGENCY SUPPORT FUNCTION #14—LONG-TERM COMMUNITY RECOVERY ANNEX, JANUARY 2008

- ESF Coordinator: Department of Homeland Security/Federal Emergency Management Agency
- Primary Agencies: Department of Agriculture, Department of Homeland Security, Department of Housing and Urban Development, Small Business Administration
- Support Agencies: Department of Commerce, Department of Defense, Department of Energy, Department of Health and Human Services, Department of the Interior, Department of Labor, Department of Transportation, Department of the Treasury, Environmental Protection Agency, Corporation for National and Community Service, Delta Regional Authority, American Red Cross, National Voluntary Organizations Active in Disaster.

INTRODUCTION
Purpose
Emergency Support Function (ESF) #14—Long-Term Community Recovery provides a mechanism for coordinating federal support to state, tribal, regional, and local governments; nongovernmental organizations (NGOs); and the private sector to enable community recovery from the long-term consequences of extraordinary disasters. ESF #14 accomplishes this by identifying and facilitating availability and use of sources of recovery funding and providing technical assistance (such as impact analyses) for community recovery and recovery planning support.

Scope

ESF #14 may be activated for incidents that require a coordinated federal response to address significant long-term impacts (e.g., impacts on housing, government operations, agriculture, businesses, employment, community infrastructure, the environment, human health, and social services) to foster sustainable recovery. ESF #14 support will vary depending on the magnitude and type of incident.

Policies

ESF #14 recognizes the primacy of affected state, tribal, and local governments and the private sector in defining and addressing risk reduction and long-term community recovery priorities, and in leading the community recovery planning process. ESF #14 long-term community recovery and recovery planning efforts will be coordinated with state/tribal/local-level stakeholders. Federal agencies continue to provide recovery assistance under independent authorities to state, tribal, and local governments, the private sector, and individuals, while coordinating assessments of need for additional assistance and identification and resolution of issues through ESF #14.

ESF #14 excludes economic policymaking. The National Economic Council, the Council of Economic Advisors, and the Department of the Treasury develop all national economic stabilization policy. Federal support is tailored based on the type, extent, and duration of the incident and long-term recovery period and on the availability of federal resources. ESF #14 is not a funding entity, but it facilitates the identification, coordination, and use of resources to support long-term recovery.

Long-term community recovery efforts build resilience focusing on disaster resistance through permanent restoration of infrastructure, housing, agricultural industry, natural resources, community well-being, and the local economy, with attention to mitigation of future impacts of a similar nature. The lead agency in the field is designated based on the type of disaster.

CONCEPT OF OPERATIONS

Assessment

ESF #14 provides the coordination mechanisms for the federal government to support the state, tribal, and local governments' assessment of the long-term recovery needs in the impacted areas and exchange assessment information among federal departments and agencies.

Coordination

ESF #14 provides the coordination mechanisms for the federal government to do the following:

- Convene interagency recovery expertise to provide strategic guidance to long-term recovery efforts.
- Identify and address long-term recovery issues, including those that fall between existing mandates of agencies.
- Avoid duplication of assistance, coordinate program application processes and planning requirements to streamline assistance processes, and identify and coordinate resolution of policy and program issues.
- Identify programs and activities across the public, private, and nonprofit sectors that similarly support long-term recovery and promote coordination between them.

- Identify appropriate federal programs and agencies to support implementation of comprehensive long-term community planning and identify gaps in available resources.
- Identify appropriate federal programs and agencies to support and facilitate continuity of long-term recovery activities.

Technical Support

ESF #14 provides a coordination mechanism for the federal government to do the following:

- Work with state, tribal, and local governments; NGOs; and private sector organizations to support long-term recovery planning for highly impacted communities.
- Link recovery planning to sound risk reduction practices to encourage a more viable recovery.
- Strategically apply subject-matter expertise to help communities recover from disasters.

Source: FEMA. January 2008. *http://www.fema.gov/pdf/emergency/nrf/nrf-esf-14.pdf.*

Interest in long-term recovery planning has increased in the aftermath of Hurricane Katrina. It has been suggested that long-term recovery planning at the community level should be conducted prior to the next disaster instead of after the next disaster strikes as it has been done in the past. One method for conducting community long-term recovery planning is presented below.

Community Long-Term Recovery Planning

The time to conduct long-term recovery planning is before the next disaster strikes. If a jurisdiction engages in predisaster long-term recovery planning, it provides the following benefits:

- Identifies the most vulnerable areas of the community
- Accelerates approval of federal funding for rebuilding in the post disaster environment
- Anticipates/compensates for regulatory and environmental requirements for rebuilding
- Minimizes economic and social disruption to the community
- Maximizes postdisaster funding in the public and private sectors
- Promotes a favorable climate for municipal bond and insurance portfolios

Planning Process

The purpose of building a long-term recovery plan is to identify what impact a major disaster will have on a community's residents, homes, infrastructure, economy, and environment and to develop processes and procedures designed to ensure that the community is rebuilt safer and stronger. The process would include at a minimum the following activities:

1. Establish a long-term recovery planning committee that includes all community stakeholders from government (local, state, and federal), the private sector, community groups, voluntary organizations, nonprofit groups, unions, churches, the media, and so on.
2. Conduct a risk vulnerability assessment that provides an estimate of the damage that a major disaster will inflict on the community's residents, institutions, critical infrastructure, economy, and environment.
3. Identify and prioritize those actions that can be taken prior to the next disaster to reduce the future disaster impacts.
4. Identify and prioritize the actions to be taken after the next disaster to rebuild the community safer and stronger.
5. Identify regulatory and environmental data needs in the recovery phase.
6. Identify the potential sources of recovery resources (i.e., state and federal government, local government funding sources, mutual aid agreements, private sector, foundations, voluntary organizations, nongovernmental organizations, etc.) and determine the types of information needed to successfully apply for these resources in a timely way.
7. Identify potential barriers to a timely recovery and put in place emergency waivers and authorities that will overcome these barriers in the recovery phase.
8. Establish and implement an aggressive public outreach and information campaign that involves the public in the planning process, data collection, and the implementation phase in the recovery.
9. Develop an Implementation Plan for the recovery phase that includes:
   a. Establishment of a community long-term recovery committee
   b. A notification process
   c. Data collection and analysis procedures
   d. Procedures for instituting emergency waivers and authorities
   e. Roles and responsibilities among stakeholders in preparing applications for recovery aid
   f. Procedures for tracking recovery aid applications
   g. A process for distributing and spending recovery aid
   h. Internal and external communications procedures and support
10. Update and refine the long-term recovery plan annually.

CRITICAL THINKING

Why is the recovery period often called a "risk-reduction window of opportunity"? What kinds of risk-reduction measures are easier to perform during recovery than other times, and why are they easier?

Conclusion

As this chapter demonstrates, the federal government plays a significant role in initiating and funding the disaster recovery process. But for recovery to be effective, the planning and decision making must be done at the local level. With a disaster comes disruption and tragedy, but in the aftermath comes opportunity. Changes to FEMA's Stafford Act now require communities and states to have mitigation plans approved before the disaster. These plans, developed in the calm before an event happens, can become the blueprint for facilitating recovery and making communities less vulnerable in the postdisaster environment. Communities should strive to integrate preevent recovery and mitigation planning into their ongoing planning efforts. Such integration will allow for the political process to work, to include citizen participation, and to garner support for changes that will make their communities safer and more secure.

CASE STUDY: ECONOMIC RECOVERY IN NEW YORK CITY AFTER SEPTEMBER 11, 2001

Prior to September 11, the World Trade Center was the heart of a vibrant downtown business district. The massive complex consisted of seven buildings, including the twin World Trade Center towers. These 110-story skyscrapers, built in 1970 by the New York Port Authority, contained nearly an acre of space on each floor. Combined, they represented 12 million square feet of office space—14 percent of the office space in downtown Manhattan—and were the workplace of 50,000 employees. Together with the other buildings destroyed or damaged on that date, over 25 percent of the commercial office space in lower Manhattan was immediately uninhabitable.

The economic impact of the attack was immediate and severe. In addition to their physical space, many companies lost all or a large percentage of their workforce and operational equipment. The transportation system on which employees depended was destroyed. The nation's financial system was shut down, and air travel was suspended. Shipping ground to a halt, and companies that relied on just-in-time products for production were left without many necessary parts. TV and radio stations lost advertising revenue as reports of the attack went commercial-free for days. Consumer spending and confidence were devastated and didn't return for weeks. And the insurance industry, heavily invested in the city, realized the costliest single event in its history.

The exact financial impact figures related to the attack are still hard to obtain, as the means to measure them are not standardized. The human casualty figure, in flux for months, was finally set at 2,749. The economic figures are much more amorphous, due to a number of reasons. First, the economy is dynamic, and was affected by several other factors, such as the ongoing recession and various scandals (Enron, WorldCom), among other issues. Second, the recovery effort is still under way, and costs related to it will likely remain open until as late as 2015, when all the WTC construction is scheduled to be completed. Insurance payments are still outstanding, and the federal government still has money yet to be allocated.

The economic recovery from the WTC attacks started immediately. To limit the immediate impact on shareholder confidence, the New York financial markets were shut for a period of several days. The Federal Reserve bolstered the system by preparing to inject liquidity into the system to prevent defaults, and interest rates for short-term borrowing were lowered. The Fed also ensured the availability of U.S. dollars overseas, and Congress supported U.S. airlines with $10 billion in guaranteed loans. After electricity and communication were restored, just a few days later, the markets were ready to open and begin returning to normal operations.

These initial actions, however, were superficial, intended to limit the extent of damage that had already been sustained. It was apparent from the start that a much greater amount of recovery actions would be needed in the years to follow. Numerous organizations, governmental agencies, and other groups have participated in this recovery, several of which are profiled next.

FEMA

The response to the attacks on the WTC marked a significant change in the way in which FEMA allocated funds. In a "normal" disaster, FEMA first determines the needs as defined by established eligibility criteria, and then distributes funds from its general disaster relief fund. Congress does not give money for a specific disaster; rather, they allocate money to this pool, from which FEMA operates. There is no predefined upper limit for the disaster; as a result, disaster funding projects can be open for years after the event occurs (events related to the Northridge earthquake, for example, were still being funded nearly ten years after the event).

In this incident, however, the amount of money that was to be allocated was established early in the process. FEMA received $8.80 billion of the $20 billion in federal funds allocated by Congress, and FEMA was given enhanced flexibility in determining how the money should be used. This strategy allowed FEMA to establish an early closeout process, forcing the city and state to establish priorities early on. It also allowed FEMA to distribute funds in ways that normally would not have been possible under the Stafford Act, such that all of the $8.80 billion would be allocated. This flexibility has also been vital to the economic recovery of the area. It has gone beyond simply getting people back on their feet, to helping lower Manhattan reestablish itself as core of the New York City economy. FEMA funds have been used to assist owners with the cleaning of WTC dust from their private residences, reimburse the city from losses associated with a reduction in tourism, pay for increased security as a result of the attacks, and fund cost-of-living allowances for the beneficiaries of the pensions of the firefighters and police officers killed in the attack.

HUD

The Department of Housing and Urban Development is responsible for the second largest allocation of funds to the WTC site. HUD funds were used to reimburse utility companies for emergency repairs immediately after the attacks. They assisted both individuals and businesses with compensation for disaster-related losses, through mortgage and rental insurance, crisis counseling, grants for disaster-related expenses, and businesses recovery grants and loans. HUD has also been instrumental in both the infrastructure and economic recovery of the WTC site. It has spent $568 million not only to return the utility infrastructure of the site to normal but to improve it. HUD's Community Development Block Grant (CDBG) has been used to fund several programs, among them the Small Firm Attraction and Retention Grant Program (SFARG), the Job Creation and Retention Program (JCRP), the Employee Training and Assistance Program (ETAP), and the Business Recovery Loan Fund. These funds have been vital to retaining the businesses that make up the economic heart of lower Manhattan.

DOT

The U.S. Department of Transportation has been involved with the effort to rebuild and improve the transportation systems damaged and destroyed at the WTC site. Because of the large number of workers that commute there, having a robust and efficient system is vital to the economic recovery of the site. DOT has been involved in restoring operation to the transportation systems and providing temporary repairs to the roads during the response phase. It is now involved in the permanent replacement of the Port Authority Trans-Hudson (PATH) terminal and improvements to the Fulton Street Transit Center and South Ferry Subway Station.

IRS

As part of the $20 billion package allocated for New York City, Congress approved the Liberty Zone tax benefit, worth approximately $5 billion. This amount is not money provided by the government but rather is a tax break targeted specifically to companies surrounding the WTC site in lower Manhattan, deemed the Liberty Zone. Among its provisions are a business employee credit, special depreciation allowance, tax-exempt private activity bonds (Liberty Bonds), and increased expensing. Some of these breaks have already expired, whereas others will continue on for several more years. The $5 billion figure is an estimate, and the IRS is not tracking the actual usage of these benefits.

State and Local: Empire State Development Corporation

The state of New York's Economic Development Corporation is aiding in the economic recovery of the region through its NY Incentives program, designed to help small business owners realize the benefits of doing business in the area by assisting with the various economic incentive programs.

Lower Manhattan Development Corporation

The Lower Manhattan Development Corporation (LMDC) is a state-city corporation designed to oversee the redevelopment and improvement of the WTC site and the entire lower Manhattan area. It was created shortly after the attack by Mayor Giuliani and Governor Pataki, and consists of eight board members appointed by the state, and eight appointed by the city. It consults with citizen groups on issues such as transportation and infrastructure, residential and commuter concerns, economic development, tourism and the arts, and memorial planning. It approved the plans for the rebuilding of the WTC site, and the included memorial site. Most important, it is in charge of channeling the funds received from the federal government.

Port Authority

The Port Authority of New York and New Jersey was founded in 1921 to enhance regional commerce and transportation in the New York City metropolitan area. It is a 12-member board, with six members appointed by the governor of each state. The Port Authority built the World Trade Center in 1970 and owned it until July 2001, when it leased it to a private party. It owns the land today, and is working closely with the LMDC to rebuild the World Trade Center and its transportation infrastructure.

Other Agencies

Numerous other agencies are involved in the rebuilding of the WTC site and lower Manhattan. Among them are the Metropolitan Transit Authority, NYC Planning Commission, NYC DOT,

NYC Department of Environmental Protection, and NYC Economic Development Corporation. Local community groups, arts societies, architects, and regional planning associations are also involved.

INSURANCE

Many of the insurance claims from the WTC attack have yet to be settled. Estimates of actual payout range from $30 to $70 billion, depending on the estimate source and date. The two World Trade Center towers, each insured for $3.5 billion, were reimbursed for only $3.5 billion total because the two attacks were considered to be part of a single event. For the insurance industry as a whole, this attack was a watershed event. Insurance companies normally operate with thin profit margins and a reliance on actuary tables to determine the likelihood of events, but acts of terrorism are potentially bankrupting and nearly impossible to predict. The U.S. government's answer has been the passage of the Terrorism Risk Insurance Act of 2003, which provides federal sharing of public and private compensation for insurance of commercial property.

CHARITABLE CONTRIBUTIONS

Although charity is present at most disasters, it was especially prevalent in the WTC disaster, especially in regards to funds collected for victims and victims' families. An estimated 600 charities registered with the IRS with the explicit intention of collecting funds related to the disaster. The top 35 of these funds had collected nearly $2.7 billion by October 2002. The largest of these, the American Red Cross Liberty Fund, had collected over $1 billion. (In addition to the funds collected, the American Red Cross served an estimated 11.5 million meals and provided 50,423 disaster workers in the first two months of the disaster.)

Of the money collected by the charities, over 70 percent had been distributed by October 2002. Much of the money went to victims' families, in an effort to recoup lost salaries. The GAO reports that the average nonuniformed victims' families received $90,000 in cash assistance, and uniformed victims' families, because of charities established especially for them, received an average assistance of $715,000 (Port Authority police), $905,000 (NYC police), and $938,000 (NYC firefighters). Other examples of areas where charities donated money to help include mental health counseling, health care provision, employment assistance, and legal and financial help.

Sources:

Cooper, J.C., & Madigan, K. 2002. "Consumers have done their part. Now, businesses will have to pitch in as faster recovery requires more capital spending and hiring," *Business Week*, September 16, 3799, 19.

Fiscal Policy Institute. 2001. *Economic Impact of the September 11 World Trade Center Attack*, Preliminary Report, September.

Lowenstein, Ronnie. 2002. "Federal aid to New York City in the aftermath of September 11: How much, and for what?" February 11. *Testimony of Ronnie Lowenstein, Director, New York City Independent Budget Office before the Joint Hearing of the City Council Finance, Lower Manhattan Redevelopment, and State and Federal Legislation Committees.*

New York Senate Finance Committee. 2002. *Financial Impact of the World Trade Center Attack*, January.

Office of the State Comptroller. 2002. *The impact of the World Trade Center tragedy on the Metropolitan Transit Authority*. Report 9–2002.

Kadlec, D., Baumohl, B., Sieger, M., & Zagorin, A. 2001. "Up from the ashes," *Time*, September 24, V. 158, 13, 80–82.

Lenain, P., Bonturi, M., & Keon, V. 2002. "The fallout from terrorism: Security and the economy," *Organization for Economic Cooperation and Development. The OECD Observer*, May, 2002, 231/232, 9–13.

Civic Alliance to Rebuild Downtown New York. 2002. *Listening to the city*. February 7.

Loomis, C.J. 2002. "Insurance after 9/11," *Fortune*, June 10. V. 145, 12, 110–115.

Malik, A. 2002. World Trade Center. *GBER*. V. 2, 1, 5–10.

GAO. 2002. More effective collaboration could enhance Charitable Organizations' Contributions in disasters. December. GAO-03-529.

Wall Street Journal. 2001. "New York City expected to recoup most losses of Sept. 11," November 16, A2.

GAO. 2003. *Overview of federal disaster assistance to the New York City area*, October, GAO-04-72.

Ratajczak, D. 2002. "Will insurance be a buffer or a drag to the economy during this recovery?" *Journal of Financial Service Professionals*, May, V. 56, 3, 18–20.

Wikipedia.com. N/D. "Rescue and recovery effort after the September 11, 2001 attacks." At *www.wikipedia.com*.

GAO. 2002. *Review of studies of the economic impact of the September 11, 2001, terrorist attacks on the World Trade Center*, May, GAO-02-700R.

Starkman, D. & Frangos, A. 2004. "Before Ground Zero rebuilding, $1.3 billion has already been spent," *Wall Street Journal*, February 25, A1.

2003. "United States: two years on; New York City," *The Economist*, September 13, V. 368, 8341.

NYCP and CC. 2002. Working together to accelerate New York's recovery: Update of the NYC partnership's economic impact analysis of the September 11 attack on New York City, February 11. *New York City Partnership and Chamber of Commerce.*

New York City Independent Budget Office. 2003. "World Trade Center assistance: aid received, aid to come," *New York City Independent Budget Office: Inside the Budget*, July 31, 117.

New York City Independent Budget Office. 2001. "World Trade Center disaster: tracking federal aid for cleanup and rebuilding," *New York City Independent Budget Office: Inside the Budget*, September 28, 89.

NYCEDC. 2003. "WTC business assistance report," *New York City Economic Development Corporation and New York State Empire State Development Corporation*, February 13.

LMDC. 2003. World Trade Center memorial and cultural program, amended general project plan, September 16. *Lower Manhattan Development Corporation.*

Important Terms

Disaster Recovery Center

Federal Coordinating Officer (FCO)

Joint Field Office (JFO)

National Processing Service Center (NPSC)

Recovery

State Coordinating Officer

Zoning

Self-Check Questions

1. Who plays the largest role in providing the technical and financial support for recovery?
2. What is a Disaster Recovery Center?
3. Which office is the central coordination point among federal, state, local, and tribal agencies and voluntary organizations for delivering recovery assistance programs?
4. What is the purpose of the National Processing Service Centers in Texas, Virginia, and Maryland?
5. What are the four types of assistance provided by the Disaster Housing Program?
6. What is covered under the Individual and Households Program?
7. What is the minimum federal share for FEMA Public Assistance Grants?
8. What entities are eligible for Public Assistance grant funding?
9. What is the difference between emergency work and public work?
10. What federal agencies besides FEMA provide recovery assistance, and what kind of assistance does each provide?
11. What is a VOAD, and what does it do?
12. Name some examples of policy areas and tools that should be considered by decision makers as they develop their recovery plan. Explain why each should be considered.

Out-of-Class Exercises

1. Visit the NVOAD website, and find out what organizations are members of your state VOAD (*http://www.nvoad.org/membersdb.php?members=state*).
2. Contact your state office of emergency management, and ask them if your state has any active recovery operations related to presidentially declared disasters. Find out how much money was granted toward the state, where it went, and what kinds of recovery and mitigation measures it covered.

International Disaster Management

What You'll Learn

- How developing nations are affected by disasters
- Why and how national, international, and nongovernmental organizations assist countries that are affected by major disasters
- Important issues that influence how international disasters are managed
- How several of the United Nations components respond to disasters
- The nongovernmental response to international disasters
- Assistance provided by the United States government to other nations affected by disasters
- Involvement of the international financial institutions, including the World Bank and the International Monetary Fund, in the funding of disaster response, relief, and reconstruction

Introduction

People of all nations face risks associated with the natural and technological hazards described throughout this book, and almost all nations eventually become victims to disaster. Throughout history, civilizations have adapted to their surroundings in the hopes of increasing the likelihood of survival. As societies became more organized, complex systems of response to these hazards were developed on local, national, and regional levels. Response capacity of individual nations can been linked to several factors, including propensity for disaster, local and regional economic resources, government structure, and availability of technological, academic, and human resources. However, as hazards and human settlements change, it is becoming increasingly common that the response capabilities of individual nations fall short in the face of large-scale disasters, and outside international assistance is required. Furthermore, there appears to be an increase in the number of disasters that affect entire regions, which calls upon a global response structure that is still in its infancy.

This chapter describes the international disaster concept and introduces the conglomeration of participants in the international disaster management domain (which includes governmental agencies, international organizations, nongovernmental organizations (NGOs), and financial institutions) that prepare for, respond to, and bring about recovery from them. The mission and goals of each of these entities and groups are described (although their performance is not detailed). In conclusion, a comprehensive case study is presented on the international response to the Gujarat, India, earthquake of January 26, 2001.

Disasters in Developing Nations

Disasters of all kinds strike literally every nation of the world, although these events do not occur with uniformity of distribution. The developing nations suffer the greatest impact of nature's fury, and these same nations are also most often subject to the internal civil conflict that leads to Complex Humanitarian Emergencies (CHEs). Furthermore, the greatest incidence of natural disasters occurs within developing countries, with 90 percent of disaster-related injuries and deaths sustained in countries with per-capita income levels that are below $760 per year (UNICEF, n.d.).

Although disaster preparedness and mitigation are widely accepted by international development agencies to be integral components in the overall development process, it comes as no surprise that countries ranking lower on development indices have placed disaster management very low in budgetary priority. These nations' resources tend to be focused on more socially demanded interests such as education and infrastructure, or on the military, rather than on projects that reduce short- or long-term hazard risk. Because disasters are chance events, and thus not guaranteed to occur, disaster management programs in poor countries tend to be viewed as superfluous. Delegating disaster management responsibilities to the military is also commonly seen even in countries with a moderate level of development, although these agencies rarely are trained to carry out the necessary response tasks required. To compound the situation further, poverty and uncontrolled urbanization often force large populations to concentrate in perilous, high-risk urban areas that contain little or no defense against disasters.

International Disasters

In earlier chapters, the term *disaster* was defined as an adverse event that overwhelms an individual, agency, or jurisdiction's capacity to respond. As each successive jurisdictional level is overwhelmed, the disaster grows in size and scope. When the response capacity of the entire nation's emergency management structure is overwhelmed, that event becomes known as an *international disaster,* and involvement of the international community of responders is required.

The threshold beyond which a disaster becomes international in size and scope is unique to each country and driven by a number of factors, including the severity of hazard consequences, the availability of economic resources, the comprehensiveness and appropriateness of responder training, the built-in resilience of infrastructure, the actual ability and the public impression of the government's ability to manage the situation, and the availability of specialized assets, among many others. Such a threshold is crossed much earlier in poorer countries where deficiencies exist in each of these areas. But even the wealthiest nations find themselves in need of help from the international community from time to time, whether for supplies, manpower, money, or a specific skill or asset that cannot be found locally.

Due to the sheer number of events that have escalated to this level, systems and procedures have emerged by which appeals for assistance are made and offers of support (both unsolicited and solicited) are communicated and enacted. In today's globally interconnected world, driven by instantaneous television (the so-called CNN effect), Internet, and new media, news of a disaster can circle the globe within minutes, stirring the machine of response into action.

Three types of emergencies normally spur an international humanitarian response: natural disasters, technological disasters, and complex humanitarian emergencies (CHEs). The first two are clearly defined, but CHEs have been subject to diverse interpretations and changing standards and thus, for the purposes of this book, are characterized by the definition established by the United Nations (UN). It classifies a CHE as a "humanitarian crisis in a country or region where there is total or considerable breakdown of authority resulting from the internal and/or external conflict and which requires an international response that goes beyond the mandate or capacity of any single agency" (DODCCRP, n.d.). Andrew Natsios (1997), a former director of the U.S. Agency for International Development (USAID), identified five characteristics most commonly seen in CHEs in varying degrees of intensity:

- Civil conflict, rooted in traditional ethnic, tribal, and religious animosities (usually accompanied by widespread atrocities)
- Deteriorated authority of the national government such that public services disappear and political control dissolves
- Mass movements of population to escape conflict or search for food, resulting in refugees and internally displaced people (IDPs)
- Massive dislocation of the economic system, resulting in hyperinflation and the devaluation of the currency, major declines in gross national product, skyrocketing unemployment, and market collapse
- A general decline in food security, often leading to severe malnutrition and occasional widespread starvation

Although these emergencies are fundamentally different from natural and technological disasters in regards to their generally political and intentional sources, they share many characteristics in terms of their requirements for response and recovery. In accordance, many of the organizations and entities described in this chapter respond to all three types of disasters indiscriminately.

Important Issues Influencing the Response Process

Several issues must be addressed when responding to international disasters. The first, *coordination*, is a vital and immediate component because of the sheer numbers of responding agencies that almost always appear. It is not uncommon in larger disasters to see several hundred local and international NGOs, each with a particular skill or service to offer. Successful coordination and cooperation can lead to great success and many lives saved, but infighting, turf battles, and nonparticipation can lead to confusion and even cause a second disaster (PAHO, n.d.).

The UN has become widely recognized as the central coordinating body, with specialized UN agencies handling the more specific needs associated with particular disaster consequences. Most often, the UN capitalizes on long-standing relationships with the host country to form a partnership on which it establishes joint control. However, UN coordination has limited statutory authority, and many of the nongovernmental and faith-based organizations that respond to international disasters continue to operate outside of any such structure. In fact, several organizations and associations have come up with their own standards on coordination and conduct, including the Red Cross Code of Conduct (*www.ifrc.org/publicat/conduct/index .asp*), the Sphere Project Humanitarian Charter and Minimum Standards in Disaster Response (*www.sphereproject.org/handbook_index.htm*), and the Oxfam Code of Conduct for NGOs (*www.oxfam.org*).

The second issue is that of *sovereignty of the state*. State sovereignty is based on the recognition of political authority characterized by territory and autonomy. Accordingly, a foreign nation or organization cannot intercede in domestic matters without the prior consent of the ruling government. This can be a major hurdle in response to CHEs that have resulted from civil war, as continues to plague efforts in Somalia where there is no established or stable government with which stakeholders may work. Although less commonly seen, sovereignty has also been an issue in matters of natural and technological disasters, particularly when a nation does not want to be viewed as weak or unable to take care of its people. Examples of such behavior include Japan's refusal to allow access to international agencies for several days after the earthquake in Kobe, the actions of the former Soviet Union following the nuclear power plant accident in Chernobyl, and most recently the government of Burma's refusal to allow entry of humanitarian aid workers in the aftermath of Cyclone Nargis.

The third issue is *equality in relief distribution*, and this factor also applies to all disaster types. Situations often arise where, for any number of cultural or political reasons, certain groups in need of aid are favored over others. There are two primary causes of such inequality. The first example is discrimination as a result of gender bias, which is most commonly found in societies where gender roles are strictly defined and women are traditionally tasked with duties related to the home and children (which tend to be increased in times of crisis). In these cultures, the men are more likely to have opportunities to wait in relief lines for supplies, and the women (as well as children and the elderly) become even more dependent on them for survival. This situation is exacerbated if a woman is a widow or single parent and has no ability to compete for distributed aid.

ADDITIONAL RESEARCH

Considerable effort has been expended in assessing the effect of gender on disaster vulnerability and the recovery abilities of individuals living in societies where gender bias is prevalent. The following reports shed considerable light on the plight of women affected by disasters throughout the world:

- The Pan American Health Organization fact sheet "Gender and Natural Disasters." *http://www.paho.org/English/DPM/GPP/GH/genderdisasters.pdf*
- The World Health Organization assessment tool "Gender Considerations in Disaster Assessment." *http://www.who.int/gender/other_health/en/gwhdisasterassessment.pdf*
- The World Health Organization paper "Gender and Health in Disasters"

The second form of inequality in relief is that of class bias. Although most obvious in social systems explicitly based on caste identity, underlying ethnic and racial divides often present similar problems. Avoiding these forms of bias is difficult because the agencies involved must be aware of the discrimination in order to counteract its influence. Often, host-country nationals are "hired" by humanitarian agencies to assist in relief distribution, and inadvertent hiring of specific ethnic or social groups can lead to unfair distribution along those same ethnic/social lines. At the same time, humanitarian agencies are quick to focus on those groups most visibly affected by a CHE, such as IDP populations, causing an inordinate percentage of aid to be directed to them while other needy groups go unnoticed.

Many of the international response agencies are continuously developing systems of relief and distribution that work to counteract the complex problems associated with these biases; however, the difficult nature of this issue is highlighted in the fact that specifically targeting groups, such as women or children, can lead to reverse discrimination. Any of these biases can lead to a decline in perceived legitimacy or impartiality of the assisting agency and/or result in exacerbation of the needs being addressed (Maynard, n.d.).

A fourth issue is the importance of *capacity building* and *linking relief with development*. Responding agencies have an obligation to avoid using a bandage approach in assisting the affected country. Disasters almost always present a window of opportunity to rebuild old, ineffective structures and develop policy and practice in a way that leaves behind a more empowered, resilient community. Because these goals mirror those of most traditional development agencies, linking relief and development should not be a major deviation from either type of agencies' missions. These opportunities are greatest in situations that require the complete restoration of infrastructure and basic social services, and are found equally in disaster and CHE scenarios. In the reconstruction phase, it is vital that training and information exchanges occur and that local risk is fully incorporated to mitigate for repeat disasters. These repeat disasters often contribute greatly to a nation's lag in development, and therefore fully addressing them is vital to increasing the nation's likelihood of being developed sustainably.

CRITICAL THINKING

- Do problems associated with equality in distribution of relief occur only in developing countries, or can they occur in any country? Can you find any examples of times when there has been inequality in relief distribution in the United States?
- Why is it imperative that relief is linked with development? Do you think that disaster relief makes recipient nations more dependent or more independent? Explain your answer.

The United Nations System

The UN began in 1945, when representatives from 51 countries met in San Francisco to establish the United Nations Charter as a commitment to preserve peace in the aftermath of World War II. Later that year, the Charter was ratified by the five permanent members: China, France, the Soviet Union, the United Kingdom, and the United States, as well as several other countries. Today, 192 countries are members of the UN, and the Charter (which is similar to a sovereign state's constitution and establishes the rights and responsibilities of member states) is amended as is necessary to reflect the changing needs of current world politics.

The UN itself is not a government body, nor does it write laws; however, the autonomous member states do have the ability through the UN to resolve conflict and create international policy. No decision or action can be forced on a sovereign state, but as global ideals are naturally reflected through these collaborative policies, they usually are given due consideration.

Through the major UN bodies and their associated programs, the UN has established a presence in most countries throughout the world and fostered partnerships with Member State governments. Although more than 70 percent of UN work is devoted to development activities, several other issues are central in their mission, including disaster mitigation, preparedness, response, and recovery. In the event of a disaster, the UN is quite possibly the best equipped to coordinate disaster relief and to work with the governments to rehabilitate and reconstruct. This is especially true in the case of the developing countries, where regular projects are ongoing and must be adjusted to accommodate for damages to infrastructure and economy caused by recurrent disasters, and where disasters quickly exhaust the response capabilities.

Upon onset of a disaster, the UN responds immediately and on an ongoing basis by supplying aid in the form of food, shelter, medical assistance, and logistical support. The UN Emergency Relief Coordinator heads the international UN response to crises through a committee of several humanitarian bodies, including the UN Children's Fund (UNICEF), the UN Development Programme (UNDP), the World Food Programme (WFP), the UN High Commissioner for Refugees (UNHCR), and other associates as deemed necessary in accordance with the problems specific to the event. Each of these agencies, as shown in this section, fulfills a specific need presented by most humanitarian emergencies, be they natural or man-made.

The UN also promotes prevention and mitigation activities through its regular development projects. By encouraging the building of early warning systems and the conducting of monitoring and forecasting routines, they are working to increase local capacity to adequately boost local and regional preparedness. In conclusion of the International Decade for Natural Disaster Reduction of the 1990s (which strove to focus on a shift from disaster response–oriented projects to disaster mitigation), the UN adopted its International Strategy for Disaster Reduction (ISDR) to promote the necessity of disaster reduction and risk mitigation as part of its central mission. This initiative seeks to enable global resilience to the effects of natural hazards in order to reduce human, economic, and social losses, through the following mechanisms:

- Increasing public awareness
- Obtaining commitment from public authorities
- Stimulating interdisciplinary and intersectoral partnership and expanding risk-reduction networking at all levels
- Enhancing scientific research of the causes of natural disasters and the effects of natural hazards and related technological and environmental disasters on societies

These strategies are carried out through the country offices and local governments in the most vulnerable communities. Mitigation and preparedness strategies are implemented at all levels of society via public awareness campaigns, secured commitment from public authorities, intersectoral cooperation and communication, and technical knowledge transfer.

The United Nations Development Programme

The UNDP was established in 1965 during the UN Decade of Development to conduct investigations into private investment in developing countries, to explore the natural resources of those countries, and to train the local population in development activities (such as mining and manufacturing). As the concept and practice of development expanded, the UNDP assumed much greater responsibilities in host countries and in the UN as a whole.

The UNDP was not originally considered an agency on the forefront of international disaster management and humanitarian emergencies because, while it addressed national capacities, it did not focus specifically on the emergency *response* systems (previously considered to be the focal point of disaster management). However, as mitigation and preparedness received their due merit, the UNDP gained increased recognition for its vital risk reduction role. Capacity building has always been central to the UNDP's mission in terms of empowering host countries to be better able to address issues of national importance, eventually without foreign assistance.

International disaster management gained greater attention as more disasters affected larger populations and caused greater financial impacts. Developing nations, where the UNDP worked, faced the greatest inability to prepare and/or respond to these disasters. The UNDP's projects have shifted toward activities that indirectly fulfill mitigation and preparedness roles. For instance, projects seeking to strengthen government institutions also improve those institutions' capacities to respond with appropriate and effective policy, power, and leadership in the wake of a disaster.

The UNDP now recognizes that disaster management must be viewed as integral to their mission in the developing world, as well as to civil conflict and Complex Humanitarian Emergency (CHE) scenarios. As excerpts from the UNDP mission show, there are implicit similarities between UNDP ideals and those of agencies whose goals specifically aim to mitigate and manage humanitarian emergencies. Here are some examples:

- [The UNDP] is committed to the principle that development is inseparable from the quest for peace and human security and that the UN must be a strong force for development as well as peace.
- UNDP's mission is to help countries in their efforts to achieve sustainable human development by assisting them to build their capacity to design and carry out development programs in poverty eradication, employment creation and sustainable livelihoods, the empowerment of women and the protection and regeneration of the environment, giving first priority to poverty eradication.
- UNDP strives to be an effective development partner for the UN relief agencies, working to sustain livelihoods while they seek to sustain lives. It acts to help countries to prepare for, avoid and manage complex emergencies and disasters.
- UNDP supports [development] cooperation by actively promoting the exchange of experience among developing countries.

The UNDP links disaster vulnerability to a lack of or weak infrastructure, poor environmental policy, land misuse, and growing populations in disaster-prone areas. When disasters occur, a country's national development, which the UNDP serves to promote, can be set back years, if not decades. Even small to medium-size disasters in the least developed countries can "have a cumulative impact on already fragile household economies and can be as significant in total losses as the major and internationally recognized disasters" (SARPN, n.d.). It is the UNDP's objective to "achieve a sustainable reduction in disaster risks and the protection of development gains, reduce the loss of life and livelihoods due to disasters, and ensure that disaster recovery serves to consolidate sustainable human development" (UNDP, n.d.).

In 1995, as part of the UN's changing approach to humanitarian relief, the Emergency Response Division (ERD) was created within the UNDP, augmenting the organization's role in disaster response. Additionally, 5 percent of UNDP budgeted resources were allocated for quick response actions in special development situations by ERD teams, thus drastically reducing bureaucratic delays. The ERD was designed to create a collaborative framework among the national government, UN agencies, donors, and NGOs that will immediately respond to disasters, provide communication and travel to disaster management staff, and distribute relief supplies and equipment. It will also deploy to disaster-affected countries for 30 days to create a detailed response plan on which the UNDP response will be based.

In 1997, under the UN Programme for Reform, the mitigation and preparedness responsibilities of the OCHA Emergency Relief Coordinator were formally transferred to the UNDP. In response, the UNDP created the Disaster Reduction and Recovery Programme (DRRP) within the ERD. Soon after, the UNDP again reorganized, creating a Bureau of Crisis Prevention and Recovery (BCPR) with an overarching mission of addressing a range of nonresponse-related issues:

- Natural disaster reduction
- Recovery
- Mine action
- Conflict prevention and peace building
- Justice and security sector reform
- Small arms and demobilization

The BCPR helps the UNDP country offices prepare to activate and provide faster and more effective disaster response and recovery. It also works to ensure that the UNDP plays an active role in the transition between relief and development. The UNDP's disaster management activities focus primarily on the development-related aspects of risk and vulnerability and on capacity-building technical assistance in all four phases of emergency management.

The UNDP has created the Disaster Reduction Unit (DRU) within the BCPR, which includes a team of seven Geneva-based officials and four regional disaster reduction advisors located in Bangkok, Nairobi, New Delhi, and Panama. The DRU works to reduce disaster risk and increase sustainable recovery in countries where the UNDP operates. It strengthens national and regional capacities by ensuring that new development projects consider known hazard risks, that disaster impacts are mitigated and development gains are protected, and that risk reduction is factored into disaster recovery. The DRU provides the UNDP country offices with technical assistance and financial support for the design and implementation of disaster reduction strategies and capacity-building programs to carry out these goals.

The UNDP Recovery Unit

Following conflict, crises, and disasters, countries must eventually (and as quickly as possible) transition from response to recovery. Many countries are unable to manage the difficult and diverse needs of recovery on their own, as they may have experienced widespread loss of infrastructure and services. Displaced persons and refugees may have little to return to, and economies may be damaged or destroyed. The Recovery Unit (under the

BCPR) operates during the period when the response or relief phase of the disaster has ended but recovery has not fully commenced (sometimes referred to as the "early recovery period").

The Recovery Unit addresses problems normally encountered in this postcrisis period through its Transition Recovery Programme. This program works to restore government and community capacities to rebuild and recover so as to prevent a return to a crisis situation. Sustainable risk reduction as a component of recovery is central to this mission. The UNDP has recognized that local expertise in risk management and reduction may not be available, and that the technical assistance they provide may be the only option these communities have to increase their resilience to future disasters. This program has proven effective in many recovery operations, including Cambodia after three decades of civil war; Afghanistan after the 2001 conflict; Gujarat, India, after the 2001 earthquake; and from 2008 to 2010 in Sri Lanka after the 26 years of civil war. Specific activities of the UNDP Recovery Unit include the following:

- Performing early assessments of recovery needs and designing integrated recovery frameworks
- Planning and assistance in area-based development and local governance programs
- Developing comprehensive reintegration programs for former Internally Displaced Persons (IDPs), returning refugees, and ex-combatants
- Supporting economic recovery both at the local and national levels
- Supporting in-country capacity building, UN system coordination, resource mobilization, and partnerships

To meet these recovery priorities, five support services have been developed within the Recovery Unit to assist the UNDP country offices and other UNDP/UN agencies to identify areas where the BCPR and the Recovery Unit can provide assistance. These support services include the following:

- Early assessment of recovery needs and the design of integrated recovery frameworks
- Planning and assistance in area-based development and local governance programs
- Developing comprehensive reintegration programs for IDPs, returning refugees, and ex-combatants
- Supporting economic recovery and revitalization
- Supporting capacity building, coordination, resource mobilization, and partnerships

When required to assist in recovery operations, the Recovery Unit may deploy a special Transition Recovery Team (TRT) to supplement UNDP operations in the affected country. These teams' focus varies according to specific needs. For instance, when neighboring countries have interlinked problems (such as cross-border reintegration of ex-combatants and displaced persons), the TRT may support a subregional approach to recovery.

It is important to note that the UNDP has no primary role in the middle of a CHE peacekeeping response; rather, they fulfill a supportive role by ensuring development is tied into relief. During recovery and reconstruction, together with others, they take the lead. In addition to the roles and responsibilities just mentioned, the UNDP leads several interagency working groups. One such group (which consists of representatives from the World Food Programme, the World Health Organization, the Food and Agriculture Organization, the UN Populations Fund, and the UN International Children's Emergency Relief Fund) develops principles and guidelines to incorporate disaster risk into the Common Country Assessment and the UN Development Assistance Framework. The International Strategy for Disaster Reduction Working Group on Risk, Vulnerability and Disaster Impact Assessment sets guidelines for social impact assessments. The UNDP also coordinates a Disaster Management Training Programme in Central America, runs the conference "The Use of Microfinance and Micro-Credit for the Poor in Recovery and Disaster Reduction," and has created a program to elaborate financial instruments to enable the poor to manage disaster risks.

The UNDP has several reasons for its success in fulfilling its roles in the mitigation, preparedness, and recovery for natural and man-made disasters. First, as a permanent in-country office with close ties to most government agencies, activities related to coordination and planning, monitoring, and training are simply an extension of ongoing relationships. Second, the UNDP functions as a coordinating body of the UN agencies concerned with development, so when crisis situations appear, there is an established, stable platform from which it may lead. And third, the UNDP has experience dealing with donors, be they foreign governments or development banks, and therefore can handle the outpouring of aid that usually results during the relief and recovery period of a disaster. This contributes greatly to reducing levels of corruption and increasing the cost-effectiveness of generated funds. In several recent events, the UNDP has established formalized funds to handle large donor contributions, which have been used for long-term postdisaster reconstruction efforts.

The United Nations Office for the Coordination of Humanitarian Affairs

Prior to 1991, the UN Disaster Relief Coordinator managed natural disasters, and special representatives of the UN Secretary General coordinated CHEs. However, UN Resolution 46/182, adopted in December 1991, merged these two roles to create the Emergency Relief Coordinator (ERC). The Department of Humanitarian Affairs was created soon after, with the ERC elevated to the status of Under Secretary General for Humanitarian Affairs. The UN Office for the Coordination of Humanitarian Affairs (OCHA) replaced the Department of Humanitarian Affairs under the UN Secretary General's Program for Reform in 1998. OCHA was established to accommodate the needs of victims of disasters and emergencies, with its specific role in disaster management the coordination of assistance provided by the UN system (in emergencies that exceed the capacity and mandate of any individual agency). OCHA response to disasters can be categorized under three main groupings:

- Coordinating the international humanitarian response
- Providing support and policy development to the humanitarian community
- Advocating for humanitarian issues to ensure that the overall direction of relief reflects the general needs of recovery and peace building

OCHA operations are carried out by a staff of approximately 1,795 people in New York, Geneva, and in the field. OCHA's 2009 budget was $239,617,000, of which only slightly more than 5 percent was from the regular UN budget. The remaining 95 percent is from "extra-budgetary resources," primarily donations from member states and donor organizations.

As head of OCHA, the Under Secretary General for Humanitarian Affairs/UN Emergency Relief Coordinator is responsible for the coordination of UN response efforts through the Inter-Agency Standing Committee (IASC). The IASC consists of UN and outside humanitarian organization leaders, and analyzes crisis scenarios to formulate joint responses that maximize effectiveness and minimize overlap. The ERC works to deploy appropriate personnel from throughout the UN to assist UN resident coordinators and lead agencies to increase on-site coordination. In March 2007, the Secretary General appointed John Holmes of the United Kingdom to replace Jan Egeland of Norway as Under Secretary General for Humanitarian Affairs and Emergency Relief Coordinator.

OCHA's Disaster Response System monitors the onset of natural and technological disasters. This system includes training assessment teams before disasters strike, as well as conducting postdisaster evaluations. When a disaster is identified, OCHA activates a response and generates a situation report to provide the international response community with detailed information (including damage assessment, actions taken, needs assessment, and current assistance provided). If necessary, OCHA may then deploy a UN Disaster Assessment and Coordination (UNDAC) team to assist relief activity coordination and assess damages and needs.

If a disaster appears inevitable or is already significant, the ERC in consultation with IASC may designate a humanitarian coordinator (HC), who becomes the most senior UN humanitarian official on the ground for the emergency. The HC is directly accountable to the ERC, thereby increasing the likelihood that the humanitarian assistance provided is quick, effective, and well coordinated. The HC appointment generally signals that the event merits a long-term humanitarian presence. The criteria used by the ERC in deciding whether to appoint an HC are based on recognition of a need for the following:

- Intensive and extensive political management, mediation, and coordination to enable the delivery of humanitarian response, including negotiated access to affected populations

- Massive humanitarian assistance requiring action by a range of participants beyond a single national authority
- A high degree of external political support, often from the UN Security Council

An On-Site Operations Coordination Center (OSOCC) may be set up in the field to assist local first-response teams to coordinate the often overwhelming number of responding agencies. Finally, OCHA can set up communications capabilities if they have been damaged or do not exist at an adequate level, as required by the UN responding agencies. OCHA generally concludes its responsibilities when the operation moves from response to recovery.

Overall, OCHA coordinates humanitarian affairs to maximize response and recovery operations and minimize duplications and inefficiencies through established structures and policies set forth by the IASC (adapted from OCHA, 2005):

- Developing common strategies
- Assessing situations and needs
- Convening coordination forums
- Mobilizing resources
- Addressing common problems
- Administering coordination mechanisms and tools

The Field Coordination Support Unit in Geneva manages the human, technical, and logistical resources OCHA uses. These resources are primarily provided by the Danish and Norwegian Refugee Councils, the Danish Emergency Management Agency, the Swedish Rescue Services Agency, and the Emergency Logistics Management Team of the United Kingdom Overseas Development Administration.

The Emergency Relief Coordinator

The Under Secretary General for Humanitarian Affairs/Emergency Relief Coordinator advises the UN Secretary General on disaster-related issues, chairs the Executive Committee on Humanitarian Affairs (ECHA), and leads the IASC. The coordinator is assisted by a deputy, who holds the position of Deputy Emergency Relief Coordinator (DERC) and is responsible for key coordination, policy, and management issues.

The Inter-Agency Standing Committee (IASC)

The IASC was established in 1992 under UN Resolution 46/182. It serves as a platform within which the broad range of UN and non-UN humanitarian partners (including UN humanitarian agencies, the International Organization for Migration, three consortia of major international NGOs, and the Red Cross movement) may come together to address the humanitarian needs resulting from a disaster. The IASC's primary role is to formulate humanitarian policy that ensures a coordinated and effective response to all kinds of disaster and emergency situations. The primary objectives of the IASC are to (OCHA, 2005):

- Develop and agree on systemwide humanitarian policies
- Allocate responsibilities among agencies in humanitarian programs
- Develop and agree on a common ethical framework for all humanitarian activities
- Advocate common humanitarian principles to parties outside the IASC
- Identify areas where gaps in mandates or lack of operational capacity exist
- Resolve disputes or disagreement about and between humanitarian agencies on systemwide humanitarian issues

The Executive Committee on Humanitarian Affairs (ECHA)

ECHA was created by the UN Secretary General to enhance coordination among UN agencies working on humanitarian affairs issues. ECHA meets on a monthly basis in New York to add a political and peacekeeping dimension to humanitarian consultations.

The OCHA Donor Relations Section

The OCHA Donor Relations Section (DRS), separated from the Consolidated Appeals Process in 2003, is the focal point for all relations with donors, particularly for funding-related issues. DRS advises the senior management team on policy issues related to inter-action with donors and resource mobilization. In addition, it plays a key role in facilitating the interaction of all OCHA entities with donors, both at headquarters and in the field level.

The Coordination and Response Division

The Coordination and Response Division (CRD) was created in 2004 by joining the former New York–based Humanitarian Emergency Branch and the Geneva-based Response Coordination Branch. The CRD is responsible for providing disaster-related direction, guidance, and support to the ERC, the UN Resident/Humanitarian Coordinators, and OCHA's field offices (including the deployment of extra personnel as necessary or emergency cash grants).

The OCHA Emergency Services Branch (ESB)

Based in Geneva, the ESB was created to expedite the provision of international humanitarian assistance. The ESB develops, mobilizes, and coordinates the deployment of OCHA's international rapid response "tool kit"—the expertise, systems, and services that aim to improve humanitarian assistance in support of disaster-afflicted countries. The ESB's humanitarian response activities include the coordination of disaster response and assessment (UNDAC), the setting of international urban search and rescue standards (INSARAG), and the establishment of OSOCCs.

The *Field Coordination Support Section (FCSS)* was established within the ESB in 1996 to support national governments and the UN Resident Coordinators in developing, preparing, and maintaining "standby capacity" for rapid deployment to sudden-onset emergencies to conduct rapid needs assessments and coordination. The FCSS manages several programs and offices to improve international disaster coordination and cooperation, including the following:

- *The United Nations Disaster Assessment and Coordination (UNDAC) Team.* The UNDAC team is made up of disaster management specialists selected and funded by the governments of UN member states, OCHA, UNDP, and operational humanitarian UN agencies (such as WFP, UNICEF, and WHO). It provides rapid needs assessments and supports national authorities and the UN Resident Coordinator in coordinating international relief. UNDAC teams are on permanent standby status so that they can deploy within hours.
- *The International Search and Rescue Advisory Group (INSARAG).* INSARAG is an intergovernmental network within the UN that manages urban search-and-rescue (USAR) and related disaster-response issues. It promotes information exchange, defines international USAR standards, and develops methodologies for international cooperation and coordination in earthquake response.
- *The Virtual On-Site Operations Coordination Centre (Virtual OSOCC).* The Internet has made it possible for humanitarian relief agencies to share and exchange disaster information continuously and simultaneously, and between any locations where Internet access can be obtained. The Virtual OSOCC is a central repository of information maintained by OCHA that facilitates this exchange of information with NGOs and responding governments. The information is stored on an interactive Web-based database, where users can comment on existing information and discuss issues of concern with other stakeholders.
- *The Surge Capacity Project (including the Emergency Response Roster).* OCHA's Surge Capacity Project seeks to ensure that OCHA always has the means and resources to rapidly mobilize and deploy staff and materials to address the needs of countries affected by sudden-onset emergencies. The Emergency Response Roster (ERR), which became active in June 2002, aims to rapidly deploy OCHA staff to sudden-onset emergencies to conduct assessments and establish initial coordination mechanisms. Staff included in the ERR are deployable within 48 hours of a request for their services through a deployment methodology based on the UNDAC model. Staff serve on the roster for two months at a time.

Established by the IASC in 1995, the *Military and Civil Defense Unit (MCDU)* supports humanitarian agencies by providing military and/or civil defense assets. The MCDU conducts civil-military coordination courses and coordinates UN participation in major humanitarian emergency exercises. The MCDU also maintains the UN's Central Register, which is a database of noncommercial, governmental, and other resources that may be called on for humanitarian response and includes a full range of equipment and supplies, teams of experts, and disaster response contacts.

The *Logistics Support Unit (LSU)* manages stocks of basic relief items that can be dispatched immediately to disaster- or emergency-stricken areas. The stockpile, which is located at the UN Humanitarian Response Depot in Brindisi, Italy, includes nonfood, nonmedical relief items (such as shelter, water purification and distribution systems, and household items) donated by UN member governments. The LSU is also involved in other logistical challenges, such as designing contingency plans for the rapid deployment of emergency relief flights and providing interface on logistical matters with other humanitarian agencies (such as WFP, WHO, UNHCR, IFRC, and ICRC). The LSU participates in the operation of a UN Joint Logistics Center and has cosponsored an effort to adopt a UN-wide system for tracking relief supplies and common procedures for air operations. Finally, the LSU contributes information to the CRR related to stockpiles and customs facilitation agreements (which helps speed up the delivery of relief items).

The Environmental Emergencies Section, or the Joint UN Environmental Programme (UNEP)/OCHA Environment Unit, serves as the integrated UN emergency response mechanism that provides international assistance to countries experiencing environmental disasters and emergencies. The joint unit can rapidly mobilize and coordinate emergency assistance and response resources to countries facing environmental emergencies and natural disasters with significant environmental impacts. The unit performs several key functions geared toward facilitating rapid and coordinated disaster response, including the following:

- Monitoring
- Notification
- Brokerage
- Information clearinghouse
- Mobilization of assistance
- Assessment
- Financial assistance

OCHA Preparedness and Mitigation Measures

Although OCHA's efforts primarily focus on coordinating humanitarian emergency response, the agency also serves a risk-reduction function. For instance, OCHA representatives work with operational humanitarian agencies to develop common policies aimed at improving how the humanitarian response network prepares for and responds to disasters. It also works to promote preparedness and mitigation efforts in member states to decrease vulnerability. CRD and ESB work closely with the UN Development Programme, other UN programs as necessary, and outside organizations on various projects and activities to increase working relationships with national governments and apply lessons learned from completed disaster responses.

OCHA's Geneva offices are continually monitoring geologic and meteorological conditions, as well as major news services, for early recognition or notification of emerging disasters. Working with UN resident coordinators, country teams and regional disaster response advisers, OCHA maintains close contact with disaster-prone countries in advance of and during disaster events. OCHA's Regional Disaster Response Advisers work with national governments to provide technical, strategic, and training assistance. They also provide this assistance to other UN agencies and regional organizations to improve international disaster management capacity.

OCHA Information Tools and Services

Clearly, information is key to disaster management, and information must be timely and accurate to be useful. This is especially true in the case of early warning and disaster prevention initiatives. OCHA maintains several information management activities in support of its humanitarian efforts, and provides systems to collect, analyze, disseminate, and exchange information. These functions are performed jointly by the Early Warning and Contingency Planning Unit, the ReliefWeb project, the Field Information Support Project, and the Integrated Regional Information Networks.

Department of Economic and Social Affairs (DESA)

DESA is another component within the Secretariat that addresses disaster management, primarily in regards to predisaster capacity building. DESA addresses a full range of issues under three general areas:

- It compiles, generates, and analyzes a wide range of economic, social, and environmental data and information from which member states draw to review common problems and evaluate policy options.
- It facilitates the negotiations of member states in many intergovernmental bodies on joint courses of action to address ongoing or emerging global challenges.
- It advises national governments on translating UN-developed policy frameworks into country-level programs and, through technical assistance, helps build national capacities.

This final area is where DESA addresses disaster management activities within its Division for Sustainable Development. As part of this effort, DESA launched a plan of action during the 2002 World Summit on Sustainable Development in Johannesburg, South Africa, that included commitments to disaster and vulnerability reduction.

The UN Centre for Regional Development (UNCRD) is another component of DESA that addresses disaster management issues. Through its headquarters in Nagoya, Japan, and its regional offices in Nairobi, Kenya, and Bogotá, Colombia, UNCRD supports training and research on regional development issues and facilitates information dissemination and exchange. UNCRD maintains a Disaster Management Planning Office in Hyogo, Japan, that researches and develops community-based, sustainable projects for disaster management planning and capacity building in developing countries. Examples of ongoing projects maintained by the Hyogo office include the Housing Earthquake Safety Initiative in Algeria, Indonesia, Nepal, and Peru, and the School Earthquake Safety Initiative in Fiji, India, Indonesia, and Uzbekistan.

The Regional Commissions

Five regional economic commissions are within the Economic and Social Council. The secretariats of these regional commissions are part of the UN Secretariat and perform many of the same functions (including the disaster management functions just listed). The five commissions promote greater economic cooperation in the world and augment economic and social development. As part of their mission, they initiate and manage projects that focus on disaster management. While their projects primarily deal with disaster preparedness and mitigation, they also work in regions that have been affected by a disaster to ensure that economic and social recovery involves adequate consideration of risk reduction measures. These are the five regional commissions:

- The Economic and Social Commission for Asia and the Pacific (ESCAP)— *www.unescap.org*
- The Economic Commission for Latin America and the Caribbean (ECLAC)— *www.eclac.cl/*
- The Economic Commission for Europe (ECE)—*www.unece.org/*
- The Economic Commission for Africa (ECA)—*www.uneca.org/*
- The Economic and Social Commission for Western Asia (ESCWA)—*www.escwa.org.lb*

The United Nations Children's Fund

Like most other major UN agencies, the UN Children's Fund (UNICEF, formerly known as the United Nations International Children's Emergency Fund) was established in the aftermath of World War II. Its original mandate was to aid the children suffering in postwar Europe, but its mission has been expanded to address the problems that affect poor children throughout the world. UNICEF is mandated by the General Assembly to serve as an advocate for children's rights, to ensure that each child receives at least the minimum requirements for survival, and to increase their opportunities for a successful future. Under the Convention on the Rights of the Child (CRC), a treaty ratified by 194 countries (all countries except the United States), the UNHCR holds wide-reaching legal authority to carry out its mission.

Before the onset of disasters, it is not uncommon for UNICEF to have established itself as a permanent in-country presence, with regular budgetary resources. In the situations of disaster or armed conflict where this is the case, UNICEF is well poised to serve an immediate role as aid provider to its specific target groups. This rapid response is important because young mothers and children are often the most marginalized groups in terms of aid received. UNICEF works on a regular basis to ensure that children have access to education, healthcare, safety, and protected child rights. In the response and recovery periods of humanitarian emergencies, these roles are merely expanded to suit the rapidly extended requirements of victims. In countries where UNICEF has not yet established a permanent presence, the form of aid is virtually the same; however, the timing and delivery are affected, and reconstruction is not nearly as comprehensive.

UNICEF maintains that humanitarian assistance should include programs aimed specifically for child victims. Relief projects generally work to provide a rapidly needed response in the form of immunizations, water and sanitation, nutrition, education, and health. Women are recipients of this aid as well because UNICEF considers them to be vital in the care of children. UNICEF also works through recovery and reconstruction projects, providing for the basic rights of children. UNICEF is currently active in 186 countries.

The World Food Programme

The World Food Programme (WFP) is the arm of the UN tasked with reacting to hunger-related emergencies throughout the developing world. The WFP was created late in 1961 by a resolution adopted by the UN General Assembly and the UN Food and Agriculture Organization (FAO). Chance enabled the program to prove the necessity of their existence when the WFP provided relief to more than 5 million people several months before they were deemed officially operational in 1963. In the year 2009 alone, the WFP fed more than 108 million people in 74 countries, up from 102 million in 78 countries in 2008. Over the course of its existence, the WFP has provided more than 50 million metric tons of food to countries worldwide.

Because food is a necessity for human survival, it is a vital component of development. The WFP works throughout the world to assist the poor who do not have sufficient food to survive "to break the cycle of hunger and poverty." Hunger alone can be seen as a crisis because more than 1.02 billion people across the globe receive less than the minimum standard requirement of food for healthy survival. Hunger is often associated with other crises, including drought, famine, and human displacement, among others.

In rapid-onset events such as natural disasters, the WFP is activated as a major player in the response to the immediate nutritional needs of the victims. Food is transported to the affected location and delivered to storage and distribution centers. The distribution is carried out according to preestablished needs assessments performed by OCHA and the UNDP. The WFP distributes food through contracted NGOs who have vast experience and technical skills required to plan and implement such projects of transportation, storage, and distribution. The principal partners in their planning and implementation are the host governments (who must request the aid of the WFP to begin with, unless the situation is a CHE where there is no established government, and the UN Secretary General makes the request). The WFP works closely with all responding UN agencies to coordinate an effective and broad-reaching response because food requirements are so closely linked to every other vital need of disaster victims.

In the aftermath of disasters, during the reconstruction phase, it is often necessary for the WFP to remain an active player through continued food distribution. Rehabilitation projects are implemented in a way that fosters increased local development, and include providing food aid to families, who as a result will have extra money to use in rebuilding their lives, and food for work programs, which break the chains of reliance on aid as well as provide an incentive to rebuild communities.

The World Health Organization

The idea for the World Health Organization (WHO) was proposed during the original meetings to establish the UN system in San Francisco in 1945. In 1946, at the United Health Conference in New York, the WHO constitution was approved, and on April 7 (World Health Day), it was signed and made official. Like the WFP, WHO proved its value by responding to an emergency (a cholera epidemic in Egypt) months before it was an officially recognized organization.

WHO was established to serve as the central authority on sanitation and health issues throughout the world. It works with national governments to develop medical capabilities and health care and assist them in the suppression of epidemics. WHO supports research for the eradication of disease and provides expertise on these subjects when requested. It also provides training and technical support and develops standards for medical care.

In the event of a disaster, WHO responds in several ways that address the health of victims. Most important, it provides ongoing monitoring of diseases traditionally observed within the unsanitary conditions of disaster aftermath. WHO also provides technical assistance to the responding agencies and host governments that are establishing disaster medical capabilities and serves as a constant source of expertise as needs arise.

CRITICAL THINKING

Is the United Nations the organization best suited to coordinate the response to international disasters? Why or why not? If not, who do you believe should be tasked with coordination?

Nongovernmental Organizations

The number of nongovernmental organizations (NGOs) focusing on international humanitarian relief has grown exponentially in the past few decades. These organizations have come to play a vital role in the response to and recovery from disasters, filling gaps left by national and multilateral organizations. They have significantly improved the ability of international relief efforts to address the needs of victims with a diverse range of skills and supplies. Some of the larger NGOs, like the International Committee of the Red Cross (ICRC), have established an international presence similar to that of the UN and have developed strong local institutional partnerships and a capacity to respond almost immediately with great effectiveness. These grassroots-level organizations are so successful in their activities that the major funding organizations such as USAID, OFDA, and the UN regularly arrange for relief projects to be implemented by them rather than their own staff.

There are several classifications of humanitarian organizations, and for the purpose of clarification, they are described as follows. The following broad categorical definitions are widely accepted among the agencies of the international relief community. These are not definitive categories into which each organization will neatly fit, but they have become part of standardized nomenclature in disaster response:

- *Nongovernmental organization (NGO).* The general term for an organization made up of private citizens, with no affiliation with a government of any nation other than the support from government sources in the form of financial or in-kind contributions. These groups are motivated by greatly varying factors, ranging from religious beliefs to humanitarian values. NGOs are considered national if they work in one country, international if they are based out of one country but work in more than four countries, and multinational if they have partner organizations in several countries. Oxfam and the ICRC are examples of multinational NGOs. NGOs can be further defined according to their functionality. Examples of these would be the religious groups, such as the Catholic Church; interest groups, such as Rotary International; residents' organizations; occupational organizations; educational organizations; and so on.
- *Private voluntary organization (PVO).* An organization that is nonprofit, tax-exempt, and receives at least a part of its funding from private donor sources. PVOs also receive some degree of voluntary contributions in the form of cash, work, or in-kind gifts. This classification is steadily being grouped together under the more general NGO classification. It should be mentioned that although all PVOs are NGOs, the opposite is not true.
- *International organization (IO).* An organization with global presence and influence. Although both the UN and ICRC are IOs, only the ICRC could be considered an NGO. There exists international law providing a legal framework under which these organizations can function.
- *Donor agencies.* Private, national, or regional organizations whose mission is to provide the financial and material resources for humanitarian relief and subsequent rehabilitation. These donated resources may go to other NGOs, other national governments, or to private citizens. Examples of donor agencies are USAID, the European Community Humanitarian Organization (ECHO), and the World Bank.
- *Coordinating organizations.* Associations of NGOs that coordinate the activities of hundreds of preregistered member organizations to ensure response with maximized impact. They can decrease the amount of overlap and help distribute assistance to the greatest range of victims. Also, they have the ability to analyze immediate needs

assessments and recommend which member organizations would be most effective in response. Examples of coordinating organizations include InterAction and the International Council for Voluntary Agencies (ICVA).

NGOs bring to the field several resources. First, they are well regarded as information-gathering bodies and thus are vital in establishing accuracy in the development of damage and needs assessments. They tend to provide a single skill or group of specific technical skills, such as the medical abilities of Medicin sans Frontiers (MSF, Doctors without Borders) or Oxfam's ability to address nutritional needs. The sheer number of helping bodies that are provided by the involvement of NGOs allows for a greater capability to reach a larger population in less time. Finally, the amount of financial support provided as a result of the fundraising abilities of NGOs brings about much greater cash resources to address the needs of victims.

These organizations can be characterized by several commonly seen characteristics:

1. They value their independence and neutrality.
2. They tend to be decentralized in their organizational structure.
3. They are committed.
4. They are highly practice-oriented.

The most well-known and most widely established NGO is the Red Cross.

The International Red Cross

The International Red Cross/Red Crescent Movement consists of the International Federation of Red Cross and Red Crescent Societies (IFRC) and the International Committee of the Red Cross (ICRC). The concept of the Red Cross was initiated by Henry Dunant in 1859, following a particularly brutal battle in Italy that he witnessed. Dunant gathered a local group to provide care for the battle-wounded through medical assistance, food, and ongoing relief. Upon returning to Switzerland, he began the campaign that led to the International Committee for Relief of the Wounded in 1863 and, eventually, the ICRC. The Committee, and their symbol of a red cross on a white background, has become the standard of neutral wartime medical care of wounded combatants and civilians.

The IFRC was founded in 1919 and has grown to be the world's largest humanitarian organization. After World War I, American Red Cross War Committee president Henry Davison proposed a creation of a League of Red Cross Societies so the expertise of the millions of volunteers from the wartime efforts of the ICRC could be used in a broader scope of peacetime activities. Today, the IFRC includes 195 member societies, a Secretariat in Geneva, and more than 60 additional delegations dispersed throughout the world.

The IFRC conducts complex relief and recovery operations in the aftermath of disasters throughout the world. Their four areas of focus include promoting humanitarian values, disaster response, disaster preparedness, and health and community care. Through their work, they seek to "improve the lives of vulnerable people by mobilizing the power of humanity," as stated in their mission. These people include those who are victims of natural and man-made disasters and postconflict scenarios.

Like the UN, the IFRC is well established in most countries throughout the world and is well poised to assist in the event that disaster strikes. Volunteers are continuously trained and utilized at the most local levels, providing a solid knowledge base before a major need presents itself. Cooperation among groups, through the federation, provides an enormous pool of people and funds from which to draw when local resources are exhausted.

When a disaster strikes and the local capacity is exceeded, an appeal by that country's national chapter is made for support to the Federation's Secretariat. As coordinating body, the Secretariat initiates an international appeal for support to the IFRD and many other outside sources and provides personnel and humanitarian aid supplies from its own stocks. These supplies, which can be shipped in if not locally available, pertain to needs in the areas of health, logistics and water specialists, aid personnel, and relief management.

The appeal for international assistance is made an average of 30 times per year, and these assistance projects can continue for years. Long-term rehabilitation and reconstruction projects, coupled with the goal of sustainable development and increased capacity to handle future disasters, have become the norm in regards to major disasters in the poorer countries. The following is how the IFRC responds to international disasters.

Depending on the complexity of the required response, a Field Assessment and Coordination Team (FACT) may be deployed to assist the local chapter in determining the support needs for the event. The teams, which are deployable to any location with only 24 hours' notice, consist of Red Cross/Red Crescent disaster managers from throughout the IFRC, bringing with them skills in relief, logistics, health, nutrition, public health, epidemiology, water and sanitation, finance, administration, and psychological support. The team works in conjunction with local counterparts and host-government representatives to assess the situation and determine what the IFRC response will consist of. An international appeal is drafted, and then launched, by the Secretariat in Geneva. The teams stay in-country to coordinate the initiation of relief activities. Once the effort has stabilized and has become locally manageable, the FACT concedes its control to the local Red Cross headquarters.

In 1994, following a spate of notably severe disasters (i.e., the Armenian earthquake, the Gulf War Kurdish refugee problem, and the African Great Lakes Region crisis), the IFRC began to develop an Emergency Response Unit (ERU) program to increase disaster response efficiency and efficacy. These ERUs are made up of preestablished supplies, equipment, and personnel, who respond as a quick-response unit on a moment's notice and are trained and prepared to handle a much wider range of scenarios than before. This concept, similar to the UNDP Emergency Response Division (ERD), has already proven effective in making IFRC response faster and better, through several deployments, including Hurricane

Mitch in Honduras. The teams, upon completion of their response mission, remained in-country to train the locals in water and sanitation issues, thus further ensuring the sustainability of their efforts. ERU teams are most effective in large-scale, sudden-onset, and remote disasters.

The IFRC is in the final stages of wrapping up a decade-long strategic effort called Strategy 2010. This effort focused on three "Directions":

1. National Society programs that are responsive to local vulnerability and focused on the areas where they can add the greatest value. The four core areas of this effort are:
   a. Promotion of humanitarian values and principles
   b. Disaster response
   c. Disaster preparedness
   d. Health and care in the community
2. Well-functioning national societies which can mobilize support and carry out their humanitarian mission, contributing to the building of civil society.
3. Working together effectively through program cooperation, long-term partnerships and funding as well as more active advocacy.

As a result of this strategy the IFRC has become more heavily engaged in disaster preparedness and has identified several mitigation strategies in the communities where they operate. These activities, which focus on consequence reduction and working toward better prediction and prevention methods, are becoming a fundamental component of local Red Cross/Red Crescent Society programs. The IFRC has recognized the following four points of action as most vital:

- Reducing the vulnerability of households and communities in disaster-prone areas and improving their ability to cope with the effects of disasters
- Strengthening the capacities of National Societies in disaster preparedness and postdisaster response
- Determining a role and mandate for National Societies in national disaster plans
- Establishing regional networks of National Societies that will strengthen the Federation's collective impact in disaster preparedness and response at the international level

The plan is to increase local capacity to handle disasters in order to decrease the magnitude of international assistance required on disaster onset. This increase in capacity eventually results in a decreased loss of life and property, as development progresses in each country and resilience from catastrophe grows. The IFRC aims to accomplish these results through their regular local capacity-building projects, performed in conjunction with research and analysis. IFRC is in the process of developing Strategy 2020, which will guide the actions of the organization and its National Societies over the decade spanning 2011–2020.

CRITICAL THINKING

- Should nongovernmental organizations be required to adhere to the UN or another governmental coordination system that is in place during the response to international disasters? Why or why not?
- What are the major risks for an NGO that refuses to participate in the coordination mechanism in place in the disaster-affected country or region? What does it gain and what does it lose by choosing to participate?

Assistance Provided by the U.S. Government

U.S. Agency for International Development

The United States has several means by which it provides assistance to other nations requiring aid in the aftermath of a disaster, accident (transportation-based, nuclear, biological, chemical, or other), or conflict. The U.S. agency tasked with providing development aid to other countries, the U.S. Agency for International Development (USAID), has also been tasked with coordinating the U.S. response to international disasters. USAID was created in 1961 through the Foreign Assistance Act, which was drafted to organize U.S. foreign assistance programs and separate military and nonmilitary assistance. One branch of USAID, the Bureau for Democracy, Conflict, and Humanitarian Response (DCHA), manages the various mechanisms with which the United States can respond to humanitarian emergencies of all types. The office under DCHA that most specifically addresses the needs of disaster and crisis victims by coordinating all nonfood aid provided by the government is the Office of U.S. Foreign Disaster Assistance (OFDA) (see Figure 8–1).

Office of Foreign Disaster Assistance

OFDA is divided into three distinct subunits: Operations Division (OPS); Program Support Division (PS); and Disaster Response and Mitigation (DRM). The Disaster Response and Mitigation Division is responsible for coordinating the provision of humanitarian assistance and relief supplies. The Operations Division develops and manages logistical, operational, and technical support for field offices and disaster responses, including Urban Search & Rescue (USAR) teams, Disaster Assistance Response Teams (DARTs), and Response Management Teams (RMTs). The Program Support Division provides programmatic and administrative support, including budget and financial services, procurement planning, contracts and grants administration, training support, information technology, communications support, and information services.

The administrator of USAID holds the title of President's Special Coordinator for International Disaster Assistance. When a disaster is declared in a foreign nation by the resident U.S. ambassador (or by the Department of State, if one does not exist), the USAID administrator is appealed to for help. This can be done when the magnitude of the disaster has overwhelmed a country's local response mechanisms, the government has requested assistance or will at least accept it, and it is in the interest of the U.S. government to assist. OFDA is authorized to immediately disburse $50,000 in emergency aid to the U.S. Embassy to be spent at the discretion of the ambassador for immediate relief, and given that the disaster satisfy three criteria: (1) the magnitude of the disaster is beyond the capacity of the host country to respond; (2) the host country accepts, or is willing to accept, assistance; and (3) a response is in the best interest of the U.S. government. OFDA also can immediately send regional advisors with temporary shelter and medical aid supplies from one of four OFDA stockpiles in Guam, Italy, Honduras, and the United States (see Figure 8–2).

If the disaster is considerable in size, the U.S. ambassador or USAID Mission Director posted in the affected country will appoint a Mission Disaster Relief Officer to oversee the developing response effort. A Disaster Assistance Response Team (DART) is deployed to the country to assess the damages and recommend the level of assistance that should be made by the U.S. government. DARTs work quickly to develop a strategy to coordinate U.S. relief supplies; provide operational support; coordinate with other donor countries, UN agencies, NGOs, and the host government; and monitor and evaluate projects carried out with U.S. funds. In the largest of disasters, Response Management Teams (RMTs) may be established in both Washington, D.C., and the disaster site to coordinate and offer administrative assistance and communication for the several DARTs that would be deployed.

OFDA developed a Technical Assistance Group (TAG) to increase its capabilities in planning and programming. TAGs consist of scientists and specialists in agriculture and food security, emergency and public health, water and sanitation, geoscience, climate, urban planning, contingency planning, cartography, and so on. TAGs work with DARTS and RMTs in response, as well as USAID development missions in preparation and mitigation for future disasters.

In addition to the direct aid and logistical and operational support offered, OFDA provides grants for relief assistance projects. These projects are carried out primarily by PVOs and NGOs, as well as IOs, the UN, and other various organizations (such as a pilots' club that is hired to transport supplies). Not all this monetary aid goes to response, however. The DRM works to facilitate projects that aim to reduce the impact of disasters before they happen again. These types of projects seek to empower national governments to make them less likely to need international assistance in subsequent events. All these organizations are monitored carefully by OFDA to ensure that they are working efficiently and are spending monetary resources sensibly.

Other USAID Divisions

Under the USAID DCHA, several other offices provide humanitarian aid. The Office of Food for Peace (FFP) handles all the U.S. government's food assistance projects (U.S. food aid is categorized as Title II or Title III, with the first having no repayment obligations and the second considered a bilateral loan). The Office of Transition Initiatives (OTI) works

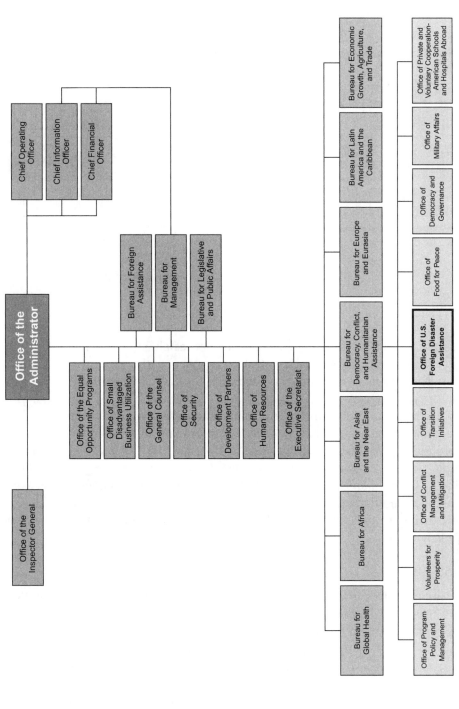

FIGURE 8-1 The USAID organizational chart.

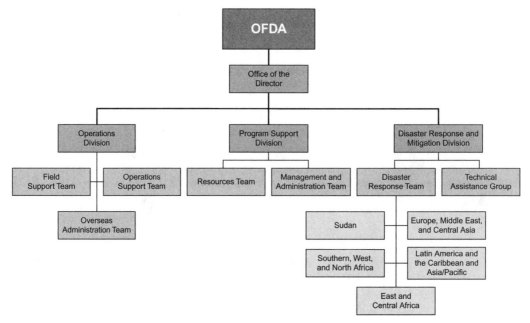

FIGURE 8-2 The OFDA organizational chart.

in postconflict situations to help sustain peace and establish democracy. The Office of Conflict Management and Mitigation (CMM) supports early responses to address the causes and consequences of conflict and war.

The Office of Military Affairs (OMA) helps to build partnerships for humanitarian relief with U.S. Department of Defense officials and offices for planning, training, mitigation, response, and recovery. The Department of State Bureau for Population, Refugees, and Migration (PRM) provides monetary grants to NGOs, PVOs, IOs, and the UN to respond to emergency refugee emergencies. A good portion of this assistance goes directly to the UNHCR. The Department of Defense (DOD) responds through its Office of Peacekeeping and Humanitarian Affairs (PK/HA). It is important to note that the developed nations of the world are highly unlikely to receive U.S. assistance on the level that is provided to the developing nations.

The U.S. Military

The U.S. military often is involved in relief efforts of natural and technological disasters and CHEs. The involvement of the military, a well-funded and equipped force whose primary function is national defense, brings about an entirely new perspective to the area of operations. It often is argued that nobody is better equipped to handle disasters than the military, with their wide assortment of heavy equipment, enormous reserve of trained personnel, and common culture of discipline and mission-oriented standard operation; however, it is also said that the military is a war agency, not a humanitarian assistance agency, and that these two organizational ideals are too fundamentally and diametrically opposed in practice to allow for effective military involvement.

The assistance of the military normally is requested by USAID/OFDA through the DOD Office of Political/Military Affairs. The chain of command for military operations begins with the President of the United States and the Secretary of Defense, collectively referred to as the National Command Authority (NCA). The NCA, which directs all functions of the U.S. military, is advised by the Joint Chiefs of Staff (JCS) of the Army, Navy, Air Force, and Marines.

The U.S. military is heavily involved in the response to international disasters through organized operations termed Foreign Humanitarian Assistance (FHA) or Humanitarian Assistance Operations (HAO). FHAs are authorized by the DOD Office of Political/Military Affairs (DODPM) at the request of OFDA (the president, as commander in chief, gives final authorization for any support operation). Assistance may be provided in the form of physical or technical support, such as logistics, transportation, communications, relief distribution, security, and emergency medicine. In emergencies of natural or manmade origin that do not involve conflict, the role of the military is to provide support, rather than leadership, to the national government and the overall relief community.

The military is known for its self-contained operational abilities, arriving on-scene with everything they need, so to speak. Usually, they provide more than adequate personnel and supplies for the mission they were called to act upon. Once in-country, they work under the strict guidelines of Force Protection (enforced security of all military and civilian personnel, equipment, and facilities associated with their mission) and Rules of Engagement (ROE, a structured, preestablished guideline of "circumstances and limitations under which the military will initiate or continue combat engagement"). The ROE dictate military action in both peacekeeping and disaster operations.

If a particular command unit is tasked with assisting a relief operation, they may deploy a Humanitarian Assistance Survey Team (HAST) to conduct a needs assessment, which relates to the specific functions the military is suited to address. These assessments are occasionally much different than those generated by more humanitarian-based organizations, such as the UN or OFDA, because the military operates in such a fundamentally different fashion. The concerns of the HAST tend to focus on the military support requirements and the logistical factors involving deployment of troops. A Joint Task Force (JTF) will be established soon after to handle the management and coordination of military personnel activities, with a commander for the JTF designated as the person in charge of the operation on-site; however, if an operation involves only one military service, or is minimal in size, a JTF may not be needed.

One of the main roles of the JTF is to establish a Civil Military Operations Center (CMOC). This center effectively functions to coordinate the military support capabilities in relation to the overall response structure involving all other players involved. The CMOC mobilizes requests for assistance from OFDA, the UN, NGOs, and the host government. All intermilitary planning is conducted through this center, including those operations involving cargo transportation and food logistics. This center is the primary node of information exchange to and from the JTF. CMOCs have taken on expanded responsibility in the past, including the reestablishment of government and civil society and the repair or rehabilitation of critical infrastructure.

CRITICAL THINKING

- The Posse Comitatus Act limits the involvement of the U.S. military in domestic operations, but not international disasters. Do you believe that the U.S. military would be better equipped than DHS to lead the federal response to domestic disasters? Why or why not?
- What aspects of the military make it so effective overseas?
- Why do you think OFDA is a component of the U.S. Department of State and not the DHS?

The International Financial Institutions

The international financial institutions (IFIs) provide loans for development and financial cooperation throughout the world. They exist to ensure financial and market stability and to increase political balance. These institutions are made up of member states, arranged on a global or regional basis, which work together to provide financial services to national governments through direct loans or projects. In the aftermath of disasters, it is common for nations with low capital reserves to request increased or additional emergency loans to fund the expensive task of reconstruction and rehabilitation. Without these IFIs, most developing nations would have no means with which to recover. The largest of these IFIs, the World Bank, and one of its subsidiaries, the International Monetary Fund (IMF), are detailed as follows. Other regional IFIs with similar functions include the Inter-American Development Bank (IDB), which works primarily in Central and South America, and the Asian Development Bank (ADB), based in Manila, Philippines, which works throughout the Asian continent.

The World Bank

The World Bank was created in 1944 to rebuild Europe after World War II. In 1947, France received the first World Bank loan of $250 million for postwar reconstruction. Financial reconstruction assistance has been provided regularly since that time in response to countless natural disasters and humanitarian emergencies.

Today, the World Bank is one of the largest sources of development assistance. In the 2008 fiscal year, it committed more than $38.2 billion in loans, funding hundreds of ongoing and new projects in scores of developing countries. The World Bank is owned collectively by 186 countries and is based in Washington, D.C. It comprises several institutions referred to as the World Bank Group (WBG):

- International Bank for Reconstruction and Development
- International Development Association

- International Finance Corporation
- Multilateral Investment Guarantee Agency
- International Centre for Settlement of Investment Disputes

The World Bank's overall goal is to reduce poverty, specifically, to "individually help each developing country onto a path of stable, sustainable, and equitable growth, [focusing on] helping the poorest people and the poorest countries" (The World Bank, n.d.). As disasters and CHEs take a greater and greater toll on the economic stability of many financially struggling countries, the Bank is taking on a more central role in mitigation and reconstruction.

Developing nations, which are more likely to have weak disaster mitigation or preparedness capacity and therefore little or no affordable access to disaster insurance, often sustain a total financial loss. In the period of rehabilitation that follows a disaster, loans are essential to the success of programs and vital to any level of sustainability or increased disaster resistance. The Bank lends assistance at several points along this cycle.

First, for regular financial assistance, the Bank ensures that borrowed funds are applied to projects that give mitigation a central role during the planning phase. It utilizes its privilege as financial advisor to guide planners, who otherwise might forego mitigation measures in an effort to stretch the loaned capital as far as possible. Ensuring that mitigation is addressed increases systems of prediction and risk analysis in World Bank–funded projects.

Since its inception, the World Bank has been heavily involved in national reconstruction efforts. Over time, these postdisaster programs have not only grown in number and scope, but have also shifted in focus from that of post conflict scenarios to that of a more diverse hazard portfolio—with natural disasters emerging as the prominent instigating factor. The Bank has established and adjusted its policy on managing the postdisaster needs of member nations through successive policy adjustments that point to an evolution in thinking about how the bank assists its "customers" facing disasters.

The range of disaster events the Bank has addressed through its various response and reconstruction programs has grown over time. All Bank policy stipulates that postdisaster projects should concentrate on restoring assets and productivity levels, thereby focusing on reconstruction (with explicit specification that relief and consumption cannot be financed—under the guiding theory that lending should be reserved for economically productive activities, thereby leaving relief managed by local groups, affected governments, bilateral relief programs, NGOs, and specialized relief organizations). Bank policy, in fact, restricts the Bank from participating in the financing of any of the following:

- Temporary shelter
- Search and rescue
- Evacuation
- Health care
- Food and water distribution
- Temporary sanitation
- Restoration of access to transport

Within the framework of these restrictions, the Bank is able to offer effective assistance to disaster-affected nations through a range of loan and technical assistance instruments. The current policy describes five forms of Bank emergency assistance: emergency recovery loans (ERLs) and credits, loan reallocation, the redesign of pipeline projects, new free-standing mitigation projects, and assessments. These, and other related capabilities, are grouped into the categories of Lending Instruments, Coordination, and Technical Assistance.

World Bank Lending Instruments

Since 1980, the Executive Board of the World Bank has approved more than 500 projects involving the management of disasters in some capacity. Through these projects, a total of more than $40 billion of bank lending—representing about 10 percent of all Bank loan commitments—was provided. Among these projects, the amount of disaster-related support ranges from a few thousand to a half-billion dollars. While some projects were entirely devoted to natural disasters, such as the Emergency Recovery Loans (ERLs; described following), more than two-thirds involved disasters as a component of more comprehensive development goals. The value of the projects dedicated entirely to disasters totals $12.2 billion. The various disaster-related loan instruments are as follows.

The Emergency Recovery Loan (ERL) Program
The Emergency Recovery Loan is a loan instrument designed to reduce the time required to complete the project appraisal process in order to meet the disaster-affected borrowers' urgent needs. The goal of an ERL is to implement the funded emergency projects within a period of two to three years. Borrower nations are limited in how they can use ERL funds for reconstruction. Projects funded must be limited to the rapid restoration of physical structures and productive activities. Policy discourages the creation of permanent new institutions for project implementation, but limited changes, such as those that reduce vulnerability, are advocated. ERLs are not intended to address long-term economic problems that require major policy adjustments. They are also not intended for projects addressing broad sectoral, structural, or institutional goals. ERLs, as a disaster response instrument, are designed for more rare disasters, rather than recurrent or longer-term events such as flooding and drought (which are better managed through the use of more traditional development loan programs). ERLs must make every effort to incorporate policy and action that result in an overall reduction in vulnerability from the hazard encountered. Bank policy calls for detailed study, planning, and preparation in advance of and during the implementation of funded projects to ensure overall risk is reduced.

Retroactive Financing
Bank policy normally restricts financing for payments made by borrowers for a project before the date of a loan agreement. However, the disaster policies allow up to 20 percent of loans to retroactively pay for emergency recovery operation expenditures, as long as they occurred after the the disaster and within four months before the expected date of

loan signing. And, in extraordinary circumstances, exceptions to the 20 percent limit may be granted.

Loan Reallocations

When a government requests post-disaster assistance, Bank country staff begin by examining the existing country portfolio to identify loans for which reallocation for reconstruction is possible. Because not all emergency situations demand ERLs, the Bank often uses the reallocation of existing loans to quickly provide smaller amounts of funding as appropriate, or to supplement ERLs in larger disasters. Reallocation works so quickly because the source projects are already approved; therefore funds can be very quickly rededicated to disaster-specific needs (often within the broad sector into which they were originally dedicated). Reallocations are most appropriate in situations where the relevance of the original project has been reduced or eliminated by the disaster. Over the past 20 years, funds from 217 projects have been reallocated. In total, almost $3.05 billion has been made available for disaster response through loan reallocation.

Redesign of Projects Not Yet Approved

Another way to make funds available to a disaster-affected government is to redesign projects that have not yet been approved. In doing so, newly acquired data about the country's disaster profile, and thus their vulnerability reduction needs, can be incorporated, as can new project components that contribute to postdisaster reconstruction that were not part of the original project design.

Balance of Payment Support

Balance of payment support is designed to provide quick disbursement of funds to meet the most pressing financial needs of affected countries. Designed to provide quick inputs to stabilize macroeconomic conditions and facilitate recovery following a calamity, this kind of support is not very common; only 15 loans have been made for balance of payment support following natural disasters.

Free-Standing Investment Projects for Mitigation

After a disaster occurs, when new hazard risk information is acquired through assessment and study, disaster mitigation projects can be designed in a way that more effectively limits risk. In this context, the Bank offers another lending instrument, the free-standing mitigation project loan, that nations may use to reduce their long-term risk. Though mitigation and risk analysis are considered essential components of regular loan programs, free-standing mitigation loans designed specifically to help prevent foreseeable disasters from occurring and/or limiting their destructive impact allow for a more targeted outcome.

Disaster Lending Instruments under Development

The Bank has been developing promising alternatives to these lending instruments. For instance, increasing the amount of lending for existing projects, which is already in use for nondisaster-related projects, is being explored in the disaster context. Another specialized form of development policy lending, the Contingent Hazard Recovery and Management Loan, is currently in development. It is hoped that these alternatives will help to avoid the diversion of funds from their original purposes, as occurs with reallocation.

World Bank Coordination

The Bank is one of a large number of institutions that governments can call upon to offer coordination assistance following a disaster. Bank policy states that it is within both the ability and interest of the Bank to assist disaster-affected borrowers in the coordination of overall donor efforts—especially as they relate to the gathering of damage assessment information. The policy requires that following a disaster, the Bank should facilitate collaboration between the government, the Bank, multilateral and bilateral donors, and NGOs to develop a common recovery strategy. Coordination can help to ensure that prevention and mitigation activities are incorporated in all reconstruction projects, Bank-funded or otherwise, and that neither duplication nor omission of coverage occurs.

The Bank has and continues to work with other donors in post-disaster situations on several different levels—cofinancing Bank-supported projects, cofinancing others' projects, donors working on related projects of their own, or by performing joint damage assessments. At present, the Bank fulfills this coordination role through partnership with the UNDP and other international agencies, bilateral donors, and local nongovernmental organizations as appropriate and possible.

The Bank's coordination role in the immediate aftermath of disasters has been somewhat limited. However, it has maintained a more prominent role in longer-term reconstruction efforts. The Bank typically concentrates on infrastructure and housing during the reconstruction, given its comparative advantage in that area. However, the Bank also has considerable experience with disaster recovery, as well as an important role in assisting with coordination that ensures that country needs are met with as few overlaps and conflicts of priorities as possible.

World Bank Technical Assistance

The World Bank assists countries managing their disaster risk, or facing an actual disaster, through the provision of several technical assistance programs. These programs include the following:

- *Analytical Work:* Through the generation of publications, working papers, articles, and reports on natural disaster topics, the Bank continues to advance the study of and knowledge about disasters and their management. These publications have explored a range of topics that have included risk management and financing mechanisms.
- *Application of the Country Assistance Strategy (CAS):* The Bank's Country Assistance Strategy (CAS) is designed to synthesize the country situation, government priorities, Bank Group strategy, and Bank partner activities into a coherent program for future work together. In countries with significant disaster-related issues, the CAS has been

used to incorporate a hazard risk component in order to elevate the importance of disasters in overall development strategy planning.

- *The Disaster Risk Management Team:* In 1999, in response to an increase in disaster-related lending, the Disaster Management Facility was established, which later became the Hazard Management Unit (HMU). This office provided Bank task managers with disaster-specific technical assistance, thereby allowing them to provide a more strategic and rapid response. In 2005, this unit was drastically modified to reflect a decentralized structure, and given the new title of Hazard Risk Management Team (within the Urban Unit), later changed to the Disaster Risk Management Team. The Disaster Risk Management Team, which is considered the anchor for the much larger Hazard Risk Management Thematic Group (which consists of more than 100 Bank staff in the various organizational units with a particular interest in hazard risk management), works to facilitate greater adherence to prevention and mitigation objectives in Bank-funded development projects. The Disaster Risk Management team provides technical support to Bank operations in promoting capacity building and establishing partnerships with the international and scientific community working on disaster issues.

- *Disaster Damage and Needs Assessment Assistance:* Bankwide experience has shown it is important to identify local vulnerabilities and determine how to reduce them in ways that lead to durable solutions. With increasing frequency, the Bank has helped borrowers to assess disaster damages and to develop a recovery strategy. Almost three-quarters of all the disaster assessments (23 out of 32) in which the Bank was involved led to a more rapid granting of an ERL.

- *Emergency Preparedness Studies:* Disaster projects often have a studies component related to the achievement of an important project objective. These studies may be used to increase disaster resilience for the project goals. Because so many disaster projects either have experienced or are expected to face repeat or new disasters in the future, disaster studies are necessary for proper hazard risk consideration to be incorporated.

- *Institutional Development:* Through its disaster-related projects, the Bank has worked in member countries to strengthen hazard management institutions, and to stress the importance of strengthening countries' institutional capacity for long-term disaster prevention and mitigation—both on its own and in cooperation with other agencies. Over the past 20 years, the Bank has formulated institutional development components for 160 completed projects that have included project management, disaster management, general research, early warning improvements, disaster-specific training programs, engineering studies, and legal and policy reform.

The International Monetary Fund

The International Monetary Fund (IMF) was established in 1946 and has grown to a current membership of 186 countries. Its goals are to promote international monetary cooperation, exchange stability, and orderly exchange arrangements; to foster economic growth and high levels of employment; and to provide temporary financial assistance to countries to help ease balance of payments adjustment. It carries out these functions using loans, monitoring, and technical assistance.

In the event of an international disaster or CHE in a member country, the IMF utilizes its Emergency Assistance Specific Facility to provide rapid financial assistance. In these situations, it is not uncommon for a country to have severely exhausted its monetary reserves. The IMF's goals are to rebuild government capacity and to return stability to the local economy. In the event of a natural disaster, funding is directed toward local recovery efforts and for any economic adjustment that may be needed. If the situation is a postconflict one, its aim is to "reestablish macroeconomic stability and the basis for long-term sustainable growth" (IMF, n.d.). The IMF will lend assistance only if a stable governing body is in place that has the capacity for planning and policy implementation and can ensure the safety of IMF resources. After stability has been sufficiently restored, increased financial assistance is offered, which will be used to develop the country in its postemergency status.

When a country wishes to request emergency assistance, it must submit a detailed plan for economic reconstruction and ensure that it will not create trade restrictions or intensify exchange. If the country is already working under an IMF loan, then assistance can come in the form of a reorganization within existing arrangements. Separate emergency assistance loans are also offered, which do not involve the regular criteria under which the countries must normally operate. These loans, although normally available only up to 25 percent of a country's preestablished lending quota, have been created in quantities reaching 50 percent of quota; however, this funding is provided only when the member country is "cooperating with the IMF to find a solution to its economic problems." These loans are required to be repaid within five years.

A country often requires technical assistance or policy advice because it is in a situation for which it has no experience or expertise. This is common in postconflict situations where a new government has been established and partnerships are being created for the first time. The IMF offers assistance in building capacity to implement macroeconomic policy. This can include tax and government expenditure capacity, the reorganization of fiscal, monetary, and exchange institutions, and guidance in the use of aid resources.

CRITICAL THINKING

- Should the IFIs be concerned with disaster management, or do you think that they should let UNOCHA and the other UN agencies handle all disaster-related concerns? Explain your answer.
- What is the risk of allowing a disaster-affected country to reprogram a regular development loan, such as one that covers the construction of a new hospital, to be used for disaster relief? Under what circumstances does this practice make sense, and in what cases should it be avoided?

CASE STUDY: THE HAITI EARTHQUAKE, JANUARY 12, 2010

On January 12, 2010, the island of Hispaniola was struck by a major earthquake measuring 7.0 on the Richter scale. The tremor, which was centered near the town of Leogane and only 16 miles from Haiti's capital, Port-au-Prince, occurred at 4:53 p.m. and at a depth of 8.1 miles.

Virtually all of Haiti's 3 million people, who were woefully unprepared for such an event, were affected by the quake. Though the exact numbers will never be known, estimates have placed the death toll at over 200,000 people, and over 300,000 people were injured. Additionally, between 800,000 and 1 million people fled the most severely affected areas, causing a massive problem with internally displaced people (IDPs) (Figure 8-3). With more than 250,000 houses and over 30,000 commercial buildings destroyed; total destruction of existing public health and medical infrastructure; damage to roads, bridges, and other transportation infrastructure; and other problems, the already heavily indebted country faces years, if not decades, of recovery.

Haiti's government and people were not completely unaware of the earthquake risk that existed, having suffered multiple major quakes in their country's history (many of which caused mass death and destruction). But because of decades of poor governance and very low development indicators, almost nothing was done to minimize risk or to prepare the population. As such, the country was immediately overwhelmed by the event, and appeals for international aid were made as soon as word could get out. Despite these calls, the country's infrastructure was so heavily damaged (including the total loss of the nation's largest port) that the delivery of foreign aid was hampered for days. Additionally, destruction of the UN offices, from where an international coordination effort would take place, and a lack of communication from the nation's top leaders caused significant confusion about who was in charge and what damages had been sustained.

Eventually the deliveries of international assistance began to arrive, and the UN cluster system was put into place to address the complex lifesaving and sustaining needs of Haiti's population. Twelve clusters were activated:

- Logistics
- Camp Coordination and Camp Management (CCCM)
- Shelter
- Nonfood items (NFI)
- Food
- Health
- WASH (water, sanitation, and health care)
- Education
- Protection
- Early recovery
- Agriculture
- Emergency telecommunications

Haiti's recovery will be an effort that requires significant investment (in the form of bilateral aid and loans from the international financial institutions), technical assistance, and materials. This effort will be a test bed of modern recovery lessons learned, since reconstruction is nearly total. If the leadership that emerges is able to effectively coordinate the recovery efforts such

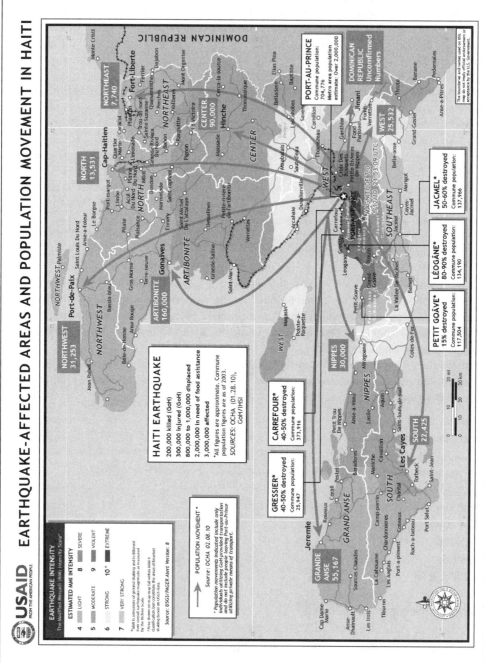

FIGURE 8-3 Map of earthquake intensity and population movement in Haiti, 2010. USAID, 2010.

that corruption is kept to a minimum, efforts are not duplicated and there are no holes in the coverage, and all recovery stakeholders are able to work in a holistic, synergistic manner, it is likely that the nation will be more resilient, more developed, and better able to recover from such events in the future.

The following is a highlight of the U.S. government's bilateral assistance provided in the first month following the quake, taken from a situation report released by USAID/OFDA on February 13, 2010 (just over one month after the event).

Haiti Earthquake
Fact Sheet #32, Fiscal Year (FY) 2010
February 13, 2010

Key Developments
FY 2010 HUMANITARIAN FUNDING PROVIDED TO DATE
Total FY 2010 USAID/OFDA Assistance to Haiti for the Earthquake............................$201,538,862
Total FY 2010 USAID/FFP2 Assistance to Haiti for the Earthquake...............................$68,000,000
Total FY 2010 USAID/OTI3 Assistance to Haiti for the Earthquake...............................$20,000,000
Total FY 2010 USAID/Haiti Assistance to Haiti for the Earthquake...............................$30,012,212
Total FY 2010 USAID/DR4 Assistance to Haiti for the Earthquake.................................$3,000,000
Total FY 2010 DoD5 Assistance to Haiti for the Earthquake...$252,000,000
Total FY 2010 USAID and DOD Humanitarian Assistance to Haiti
     for the Earthquake $574,551,074

To illustrate the complexity and comprehensive nature of the international relief efforts that were conducted in the months following the quake, the following is drawn from a UN/OCHA situation report dated February 11, 2010.

Humanitarian assistance commodities are moving at a steady rate and distribution is improving. Shelter and sanitation continue to be issues of concern as the rains begin and disease control gains prominence. The WFP food distribution surge has reached 1.6 million people with a two-week ration of rice over the past eleven days. The government and aid organizations are also focused on the needs of the estimated half-million people who have moved to outlying departments.

In the context of the upcoming rainy season, settlement location can be as much a factor in the loss of life as whether or not shelter material has been received. Sites need to be found that take the following into consideration: flood risk, congestion, clearance of rubble, and proximity to services. The CCCM Cluster is advocating with the Government to fast track the expropriation of large quantities of suitable private land within and outside the city, to enable safe decongestion in flood prone areas and move vulnerable populations to new safer sites before the start of the rains in early April.

The Petionville spontaneous settlement site (at a golf course) was assessed by a Shelter Cluster team on 9 February and is reported to be one of the most vulnerable sites for epidemics and flooding. The team estimates that 25,000 people are living at the site which is very densely populated. A large number of shelters are on unstable slopes and heavy rains will cause them to slide. Low lying areas are at significant risk of flooding, with the market area most at risk.

The team also found insufficient fire breaks with no fire risk mitigation strategy for the site. The team recommended that new sites are identified for families to move to on a voluntary basis. This must be conducted after families are registered in order to ensure coverage of assistance.

The Dominican Republic Humanitarian Country Team completed an interagency assessment of the border area. The team estimates that approximately 168,000 internally displaced persons are living along the border on the Haitian side. The majority of them are living with host families.

There are some spontaneous settlement sites, such as in Anse-a-Pitre, where there are more than 1,000 people living. Another 400 people are in a spontaneous settlement in Ganthier, very near to the road leading to Port-au-Prince. A joint assessment mission led by WFP will take place on 12 February to evaluate their needs.

The security situation throughout the country remains stable despite increased reports of isolated incidents. Security around food distributions remains a concern and requires close coordination between MINUSTAH and humanitarian partners. The government's state of emergency period is scheduled to expire on 15 February.

Logistics A small number of commercial cargo flights have started arriving at Port-au-Prince airport. The first civilian passenger flight is scheduled for 19 February. Refueling remains an issue. Las Americas airport, in the Dominican Republic, is congested. WFP, on behalf of the Logistics Cluster, is working to secure dedicated warehouse space at the airport to alleviate the current situation.

Floating docks are being established at the Port-au-Prince port and are expected to raise capacity to a possible 1,500 containers a day. A slot system is now in place for incoming ships. A British Naval vessel will be arriving in Port-au-Prince on 18 February with port enhancement equipment and vehicles for use by NGO partners. This ship will be made available for tasking by WFP and the Logistics Cluster to shuttle cargo to ports within Haiti until 15 March.

The border crossing at Jimani is severely congested. Passage is through a small gate, allowing only one vehicle at a time. The regular market on Monday and Thursday causes a severe bottleneck, and, with the increase in traffic, the market is now expanding to other days of the week. Options to help the flow of convoys across the border are being investigated, including widening the gates and extending opening hours. There is also a plan to move the market.

The road between Port-au-Prince and Jacmel suffered significant damage from the earthquake and subsequent aftershocks. Landslides have been cleared and work is ongoing by the Canadian military and MINUSTAH, but many areas remain at risk of landslides once the rainy season begins.

Camp Coordination and Camp Management (CCCM) The CCCM cluster is working to support three categories of sites: 10 organized settlement sites; 19 priority sites for decongestion; 8 government-identified sites for the establishment of organized settlements (see attached map for details).

The CCCM Cluster has identified 19 priority sites for decongestion. The total estimated population in these sites is 180,000 people. The cluster will be working with these populations to move them to organized settlements in periphery locations. This relocation will be on a voluntary basis. Some 900 hectares of land are needed to relocate all 180,000 people (based on 45 m^2 of space per person). Due to the scarcity of available space, the cluster will be focusing only on decongestion. An additional constraint is the lack of partners that work in these sites—for example, 11 out of the 19 priority sites don't have a camp management organization reporting to the CCCM Cluster.

Ten organized sites are being managed by the cluster. The ten sites host an estimated 76,000 people and are run by dedicated cluster partners that are working on improving site conditions. Some of the organized sites have been included in the list of 19 priority sites that require decongestion (Champ de Mars, Aviation/Parc de la Paix, Place de la Paix, Terrain Acra). The preliminary assessments for five out of the eight government-identified sites have been finalized. This includes Tabarre 1 and 2, Sibert, Croix de Bouquets, Santo 17 (a 20,000 m^2 site recently made available by the mayor). In addition, a site has been made available in Tabarre to expand the Congres Charismatique site. Assessments of sites especially with regard to rainy season preparedness are ongoing but prove to be difficult due to the overcrowding of most sites.

Shelter/Nonfood Items (NFI) Distribution of plastic sheeting for emergency shelter remains a high priority. There are now close to 400,000 plastic sheets in stock and in the pipeline. As of 11 February, over 49,000 tarps have been distributed along with 23,000 family size tents. Key household NFIs include kitchen sets (26,500 distributed), hygiene kits (83,000 distributed), blankets (79,500 distributed) and mosquito nets (10,300 distributed). Now that there is more shelter material in stock and in the pipeline, the cluster is working to increase distribution capacity. NFI distributions are planned for sites along the border including in Ganthier and in Fond Parisien. Transitional shelter items intended for the medium term are needed urgently to support the process of reconstruction; major procurements have yet to be placed. Joint procurement options are being discussed.

UN-HABITAT will be working with the CCCM, Shelter and Protection Clusters to identify sites for transitional shelters. UN-HABITAT is also working to coordinate agencies planning to conduct building assessments and inspections. Clear and informative public information regarding structural safety as well as building inspections are needed to provide people with the reassurance to return home where possible.

Detailed information regarding allocation of life items in stock and in the pipeline is improving. GPS capacity of smaller NGOs needs to be strengthened to improve coordination of the response. The movement of displaced people between spontaneous sites makes it difficult for agencies to plan distributions. Local NGO focal points are working actively with partners to help identify gaps and needs and hosting regular coordination meetings in Petit Goave, Grand Goave, Jacmel, and Leogane with the support of OCHA.

Food On day 11 of the food surge operation, a total of 28,368 families were reached out of the planned 29,150 families through the 15 sites that were operational. This represents a total of 170,208 people for the day. A total of 6,734 metric tons of rice has been distributed over the 11 days. WFP reports that 1.6 million people have received a two-week ration of rice since the beginning of the food surge operation.

It has been agreed to extend the surge at four of the distribution sites which are in Cite Soleil and Carrefour. These sites became operational on day four of the operation and are being extended in order to reach the target population. The extension is planned for four days for a daily cumulative caseload of 13,000 households. In addition, the government has proposed adding two sites: one is located in Croix de Bouquets and will be covered by World Vision; the second is located in Kenscoff for which a partner has not yet been identified.

As of 9 February, WFP and its partners have reached 2.3 million persons with varying levels of food since the start of the response.

Health Reports from medical teams continue to show a decline in trauma injuries requiring treatment but the need for overall medical care is rising. The cluster is developing a referral system with a list of functional hospitals and contact details which will be available by the end of the week.

The vaccination campaign that started on 2 February is ongoing. Vaccines against measles/ rubella and diphtheria, tetanus, and pertussis (with vitamin A) are being provided for children under 7 years of age, and diphtheria and tetanus vaccines are being provided for everyone over 8 years. Activities are ongoing in at least four large settlements in Port-au-Prince and outside the capital in Jacmel and Grand Goave as of 9 February.

The Ministry of Health's surveillance system reports acute respiratory infections as the main cause of morbidity. The Health Cluster will continue to monitor morbidity rates to track whether the health situation is improving.

Malaria and dengue are widespread in Haiti in the rainy season, and the current conditions in which the displaced populations are living will increase the risks of outbreaks. PAHO/WHO is collaborating with the Ministry of Public Health to develop comprehensive programs in integrated vector control management and surveillance of vector-borne diseases. A PAHO/ WHO stock of 15,000 LLINs (long-lasting impregnated bed nets) is available for hospitals and health care centers to protect patients and families from vectors (mosquitoes, flies, etc.). Priority is given to high-risk areas as well as pregnant women or mothers with children under 5.

PAHO/WHO is also supporting a mental health team deployed by the Dominican Republic in the border region at the General Hospital of Jimani. The team consists of one psychiatrist, four psychologists, and three nurses specialized in mental health. Mental health and psychosocial support provides two services: psychological/psychiatric interventions and social support.

A meeting of the cluster's reproductive health subgroup was held with the Ministry of Health (MoH) on 8 February to exchange strategies for integrating reproductive health into patient care. The MoH will soon make available national protocols in the areas of family planning, treatment of sexually transmitted diseases, prenatal care, delivery, and responses to rape. The Ministry of Health is reviewing the medical care provider salary scale. The cluster is considering the effect on the human resources and health care structures when international NGOs hire medical staff. The Ministry of Health has said that health care will be provided for free during this three-month period.

WASH As of 9 February, the WASH Cluster reports that 911,200 people are being provided with safe drinking water (on the basis of 5 litres per person per day) through water tankering and water treatment in 300 sites across Port-au-Prince, Leogane, and Jacmel. Water coverage is actually greater than this figure as many other mechanisms to access water are now available.

With a target of 1.1 million persons with 5/l/p/d, the estimated gap is approximately 188,800 persons in need of the minimum coverage. Coverage of water supply prior to the earthquake was limited with the piped system only reaching 25 percent of people in Port-au-Prince and the rest getting water from water kiosks.

The cluster reports that 3,000 portable and/or latrines that can be emptied (which enables maintenance) will be installed within the coming weeks in Port-au-Prince. The goal is to have 50 percent of latrines completed by 28 February. Cases of diarrheal diseases in children continue to be reported. As of 9 February, approximately 250,000 people have benefited from the distribution of 44,850 hygiene kits with an estimated gap of close to 950,000 persons in need, according to UNICEF.

Health care waste continues to be a priority, due to the large amount of medical waste. If waste is not handled properly, it increases risks of vector proliferation and infection of workers and/or patients. PAHO/WHO and partners have set up a system to collect and remove medical waste in all hospitals and dispose them in a safe and organized landfill site. Two teams of four people each are hired to work on the dumping site and to ensure that the disposal site for health care waste and excreta are kept clean.

Due to the large number of patients and families living around hospitals, additional toilets have been built or portable ones brought in to respond to the urgent needs. Sanitation outside the hospitals is a top priority, as the rainy season will begin in a few weeks, thus increasing the risk of fecal contamination.

Education   In some areas close to the border with Haiti, such as Jimaní, students have not returned to school out of fear of another earthquake. Some teachers are reportedly giving classes outside. The Dominican Republic has donated 15 mobile schools with a capacity of 40 students each. An assessment mission is needed to understand the conditions of schools located in the border area, especially in Jimaní where schools have been severely affected.

Protection   The Protection Cluster reports that in Jacmel there is an increasing concern over the plight of persons living with disabilities. There have not been sufficient assessments and programmes targeted to assist this group. In Gonaives, there is increased concern for children in the streets, either due to separation or lack of access to schools.

Given identified security concerns in the spontaneous settlements, particularly with regards to the safety of women and the lack of lighting, the cluster has arranged for a shipment of 17,000 solar powered torches to be distributed through partners to women across sites in Port-au-Prince and possibly other locations. The cluster partners continue to address protection concerns in the work of other clusters, particularly food distribution, site planning, and NFIs.

The Child Protection subcluster and MINUSTAH have been working on a common strategy to tackle the issue of trafficking of children and a system for registration of children. The subcluster has assessed the Haiti/Dominican Republic border to be very porous with limited identification checks of people crossing. Cases of trafficking have been reported, but there is no system in place to gather facts and figures. The subcluster and UNICEF are considering actions to address this gap. In the Dominican Republic, protocols for protecting Haitian children are being finalized as of 11 February.

The subcluster on Prevention and Response to GBV has started trainings for mobile teams to be deployed in settlement sites to provide support and counseling to survivors of gender-based violence.

Early Recovery   As of 9 February, 35,185 people have been employed through UNDP's cash-for-work programme. The main activities include the removal of debris and cleaning drainage canals in Bel Air, Carrefour, Carrefour Feuilles, Petit Goave, Grand Goave, Gressier, Leogane, Martissant, Tabarre, Cite Soleil and Delmas. The programme is indirectly benefiting 175,000 people based on a five-person family.

The Steering Committee (Ministry of Planning, DINEPA and UNDP) for UNDP's cash-for-work programme has approved 12 out of 14 cash-for-work projects submitted by national and international NGOs. The new projects are expected to start shortly. One such project will be run by World Stove and International Lifeline Fund who are planning to develop a fuel efficient stove factory in Carrefour Feuilles. The factory will distribute stoves and fuel (in the form of biomass pellets), which will create jobs, reduce consumption of charcoal, and eliminate biomass waste.

The main priorities for the cluster remain the extension of cash-for-work activities for debris/rubble removal and the clearing of streets and drainage canals.

Agriculture As part of the ongoing assessments, over 3,000 interviews have been carried out by cluster partners in order to assess the effect of displaced populations on poor rural households. The findings confirm the reported increases in household size as a result of relatives arriving from affected urban areas. The food market has contracted in surveyed areas due to reduced demand in terms of purchasing power and preference of population for free food aid (available in the market in some areas).

Emergency Telecommunications (ETC) The ETC Cluster reports that two ICT staff deployed to Jacmel on 9 February. The staff will support the WFP office and be available as a resource to the ETC community. An assessment of the two new ETC sites in Leogane was carried out. WFP through the ETC Cluster will deploy BITSAT to provide internet connectivity. Connectivity is currently being provided by Télécoms Sans Frontières.

Coordination The following eight clusters are operational in Leogane: camp coordination and camp management (IOM); early recovery (UNDP); education (UNICEF); health (Save the Children); food (WFP); protection (UNICEF); shelter/NFI (IFRC); and WASH (DINEPA). Humanitarian partners are currently discussing with MINUSTAH the establishment of a common humanitarian compound in Leogane, which would include office and accommodation space.

The OCHA sub-office in Jacmel is offering coordination support to more than 21 partners, organized in seven clusters: early recovery, education, food, health, protection, shelter/NFI, and WASH. The Food Cluster has been activated in Gonaives. OCHA has established a presence in the Dominican Republic in order to support the work of the RC/HC. Regular meetings are held with the participation of clusters. Eleven clusters are functioning: agriculture, early recovery, education, emergency telecommunication, food, health, logistics, nutrition, protection, shelter/NFI, and WASH.

Funding According to the Financial Tracking Service (FTS), the current Flash Appeal is 95 percent funded with $548 million received out of $575 million, and $29 million pledged. Donors are urged to convert all pledges into cash. FTS also documents all contributions and pledges to projects not listed in the Flash Appeal. To date, the combined total is above $1 billion in funding and over $860 million in uncommitted pledges. A revised Flash Appeal for 12 months will be launched next week.

The Emergency Relief Response Fund for Haiti has over $76 million in pledges, of which $63 million has been received. To date, Saudi Arabia is the largest contributor with $50 million. Over 40 project proposals are in the pipeline for consideration, amounting to $31 million, of which $7 million has been approved for disbursement (cash-for-work activities). NGOs account for 75 percent of the total project proposals received. In addition to the proposals under review, the HC has announced strategic allocations for priority and underfunded clusters, including logistics, shelter, camp coordination and management, agriculture, protection, and early recovery.

Countries of the Union of South American Nations (UNASUR) will create a fund for the reconstruction and rehabilitation of Haiti. The decision was announced at an UNSAR Extraordinary Summit, held on 11 February in Quito, Ecuador. According to a plan developed at the summit, the 12 UNASUR members will set up a $100 million fund and request a no-interest $200 million loan from the Inter-American Development Bank.

Conclusion

As global populations converge into more concentrated urban settlements, their collective hazard risks amplify. Loss of life and property caused by the realization of these hazard risks will overwhelm the response and recovery capacities of individual sovereign nations to an ever-increasing degree. Many of these disasters, particularly in the lesser-developed nations, will contribute to existing development obstacles and regional instability unless trends toward increased multilateral cooperation in disaster assistance are recognized more widely for their importance. The capabilities and organizational capacities of the international disaster management agencies listed in this chapter, namely national governments, nonprofit organizations, international organizations, and the international financial institutions, are vital for both the preparation and mitigation of hazard risks, and the response and recovery of actualized disasters.

Important Terms

Complex humanitarian emergency
Coordinating organization
Developing nation
Donor agency
International financial institution
International organization
Nongovernmental organization
Private voluntary organization
Sovereignty

Self-Check Questions

1. What percentage of all disaster-related injuries and deaths are sustained in countries with per-capita income levels below $760 per year?
2. Why do poor nations often place disaster management so low in terms of budgetary priority?
3. When does a disaster require international involvement?
4. How are complex humanitarian emergencies different from those caused by natural or technological disasters?

5. What are the four important issues influencing the response process that are listed in this chapter? Describe each.
6. What was the goal of the International Decade for Natural Disaster Reduction?
7. How does the United Nations Development Programme contribute to international disaster management?
8. What is the purpose of the UNDP Recovery Unit?
9. What are the three main groupings of disaster response performed by UNOCHA?
10. How does UNOCHA help nations mitigate and prepare for disasters?
11. Name the various classifications of nongovernmental organizations, and describe each.
12. What are the four common characteristics shared by the NGOs?
13. How does the U.S. government provide assistance to disaster-affected nations?
14. Name one international financial institution, and describe how it assists in the aftermath of an international disaster.

Out-of-Class Exercises

1. Visit the UN Consolidated Appeals Process (CAP) website at *http://ochaonline.un.org/humanitarianappeal/*. Navigate into the appropriate hyperlinks. Make a list of each emergency, and determine what percentage of the appeal has been funded. From this list, try to determine why some countries' appeals are fully funded, while others fall very far short of their request. Is this an issue of inequality in relief distribution, or is it something else?
2. Visit the Interaction website at *www.interaction.org*. Select a member organization from their member list, and go to that organization's website. Investigate what that organization does in response to disasters. In what countries around the world is that organization working right now? If a disaster happened in the United States, would that organization respond? Why or why not?

Emergency Management and the Terrorist Threat

What You'll Learn

- How the government's hazard focus has been affected by the changing risk of terrorism
- The events of September 11, 2001, the consequences of those events, and how the government responded
- How the Department of Homeland Security was formed, its components, its role in the emergency management and counterterrorism efforts, and its accomplishments
- How the federal government funds first responders
- How the U.S. government communicates terrorist threat information to the public
- Why the 9/11 Commission was formed and what was found as a result of its investigation
- How state and local governments manage the risk of terrorism
- How Hurricane Katrina affected terrorism preparedness and response

Introduction

The terrorist attacks of September 11, 2001, prompted dramatic changes in emergency management in the United States. These attacks and the subsequent anthrax scare in Washington, D.C., in October 2001 have been the impetus for a reexamination of the nation's emergency management system, including its priorities, funding, and practices. Many feel that sentiment about these events steered emergency management away from a risk-based system to one that gave inordinate attention to terrorism at the expense of proportionate treatment of natural hazard risks. In 2005, the disasters associated with Hurricanes Katrina and Rita partially corrected the course, but the changes inspired by 9/11 are ongoing and will continue for the foreseeable future.

Prior to 9/11, the Nunn-Lugar legislation provided the primary authority and focus for domestic federal preparedness activities for terrorism. Several agencies, the Federal Emergency Management Agency (FEMA), the Department of Justice (DOJ), the Department of Health and Human Resources (HHS), the Department of Defense (DOD), and the National Guard were all involved, and jockeying for leadership of the terrorism issue. There were some attempts at coordination but, in general, agencies pursued their own agendas. The biggest difference among the agencies was the level of funding available, with the

DOD and DOJ controlling the most funds. State and local governments were confused, felt unprepared, and complained of the need to recognize their vulnerability and needs should an event happen. The TOPOFF exercise, held in 2000, reinforced these concerns and vividly demonstrated the problems that could arise in a real event. The events of September 11, unfortunately, validated their concerns and visibly demonstrated the need for changes in the federal approach to terrorism.

The changes fall into five general categories: (1) first responder practices and protocols, (2) preparing for terrorist acts, (3) funding the war on terrorism, (4) creating the Department of Homeland Security, and (5) the shift in focus of the nation's emergency management system to the war on terrorism. This chapter explores these categories, identifies issues, and discusses the implications of this new direction for emergency management. Where appropriate, a historic perspective to these changes is provided.

Changes in Emergency Management and the War on Terrorism

Five groups must be fully engaged in the nation's war on terrorism: the diplomatic community, the intelligence community, the military, law enforcement agencies, and emergency management. The principal goal of diplomats, intelligence agencies, the military, and law enforcement agencies is the reduction if not elimination of the possibility of future terrorist attacks on American citizens inside our borders and abroad (Figure 9-1).

FIGURE 9-1 Oklahoma City, Oklahoma, April 26, 1995. A scene of the devastated Murrah Building following the Oklahoma City bombing.
FEMA News Photo.

The emergency management community, on the other hand, is much more concerned with actions that increase preparedness for future attacks (should they occur) or that mitigate the impacts of those events (to life, property, the economy, or the environment) through engineered and nonengineered solutions. President George W. Bush and many of his advisors constantly reiterated that his administration operated under the assumption that the next terrorist attack was not a question of *if* but rather *when*, and the current administration has taken the same approach.

Emergency management is a risk-based discipline, and the dedication of funding, equipment, staff efforts, and other factors should be made according to the outcome of scientific risk analysis as described in previous chapters of this book. However, emergency management policy and strategy is, to an increasing degree, dictated by the policy agenda of government administrations, which are more closely aligned to public opinion than any scientific assessment. It is therefore incumbent upon emergency managers to apply a level of attention to preparing for the next bombing or biochemical event that may be disproportionate to that of preparing for the next hurricane or flood or tornado, as such decisions are dictated by grant requirements, regulations, and other legal and statutory provisions.

The focus of emergency management in the war on terrorism can have many crossover benefits into natural and technological hazards management, as many of the actions taken bring about a net reduction in risk for our first responders, the public, the business community, the economy, and our way of life. Initiatives such as interoperable communications, credentialing, standardization of incident management protocols, and others that were created in the aftermath of 9/11 to manage the terrorist threat all have extensive dual-use applications at all government levels.

The war on terrorism has brought about the most fundamental change in nationwide emergency management capacity since the creation of FEMA due to the unprecedented funding resources that have been made available to the state and local emergency management communities. The federal government recognized the vital role that state and local first responders played in responding to the September 11 events, but it also recognized that most agencies do not have the capacity to handle the growing terrorist threat. As such, and for the first time in memorable history, vast sums of money have been provided by the federal government to first responders for the purchase of equipment and training, to conduct planning and exercises, and for the development of new technologies. Funding for FEMA has increased, as has the amount of funds FEMA delivers to state and local emergency management organizations.

Prior to 2001, FEMA distributed approximately $175 million annually to its state and local emergency management partners. Since the September 11 attacks, the amount of money granted to these agencies has been measured in the billions of dollars each year, with the FY 2010 budget request for such items and activities totaling almost $3.87 billion. New federal funding sources also have opened up for emergency managers from the Department of Defense, the Department of Justice, and the Department of Health and Human Resources to fund contingency plans, technology assessment and development, and bioterror equipment and training. These changes in funding for emergency management have been felt most significantly at the state and local levels.

The creation of the Department of Homeland Security (DHS) represented a landmark change for the federal community, especially for emergency management. The consolidation of all federal agencies involved in fighting the war on terrorism follows the same logic that first established FEMA in 1979. At that time, then-president Carter, at the request and suggestion of the nation's governors, consolidated all the federal agencies and programs involved in federal disaster relief, preparedness, and mitigation into one single federal agency, FEMA.

The director of the new agency, FEMA, reported directly to the president. However, now that FEMA is a component of DHS, the FEMA director no longer reports directly to the president but rather to the DHS secretary. The impact of this change was not fully understood until Hurricane Katrina struck the Gulf Coast with devastating impact in 2005. This was the first post-9/11 emergency where there was a need for a strong voice leading emergency management, and that voice did not exist.

Following the 2005 hurricane season, Congress addressed leadership and capacity shortfalls through the Post-Katrina Emergency Management Reform Act of 2006 (PKEMRA) legislation, which again reorganized federal emergency management structures in a way that was closer aligned to the function of the agency as a leader in emergency management rather than as a component of security enforcement. These changes continue, and they likely will for some time until the terrorism risk abates or the relativity of terror risk versus more traditional natural and technological hazard risk is better understood. Either way, now that the move has been made, it is highly unlikely that FEMA will soon be independent from the terror- and security-focused DHS.

The rapid move toward a security-focused emergency management structure and system began in 2001, prior to the September 11 terrorist attacks, when President Bush requested the creation of an Office of National Preparedness within FEMA that would focus attention on the then-undetermined terrorist threat and other national security issues. This had the effect of reinforcing the administration's desire to shift FEMA's mission and attention away from the all-hazards approach that was established by the Clinton administration. The gradual shift was accelerated by the events of September 11, which encouraged adoption of similar changes by state and local emergency management operations across the country. This wasn't the first time such a shift occurred, though. In 1981, at the beginning of the Reagan administration, emergency management efforts shifted in focus from disaster management to planning for a nuclear war due to the fear of a nuclear-armed Soviet Union. For the remaining years of the Reagan administration and the four years of President George H. W. Bush's administration, FEMA resources and personnel focused their attention on ensuring continuity of government operations in the event of a nuclear attack. Little attention was paid to natural hazard management, and FEMA was left unprepared to deal with a series of catastrophic natural disasters starting with Hurricane Hugo in 1989 and culminating with Hurricane Andrew in 1992.

But 2005 demonstrated how emergency management policy decisions that neglect to fully account for comprehensive risk information can ultimately lead to poor preparedness and response debacles as were witnessed by the world following Hurricane Katrina. The rapid change in focus away from the diversified, comprehensive risk management approach of the 1990s is undoubtedly what resulted in a dramatic weakening of FEMA's natural disaster management capabilities. And while the lessons of Hurricane Katrina continue to be applied through fulfillment of the provisions of PKEMRA, the FEMA organizational capacity still has far to go before management capacity is aligned with the actual risk posed by the nation's full portfolio of natural, technological, and intentional hazard risks.

September 11, 2001

Summary of Events

Measuring the far-reaching impacts of the events of September 11 on emergency management can be done in a wide variety of ways. In the following sections of this chapter, we will discuss some of the organizational, funding, technology, and operational changes that these events initiated. We will also expand upon how the focus of the emergency management in this country shifted because of these events.

In this section we will examine the size and breadth of these events through an examination of some of the financial costs, principally spending by FEMA and other federal government agencies, in responding to and assisting in the recovery from these events. When considering the impacts of the September 11 events, perhaps the most devastating impact is the horrific loss of life in New York City, Virginia, and Pennsylvania. After years of painstaking research to determine who was actually present at each of the three attack locations, a final tally of 2,976 fatalities was determined. Of this amount, 184 died at the Pentagon, 40 in Pennsylvania, and the remaining 2,752 at the World Trade Center (Figure 9-2).

FIGURE 9-2 New York City, New York, September 25, 2001. Fragments of the World Trade Center facade are all that remain of the 110-story structures that once dominated the skyline of lower Manhattan. Photo by Mike Rieger/ FEMA News Photo.

The attacks on the World Trade Center and the Pentagon, considered together, are arguably the first national disaster event to have occurred in the United States outside of wartime. It was the first disaster event to have impacted all citizens, leaving all communities with a lingering sense of vulnerability. However, it was the economic consequences of these attacks that had the most far-reaching direct impacts, affecting people not only nationwide but also throughout the world.

Costs Associated with Federal/State Disaster Assistance

The cost to the federal government for the response and recovery of the World Trade Center was formally estimated to be $20 billion, though the exact number will never be known due to the complex ways in which the nation's economy, infrastructure, and social fabric was impacted by these events. FEMA provided 42 percent of this federal share, with $8.818 billion in aid. HUD gave the second largest amount, $2.48 billion, or 17 percent, while DOT ranked third at $2.37 billion (11.5 percent). All other federal agencies contributed a total of $820 million, which amounted to 4 percent of the total federal share. Also included in the federal figures of aid are the tax benefits associated with the New York City Liberty Zone—an area of the city where new tax incentives have resulted in over $5 billion in indirect economic aid to the city and its residents.

Since September 2001, the indirect costs associated with securing the nation from future acts of terrorism have eclipsed this $20 billion figure, and include the costs associated with creation of the Department of Homeland Security, government control of airport security, overtime of police and fire department staff, increased security at special events and at critical facilities, preparedness grants for equipment and training provided to state and local governments, technology research, and port security, among many others. Include the cost of the wars in Iraq and Afghanistan, considered preemptive action to mitigate the risk of an attack on domestic soil, and the costs of these combined measures, across the nine years since the terrorist attacks, reaches above $1 trillion.

Post-9/11 First Responder Valuation

In July and August 2002, two September 11–related after-action reports were released: "Improving NYPD Emergency Preparedness and Response," which was prepared by McKinsey & Company for the New York City Police Department, and "Arlington County After-Action Report on the Response to the September 11 Terrorist Attack on the Pentagon," which was prepared for Arlington County, Virginia, by Titan Systems Corporation. Both reports are based on hundreds of interviews with event participants and reviews of organizational plans, and they have served to provide many lessons and recommendations through which change in the emergency discipline has emerged.

The NYPD report (McKinsey & Company, 2002) did not pass judgment on the success or failure of the NYPD on September 11 but rather assessed the NYPD's response objectives and instruments in order to identify 20 improvement opportunities for the NYPD, of which 6 merited immediate action:

- Clearer delineation of roles and responsibilities of organizational leaders
- Better clarity in the chain of command
- Radio communications protocols and procedures that optimize information flow
- More effective mobilization of response staff
- More efficient provisioning and distribution of emergency and donated equipment
- A comprehensive disaster response plan, with a significant counterterrorism component

The "Arlington County After-Action Report" did declare the response by the county and others to the Pentagon terrorist attack a success that "can be attributed to the efforts of ordinary men and women performing in extraordinary fashion" (Titan Systems Corporation, 2002). The terrorist attack on the Pentagon provided an extreme test of the plans and skills of responders from Arlington County, Virginia; the federal government; and other jurisdictions and organizations that responded. Select notable facts about the response to the September 11 attack at the Pentagon, as compiled in the report, include the following:

- The first Arlington County emergency response unit arrived at the crash site less than three minutes after impact.
- Over 30 urban search and rescue teams, police departments, fire departments, and federal agencies assisted Arlington's police and fire in the rescue. Some of these important partners included the FBI, the Federal Emergency Management Agency, U.S. Park Police, the Defense Protective Service, the Military District of Washington, the Metropolitan Washington Airport Authority, the Virginia Department of Emergency Management, and USAR teams from Albuquerque, New Mexico; Fairfax County, Virginia; Montgomery County, Maryland; and Memphis, Tennessee.
- Captain Dennis Gilroy and the team on Foam Unit 161 from the Fort Meyer Fire Station were on-site at the Pentagon when Flight 77 crashed into the building. Firefighters Mark Skipper and Alan Wallace, who were next to the unit, received burns and lacerations but immediately began helping Pentagon employees, who were trying to escape through first-floor windows.
- Captain Steve McCoy and the crew of Engine 101 were on their way to fire staff training in Crystal City when they saw the plane fly low overhead and an explosion from the vicinity of the Pentagon. McCoy was the first person to call Arlington County's Emergency Communications Center to report the plane crash.
- The Arlington County American Red Cross Chapter coordinated support from the Red Cross. The chapter had 80 trained volunteers at the time of the attack, but the organization's mutual-aid arrangements with other chapters garnered nearly 1,500 volunteers who helped support the emergency services personnel, victims, and their families.

- Business supporters set up temporary food service on the Pentagon parking lot for rescue workers. Over 187,940 meals were served to emergency workers. Many other businesses brought phones for rescuers to call home, building materials, and other vital necessities.
- Over 112 surgeries on nine burn victims were performed in three weeks. One of the nine burn victims died after having over 60 percent of her body burned. There were 106 patients that reported to area hospitals with various injuries.

The "Arlington County After-Action Report" contains 235 recommendations and lessons learned, each of which must be understood within the context and setting of the Pentagon response. Some specifically apply to a particular response element or activity. Others address overarching issues that apply to Arlington County and other jurisdictions throughout the country, particularly those in large metropolitan areas. These recommendations are not weighted or prioritized, since their intent was to leave such decisions up to the operational staff drawing lessons from the report. What is interesting about these recommendations is that while they were developed in response to a terrorist attack, they are fully transferable into the all-hazards context. These are some of their recommendations:

1. **ICS and Unified Command.** The primary response participants understood the ICS, implemented it effectively, and complied with its provisions. The ACFD, an experienced ICS practitioner, established its command presence literally within minutes of the attack. Other supporting jurisdictions and agencies, with few exceptions, operated seamlessly within the ICS framework. For those organizations and individuals unfamiliar with the ICS and Unified Command, particularly the military, which has its own clearly defined command and control mechanisms, the Incident Commander provided explicit information and guidance early during the response and elicited their full cooperation.

2. **Mutual Aid and Outside Support.** The management and integration of mutual-aid assets and the coordination and cooperation of agencies at all government echelons, volunteer organizations, and private businesses were outstanding. Public safety organizations and chief administrative officers (CAOs) of nearby jurisdictions lent their support to Arlington County. The response to the Pentagon attack revealed the total scope and magnitude of support available throughout the Washington metropolitan area and across the nation.

3. **Arlington County CEMP.** The CEMP proved to be what its title implies. It was well thought out, properly maintained, frequently practiced, and effectively implemented. Government leaders were able to quickly marshal the substantial resources of Arlington County in support of the first responders, without interfering with tactical operations. County board members worked with counterparts in neighboring jurisdictions and elected federal and state officials to ensure a rapid economic recovery, and they engaged in frequent dialogue with the citizens of Arlington County.

4. **Employee Assistance Program (EAP).** At the time of the Pentagon attack, Arlington County already had in place an aggressive, well-established EAP offering critical

incident stress management (CISM) services to public safety and other county employees. In particular, the ACFD embraced the concept and encouraged all of its members to use EAP services. Thus, it is not surprising that the EAP staff was well received when they arrived at the incident site within three hours of the attack. During the incident response and in follow-up sessions weeks afterward, the EAP proved invaluable to first responders, their families, and the entire county support network. This is a valuable resource that must be incorporated in response plans.

5. **Training, Exercises, and Shared Experiences.** The ACED has long recognized the possibility of a weapons of mass destruction (WMD) terrorist attack in the Washington metropolitan area and has pursued an aggressive preparedness program for such an event, including its pioneering work associated with the MMRS. In preparation for anticipated problems associated with the arrival of Y2K, Arlington County government thoroughly exercised the CEMP. In 1998, the FBI Washington Field Office (WFO) established a fire liaison position to work specifically with area fire departments. Washington metropolitan area public safety organizations routinely work together on events of national prominence and shared jurisdictional interests, such as presidential inaugural celebrations, heads of state visits, international conferences such as the periodic International Monetary Fund (IMF) conference, and others. They also regularly participate in frequent training exercises including those hosted by the Pentagon and MDW. All this and more contributed to the successful Pentagon response.

The following challenges must be met:

1. **Self-Dispatching.** Organizations, response units, and individuals proceeding on their own initiative directly to an incident site, without the knowledge and permission of the host jurisdiction and the Incident Commander, complicate the exercise of command, increase the risks faced by bona fide responders, and exacerbate the challenge of accountability. WMD terrorist event response plans should designate preselected and well-marked staging areas. Dispatch instructions should be clear. Law enforcement agencies should be familiar with deployment plans and quickly establish incident site access controls. When identified, self-dispatched resources should be immediately released from the scene, unless incorporated into the Incident Commander's response plan.

2. **Fixed and Mobile Command and Control Facilities.** Arlington County does not have a facility specifically designed and equipped to support the emergency management functions specified in the CEMP. The conference room currently used as the EOC does not have adequate space and is not configured or properly equipped for that role. The notification and recall capabilities of the Emergency Communications Center are constrained by equipment limitations and there are no protected telephone lines for outside calls when the 9-1-1 lines are saturated. The ACED does not have a mobile command vehicle and relied on the use of vehicles belonging to other organizations and jurisdictions. The ACPD mobile command unit needs to be replaced or extensively modernized.

3. **Communications.** Almost all aspects of communications continue to be problematic—from initial notification to tactical operations. Cellular telephones were of little value in the first few hours and cellular priority access service (CPAS) is not provided to emergency responders. Radio channels were initially oversaturated, and interoperability problems among jurisdictions and agencies persist. Even portable radios that are otherwise compatible were sometimes preprogrammed in a fashion that precluded interoperability. Pagers seemed to be the most reliable means of notification when available and used, but most firefighters are not issued pagers. The Arlington County EOC does not have an installed radio capacity and relied on portable radios coincidentally assigned to staff members assigned duties at the EOC.

4. **Logistics.** Arlington County, like most other jurisdictions, was not logistically prepared for an operation of the duration and magnitude of the Pentagon attack. The ACED did not have an established logistics function, a centralized supply system, or any experience in long-term logistics support. Stock levels of personal protective equipment (PPE), critical high-demand items (such as batteries and breathing apparatus), equipment for reserve vehicles, and medical supplies for EMS units were insufficient for sustained operations. These challenges were overcome at the Pentagon with the aid of the more experienced Fairfax County Fire and Rescue Department logistics staff. A stronger standing capacity, however, is needed for a jurisdiction the size of Arlington County.

5. **Hospital Coordination.** Communications and coordination were deficient between EMS control at the incident site and area hospitals receiving injured victims. The coordination difficulties were not simple equipment failures. They represent flaws in the system that were present on September 11. Regional hospital disaster plans no longer require a clearinghouse hospital or other designated communications focal point for the dissemination of patient disposition and treatment information. Thus, hospitals first learned of en route victims when contacted by transporting EMS units, and EMS control reconstructed much of the disposition information by contacting hospitals after the fact. Although the number of victims of the Pentagon attack were fewer than many anticipated, they were not insignificant. An incident with more casualties would have seriously strained the system.

The events at the World Trade Center and the Pentagon varied significantly in size and impact but, from a responder's perspective, they were similar in terms of their no-notice nature and the challenges associated with their response and recovery. There are striking similarities between the "improvement opportunities" listed in the NYPD report and the "lessons learned" in the Arlington County report (Figure 9-3).

Although the specifics vary, in both response operations, five key areas of improvement were noted: command, communications, coordination, planning, and dispatching personnel. Many of the actions taken after September 11 by government officials and emergency managers at the federal, state, and local levels reflected a perception that the terrorist threat existed in all communities and that there was a significant need for changes in order to prepare for the next terrorist event.

FIGURE 9-3 New York City, New York, October 13, 2001. A month later, New York firefighters were still at work putting out fires at the site of the World Trade Center.
Photo by Andrea Booher/FEMA News Photo.

CRITICAL THINKING

Do you feel that the recommendations of the Arlington County report are relevant to small communities, or do they apply only to large metropolitan areas? Explain your answer.

Federal Government Terrorism Activity

For FEMA and its partner agencies in the National Response Framework (NRF—formerly the National Response Plan—see Chapter 6), the most significant actions taken by the federal government to combat terrorism were the creation of the Department of Homeland Security (DHS) and the Global War on Terrorism (which has involved sustained military campaigns in both Afghanistan and Iraq in addition to the diplomatic and other nonmilitary actions conducted throughout the rest of the world).

For state and local emergency managers, the most significant effect of these actions taken since September 11 has been the ongoing increase in available funding under new and existing funding vehicles that has provided significant support to first responders and emergency management officials for terrorism planning and prevention activities. However, as was stated earlier in this chapter, that has represented a concurrent and fundamental shift in funding from a more traditional all-hazards management approach to one that favors the terrorist threat.

Risk perception about a hazard is a primary driver behind government policy, and that is especially true in the case of the high-profile terrorist hazard exposed by the 9/11 attacks. In the first years after the attacks occurred, it was difficult for the American people to formulate accurate impressions of risk, and given the actions taken by the government to combat such risk and keep them informed (most notably through the use of the color-coded Homeland Security Advisory System), these impressions tended to be that such risk warranted a sustained and significant government effort. Whether due to diligent intelligence and security efforts or the absence of a serious ongoing terrorist threat within the nation's borders, the years since September 11 have seen no new major terrorist activity. In those same years, however, the American public has seen the effects related to several major natural hazards, including Hurricanes Katrina, Rita, Ivan, and others.

Despite a sustained government effort to inform the public of ongoing counterterrorism actions (including the wars in Iraq and Afghanistan), the levels of public support for spending on homeland security activities and equipment has waned considerably—a trend that is likely to increase each year as long as the time since the terrorist attacks grows. Such changes in sentiment have the greatest impact on the activities of the federal government, which are guided by congressional incentives (and funding). In the following section, specific examples of the influence of the terrorist threat on emergency management will be explored.

ADDITIONAL RESEARCH

Scientist Amy Ding at the University of Illinois studied the effect of a sustained heightened state of readiness for acts of terrorism, as instructed by the perpetual "yellow" status of the Homeland Security Advisory System that has existed for several years. Their findings, published in the article "A Theoretical Model of Public Response to the Homeland Security Advisory System" in the *Journal of Defense Modeling and Simulation*, suggest that the public has lost interest in the system and is no longer paying attention (nor are they taking the recommended actions). This study can be found at *http://www.scs.org/pubs/jdms/vol3num1/JDMSvol3no1Ding45-55.pdf*.

The Department of Homeland Security (DHS)

On November 25, 2002, President Bush signed into law the Homeland Security Act of 2002 (HS Act) (Public Law 107–296) and announced that former Pennsylvania governor Tom Ridge would become secretary of a new Department of Homeland Security (DHS) to be created through this legislation. This act, which authorized the greatest federal government reorganization since President Harry Truman joined the various branches of the armed forces under the Department of Defense, was charged with a threefold mission of protecting the United States from further terrorist attacks, reducing the nation's vulnerability to terrorism, and minimizing the damage from potential terrorist attacks and natural disasters.

The sweeping reorganization into the new department, which officially opened its doors on January 24, 2003, joined together over 179,000 federal employees from 22 existing federal agencies under a single, cabinet-level organization. The legislation also included several changes within other federal agencies that were only remotely affiliated with DHS.

The creation of DHS was the culmination of an evolutionary legislative process that began largely in response to criticism that increased federal intelligence interagency cooperation could have prevented the September 11 terrorist attacks. The White House and Congress both had recognized that a homeland security czar would require both a staff and a large budget in order to succeed, and thus began deliberations to create a new cabinet-level department that would fuse many of the security-related agencies dispersed throughout the federal government.

For several months during the second half of 2002, Congress jockeyed between different versions of the Homeland Security bill in an effort to establish legislation that was passable yet effective. Lawmakers were particularly mired on the issue of the rights of employees—an issue that prolonged the legal process considerably. Furthermore, efforts to incorporate many of the intelligence-gathering and investigative law enforcement agencies—namely, the National Security Agency (NSA), the FBI, and the CIA—into the legislation failed.

Despite these delays and setbacks, after the 2002 midterm elections, the Republican seats gained in both the House and Senate gave the president the leverage he needed to pass the bill without further deliberation (H.R., 299-121 on November 13, 2002; Senate, 90–9 on November 19, 2002). Although the passage of this act represented a significant milestone, the implementation phase presented a tremendous challenge—a concern expressed by several leaders from the agencies that were to be absorbed. On November 25, 2002, President Bush submitted his Reorganization Plan (as required by the legislation), which mapped out the schedule, methodology, and budget for the monumental task.

Beginning March 1, 2003, almost all of the federal agencies named in the Act began their move, whether literally or symbolically, into the new department. Those remaining followed on June 1, 2003, with all incidental transfers completed by September 1, 2003. Although a handful of these agencies remained intact after the move, most were fully incorporated into one of four new directorates: Border and Transportation Security (BTS), Information Analysis and Infrastructure Protection (IAIP), Emergency Preparedness and Response (EP&R), and Science and Technology (S&T). A fifth directorate, Management, incorporated parts of the existing administrative and support offices within the merged agencies. Secretary Ridge was given exactly one year to develop a comprehensive structural framework for DHS and to name new leadership for all five directorates and other offices created under the legislation.

In addition to the creation of the Department of Homeland Security, the HS Act made several changes to other federal agencies and their programs and created several new programs. Here are some of the most significant ones:

- Established a National Homeland Security Council within the Executive Office of the President, which assesses U.S. objectives, commitments, and risks in the interest of Homeland Security; oversees and reviews federal homeland security policies; and makes recommendations to the president.
- Transferred the Bureau of Alcohol, Tobacco, and Firearms (ATF) from the Department of the Treasury to the Department of Justice (DOJ).
- Explicitly prohibited both the creation of a national ID card and the proposed Citizen Corps "Terrorism Information and Prevention System" (Operation TIPS, which encouraged transportation workers, postal workers, and public utility employees to identify and report suspicious activities linked to terrorism and crime). The Act also reaffirmed the Posse Comitatus Act, which prohibits the use of the Armed Forces in law enforcement activities except under constitutional or congressional authority (the Coast Guard is exempt from this Act).
- The "Arming Pilots Against Terrorism Act," incorporated into the HS Act, allows pilots to defend aircraft cockpits with firearms or other "less-than-lethal weapons" against acts of criminal violence or air piracy and provides antiterrorism training to flight crews.
- The Critical Infrastructure Information Act (2002), incorporated in the HS Act, exempts certain components of critical infrastructure from Freedom of Information Act (FOIA) regulations.
- The "Johnny Michael Spann Patriot Trusts" was created to provide support for surviving spouses, children, or dependent parents, grandparents, or siblings of various federal employees who die in the line of duty as result of terrorist attacks, military operations, intelligence operations, or law enforcements operations.

On November 30, 2004, following the presidential elections, DHS Secretary Ridge announced his resignation. After an initial nomination of NYPD commissioner Bernard Kerik for the position, which was withdrawn due to questions arising during confirmation hearings, federal judge Michael Chertoff was nominated and confirmed to lead the agency. In January 2009, after the Obama administration assumed control of the executive office, Arizona governor Janet Napolitano was nominated and confirmed as the third secretary of Homeland Security.

CRITICAL THINKING

Do you think that the Department of Homeland Security can ever have a true risk-based all-hazards focus, or will its focus always be terrorism? Explain your answer.

Secretary Chertoff's Six-Point Agenda

On July 13, 2005, DHS secretary Michael Chertoff released a six-point agenda to reorganize the department. The agenda followed an initial review that Chertoff had initiated immediately upon assuming his leadership position. The review was designed to closely examine the department to find ways in which leadership could better manage risk in terms of threat, vulnerability, and consequence; prioritize policies and operational missions according to this risk-based approach; and establish a series of preventive and protective steps that would increase security at multiple levels. The resulting agenda brought about several changes that led to the present design and that focused on the following:

- Increasing overall preparedness, particularly for catastrophic events
- Creating better transportation security systems to move people and cargo more securely and efficiently
- Strengthening border security and interior enforcement and reforming immigration processes
- Enhancing information sharing (with partners)
- Improving financial management, human resource development, procurement, and information technology within the department
- Realigning the department's organization to maximize mission performance

Several new policy initiatives were included in the proposed overhaul of the department, including the following:

- A new approach to securing borders through additional personnel, new technologies, infrastructure investments, and interior enforcement—coupled with efforts to reduce the demand for illegal border migration by channeling migrants seeking work into regulated legal channels
- Restructuring the current immigration process to enhance security and improve customer service
- Reaching out to state homeland security officials to improve information exchange protocols, refine the Homeland Security Advisory System (HSAS), support state and regional data fusion centers, and address other topics of mutual concern
- Investing in DHS personnel by providing professional career training and other development efforts

One of the most significant changes that occurred as a result of the six-point agenda was an organizational restructuring of the department. Chertoff asserted that these changes were made to increase the department's ability to prepare, prevent, and respond to terrorist attacks and other emergencies:

- The creation of the Directorate of Policy, which centralized and improved policy development and coordination.
- The creation of a new Office of Intelligence and Analysis to strengthen intelligence functions and information sharing. This office was created to ensure that information

is gathered from all relevant field operations and other parts of the intelligence community; is analyzed with a mission-oriented focus; is informative to senior decision makers; and is disseminated to the appropriate federal, state, local, and private sector partners. Led by a chief intelligence officer who reports directly to the secretary, this office is comprised of analysts within the former Information Analysis directorate and draw on expertise of other DHS components with intelligence collection and analysis operations.

- The creation of a new Office of Operations Coordination to improve operational coordination and efficiency. This office works to enable DHS to more effectively conduct joint operations across all organizational elements; to coordinate incident management activities; and to utilize all resources within the department to translate intelligence and policy into immediate action. The Homeland Security Operations Center (HSOC), which serves as the nation's nerve center for information sharing and domestic incident management on a full-time basis, was moved into this new office.
- The Information Analysis and Infrastructure Protection Directorate was renamed the Directorate for Preparedness, and preparedness assets from across the department were consolidated under it. The Directorate for Preparedness now facilitates grants and oversees nationwide preparedness efforts supporting first responder training, citizen awareness, public health, infrastructure, and cyber security, and ensures that proper steps are taken to protect high-risk targets.
- FEMA was moved so it reports directly to the DHS secretary. As a result of the new DHS reorganization, FEMA now focuses on response and recovery activities rather than all four phases of emergency management.
- The Federal Air Marshal Service was moved from the Immigration and Customs Enforcement (ICE) bureau to the Transportation Security Administration to increase operational coordination and strengthen efforts to meet the common goal of aviation security.
- A new Office of Legislative and Intergovernmental Affairs was created, which merged certain functions among the Office of Legislative Affairs and the Office of State and Local Government Coordination. This was done in order to streamline intergovernmental relations efforts and better share homeland security information with members of Congress, as well as state and local officials.
- The Office of Security was moved so it is now positioned under the direction of the Under Secretary for Management in order to better manage information systems, contractual activities, security accreditation, training, and resources.

The Post-Katrina Emergency Management Reform Act

In order to correct the emergency management shortfalls that were highlighted in the inadequate response to Hurricane Katrina, Congress passed the Post-Katrina Emergency Management Reform Act, which was signed into law by President Bush on October 4, 2006.

The Act established new leadership positions within the department, created additional functions that were assumed by FEMA, created and reallocated functions to other components within DHS, and amended the Homeland Security Act in ways that directly and indirectly affect the organization and functions of various entities within DHS. These changes, which also included nonmandated actions, include the following:

- Transferred (with the exception of certain offices) the functions of the DHS Preparedness Directorate to FEMA, including:
  - The United States Fire Administration (USFA)
  - The Office of Grants and Training (G&T)
  - The Chemical Stockpile Emergency Preparedness Division (CSEP)
  - The Radiological Emergency Preparedness Program (REPP)
  - The Office of National Capital Region Coordination (NCRC)
- The Act changed the title of FEMA director to FEMA administrator and supported that position with two deputy administrators. The first is the deputy administrator and chief operating officer (the principal deputy, with overall operational responsibilities at FEMA), and the other is a deputy administrator for National Preparedness—a division that was created within FEMA by the Act.
- The National Preparedness Division (NP) was created by merging several existing FEMA programs with the legacy DHS Preparedness Directorate programs just listed. Its focus is policy, contingency planning, exercise coordination and evaluation, emergency management training, and hazard mitigation with respect to the Chemical Stockpile Emergency Preparedness (CSEP) program and the Radiological Emergency Preparedness Program (REPP). NP is described in much greater detail in Chapter 4.
- The Office of Grants and Training was moved to FEMA and renamed the Office of Grant Programs. The Training and Systems Support Divisions of the Office of Grants and Training was transferred to the National Integration Center (NIC) within NP. The Office of the Citizen Corps within the Office of Grants and Training was first transferred into the FEMA Office of Readiness, Prevention and Planning, and ultimately into NP as well.
- Additional headquarters positions created at FEMA by the Post-Katrina Act include a disability coordinator in the FEMA Office of Equal Rights, a small state and rural advocate, a law enforcement advisor to the administrator, and a National Advisory Council. The National Advisory Council, which was created in early 2007, advises the FEMA administrator on all aspects of emergency management to ensure better coordination among stakeholders. Members of the Council are appointed by the FEMA administrator, representing a geographic and disciplinary cross section of officials from emergency management and law enforcement, and include homeland security directors; adjutants general; emergency response providers from state, local, and tribal governments; private sector; and nongovernmental organizations.

Funding for First Responders and Emergency Management

For state and local government, the events of September 11 resulted in an extraordinary increase in funding for first responders—fire, police, and emergency medical technicians—and emergency management activities (Table 9-1). Also, the number of federal government agencies and programs now providing funds for these activities has increased significantly. In the first responder community, historically only the police have received significant funding from the federal government. Fire departments across the country traditionally have raised the majority of their funding from local sources. Emergency medical technicians are often private contractors paid for by local and state government sources.

Proper training and equipping of firefighters responding to a biochemical terrorist attack has been a concern among the fire services community and FEMA since the early 1990s. Passage of the Fire Prevention and Assistance Act in 2000 was the first effort by Congress to support the nation's paid and volunteer fire departments. In the spring of 2001, FEMA initiated a new Fire Grant program that provided $100 million in small grants to local fire departments for equipment, protective gear, training, and prevention programs. In 2002, the amount available for FEMA fire grants increased to $300 million. By 2004, that amount had risen to over $700,000 (though these totals have fallen every year since). In addition to the annual fire grants, the bulk of the $3 to $3.5 billion spent on first responders each year has been designated for equipping and training of first responders for future terrorist events (see the proposed 2010 budget figures in Table 9-1).

FEMA is not the only source of terrorism funding for state and local government. The Department of Justice, through a variety of programs, funds the acquisition of equipment

Table 9-1 Select Local First Responder Funding Figures: 2006–2010 (in Millions)

Funding Area	FY 2006 Enacted	FY 2007 Enacted	FY 2008 Enacted	FY 2009 Enacted	FY 2010 Enacted
State Homeland Security Grant Program (SHSGP)	$545	$525	$861	$861	$842
Urban Area Security Initiative (UASI)	$740	$770	$781	$798	$832.5
Assistance to Firefighters Grant Program (Fire Grants)	$655	$547	$560	$565	$400 (proposed)
Emergency Management Performance Grants (EMPG)	$173	$177	$291	$306	$330
Citizen Corps	$20	$15	$15	$15	$12.5
Metropolitan Medical Response System (MMRS)	$33	$32	$0	$40	$39
Public Safety Interoperable Communications Grant	$0	$0	$48	$48	$48
Staffing for Adequate Fire and Emergency Response (SAFER)	$109	$115	$190	$210	$420 (proposed)

and technology. The Department of Health and Human Resources provides substantial funding to state and local government to address the threat of biochemical terrorist attacks. The Center for Disease Control funds public health planning and capacity building and bolstering of the national pharmaceutical stockpile. The Department of Defense provides funding for emergency management training for military personnel and community officials.

Communicating Threat Information to the American People

DHS relies most heavily on the Homeland Security Advisory System (HSAS) to inform the public about the threat of terrorism. The HSAS was born out of Homeland Security Presidential Directive–3 (HSPD-3), which was issued on March 11, 2002, and states the following:

> *The nation requires a Homeland Security Advisory System to provide a comprehensive and effective means to disseminate information regarding the risk of terrorist acts to federal, state, and local authorities and to the American people. Such a system would provide warnings in the form of a set of graduated "Threat Conditions" that would increase as the risk of the threat increases. At each Threat Condition, federal departments and agencies would implement a corresponding set of "Protective Measures" to further reduce vulnerability or increase response capability during a period of heightened alert.*
>
> *This system is intended to create a common vocabulary, context, and structure for an ongoing national discussion about the nature of the threats that confront the homeland and the appropriate measures that should be taken in response. It seeks to inform and facilitate decisions appropriate to different levels of government and to private citizens at home and at work.*

The system, which is designed to combine threat information with vulnerability assessments and provide communications to public safety officials and the public, has three components:

- **Homeland Security Threat Advisories.** Contain actionable information about an incident involving, or a threat targeting, critical national networks or infrastructures or key assets. They could, for example, relay newly developed procedures that, when implemented, would significantly improve security or protection. They could also suggest a change in readiness posture, protective actions, or response. This category includes products formerly named alerts, advisories, and sector notifications. Advisories are targeted to federal, state, and local governments; private sector organizations; and international partners.
- **Homeland Security Information Bulletins.** Communicate information of interest to the nation's critical infrastructures that do not meet the timeliness, specificity, or

significance thresholds of warning messages. Such information may include statistical reports, periodic summaries, incident response or reporting guidelines, common vulnerabilities and patches, and configuration standards or tools. It also may include preliminary requests for information. Bulletins are targeted to federal, state, and local governments; private sector organizations; and international partners.

- **Color-Coded Threat Level System.** Used to communicate with public safety officials and the public at large through a threat-based, color-coded system so that protective measures can be implemented to reduce the likelihood or impact of an attack. Raising the threat condition has economic, physical, and psychological effects on the nation, so the Homeland Security Advisory System can place specific geographic regions or industry sectors on a higher alert status than other regions or industries, based on specific threat information.

Figure 9-4 provides suggestions for public action in accordance with the five color codes of the Homeland Security Advisory System. The following information, based on the same color-coded chart, provides DHS recommendations to federal departments and agencies.

Guidance for Federal Departments and Agencies

The following Threat Conditions each represent an increasing risk of terrorist attacks. Beneath each Threat Condition are some suggested Protective Measures, recognizing that the heads of federal departments and agencies are responsible for developing and implementing appropriate agency-specific Protective Measures:

1. **Low Condition (Green).** Declared when there is a low risk of terrorist attacks. Federal departments and agencies should consider the following general measures in addition to the agency-specific Protective Measures they develop and implement:
   - Refining and exercising as appropriate preplanned Protective Measures
   - Ensuring personnel receive proper training on the Homeland Security Advisory System and specific preplanned department or agency Protective Measures
   - Institutionalizing a process to assure that all facilities and regulated sectors are regularly assessed for vulnerabilities to terrorist attacks, and all reasonable measures are taken to mitigate these vulnerabilities
2. **Guarded Condition (Blue).** Declared when there is a general risk of terrorist attacks. In addition to the Protective Measures taken in the previous Threat Condition, federal departments and agencies should consider the following general measures in addition to the agency-specific Protective Measures that they will develop and implement:
   - Checking communications with designated emergency response or command locations
   - Reviewing and updating emergency response procedures
   - Providing the public with any information that would strengthen its ability to act appropriately

From The U.S. Department of Homeland Security.

Citizen Guidance on the Homeland Security Advisory System

Risk of Attack	Recommended Actions for Citizens
GREEN Low Risk	⇨ Develop a family emergency plan. Share it with family and friends, and practice the plan. Visit www.Ready.gov for help creating a plan. ⇨ Create an "Emergency Supply Kit" for your household. ⇨ Be informed. Visit www.Ready.gov or obtain a copy of "Preparing Makes Sense, Get Ready Now" by calling 1-800-BE-READY. ⇨ Know how to shelter-in-place and how to turn off utilities (power, gas, and water) to your home. ⇨ Examine volunteer opportunities in your community, such as Citizen Corps, Volunteers in Police Service, Neighborhood Watch or others, and donate your time. ⇨ Consider completing an American Red Cross first aid or CPR course, or Community Emergency Response Team (CERT) course.
BLUE Guarded Risk	⇨ *Complete recommended steps at level green.* ⇨ Review stored disaster supplies and replace items that are outdated. ⇨ Be alert to suspicious activity and report it to proper authorities.
YELLOW Elevated Risk	⇨ *Complete recommended steps at levels green and blue.* ⇨ Ensure disaster supply kit is stocked and ready. ⇨ Check telephone numbers in family emergency plan and update as necessary. ⇨ Develop alternate routes to/from work or school and practice them. ⇨ Continue to be alert for suspicious activity and report it to authorities.
ORANGE High Risk	⇨ *Complete recommended steps at lower levels.* ⇨ Exercise caution when traveling, pay attention to travel advisories. ⇨ Review your family emergency plan and make sure all family members know what to do. ⇨ Be Patient. Expect some delays, baggage searches and restrictions at public buildings. ⇨ Check on neighbors or others that might need assistance in an emergency.
RED Severe Risk	⇨ *Complete all recommended actions at lower levels.* ⇨ Listen to local emergency management officials. ⇨ Stay tuned to TV or radio for current information/instructions. ⇨ Be prepared to shelter-in-place or evacuate, as instructed. ⇨ Expect traffic delays and restrictions. ⇨ Provide volunteer services only as requested. ⇨ Contact your school/business to determine status of work day.

Developed with input from the American Red Cross.

FIGURE 9-4 The Homeland Security Advisory System.
From www.dhs.gov.

3. **Elevated Condition (Yellow).** Declared when there is a significant risk of terrorist attacks. In addition to the Protective Measures taken in the previous Threat Conditions, federal departments and agencies should consider the following general measures in addition to the Protective Measures that they will develop and implement:
   - Increasing surveillance of critical locations
   - Coordinating emergency plans as appropriate with nearby jurisdictions
   - Assessing whether the precise characteristics of the threat require the further refinement of preplanned Protective Measures
   - Implementing, as appropriate, contingency and emergency response plans
4. **High Condition (Orange).** Declared when there is a high risk of terrorist attacks. In addition to the Protective Measures taken in the previous Threat Conditions, federal departments and agencies should consider the following general measures in addition to the agency-specific Protective Measures that they will develop and implement:
   - Coordinating necessary security efforts with federal, state, and local law enforcement agencies or any National Guard or other appropriate armed forces organizations
   - Taking additional precautions at public events and possibly considering alternative venues or even cancellation
   - Preparing to execute contingency procedures, such as moving to an alternate site or dispersing their workforce
   - Restricting threatened facility access to essential personnel only
5. **Severe Condition (Red).** This reflects a severe risk of terrorist attacks. Under most circumstances, the Protective Measures for a Severe Condition are not intended to be sustained for substantial periods of time. In addition to the Protective Measures in the previous Threat Conditions, federal departments and agencies also should consider the following general measures in addition to the agency-specific Protective Measures that they will develop and implement:
   - Increasing or redirecting personnel to address critical emergency needs
   - Assigning emergency response personnel and prepositioning and mobilizing specially trained teams or resources
   - Monitoring, redirecting, or constraining transportation systems
   - Closing public and government facilities

The Department of Homeland Security also helps citizens and business owners to prepare for future acts of terrorism through their Ready.gov campaign, as described in Chapter 4. This Internet-based public education campaign provides "a commonsense framework designed to launch a process of learning about citizen preparedness."

DHS urges citizens to stay informed about how to react to various terrorism incident scenarios. These include biological, chemical, explosive, nuclear, and radiological, disasters. Ready.gov states:

Terrorists are working to obtain biological, chemical, nuclear, and radiological weapons, and the threat of an attack is very real. Here at the Department of Homeland

Security, throughout the federal government, and at organizations across America we are working hard to strengthen our nation's security. Whenever possible, we want to stop terrorist attacks before they happen. All Americans should begin a process of learning about potential threats so we are better prepared to react during an attack. While there is no way to predict what will happen, or what your personal circumstances will be, there are simple things you can do now to prepare yourself and your loved ones.

Some of the things you can do to prepare for the unexpected, such as assembling a supply kit and developing a family communications plan, are the same for both a natural or man-made emergency. However, as you will see throughout the pages of Ready.gov, there are important differences among potential terrorist threats that will impact the decisions you make and the actions you take. With a little planning and common sense, you can be better prepared for the unexpected.

Appendix A illustrates the recommendations for citizens to stay prepared that have been provided by Ready.gov. More detailed recommendations for each step are provided at *www.Ready.gov.*

CRITICAL THINKING

Since its creation, the Homeland Security Advisory System has been raised to Orange eight times, and to Red one time. During these periods of elevated status, there were no attacks. Do you think that the absence of attacks makes citizens ignore future threats? Why or why not?

Accomplishments of the Department of Homeland Security

Since 2001, the Department of Homeland Security has accomplished the following:

- Hired over 5,700 new Border Patrol agents and acquired nearly 7,800 new detention beds.
- Provided over $27 billion to state, local, and tribal governments to enhance first responder preparedness.
- Created the Domestic Nuclear Detection Office to detect, identify, and track down the origins of nuclear and radiological materials.
- Hired a workforce and deployed sufficient technology to electronically screen 100 percent of airline passengers and checked baggage.
- Strengthened marine transportation systems and the cargo supply chain through the Container Security Initiative, Customs Trade Partnership Against Terrorism, and the Maritime Transportation Security Act.
- Awarded billions of dollars in port security grants to enhance the physical security of the nation's seaports.

During 2008, DHS accomplished the following:

- The Office of Intelligence and Analysis (I&A) expanded deployment of training to state and local government as well as private sector personnel handling classified and sensitive information received from the department.
- The *DHS Small Vessel Security Strategy* (SVSS) was released with the intent to reduce potential security and safety risks from small vessels through boater education.
- Billions of dollars in grants were provided to states and communities for IED prevention and protection, and DHS Science & Technology established a new Program Executive Office specifically to find methods to reduce the nation's vulnerability to explosives and protect infrastructure.
- More than 2,000 Behavior Detection Officers employed at the TSA worked at more than 150 of the nation's largest airports to identify potentially high-risk passengers in airports. TSA revamped its airport screening operations to emphasize the human element of security and made significant technology and process improvements. TSA deployed whole-body imaging technology at 18 airports and 500 advanced technology x-ray machines at 20 airports to more effectively screen carry-on luggage.
- During 2008, the Secret Service achieved a 100 percent success rate in safe arrivals and departures for all protectees during more than 2,000 protective visits.
- The National Protection and Programs Directorate (NPPD) established national standards for chemical facility security in a comprehensive set of regulations—the Chemical Facility Anti-Terrorism Standards—to protect high-risk chemical facilities from attack and prevent theft of chemicals that could be used as weapons.
- The Comprehensive National Cybersecurity Initiative (CNCI) was created, establishing the policy and strategy and guidelines to secure federal systems. The directive provides a comprehensive approach that anticipates future cyber threats and technologies, and requires the federal government to integrate many of its technical and organizational capabilities to better address sophisticated threats and vulnerabilities.
- The Office of Health Affairs (OHA) oversaw the development and launch of the National Biosurveillance Integration Center (NBIC), which integrates biosurveillance data and information on biological incidents. To date, NBIC has played an integral role in a number of recent biological events, including the recent *Salmonella Saintpaul* outbreak, foot-and-mouth disease, the adulteration of Chinese milk products with melamine, cases of extremely drug-resistant tuberculosis, and pet food and *E. coli* incidents.
- Through aerosol collectors strategically deployed by the Office of Health Affairs in more than 30 jurisdictions across the nation, the BioWatch program provided critical early detection capabilities of dangerous biological pathogens to enhance the nation's response to an accidental or purposeful use of biological pathogens.
- The Office of Health Affairs led the department's efforts in securing the U.S. food supply, agriculture, and animal health by coordinating and collaborating with federal entities in the food and agriculture sectors.

- DHS Science & Technology continued to develop next-generation technologies to ensure the integrity of cargo shipments, advanced detection, identification, apprehension, and enforcement capabilities along the nation's maritime borders, and technologies that support a framework for rapid, coordinated responses to maritime anomalies and threats.
- Two new biodefense facilities were constructed: the National Bio and Agro-defense Facility (NBAF) and the National Biodefense Analysis and Countermeasure Center laboratory.
- Customs and Border Protection doubled the size of the Border Patrol from approximately 9,000 in 2001 to more than 18,000 in 2008; constructed more than 520 miles of vehicle and pedestrian fencing (including approximately 93 miles in FY 2008); and apprehended 1,020,438 individuals, including 200 individuals with serious criminal records such as murder, rape, and child molestation.
- The Domestic Nuclear Detection Office (DNDO) deployed more than 1,000 radiation detection devices to U.S. land and seaports of entry, allowing for 100 percent of cargo containers crossing the southern border and 96 percent at the northern border to be scanned for radiation, and more than 98 percent scanned at seaports.
- U.S. Immigration and Customs Enforcement (ICE) launched 3,291 financial investigations into money laundering and other financial crimes, resulting in 1,596 related seizures of currency and monetary instruments in the amount of nearly $250 million. Throughout 2008, ICE seized 1,520 counterfeit items with a domestic value of $64,126,280.
- Under Operation Neptune Shield, the USCG escorts vessels carrying especially hazardous cargo to protect nearby population centers and infrastructure from an attack, including more than 1,400 vessels and barges carrying such hazardous cargo in 2008.
- The USCG removed more than 267,100 pounds of cocaine at sea, worth an estimated street value of more than $3.5 billion. Included in the removal total is cocaine seized from five semisubmersibles, which present a growing threat by drug trafficking organizations and a high level of risk to Coast Guard boarding teams. Throughout 2008, CBP seized almost 3 million pounds of narcotics and made 3 million agricultural interceptions at the ports of entry to include the exclusion of six commercial maritime vessels from U.S. waters due to Asian Gypsy Moth infestations. In FY 2008, ICE seized more than 60 tons of cocaine, nearly 2,500 pounds of heroin, more than 4,000 pounds of methamphetamine, and more than 1 million pounds of marijuana. Additionally, ICE drug investigations led to 8,396 arrests and 5,532 convictions of individuals associated with narcotics violations.
- U.S. Immigration and Customs Enforcement (ICE) removed or returned more than 323,000 illegal aliens from the United States, roughly a 20 percent increase over 2007.
- U.S. Citizenship and Immigration Services (USCIS) E-Verify program allowed automated verification of employee names, dates of birth, and Social Security numbers, as well as immigration information for noncitizens, for more than 63,000 new employers registered on the system, which verified more than 6.6 million workers' eligibilities.

- Since March 2003, FEMA has responded to 454 major natural disaster and emergency declarations. FEMA has provided direct material and financial assistance to more than 4 million individuals across the nation.
- DHS personnel worked with state and local officials to quickly distribute aid and successfully executed the evacuation of more than 2 million Gulf Coast residents in anticipation of Hurricanes Gustav and Ike. Additionally, USCG personnel from across the country responded to an unprecedented string of disasters in the Midwest and Gulf Coast from June to October. The crews of regional units, Disaster Area Response Teams (DARTs), and river cutters rescued residents trapped by floodwaters, protected critical infrastructures, and quickly rebuilt damaged aids to navigation after floods hit midwestern states. USCG personnel rescued hundreds along the Gulf Coast trapped by hurricane storm surges and opened the Houston Ship Channel to allow the flow of regional commerce. Coast Guard Maritime Safety and Security Teams nationwide provided critical water and landside security for the impacted regions, and elements of the National Strike Force deployed personnel to assist the Unified Command (federal, state, and local) with pollution response to hazardous material releases and oil discharges, salvage response, and logistics. FEMA and other federal agencies distributed nearly $700 million to southeast Texas residents and businesses to aid in recovery, and relief efforts continue.
- Through FEMA, DHS provided more than $3 billion in preparedness grant support to state and local governments to help them prepare for and mitigate the impact of natural and man-made disasters.
- FEMA developed a comprehensive strategy for the overarching vision, goals, and principles for a national disaster housing effort, the 2008 Disaster Housing Plan.
- NPPD's Office of Infrastructure Protection deployed Protective Security Advisors (PSAs) to support state and local Emergency Operations Centers. The PSAs provide infrastructure security expertise and support to local authorities responsible for domestic incident management.
- DHS hired more than 2,300 protection officers, 11,200 transportation security officers, more than 700 immigration enforcement agents, and more than 450 deportation officers. In 2008, the Federal Law Enforcement Training Center (FLETC) trained more than 61,000 students from all three branches of the federal government, as well as international, state, local, campus, and tribal law enforcement agencies.

DHS Budget

The White House has proposed a budget for fiscal year 2010 that requests a total of $55.12 billion for the Department of Homeland Security. This amount is an increase of 5 percent over what was funded by Congress in FY 2009 (excluding funds provided in emergency supplemental funding). The FY 2010 budget request targets the following five areas:

- Guarding against terrorism
- Securing our borders

Table 9-2 DHS Office Funding

Directorate/Agency/Office	Funding Amount (in Millions)	Funding Percent (%)
Customs and Border Protection	$11,437	20
U.S. Coast Guard	$9,956	18
Transportation Security Agency	$7,794	14
Federal Emergency Management Agency	$6,612	12
Immigration and Customs Enforcement	$5,763	10
FEMA Grants	$3,867	7
U.S. Citizenship and Immigration Service	$2,867	5
National Protection and Programs Directorate	$1,959	4
U.S. Secret Service	$1,709	3
Science and Technology	$968	2
Department Operations	$904	2
Domestic Nuclear Detection Office	$366	1
Analysis and Operations	$357	1
Federal Law Enforcement Training Academy	$288	1

- Smart and tough enforcement of immigration laws and improving immigration services
- Preparing for, responding to, and recovering from natural disasters
- Unifying and maturing DHS

Under this budget, DHS offices would be funded as shown in Table 9-2.

The 911 Commission

In late 2002, in an effort to "prepare a full and complete account of the circumstances surrounding the" terrorist attacks that occurred on September 11, 2001, the National Commission on Terrorist Attacks Upon the United States (more commonly known as the 911 Commission) was formed. This commission set out to determine the shortfalls and the lessons learned from the preparedness for and response to international terrorism within the United States and to formulate recommendations for activities that would help to improve these systems in case of future threats and attacks.

The Commission, which consisted of five Republicans and five Democrats, interviewed over 1,200 people from 10 countries, including several past and present government officials at the federal, state, and local levels, and studied millions of pages of documentation, to accurately assess the events. On July 22, 2004, the 911 Commission released its long-awaited report. Although there was initial criticism of earlier Commission reports and its members—including claims of bias, difficulty in attaining cooperation from White House officials, and partisanship, among others—the final report's findings generally have been met with approval and acceptance for their recommendations.

The report found many opportunities that could have been exploited by the federal government to stop the terrorists who attacked in 2001:

- Not watchlisting future hijackers Hazmi and Mihdhar, not trailing them after they traveled to Bangkok, and not informing the FBI about one future hijacker's U.S. visa or his companion's travel to the United States.
- Not sharing information linking individuals in the *Cole* attack to Mihdhar.
- Not taking adequate steps in time to find Mihdhar or Hazmi in the United States.
- Not linking the arrest of Zacarias Moussaoui, described as interested in flight training for the purpose of using an airplane in a terrorist act, to the heightened indications of attack.
- Not discovering false statements on visa applications.
- Not recognizing passports that had been manipulated in a fraudulent manner.
- Not expanding no-fly lists to include names from terrorist watchlists.
- Not searching airline passengers identified by the computer-based CAPPS screening system.
- Not hardening aircraft cockpit doors or taking other measures to prepare for the possibility of suicide hijackings.

The report also identified failures on the part of U.S. government policy that could have prevented the attacks:

- **Imagination.** The Commission saw this as the most important failure. They do not believe leaders understood the gravity of the threat or that terrorist danger from Bin Ladin and al Qaeda was a major topic for policy debate among the public, the media, or in Congress. Al Qaeda's new brand of terrorism presented challenges to U.S. governmental institutions that they were not well designed to meet. Though top officials all told the Commission that they understood the danger, the Commission believed there was uncertainty among them as to whether this was just a new and especially venomous version of the ordinary terrorist threat the United States had lived with for decades or if it was indeed radically new, posing a threat beyond any yet experienced.
- **Policy.** The Commission felt that terrorism was not the overriding national security concern for the U.S. government under either the Clinton or the pre-9/11 Bush administration. The policy challenges were linked to this failure of imagination. Officials in both the Clinton and Bush administrations regarded a full U.S. invasion of Afghanistan as practically inconceivable before 9/11.
- **Capabilities.** Before 9/11, the United States tried to solve the al Qaeda problem with the capabilities it had used in the last stages of the Cold War and its immediate aftermath. The Commission claims these capabilities were insufficient. The CIA had minimal capacity to conduct paramilitary operations with its own personnel, and it did not seek a large-scale expansion of these capabilities before 9/11. The CIA also needed to improve its capability to collect intelligence from human agents.

- At no point before 9/11 was the Department of Defense fully engaged in the mission of countering al Qaeda, even though this was perhaps the most dangerous foreign enemy threatening the United States. The North American Aerospace Defense Command (NORAD) itself was barely able to retain any alert bases at all. Its planning scenarios occasionally considered the danger of hijacked aircraft being guided to American targets but only aircraft that were coming from overseas.
- The Commission saw the most serious weaknesses in agency capabilities in the domestic arena. The FBI did not have the capability to link the collective knowledge of agents in the field to national priorities. Other domestic agencies deferred to the FBI. FAA capabilities were weak. Any serious examination of the possibility of a suicide hijacking could have suggested changes to fix glaring vulnerabilities— expanding no-fly lists, searching passengers identified by the CAPPS screening system, deploying federal air marshals domestically, hardening cockpit doors, and alerting air crews to a different kind of hijacking possibility than they had been trained to expect. Yet, the FAA did not adjust either its own training or training with NORAD to take account of threats other than those experienced in the past.
- **Management.** The Commission reported that the missed opportunities to thwart the 9/11 plot were also symptoms of a broader inability to adapt the way government manages problems to the new challenges of the twenty-first century. Action officers should have been able to draw on all available knowledge about al Qaeda in the government. Management should have ensured that information was shared and that duties were clearly assigned across agencies and across the foreign-domestic divide. There were also broader management issues with respect to how top leaders set priorities and allocated resources. The U.S. government did not find a way of pooling intelligence and using it to guide the planning and assignment of responsibilities for joint operations involving entities as disparate as the CIA, the FBI, the State Department, the military, and the agencies involved in homeland security.

In addition to these general findings, the Commission also reported a description of several specific findings they claim resulted in the inability of the government to thwart the attacks and its ability to respond once they occurred:

- Unsuccessful diplomacy
- Lack of military operations
- Problems with the intelligence community
- Problems in the FBI
- Permeable borders and immigration controls
- Permeable aviation security
- Terrorist financing
- The lack of an improved homeland defense
- Problems with emergency response systems
- The poor response of Congress to the terrorist threat

In December 2005, the 9/11 Commission released a follow-up report that graded the Bush administration and Congress's handling of the Commission's recommendations. The findings, which were issued in the form of a "report card," assigned letter grades to the 41 key recommendations. The grades were as follows (with I signifying "Incomplete"):

- Homeland Security and Emergency Response
  Radio Spectrum for first responders: **F**
  Incident Command System: **C**
  Risk-based allocation of homeland security funds: **F**
  Critical infrastructure assessment: **D**
  Private sector preparedness: **C**
  National Strategy for Transportation Security: **C–**
  Airline passenger prescreening: **F**
  Airline passenger explosive screening: **C**
  Checked bag and cargo screening: **D**
  Terrorist travel strategy: **I**
  Comprehensive screening system: **C**
  Biometric entry-exit screening system: **B**
  International collaboration on borders and document security: **B**
  Standardize secure identifications: **B–**
- Intelligence and Congressional Reform
  Director of National Intelligence: **B**
  National Counterterrorism Center: **B**
  FBI national security workforce: **C**
  New missions for CIA Director: **I**
  Incentives for information sharing: **D**
  Governmentwide information sharing: **D**
  Northern Command planning for homeland defense: **B–**
  Full debate on PATRIOT ACT: **B**
  Privacy and Civil Liberties Oversight Boards: **D**
  Guidelines for government-sharing of personal information: **D**
  Intelligence oversight reform: **D**
  Homeland Security Committees: **B**
  Unclassified top-line intelligence budget: **F**
  Security clearance reform: **B**
- Foreign Policy and Nonproliferation
  Maximum effort to prevent terrorists from acquiring WMD: **D**
  Afghanistan: **B**
  Pakistan: **C+**
  Saudi Arabia: **D**
  Terrorist sanctuaries: **B**
  Coalition strategy against Islamist terrorism: **C**

Coalition detention standards: **F**

Economic policies: **B+**

Terrorist financing: **A−**

Clear U.S. message abroad: **C**

International broadcasting: **B**

Scholarship, exchange, and library programs: **D**

Secular education in Muslin countries: **D**

In early 2007, the new Democratic House presented for their first vote of the session a bill, entitled "Implementing the 9/11 Commission Recommendations Act of 2007" (H.R. 1), that would fund all of the remaining unfulfilled recommendations of the 9/11 Commission. The bill easily passed by a vote of 299–128. However, the cost of implementing these remaining recommendations—estimated to be over $21 billion between 2007 and 2012—drew considerable fire from opponents who claimed the bill's provisions were misguided. However, in July 2007, this bill was passed by the Senate, and President Bush signed it into law on August 3 of that same year. Information on this legislation can be accessed at *http://www.govtrack.us/congress/bill.xpd?bill 5 h110-1.*

CRITICAL THINKING

Do you agree with the findings of the 911 Commission, or do you think that their findings go too far? Explain your answer.

State Government Terrorism Activity

Governors, and the states they govern, are recognized for the critical role they play in homeland security. State and local law enforcement and health personnel provide the first line of defense in protecting critical infrastructure and public health and safety. Should an incident occur, state and local personnel are the first to respond to an emergency and the last to leave the scene. Governors, with the support of the federal government, are responsible for coordinating state and local resources to effectively address natural disasters, accidents, and other types of major emergencies, including terrorist incidents.

The national effort to protect the nation from acts of terrorism has been conducted with equal strength at the state level as has been seen at the federal level. As the recipients of a bulk of the homeland security funding that has been distributed by the Department of Homeland Security and other federal agencies, the states have had the ability to administer new statewide programs aimed at bringing preparedness and prevention to each and every community.

State homeland security entities were created to ensure that the states are preparing for the wide range of terrorist attacks that have been identified by DHS and other entities.

These state offices accomplish this by facilitating the interaction and coordination that is needed among each state's governor's office, the homeland security director, the state emergency management office, other state agencies, local governments, the private sector, volunteer organizations, and the federal government.

Following the attacks of September 11, the governors designated individuals from various backgrounds in state government to serve as their state homeland security directors. Among the states and territories, there is no common model; however, in several states, the homeland security director serves as an advisor to the governor in addition to coordinating state emergency management, law enforcement, health, and related public safety functions. In other models, governors designated the state's Adjutant General as homeland security advisor. Although governors generally have opted not to create unique cabinet-level positions with oversight over all state agencies, they did form homeland security task forces. The task forces typically consist of executive office staff and agency heads from law enforcement, fire and rescue, public health, the National Guard, transportation, public works, and information technology.

State offices of homeland security have been placed in all of the following state government agencies since 2001, in order of most to least common (list from the National Emergency Management Association, National Governors Association):

- Governor's office
- Military/Adjutant General
- Emergency Management
- Public Safety
- Law Enforcement
- Attorney general
- Lieutenant governor
- Land commissioner

In August 2002, the NGA Center for Best Practices of the National Governors Association released "States' Homeland Security Priorities." A list of ten "major priorities and issues" was identified by the NGA center through a survey of states' and territories' homeland security offices (NGA Center for Best Practices, 2002). Eight years later, these same priorities still apply, despite the major events that have occurred in that time:

- Coordination must involve all levels of government.
- The federal government must disseminate timely intelligence information to the states.
- States must work with local governments to develop interoperable communications between first responders and adequate wireless spectrum must be set aside to do the job.
- State and local governments need help and technical assistance to identify and protect critical infrastructure.
- Both the states and federal government must focus on enhancing bioterrorism preparedness and rebuilding the nation's public health system to address twenty-first-century threats.

- The federal government should provide adequate federal funding and support to ensure that homeland security needs are met.
- The federal government should work with states to protect sensitive security information, including restricting access to information available through "freedom of information" requests.
- An effective system must be developed that secures points of entry at borders, airports, and seaports without placing an undue burden on commerce.
- The National Guard has proven itself to be an effective force during emergencies and crises. The mission of the National Guard should remain flexible, and Guard units should remain primarily under the control of the governor during times of crises.
- Federal agencies should integrate their command systems into existing state and local incident command systems (ICS) rather than requiring state and local agencies to adapt to federal command systems.

Local Government Terrorism Activity

The Counties

Emergency preparedness, mitigation, response, and recovery all occur at the local community level. This is true for terrorism preparedness, mitigation, response, and recovery activities. It is at the local level that the critical planning, communications, technology, coordination, command, and spending decisions matter the most. The priorities of groups such as the National Conference of Mayors and the National Associations of Counties (NACo) represent what matters at the local community level in the fight against terrorism. The fight against terrorism has spawned a series of new requirements in preparedness and mitigation planning at the local level.

NACo has created a "Policy Agenda to Secure the People of America's Counties." This policy paper states, "Counties are the first responders to terrorist attacks, natural disasters and major emergencies" (NACo, 2004). NACo has established a 43-member NACo Homeland Security Task Force that in July 2004 reaffirmed a set of 21 recommendations concerning homeland security issues:

1. National Strategies for the Nation
2. Sustained Funding for Homeland Security
3. Base Level of Preparedness for All Communities
4. High Threat Funding to Most Critical Areas
5. Expediting Assistance at All Levels of Government
6. Fund Local Public Health Emergency Preparedness
7. Ensure an Adequate Supply of Vaccines and Antibiotics
8. Train Health Personnel
9. Ensure That Adequate Medical Surge Capacity Exists
10. Sharing of Intelligence

11. Balance Heightened Border Security with Economic Activity
12. Securing Critical Infrastructure
13. Help Localities Secure Public Utilities and a Safe Water Supply
14. Reimburse Counties for Costs Incurred on Behalf of the Federal Government
15. Assist Counties to Develop Evacuation Capacity
16. Train County Elected and Appointed Officials to Prepare for and Respond to Acts of Terror
17. One-Stop Clearinghouse
18. Assist Public Safety Communications Interoperability and Interference Issues
19. Establish a Public Communication Network
20. Urge the Release of Federal Research to Assist Counties
21. Provide Immunity to Encourage Mutual Aid and Support

Cities and Towns

Other than the largest cities, most local communities do not have specially designated offices of homeland security or any other terrorism-specific government office or agency. In general, local communities rely on the skills and training of their teams of first responders, who include the fire, police, emergency management, emergency medical, and other officials that live within their jurisdictions.

However, these first responders are the heart of the system that the nation depends on for the protection from and response to terrorist attacks. Local communities are instructed that they may have to manage the aftermath of a terrorist attack for a full 24 to 48 hours on their own before state or federal backup arrives. As should be obvious by the levels of funding that have been described in copious detail throughout this text, the federal government has recognized and responded to such facts.

Local first response still has much catching up to do in order to be able to fulfill the preparedness and response needs of the federal government. Interoperable communication, the condition where all responders and emergency management within and without each community can talk to each other, is still not possible. Many communities lack the equipment and training necessary to respond to attacks involving weapons of mass destruction. Efforts to vaccinate health care workers from biological weapons such as smallpox have failed, and there are still questions about whether communities could handle an outbreak of one of these diseases even if sufficient vaccines were available to them.

In the larger communities, where the training and equipment are better funded and considered adequate, there are other issues that have presented themselves. Large ports are still not passing minimum security requirements to keep out potential weapons of mass destruction; financial woes are sounded each time the Homeland Security Alert System is raised for specific terrorist threats due to the need for police overtime and the loss of other essential services to reassigned officials; and contentious battles over the appropriation of both federal and state funding have soured many preexisting relationships.

But, the will to prepare exists, and the growing pains are becoming less severe as more and more funds reach deeper into American communities. Cooperation and intelligence sharing has made the state and local responders a more integral part of the counterterrorism team that will be necessary to prevent or contain future terrorist attacks, whether they be internationally based or homegrown.

The DHS Office of State and Local Coordination was established to serve as a single point of contact for facilitation and coordination of departmental programs that impact state, local, territorial, and tribal governments. Through this office, DHS has brought together many organizations with a long history of interaction with, and support to, state, local, territorial, and tribal government organizations and associations, and the office is working hard to consolidate and coordinate that support. Today, this office facilitates the coordination of DHS-wide programs that impact state, local, territorial, and tribal governments; serves as the primary point of contact within DHS for exchanging information with state, local, territorial, and tribal homeland security personnel; identifies homeland security–related activities, best practices, and processes that are most efficiently accomplished at the federal, state, local, or regional levels; and utilizes this information to ensure that opportunities for improvement are provided to our state, territorial, tribal, and local counterparts.

The events of September 11 established the security of community infrastructure as a potential target for terrorist attacks. Community infrastructure has always been vulnerable to natural and other technological disaster events—so much so that FEMA's largest disaster assistance program, Public Assistance, is designed to fund the rebuilding of community infrastructure damaged by a disaster event. Local government officials and local emergency managers must now increase the attention they give to protecting and securing community infrastructure from a terrorist attack. They must also include in these preparedness efforts the local public health system.

The Effect of Hurricane Katrina on Terrorism Preparedness and Response

Both the government and the public interpreted the lack of preparedness for September 11 to mean that too little was being done to plan for and protect the nation from the suddenly obvious terrorist threat. The resulting action included a fundamental shift in the focus of emergency management that many considered to be knee-jerk and that included among other changes the restructuring of a significant number of U.S. government agencies and offices, and a redrafting of all U.S. emergency operations plans at all levels of government. Many proponents of "all-hazards emergency management" contended that this shift was so great that it would leave the country more vulnerable to the effects of natural disasters than it was before the changes occurred.

After a period of relatively few major disaster events—during which time the nation's focus on all accounts was the global war against terrorism—the fears of all-hazards proponents were confirmed when Hurricane Katrina (an anticipated and previously exercised natural hazard event) struck on August 29, 2005, and quickly overwhelmed response mechanisms at all government levels. As with all devastating disasters, the subsequent aftermath was rife with finger pointing and wide denials of blame—with the federal government accusing local responders of poor decision making and local and state officials claiming that FEMA ignored their pleas for help. Upon closer examination, however, the general consensus was that FEMA had been diluted too much as an effective response organization within the Department of Homeland Security, much of which came as a result of the terror focus (both programmatically and in relation to the targeting of disaster preparedness grants) and that major changes would have to be made if such weaknesses were ever to be addressed.

ATTACKS THWARTED: GOOD INTELLIGENCE AND GOOD LUCK

Since the attacks of September 11, 2001, and the anthrax attacks in October of that same year, there have been several attempts at terrorism, yet all have failed thus far. While a good measure of this can be credited to the increased level of intelligence and investigations supported by the changes brought about by the legislation described in this text (including, for instance, the PATRIOT Act and the Homeland Security Act of 2002), a certain amount of credit can also be attributed to the actions of the public and just plain luck. None of these has required any of the emergency services to respond, given that they were all prevented or failed to achieve their mission. Here are some of the more notable events:

- *Shoe Bombing:* British citizen Richard Reid attempted to detonate explosives hidden in his shoes on a transatlantic flight, but flight attendants and fellow passengers subdued the bomber as he tried to light the fuse.
- *Intent to Create a Dirty Bomb:* Jose Padilla was arrested in 2002 upon his return to the United States following a trip to Pakistan after investigations determined he was intent on acquiring and using radioactive materials for terrorism purposes. Padilla was ultimately convicted of conspiring with terrorist groups in 2007.
- *Terrorist Training:* Six men from the Buffalo, New York area, dubbed the "Lackawanna Six," were arrested in 2002 after attending terrorist training in Pakistan. All six pled guilty to supporting al Queda.
- *Bridge Attack:* Iyman Faris was arrested and convicted in 2003 for planning to attack the Brooklyn Bridge with blowtorches in an attempt to collapse the structure.
- *Stock Market Attack:* Dhiren Barot was arrested in 2004 for plotting to attack the New York Stock Exchange using, among other weapons, a dirty bomb. Barot was convicted in the United Kingdom for conspiracy to commit mass murder.
- *Subway Bombing:* James Elshafay and Shahawar Siraj were arrested and convicted for planning to detonate explosives in the New York subway system. The investigation was led by the New York City Police Department, who used undercover work to infiltrate the group.
- *Various Attacks:* Four individuals were arrested in California for plotting to attack a number of sites in the United States, including the Los Angeles National Guard, synagogues, and other targets in the area. The four remain in jail awaiting trial.

- *Infrastructure Attack:* Michael Reynolds was arrested in 2005 for plotting to attack a Wyoming gas refinery and the Transcontinental Pipeline. Reynolds was convicted of providing material support to terrorists, among other charges.
- *Sears Tower Attack:* Seven individuals were arrested in 2006 for plotting to blow up the Sears Tower in Chicago and FBI offices. All await trial.
- *Multiple Airliner Attack:* British police arrested 24 people in that country for planning an attack on ten airplanes headed to the United States, using liquid explosives. This planned attack led to a ban on liquids in carry-on luggage on airliners worldwide.
- *Army Base Attack:* Six young men were arrested for planning an attack on Fort Dix in New Jersey. The arrests were made after an investigation that began with a video store clerk's tip that led to information that the men were training in nearby mountains for the attack.
- *Airport Fuel Line Attack:* Four men were arrested in 2007 for plotting to attack a fuel line that supplies JFK Airport in New York. One of the planners was a former airport employee, while others lived in various countries in Central and South America.
- *Airplane Bombing:* A Nigerian national was arrested on Christmas Eve 2009, after explosives hidden in his underwear failed to explode as the airplane he was riding in approached the airport in Detroit, Michigan. Fellow passengers subdued the 23-year-old, who had received terrorist training in Yemen.

Sources: Carafano, 2007; *Fox News,* 2009.

ANOTHER VOICE

In 2009, the Department of Homeland Security Office of the Inspector General released a report titled "FEMA: In or Out?" that tackled the questions surrounding whether FEMA should be a standalone agency or remain a component of DHS (OIG-09-25). The findings of this report do not take a stance on the answer to this question, but they do claim to give consideration to both sides of the argument surrounding this issue. However, this internal report clearly takes a strong stance that favors FEMA's steadfast inclusion within DHS, which stands to benefit the agency incredibly (due to FEMA's virtually limitless budget under the provisions of the Stafford Act). This report is far from being impartial, and moreover, it heavily downplays the arguments in favor of FEMA's reinstatement as an independent, cabinet-level agency. The following excerpt is taken verbatim from this report.

Arguments for Keeping FEMA in DHS

Despite generally positive reviews of FEMA's performance in the most recent disasters, calls to return FEMA to its independent-agency status have been renewed. The arguments for this proposal are discussed following, but before addressing them, we will outline the arguments for leaving FEMA in DHS. These include, especially, the nation's current vulnerability to terrorism, the synergy and resources FEMA enjoys as part of DHS, and the importance of avoiding the stovepiping of preparedness and response functions.

Vulnerability to Terrorism

Our last two presidents, Bill Clinton and George W. Bush, and the current U.K. prime minister, Gordon Brown, all had to deal with a major terrorist attack in their respective countries during their first year in office. While there have been no recent reports of a specific imminent threat, some argue that the United States faces an increased risk of a terrorist event during the first year of the new presidency. In November 2008, shortly before the presidential election, Director of National Intelligence Mike McConnell told intelligence officials that the new administration might be tested by a terrorist attack during its first year, citing, "the World Trade Center was attacked in the first year of President Clinton, and the second attack was in the first year of President Bush." President-elect Barack Obama made a statement to this effect during a recent interview, saying that it was "important to get a national security team in place, because transition periods are potentially times of vulnerability to a terrorist attack," and vice president-elect Joe Biden warned that "it will not be six months before the world tests Barack Obama like they did John Kennedy."

We simply cannot predict whether there will be a terrorist attack in this country in the next year. Given that there is an elevated risk of this happening, however, we must consider whether it makes sense to make major changes to our homeland security apparatus during this period. It is critical to note here that the talk of removing FEMA from DHS generally focuses on the perceived benefits to FEMA—on which not all sides agree. What is not always included in the debate is consideration of the effect that FEMA's removal would have on the department.

Since 2003, a number of support functions for the different components of DHS have been interwoven. A reorganization would impact not only FEMA, which would have to reconstitute itself as a standalone agency, but also DHS as a whole, which would have to adjust to losing an important component. Don Kettl warns that "FEMA has gone through a long and wrenching series of reorganizations.... Change for the sake of change could simply induce organizational whiplash and further destabilize an already unstable organization." John Harrald warns that pulling FEMA out of DHS would mean a difficult transition period and the rewriting of doctrine and the redesign of systems, "but natural hazards and terrorists are not going to wait for us to reorganize yet again."

Ongoing Reviews

It is clear that removing FEMA from DHS at this point would cause considerable upheaval, to both FEMA and the department. Such action should not be taken without very careful consideration. At this time, the Quadrennial Homeland Security Review (QHSR) is underway at DHS, and the first QHSR report is due in December 2009. This comprehensive review of the department was mandated by Congress in the Implementing the Recommendations of the 9/11 Commission Act of 2007 (P.L. 110–53). The National Academy of Public Administration has just begun an independent assessment of preparedness and response integration, with a focus on FEMA's ten regional offices, and will provide recommendations on the integration, synchronization, and strengthening of preparedness programs between FEMA and its regional offices.

Experts have cautioned that "major structural changes, such as bureaucratic adjustments involving the Department of Homeland Security, should follow a detailed strategic review and be addressed later in the first term." The formal recommendation of the Homeland Security Presidential Transition Initiative is that "a decision to remove FEMA should be deferred until the completion of the Quadrennial Homeland Security Review in late 2009. Maintaining the status quo in the first year avoids unnecessary instability and confusion at a time of elevated risk. It also provides time for the new administration to consult with congressional leadership and build support for any major changes that may be contemplated within the QHSR process."

Synergy and Resources

A primary benefit to FEMA of being part of the 200,000-plus person Department of Homeland Security is the wealth of resources available to FEMA through other DHS components. These connections create synergies that were never available to FEMA as a standalone agency. In DHS, FEMA is coupled with components that have far-reaching responsibilities and capabilities, including search and rescue, communications, law enforcement, intelligence, and infrastructure protection.

The Government Accountability Office (GAO) has cited areas of interconnectedness, including grants, through which Urban Area Security Initiative and State Homeland Security Program funding can be used for mass evacuation planning; interoperable communications; DHS Science & Technology expertise for the Equipment Standards Program; and a huge surge capacity of personnel that can be tapped in case of a disaster.

Former DHS secretary Michael Chertoff recently said that "until this department was formed, interagency planning on the civilian side was not a well-executed responsibility." In contrast, Admiral Thad Allen testified in 2006 that since DHS's creation, the relationship between the Coast Guard and FEMA has been greatly strengthened. Prior to the establishment of DHS, Coast Guard and FEMA interaction was infrequent. In 2006, the number of joint exercises had increased 354 percent, from 13 in the years 1999–2002 to 59 in the years 2003–2006.

Chertoff has also stated "the fact that FEMA and other components of DHS have had an opportunity during times of rest to plan, train, and exercise together and to build capabilities that are capable of crossing jurisdictional lines has allowed us to have the kind of capabilities to support an emergency that would not be the case if we were in different departments." Those joint capabilities were evidenced in recent disasters.

In the wake of Hurricane Katrina, the Coast Guard, the Transportation Security Administration (TSA), U.S. Customs and Border Protection (CBP), U.S. Immigration and Customs Enforcement (ICE), and the Secret Service were all vital. More recently, in responding to Hurricanes Gustav and Ike, "FEMA was supported by all of the elements and all the powers of the Department of Homeland Security." CBP provided security for the transit of life-sustaining goods and provided aerial assets that allowed surveying of damage. In the past, FEMA relied on DOD for aerial surveillance, which cost considerably more than using CBP. TSA supported 20 FEMA commodity distribution locations, augmenting FEMA staff with 366 additional employees in the field. The Coast Guard performed land, maritime, and air search-and-rescue missions. Chertoff argued that when "it's necessary to quickly call upon other agencies, the quickest way to do that is not by reaching to another department of government, … but it's to have the ability of the Secretary to immediately order assistance to be rendered in all of the elements and capabilities of the entire Department of Homeland Security."

Finally, it is important to discuss DHS grants and their importance to the emergency management community. When FEMA initially joined DHS, many of its grants functions were transferred to other parts of DHS. Since Hurricane Katrina, FEMA administers almost all DHS grants, both those focused on natural hazards and those focused on terrorism. Pulling FEMA out of DHS would almost certainly disrupt the grants function in the short term, and it could result in once again separating out "emergency management" grants from "terrorism" grants, which we know from experience leads to inefficiency, duplication, and waste. The synergies that have been realized in homeland security grants should be an important consideration when debating the merits of removing FEMA from DHS.

Preparedness and Response

The well-recognized cycle of emergency management includes preparedness, response, recovery, and mitigation. This is true of all emergency management, whether for natural or man-made hazards. It is helpful to think of these elements as a four-legged stool. Remove one of the elements, and the stool becomes unstable. Some would suggest that we need two stools: one labeled crisis management and one labeled consequence management. The problem is that we know from the past that this structure simply does not work well. It is evident in the "stovepipes" that existed prior to the creation of DHS.

Chertoff sums up the argument, stating that "the core of the argument made about FEMA is that somehow FEMA's involved with consequence management, dealing with the response, and DHS, in other respects, is dealing with preventing or protecting against a response and that if these are different functions, that therefore they ought to be under different roofs, and I really beg to differ with that. I think that is a profound misunderstanding of how one plans and prepares and executes in the face of a possible emergency and an actual emergency because the truth is emergencies don't come neatly packaged in stovepipes and if there's any lesson we've learned in dealing with terrorism or dealing with any other crisis, it is that stovepiping is the enemy of efficient and effective response."

The Hart-Rudman Commission report states, "The current distinction between crisis management and consequence management is neither sustainable nor wise. The duplicative command arrangements that have been fostered by this division are prone to confusion and delay." We would add that this duplication wastes time, energy, and resources. Preparedness and response are fundamental to homeland security. If FEMA is removed, a duplicate agency would most certainly be created in DHS, because preparedness and response are so fundamental to DHS's mission that it could not operate effectively without them.

Finally, Kettl suggests that for local frontline first responders, there is no line between terrorist and nonterrorist hazards; first responders must focus on all-hazards-plus. The federal approach and structure should match the local approach. "Separation would create deep fissures between national policy and the realities of local response."

Goldwater-Nichols Act of 1986

It is worth mentioning, in the context of merging entities and the growing pains that can result, the Goldwater-Nichols Act of 1986 (P.L. 99–433), which increased integration among the armed services. Like most "independent" agencies, the defense agencies did not want to be integrated initially, but over time, the arrangement has created a stronger DOD. The Defense components did not want their individual roles and authorities to be diminished, and they resisted integration for years. The Desert One episode—the failed attempt to rescue the hostages in Iran during the Carter administration—was the final straw in this arrangement. This failure prompted passage of the Goldwater-Nichols Act.

Just as passage of the Homeland Security Act did not automatically bring jointness to homeland security functions, neither did the Goldwater-Nichols Act immediately solve the challenges in the military. According to Wormuth, "The Department of Defense took more than 40 years to evolve from the War Department into the Defense Department and then another 20 years after passage of the 1986 Goldwater-Nichols Act to mature into the integrated agency of today."

ARGUMENTS FOR MAKING FEMA A STANDALONE AGENCY

In the past few months, emergency managers and others have called for FEMA to be removed from DHS. In November 2008, the U.S. Council of the International Association of Emergency Managers (IAEM-USA) formally adopted the position that FEMA's independent agency status should be restored, with the agency reporting directly to the president. The organization further urged that the FEMA director be included as a member of the president's cabinet.

Kettl suggests that calls for FEMA's removal may be based on a faulty premise: that James Lee Witt transformed the troubled agency and made it successful (under Witt, FEMA was independent), so FEMA should be restored to independent status. Kettl points out, however, that FEMA did not always perform well in the past, even when it was an independent agency. FEMA was an independent agency when it was roundly criticized for its response to Hurricane Andrew in 1992. Problems were also recognized during the TOPOFF 2000 exercise—again, while FEMA was an independent agency.

"When viewed against the history of emergency management, the success FEMA enjoyed in the 1990s was the exception, not the rule," Roberts states. Kettl suggests that under Witt, "success in managing FEMA flowed from the leader's ability to lead…. Restructuring cannot *substitute* for leadership." In 2006, David Walker, then-comptroller general of the United States, said, "There are pros and cons to keeping FEMA in or out, but the quality of leadership … and the quantity of resources has more to do with the success of the agency."

CALLS FOR AN INDEPENDENT FEMA, WITH CABINET-LEVEL STATUS AND A DIRECT LINE TO THE PRESIDENT

Those who would like to see FEMA removed from DHS are calling for three basic elements: (1) independent agency status, (2) including the FEMA administrator in the president's cabinet, and (3) giving the FEMA administrator a direct line to the president. Addressing the third element first, the FEMA administrator already has a direct line to the president during a disaster. Congress recognized this shortcoming in the aftermath of Hurricane Katrina and legislated this relationship in the Post-Katrina Reform Act. GAO recently found that the FEMA administrator does give advice directly to the president during meetings.

The critical thing to note here, however, is that having a direct line to the president does not necessarily mean one has the president's ear. As just pointed out, Witt had President Clinton's ear, but this likely stemmed more from his personal relationship with the president than from his status as FEMA director. The Post-Katrina Reform Act "assures that there will be direct access, but it cannot assure that the relationship with the president will be strong or that the administrator will have the president's confidence."

Including the FEMA director in the cabinet is a decision that cannot be legislated. While not defined in law, the cabinet traditionally includes the vice president and the heads of 15 executive departments. The president has the discretion to accord cabinet-level rank to other officials. Currently, in addition to the heads of the 15 executive departments, cabinet-level status has been given to the White House chief of staff, the director of OMB, the United States trade representative, the administrator of the Environmental Protection Agency, and the director of the Office of National Drug Control Policy. Executives who do not currently have cabinet-level status include the director of the Central Intelligence Agency, the administrator of the Small Business Administration, and the administrator of the National Aeronautics and Space Administration.

The first element of the argument, granting FEMA independent agency status, arguably could be accomplished legislatively or by Executive Order. But this arrangement will not necessarily solve FEMA's problems or address the concerns of those who would like to see FEMA removed from the Department of Homeland Security. As just evidenced, FEMA often performed poorly even when it was an independent agency. According to Kettl, "Structure matters. But leadership counts far more."

CRITICAL THINKING

Do you feel that the DHS inspector general report gives you sufficient and unbiased information on both sides of this argument? Could you make an informed decision based on this report, or do you feel that it would be necessary to read the viewpoints of the tens of thousands of local and state first response agencies that have been affected by this legislation, as well as the emergency management professionals and experts who are not directly associated with the Department of Homeland Security (as was the case with the authors of this report)? Explain your answer.

In FY 2006, which began just one month into the yet ongoing Hurricane Katrina disaster recovery operation, the Government Accountability Office found that over 75 percent of DHS's preparedness grants targeted state and local readiness for terrorism. These figures indicated that emergency management funds were still misaligned with the reality of risk that was much better understood by the local agency responders to be that of an all-hazards portfolio. Fortunately, since that time, changes have been made by the administration and Congress that clearly show promise that FEMA, as an emergency management organization, must be focused on all hazards and not just terrorism. FEMA is steadily regaining many of its former responsibilities that were lost to other agencies that were more narrowly focused on terrorism such as the Office of Domestic Preparedness and the DHS Preparedness Directorate. How far these corrective actions go will ultimately depend on whether another major terrorist attack interrupts the steady flow of natural disasters that are guaranteed to strike in coming years.

Conclusion

Emergency management in the United States was changed forever by the events of September 11. New foci, new funding, new partners, and new concerns associated with the fight against terrorism are changing the way emergency management functions in this country every day. At the federal government level, the new Department of Homeland Security has been established, which includes FEMA and all the federal government disaster management programs. At the state level, governors and state emergency management directors are calling for better coordination, new communications technologies, and—always—more and more funding. At the local government level, terrorism is a new threat that greatly expands their facility security requirements and is added to a long list of needs and priorities. But the threat of terrorism is one that can't be ignored. Issues of coordination, communications, and funding concern local governments as well.

The United States has taken its typical response to a new problem. It has reorganized and committed huge amounts of funding to reducing the problem. The ability of the Department of Homeland Security to achieve an enhanced level of coordination is improving, but it still has a long way to go. Preventing future terrorist attacks remains mostly outside the purview of DHS, residing with the intelligence community, the military, diplomatic corps, and law enforcement. What DHS can offer is a better prepared and equipped first responder cadre, enhanced transportation and border security, and more money for emergency management programs.

But the question of cost effectiveness will remain to be seen. The likelihood of natural and technological disasters has already proven to be far greater than that of terrorist attacks. In the years following the September 11 terrorist attacks, the United States has been affected by hurricanes, floods, wildfires, chemical accidents, transportation accidents, volcanoes, ice storms, tornadoes, severe winter weather, avalanches—the list goes on and on. The Department of Homeland Security will need to continually reassess its priorities in terms of terrorism versus other less-sinister hazards, and shift funding as appropriate. The terrorist threat will never go away completely, but over time, it should require much less of the attention of the nation's first responders, state responders, and federal government preparedness and response agencies.

ADDITIONAL RESEARCH

Redefining Readiness: Terrorism Planning through the Eyes of the Public is a study by Roz D. Lasker of the New York Academy of Medicine (September 2004). The first of its kind, the study measured how Americans might react to protective instructions in two terrorist attacks: a smallpox outbreak and the explosion of a dirty bomb. This information is considered critically important because the plans currently being developed to deal with these situations are based on expert *assumptions* about what people would be concerned about and how they would behave. If planners' assumptions about the public are wrong—as they have been in the past—the plans being developed will not work as expected, and a large number of people who should be protected will be unnecessarily harmed.

Important Terms

Adjutant General
After-action report
Critical infrastructure
Homeland Security Advisory System
Homeland Security Presidential Directive

Self-Check Questions

1. What are the five groups that must be fully engaged in the nation's war on terrorism?
2. What is the goal of emergency management in regards to the terrorism threat?
3. How much money did the federal government spend in the response to and recovery from the September 11 attacks?

4. What did the two September 11–related after-action reports say about the capabilities of first responders?
5. What has been the most significant result of the September 11 attacks for state and local emergency managers?
6. What were the names of the original five DHS Directorates? Which of these still exist today?
7. Why did Secretary Chertoff release the Six-Point Agenda? What was the purpose of the Agenda?
8. What did the Post-Katrina Emergency Management Reform Act do?
9. Other than DHS, what federal agencies provide terrorism-based funding for first responders?
10. What was the purpose of the 911 Commission? What did the Commission find?
11. How did the states respond to the terrorist threat?
12. How did Hurricane Katrina affect terrorism preparedness in the United States?

Out-of-Class Exercises

Visit the website for your state homeland security office. Where in government is this office? What grants and other assistance does it provide to local governments and citizens of the state? Is this office colocated with the office of emergency management, or is it a separate office? What is the experience of the lead executive of the office?

10

The Future of Emergency Management

French novelist and journalist Jean Baptiste Karr, reflecting on the political climate of the late 1800s is credited with the statement "The more things change, the more they stay the same." This quote seems particularly applicable to the state of emergency management in 2009. The year started full of promise with the swearing in of a new president, Barack Obama, bringing hope for major changes in Washington. Among the changes President Obama hinted at while on the campaign trail in 2008 were the reestablishment of FEMA as an independent agency, a cutting of the bureaucratic red tape faced by communities recovering from disasters, and the rebuilding of emergency management partnerships with state and local governments.

As this book goes to press, major questions remain concerning how the Obama administration will impact the discipline of emergency management. However, some of the recent decisions and actions provide insight into what can be expected in the near future. And beyond these political decisions, new trends in technology, cultural diversity, and economics will exert great influence on the future direction of emergency management. This chapter examines several of these factors, explores alternatives, and poses ideas for how the future could unfold. We will demonstrate how the field has come full circle and is again facing many of the same conditions that existed and the questions that were posed to emergency management in the 1980s. These conditions become the basis of the new ideas, promising trends, and innovative models we believe are needed to preserve the integrity of a strong emergency management system and each of its associated functions. In order to lend greater perspective to these proposed solutions, the following background material depicting the evolution of the discipline of emergency management is provided.

Understanding the Past

In the 1960s when the National Governors Association commissioned the seminal study on this discipline, comprehensive emergency management became defined as a cycle of preparedness, response, recovery, and mitigation. This cycle and its functions became what emergency managers were supposed to accomplish at the local, state, and federal levels. At this stage, emergency management was still new. Two factors were prominent at this time: The establishment of the discipline and its concepts were being driven by the reactions to a series of hazard events (Hurricane Betsy, the Three Mile Island accident, and the Mt. St. Helens eruption). Second, the individuals who initially staffed state and local emergency management positions held military or civil defense backgrounds. As a result, the response function was emergency management's dominant driving force. Skills such as logistics, command, control, and search and rescue prevailed. Preparedness as a function came second and reflected the civil defense mentality of watch and warning, sheltering, and evacuating.

In addition, what drove the importance of preparedness was the government's reaction to the accident at the Three Mile Island nuclear power plant. In this event's aftermath, adequate off-site preparedness around commercial nuclear power plants became a condition for continued licensing by the Nuclear Regulatory Commission (NRC). Hence, it was this regulatory requirement that led to the embrace of preparedness as an important emergency management function. This was especially true at the state level, where state emergency management organizations received funding for staff and operations from the commercial power plants to ensure that they could perform the necessary operations and exercises to attest to adequate preparedness for the licensing process.

The functions of recovery and mitigation were neither widely understood nor regarded within the field, and the skill set needed to support these functions (e.g., land use planning, building code design and enforcement, engineering, architecture, cartography, and geology) were not possessed by most emergency managers. Recovery was neither well understood nor supported until the late 1980s, when a major overhaul of the legislation supporting the federal government's disaster management programs occurred. Passage of the Robert T. Stafford Act in 1988 significantly expanded the role of the federal government in disaster recovery. However, it took until the 1990s, under the Clinton administration, for emergency management to assume a major role in a community's recovery from a major disaster.

Unlike response and preparedness, which were regarded as fundamental to the discipline, mitigation and recovery involved more complex political processes, problematic issues that needed to be resolved, and the reaching of a wide consensus among community leadership—all activities that the emergency manager may not have had the skills or the desire to pursue. One factor that has predisposed emergency managers to an embrace of the response and preparedness functions is the availability of or the association with financial resources for each. As previously noted, funding of preparedness by private, commercial utilities supported that function on an annual basis. In fact, this private funding for off-site preparedness planning at commercial nuclear power plants provided the impetus and model for all later preparedness planning efforts.

When it comes to response, the basis of its prominence is legal in nature. Since public health and safety are a constitutional obligation of all state and local governments, a response capability would always be supported with a discrete amount of funding and resources on an annual basis. The forces that drove mitigation and recovery were very different. For example, because the majority of recovery funding was event-driven and therefore always depended on the occurrence of actual disasters (and federal declarations to support them), most states and localities rarely received discrete recovery funds.

Mitigation fared even worse. It wasn't until the Stafford Act was enacted, thereby providing a funding source for postdisaster mitigation in communities where presidential disaster declarations were made, that mitigation funding existed. Originally, the National Flood Insurance Program (NFIP—the only national mitigation program) mandated mitigation without any financial resources to support it—or at least to support emergency management operations. What the NFIP did provide in return for passage of land use ordinances that restricted development in the floodplain was low-cost, subsidized flood insurance for individual homeowners. So in this case, mitigation supported individuals but not the emergency management organizations. Of course, there were collateral benefits to emergency managers from the NFIP, including that the federal government provided a detailed map delineating NFIP communities' flood risks (which helped guide emergency planning and response operations). During the late 1990s and early 2000s, the NFIP fund made several new mitigation programs available to communities prior to a disaster, including the Flood Mitigation Assistance, Repetitive Flood Claims, and Severe Repetitive Loss programs.

In the aftermath of September 11, 2001, when the Department of Homeland Security was established and FEMA lost its status as an independent agency, emergency management became a minor player. In a majority of states, governors established new homeland security organizations. In some cases, the state emergency management function was subsumed into these organizations, while in other cases, these new organizations became competitors for the funding. So not only did most emergency management organizations fail to get an actual increase in funds, but like FEMA, they lost authority and political clout.

The primary mission of homeland security is to prevent future acts of terrorism. This requires the inclusion and prominence of law enforcement and intelligence functions. Even in the event of an actual terrorist act, these two functions will have primacy in the immediate response. Given the national preoccupation with the events of September 11 and terrorism, all states and localities were forced to make plans and preparedness for terrorism their highest priority. These forced requirements were similar to those imposed during the 1980s when states that were unwilling to plan for nuclear attacks were denied federal funding. It wasn't until the massive failures of FEMA during the response to and recovery from Hurricane Katrina and subsequent disasters like Hurricanes Rita and Ike that the public and politicians focused on the issue of natural hazards and questioned the role of the federal government in helping people in the aftermath of natural disasters. The lack of a competent federal response and the need to enhance preparedness for catastrophic disasters became an issue in the Bush administration. And while the recovery from Katrina continued to languish, FEMA concentrated its efforts on planning for the next catastrophic disaster. Top-down federal preparedness planning requirements and compliance with federal procedures, such as compliance with the National Information Management System (NIMS), were imposed on state and local governments as requirements for continued receipt of federal funding.

The Obama Administration

With the election of Barack Obama, the emergency management community became more optimistic. Many thought that the new president might move FEMA out of DHS and make it an independent agency again. The International Association of Emergency Managers (IAEM), which represents thousands of domestic and international local emergency managers, had taken a very courageous position in supporting FEMA independence in many congressional hearings and wrote letters advocating this position to the new administration. Unfortunately, with the new administration facing much more critical economic and international problems, and strong opposition from Senators Lieberman and Collins, the Senate leadership on Homeland Security deferred to the appointed leadership at DHS and chose to keep FEMA as part of DHS. They chose Craig Fugate, the former state director of emergency management in Florida and a proven, effective emergency responder, to be the new FEMA administrator.

Fugate has made personal preparedness one of his highest priorities for the Obama FEMA administration, with (as has been described in previous chapters) operational readiness to respond representing his other significant priority. These priorities both are consistent with Fugate's tenure in Florida and reflect the concerns that the Obama administration does not want to repeat the mistakes of the Bush administration, as evidenced by Hurricane Katrina. It also indicates that efforts to reduce the impacts of future disasters by promoting existing or new mitigation programs, such as a new version of Project Impact, will not be a priority of Fugate's tenure.

The Obama administration did, however, build on an initiative that had been started under the Bush administration to make the Department of Housing and Urban Development (HUD) a bigger player in the recovery phase of disasters. Under President Bush, FEMA had engaged in a pilot project that put HUD in charge of postdisaster temporary housing, a perennially problematic responsibility for which FEMA was constantly criticized. For HUD, it allowed access to the Disaster Relief Fund to supplement existing HUD appropriations and an opportunity to rebuild its public housing administrative infrastructure without using HUD funding. The pilot program used in Hurricane Ike had some problems, but new DHS leadership under Napolitano was more than willing to pass off this perennial disaster headache to another federal agency.

"Those Who Forget the Past Are Doomed to Repeat It"

With the latest developments, it is impossible not to reflect on history and recognize that in so many ways, emergency management has truly come full circle. Before FEMA was established in 1979, HUD was responsible for many disaster assistance programs, including temporary housing. HUD's failure to effectively execute this program in multiple disasters was one of the reasons this function was transferred to the newly created FEMA, along with the other individual disaster assistance programs that HUD administered. As demonstrated by Hurricane Ike, there is no indication that HUD has the capacity to effectively execute the housing mission any better today than it did when it was in charge the last time. However, the administration seems intent on HUD becoming a major player in their disaster portfolio.

For example, the Obama administration recognized the need to do something about federal disaster recovery efforts and established a White House Task Force on Recovery that is being cochaired by the secretaries of DHS and HUD. Concurrent with this effort was the FEMA initiative, which came in response to PKEMRA legislation requirements, to create a National Disaster Recovery Framework (NDRF) that would complement the National Response Framework (NRF). Unlike the development of the NRF, the NDRF took great pains to include significant input from state and local governments, nonprofits, and the private sector. Stakeholder input was obtained through ten videoconferences that were held through the ten FEMA/HUD regions; public meetings in New York City, New Orleans, Salt Lake City, Memphis, and Los Angeles; and a website for public and stakeholder comments.

In addition, special listening sessions were convened for academics, associations, and other stakeholders. The final NDRF product is to be presented to the president of the White House Task Force in July 2010 and then to Congress. The prominence of HUD as a cochair has raised speculation that HUD may be taking on more and more of the traditional recovery responsibilities. It is no secret that DHS has questioned the prominent role of FEMA in recovery, and as the most recent reorganization of FEMA indicates, disaster recovery is no longer an equal partner of disaster response, having been subsumed into the agency's Disaster Operations Directorate.

ADDITIONAL RESEARCH

Organizations at Risk: What Happens When Small Businesses and Not-for-Profits Encounter Natural Disasters, by Daniel J. Alesch, is a report supported by federal grants funding in the aftermath of the Northridge earthquake that discusses how and why businesses fail or succeed in recovering from the impacts of natural disasters.

Like the NRF, the NDRF is not a plan of how the federal government will operate in disaster recovery. It does not detail what state and local governments can expect in the way of support from each of the federal departments and agencies, but rather it presents a conceptual framework. Unlike their predecessor, the National Response Plan, neither the NRF nor the NDRF actually require departments and agencies to agree to perform specific functions or deliver certain services. Nobody is accountable, and nobody is in charge. These are the exact circumstances under which FEMA functioned throughout the 1980s until the Federal Response Plan (the predecessor to the NRP) was finally developed and signed off on by the departments and agencies in the early 1990s.

There are, of course, several other less obvious examples of how the current emergency management system has reverted to the 1980s model. During the 1980s, for instance, FEMA took the position that it would dictate to state and local governments what measures must be taken to comply with the federal response operations, and it measured this compliance through the CARL codes. The CARL codes were discontinued in the 1990s but were soon afterward replaced during the 2001 to 2009 period with requirements for state and local NIMS compliance. Furthermore, the Integrated Planning System (IPS) implemented by FEMA in 2006 dictates to state and local governments how they should plan for disasters, irrespective of the regional differences in risk and disaster type.

Clearly, the top-down approach of the 1980s, when nuclear attack planning became the norm, was adopted in the post-9/11 era, where skewed perceptions influenced policies such that terrorism became the leading hazard risk (and, it seemed, the only disaster-related concern). The all-hazards approach, in which state and locals determined their priorities, was given lip service but not supported by policies or funding.

In 2009, FEMA announced that the advancement of personal preparedness is a top agency priority and that individuals impacted by disasters have to learn to be "survivors" rather than victims. While this is certainly a lofty goal—as it was during the 1980s when FEMA supported the construction of personal bomb shelters—the question remains: How effective are personal preparedness programs? On the other hand, as was very clearly demonstrated during the 1990s, investing similar resource levels and providing the same leadership commitment into promoting mitigation by individuals and communities is highly effective in reducing the impacts of disasters.

It is too early to determine whether the Obama administration will continue the trends seen in the 1980s or adopt the much more successful and progressive emergency management model built in the 1990s. All indications are that the Obama administration recognizes the need to rebuild the partnership with state and local governments. They have appointed a talented and qualified FEMA administrator who understands how important that partnership is and recognizes the need to adopt new technologies into emergency management. But the administration lacks any substantial strategy on the future of emergency management. Recent efforts to transfer and dilute emergency management authorities from FEMA to other federal agencies, and recognizing that mitigation programs such as the NFIP are seen as distractions and not solutions, could be indicators that a cohesive, comprehensive, and well-coordinated federal, state, and local system of emergency management will not be forthcoming soon.

CRITICAL THINKING

- What are the potential benefits to FEMA as an organization within DHS?
- Do you think that all phases of emergency management should be given equal weight in terms of resources, or should one function be a higher priority, and why?
- What do you see as the biggest challenges facing emergency management at the federal, state, or local level?

Emergency Management Ideas for the Future

Reflecting upon this detailed background and the disaster events of the past few years, the authors would like to suggest a range of emergency management ideas, trends, and structures that we feel are necessary to consider as the evolution of emergency management moves forward.

Idea One: Adopt Risk Management as an Operating Philosophy Instead of Emergency Management

This concept, which is a radical departure from traditional emergency management because it requires rigorous analysis and includes acceptance of a level of failure, is proactive instead of reactive (as is the case with emergency management). Risk management is commonly defined as being the process of the identification, assessment, and prioritization of risks, followed by the application of appropriate resources and strategies to minimize, monitor, and control the impacts of disaster events.

The common strategies for managing risk include transferring the risk to another party (insurance), avoiding the risks (land use planning), reducing the negative impacts (buyouts), and/or accepting some or all of the consequences of a particular risk (levees). Risk management is widely practiced throughout the private sector and by various public entities. There are widely adopted standards for various risk management processes established by the National Institute of Science and Technology and ISO standards. The Environmental Protection Agency publishes a *Risk Management Guidebook*. Emergency management organizations in Australia and New Zealand apply risk management principles in their operations. FEMA's Project Impact program of the late 1990s was an attempt to support communities wishing to conduct a streamlined version of the risk management process that proved very effective.

It would be valuable for FEMA to adopt a risk management approach as new threats continue to emerge and resources remain constant for addressing these threats. It would be important for FEMA to promote and support communities to engage in the risk management process to make them more resilient from future disasters. Part of the process of improving emergency management in the future is to identify the sources of problems in the past. The box below focuses on Hurricane Katrina, examining what went wrong and what we can do to avoid this kind of incident in the future.

HURRICANE KATRINA: WHAT WENT WRONG AND HOW TO FIX IT

The numerous after-action reports identified many factors that contributed to the failure of the response and recovery efforts for Hurricane Katrina. Many of these factors can be summarized as follows:

- *Lack of leadership:* Political leaders at all levels of government did not assume leadership of the response and recovery efforts as New York mayor Rudy Giuliani did in the aftermath of the World Trade Center attacks. The leadership of FEMA and the state and local emergency management operations were also found lacking.

- *Information:* During the response, there was no clear effort made to collect, analyze, and disseminate information among the various responders. As more than one report noted, there was little if any situational awareness in the early days of the response. The media became the first source of information.
- *Communications:* The elected and appointed officials involved in the response failed to communicate with one another and failed to communicate effectively with the general public.
- *Preparedness:* DHS/FEMA, the state Office of Homeland Security, and the New Orleans Office of Homeland Security were unprepared to deal with a disaster of this size and magnitude. A major contributing factor was the almost exclusive focus on homeland security and terrorism issues since September 11. These agencies and their personnel were not prepared to respond to a large natural disaster.
- *Mitigation:* The levee system is the principle flood-mitigation mechanism in the New Orleans area, and it failed. Reports indicate that the system was badly designed and poorly maintained.
- *Coordination:* Federal, state, and local emergency responders failed to work together and to effectively coordinate their actions. Part of this failure was the inability of the FEMA director to marshal and direct the full resources of the federal government in support of state and local efforts. The National Response Plan failed because FEMA, as the designated leader of the plan, was unable to direct the actions of other federal agencies.

The following questions that arose after Katrina must be considered as efforts are made to rebuild the nation's emergency management system:

- *The roles of the military and the National Guard:* With the nation at war, the resources that were available from the state and federal National Guards were much more limited than during peacetimes. What continuing role should the active duty military have in responding to future disasters?
- *Voluntary agencies, nongovernmental organizations (NGOs), and the business community:* All three sectors played big roles in the response and continue to play major roles in the recovery. How can these sectors work best with the government sector in future disasters in order to fully leverage the resources that each sector can bring to the table?
- *Who's in charge?:* Will the reforms proposed by all of the after-action reports and that are now being implemented within the federal government settle the key question of who will be in charge at the federal level during the next major disaster?
- *Vulnerable populations:* Katrina exposed the extreme vulnerability of certain populations in our society such as the elderly, the disabled, children, the economically disadvantaged, non-English-speakers, and so on. What can be done to revise emergency plans to address the issues that impact these special needs populations in a major disaster?
- *Mitigation:* With global climate change and the severity and frequency of large weather events rising, we can expect more Katrinas in the future. When will government and nongovernment leaders recognize that reducing the loss of life and the economic and environmental impacts of future disasters can be accomplished through hazard mitigation actions and provide the resources to take action across the country?

In consideration of all of these factors and questions, the authors propose consideration of the following five points that alone or in concert may contribute to rebuilding the nation's emergency management system in the wake of Hurricane Katrina:

- Move FEMA out of DHS and reestablish it as an independent executive branch agency whose director reports directly to the president.
- Elevate the FEMA director to cabinet status, and give the FEMA director the authority to direct federal disaster response resources.
- Refocus the National Response Plan to marshal the full resources of the federal government at the direction of the FEMA director in support of state and local emergency managers in a major disaster event.
- Create a new entity (it could be a new federal government agency, a quasi-government agency, or a nonprofit organization funded by the government) that focuses on building community and individual resiliency through a mix of policy/legislative initiatives and community-based programming in the areas of mitigation and preparedness. It should also include federal government involvement from FEMA, HUD, EPA, DOE, the Departments of Education and Commerce, HHS, NOAA, and so on.
- Establish an agreement with the nongovernmental sector (voluntary agencies, NGOs, and the business community) that details how government and nongovernment entities will work together in all four phases of emergency management.

Idea Two: Embrace New and Emerging Technologies

In the past, emergency managers and emergency management systems have failed to take advantage of new and emerging technologies to improve operations and enhance capabilities. GIS and GPS technologies have been staples of the emergency management tool kit, and as of late, there has been an upsurge in the use of various social networking technologies. Social networking websites like Facebook, Twitter, YouTube, and Flikr enable the real-time transfer of information about what is happening to people and places that are impacted by disasters. These technologies are already in common use among the general public, and emergency management personnel can leverage these tools to both transmit and gather public information.

One such application being piloted with the state of Florida is called Emicus (*www.emicus.com*). Emicus has been engineered to provide real-time information on the data that matters most in an emergency, such as the location of the nearest shelter that allows pets, the status of inventory at gas stations, and the location of hardware stores that have generators or plywood and the availability of such materials at these facilities. Users can input geolocated information via computer, mobile web, iPhone application, or SMS (text) message and receive information back. This information is authenticated and displayed on an interactive map. Potential sources of information include federal, state, and local governments; NGOs; businesses; news organizations; social media sites; and people who are in the impacted area. Many of these new tools are being developed as private sector business opportunities.

Emergency managers should be partnering with technology developers to design solutions for problems such as better analysis of risk, better rapid damage assessments, economic loss estimations, logistics and transportation capacities, public warnings and communications, and mitigation measures.

Idea Three: Adapt to Shifts in Sociological and Demographic Structure

The U.S. society is going through several major changes that will impact emergency management operations that include such things as the aging of the population, a higher concentration of people with mental and functional disabilities, and larger concentrations of non-English-speaking populations. The demands these various populations, who are considered the most vulnerable to hazard risk, will have on warnings, evacuations, sheltering, and communications must be anticipated *now*, and strategies and technologies must be developed to prepare emergency managers to assist and protect these populations.

Social and demographic vulnerability as it relates to disasters has been studied for years by researchers in the communication and sociology disciplines. Many institutes have studied issues like the behavior of individuals who are facing a crisis, the ability of different groups to respond to evacuation orders, the channels and messages through which different groups receive preparedness education and event warnings, the availability of recovery resources among each of the different demographic sectors, and the special disaster preparedness, response, and recovery considerations that are particular to each group (e.g., the disaster medical needs of children). A significant amount of information is available about each of these factors, but until the emergency management profession embraces such study in their planning efforts and advocates for further research into areas of deficient understanding, social and demographic factors will continue to confound operations.

Idea Four: Recreate Emergency Management with a New Entity

In light of the expanding threat environment and the impacts of global climate change, it may be time to take a fresh look at emergency management in order to better understand the limitations of the current cycle. We have already discussed the historical and cultural barriers that have led parts of the emergency management community to ignore the functions of mitigation and long-term recovery. The sacred nature of the emergency management cycle of preparedness, response, recovery, and mitigation has rested in the supposed connectivity of these factions. But as we have maintained, there has always existed disagreement as to when the mitigation function begins. Do you undertake mitigation before the disaster occurs, when the risk has been identified and delineated? Or do you wait until the hazard risk has occurred and a "window of opportunity" for mitigation is opened? To be effective, mitigation must be part of the everyday planning and decisions that individuals and communities participate in.

After a disaster, the process of long-term recovery offers the most accessible and accommodating political environment for implementing mitigation actions. By *mitigation* we speak not only about mitigation in the built environment but also about the measures individuals can take on a more personal level. For example, after a home is damaged in a disaster, the homeowner is more likely to purchase and/or retain appropriate insurance than before the experience.

Referring back to the previous discussion of the different skill sets and partnerships needed for effective mitigation and recovery, is it still logical or even necessary for these functions to be part of the emergency manager's portfolio? We would like to propose new organizational structures to address the functions of recovery and mitigation. Our idea is that the functions of mitigation and long-term recovery should be supported by a different quasi-governmental structure. One of the strongest arguments for this approach is that the private sector is a more significant player in these functions than that of either preparedness or response. The private sector owns most of the built environment that faces the hazard risk and is actually impacted in disaster events. The private sector has an enormous influence in the political environment that can support or reject certain mitigation measures, including the passage of building codes and land use ordinances. And with regards to the insurance industry, the private sector is already in control of one of the most effective vehicles that can best be used to implement mitigation measures.

When any community recovers from a disaster, the success of their efforts is very dependent on how quickly the predominantly private sector functions are restored. Businesses provide the majority of a community's employment; critical services such as health, child care, and food; and critical infrastructures, such as transportation, energy, and communications. In the event of a presidential declared disaster, recovery of many of these functions may be supported through the federally administered Disaster Relief Fund as a part of the response, such as with public transportation systems. Unfortunately, it is more often the case that these resources, which are critical to the facilitation of a quick recovery, are not supported by the federal programs.

To date, the emergency management community has not been extremely effective in engaging the private sector. Government agencies' relations with the private sector most often occur as a regulatory requirement. In the emergency management world, this is evidenced by the relationships with the commercial nuclear industry and the flood insurance industry. The National Institute of Building Sciences (NIBS) provides a potential model for this organizational structure. NIBS is a nonprofit organization created by Congress and that receives appropriations from Congress, but it is independent of the federal government. The original purpose in establishing NIBS was to support and promote affordable options within the housing sector. NIBS was expected to bring together representatives of government, industry professionals, and labor and consumer interests to focus on the identification and resolution of actual and potential problems that hampered the construction of safe, affordable structures for housing, commerce, and industry throughout the United states. NIBS has thus far been successful in bringing together representatives from government agencies, regulatory agencies, legislators, and the private sector to "seek consensus solutions to problems of mutual concern."

We are not suggesting that the functions of mitigation and recovery be added to the NIBS mission, although they have been extremely effective partners with FEMA. With NIBS, FEMA has in the past promoted mitigation through the work of the Building Seismic Safety Council (BSSC) and the Multi-Hazard Mitigation Council. While the NIBS mission is limited to the built environment, it has demonstrated that this type of structure can provide the vehicle for the private sector to work as equivalent partners with government to accomplish mutually beneficial goals.

The authors propose that Congress establish a new entity that would bring together not just the public and private building community but also the following (selected examples):

- Private and public infrastructure representatives (e.g., lifelines, transportation, energy)
- Private and public financial and risk management industries (e.g., insurance, Fannie Mae)
- Public and private environmental community stakeholders
- Public and private community development stakeholders
- Construction code design and enforcement community members
- Climate change research scientists
- NGOs, academia, and foundations
- Public and private emergency management community members

Creating a new entity is difficult, and Congress is usually reluctant to interfere in what has historically been considered a purely government function. However, the events of Katrina, the competing priorities within DHS, the changing threat environment, and the dire prospects of global climate change all require a new, fresh look and approach. This concept needs to be explored and developed with all of the partners that are essential to accomplishing the functions of mitigation and recovery.

While it may be extremely difficult to understand how mitigation and recovery can ever become effective in the current political environment, one can identify distinct positive and negative aspects of this concept. The negatives are obvious. This approach would require a major change to current governmental structure. It would require DHS/FEMA, and possibly HUD, to relinquish a level of authority that is anathema to bureaucratic politics. In the case of mitigation, the authority is minimal and the politics are major. It would require DHS/FEMA and state and local emergency management organizations to potentially give up some of their resources. It is unlikely that this would happen because each organization would claim that only minimal resources were attributed to these functions. It will also require a new pattern for making connections among the necessary partners not just at the federal level but also at the state and local levels. Because of the nature of our communities, the connections and cooperations at the local level may be the easiest to accomplish.

The most significant obstacle is overcoming the inertia and reluctance of Congress to create new governmental or quasi-governmental entities. Typically, only major events precipitate such congressional action. Without some external pressure or an external event, discussion and support for this option would be difficult to generate.

The primary positive aspect of this approach is twofold: mitigation and the benefits of long-term recovery would be given the same attention as preparedness and response, and the private sector, one of the entities that is most important to the implementation of mitigation, would have a significant role in the process. As a nation, we have cultivated, to a degree, an awareness of the need for preparedness and the necessity of response. We have not yet invested the same level of effort in mitigation and recovery. In spite of the cost-benefit analysis data and empirical evidence of the value of mitigation and its inclusion in long-term recovery, it is still a very hard sell. The "sell" is often being made by participants who do not necessarily have the expertise, skills, and comfort with the audience. It is unfair to ask the current emergency management professional to change how they operate, to change priorities when the change will require an entirely new skill set and the acceptance of considerable political risk.

To provide the opportunity for the culture of mitigation to exist, we need to engage those stakeholders who can impact this in a meaningful way and with a level of leadership that understands the risks and benefits of the process. This leadership does not exist in emergency management, and we need to find another vehicle to exercise the leadership. The usual government approaches will not work. If we are serious about reducing the impacts of future disasters and improving individual and community disaster resiliency, then we need to look at a new model.

Conclusion

What does the future hold for emergency management? As of January 2010, the future remains full of uncertainty. Will the Obama administration continue to decentralize and diffuse disaster responsibilities across the federal government, will it embrace a larger role for the military in disaster response, and will it value mitigation and make it a priority? All of these questions remain unanswered. The administration and DHS/FEMA went untested as the 2009 hurricane season was the least active in decades and the H1N1 virus was controlled without the pandemic some thought would occur.

With all of the other pressing priorities of the economic recession and two international wars, it is understandable that emergency management has not been a top priority. However, we would argue that now is the time for real leadership and an opportunity to make a radical departure from the policies of the Bush years and to reinvent emergency management. The opportunity is now to establish a proactive system that includes implementation of risk management principles; a strong, coordinated partnership of federal, state, local, private, and nonprofit sectors; and application of new and emerging technologies for more effective operations that are focused on risk reduction through mitigation. Or we can adopt the philosophy of, perhaps, the most brilliant and innovative American scientist, Albert Einstein, who said, "I never think of the future—it comes soon enough."

In this chapter, we identified several concepts and approaches that together could stimulate thoughts, ideas, and a much-needed dialogue. The evolving threats, the realities of global climate change, and our changing social, economic, and political environment all demand new and innovative approaches and leadership. We hope this book motivates each reader to accept the challenge.

Appendix A
Acronyms

AAR	After-action report
AEC	Agency emergency coordinator
AFRO	African Regional Office (WHO)
AOA	Administration on Aging
AOR	Areas of responsibility (DOD)
ARC	American Red Cross
ARES	Amateur Radio Emergency Services
BHR	Bureau for Humanitarian Response (USAID)
B-NICE	Biological, nuclear, incendiary, chemical, and explosive (weapons)
CARE	Cooperative for Assistance and Relief Everywhere
CAT	Crisis Action Team
CBDG	Community Development Block Grant
CBRN	Chemical, biological, radiological, and nuclear (weapons)
CBRNE	Chemical, biological, radiological, nuclear, and explosive (weapons)
CCP	Casualty collection point
CCP	Citizens Corps Program
CCP	Crisis Counseling Assistance and Training Program
CDC	Centers for Disease Control and Prevention, U.S. Public Health Service
CDRG	Catastrophic Disaster Response Group
CENTCOM	Central Command (DOD)
CEPPO	Chemical Emergency Preparedness and Prevention Office
CERCLA	Comprehensive Environmental Response, Compensation, and Liability Act
CFA	Catalog of Federal Domestic Assistance
CHE	Complex Humanitarian Emergency
CJTF	Commander for the Joint Task Force (DOD)
CMHS	Center for Mental Health Services
CMOC	Civil/Military Operations Center (DOD)
CMT	Crisis Management Team
CNN	Cable News Network
CRC	Convention on the Rights of the Child
CRC	Crisis Response Cell
CRM	Crisis resource manager
CRS	Catholic Relief Services
DAE	Disaster assistance employee
DART	Disaster Assistance Response Team (USAID)
DCE	Defense coordinating element

DCO	Defense coordinating officer
DCSA	Defense Support of Civil Authorities
DEA	Drug Enforcement Agency
DEST	Domestic Emergency Support Team
DFO	Disaster Field Office
DHHS	Department of Health and Human Services
DHS	Department of Homeland Security
DMAT	Disaster Medical Assistance Team
DMORT	Disaster Mortuary Response Team, National Disaster Medical System
DMTP	Disaster Management Training Programme
DOD	United States Department of Defense
DOJ	Department of Justice
DOL	Department of Labor
DOT	Department of Transportation
DRC	Disaster Recovery Center
DRD	Disaster Response Division
DRRP	Disaster Reduction and Recovery Programme
DUA	Disaster unemployment assistance
EAS	Emergency Alert System
EC	Emergency coordinator
ECHO	European Community Humanitarian Organization
ECS	Emergency communications staff
EDA	Economic Development Administration
EGOM	Empowered Group of Ministers (India)
EICC	Emergency Information and Coordination Center
EMPG	Emergency Management Performance Grants
EMRO	Eastern-Mediterranean Regional Office (WHO)
EMS	Emergency Medical Services
EOC	Emergency Operations Center
ERC	Emergency Response Coordinator (UN)
ERCG	Emergency Response Coordination Group, Public Health Service/Centers for Disease Control and Agency for Toxic Substances and Disease Registry
ERD	Emergency Response Division (UNDP)
ERL	Emergency Recovery Loan (WBG)
ERT	Emergency Response Team
ERT-A	Emergency Response Team Advance Element
ERT-N	National Emergency Response Team
ERU	Emergency Response Unit (IFRC)
ESF	Emergency Support Function
EST	Emergency Support Team
EUCOM	European Command (DOD)
EURO	Regional Office for Europe (WHO)
FAA	Federal Aviation Administration
FACT	Field Assessment and Coordination Team (IFRC)
FAO	Food and Agriculture Organization

FBI	Federal Bureau of Investigation
FCO	Federal Coordinating Officer
FECC	Federal Emergency Communications Coordinator
FEMA	Federal Emergency Management Agency
FERC	FEMA Emergency Response Capability
FESC	Federal Emergency Support Coordinator
FFP	Office of Food for Peace (BHR)
FHA	Foreign Humanitarian Assistance (DOD)
FHWA	Federal Highway Administration
FIRST	Federal Incident Response Support Team
FOC	FEMA Operations Center
FRC	Federal Resource Coordinator
FRERP	Federal Radiological Emergency Response Plan
FRN	FEMA Radio Network
FRP	Federal Response Plan
FSA	Farm Service Agency
GSN	Global Seismographic Network
HAO	Humanitarian Assistance Operations (DOD)
HAST	Humanitarian Assistance Survey Team (DOD)
HAZUS	Hazards—U.S. (FEMA Consequence Modeling System)
HET-ESF	Headquarters Emergency Transportation Emergency Support Function
HHS	Department of Health and Human Services
HSAS	Homeland Security Advisory System
HSEEP	Homeland Security Exercise and Evaluation Program (ODP)
HSOC	Homeland Security Operations Center
HSPD	Homeland Security Presidential Directive
HUD	Department of Housing and Urban Development
IAEM	International Association of Emergency Managers
IASC	Inter-Agency Standing Committee
IBRD	International Bank for Reconstruction and Development (WBG)
ICP	Incident Command Post
ICPAE	Interagency Committee on Public Affairs in Emergencies
ICRC	International Committee of the Red Cross
ICS	Incident Command System
ICVA	International Council for Voluntary Agencies
IDA	International Development Association (WBG)
IDNDR	International Decade for Natural Disaster Reduction (UN)
IDP	Internally Displaced Persons
IFC	International Finance Corporation (WBG)
IFG	Individual and Family Grant
IFRC	International Federation of Red Cross/Red Crescent Societies
IHP	Individuals and Households Program
IIMG	Interagency Incident Management Group
IMD	Indian Meteorological Department
IMF	International Monetary Fund

IMT	Incident Management Team
INS	Immigration and Naturalization Service
IO	International Organization
ISCID	International Centre for Settlement of Investment Disputes (WBG)
ISDR	International Strategy for Disaster Reduction (UN)
JCS	Joint Chiefs of Staff (DOD)
JFO	Joint Field Office
JIC	Joint Information Center
JOC	Joint Operations Center
JTF	Joint Task Force (DOD)
JTTF	Joint Terrorism Task Force
MACC	Multi-Agency Command Center
MIGA	Multilateral Investment Guarantee Agency (WBG)
MMRS	Metropolitan Medical Response System
MOA	Memorandum of Agreement
MOU	Memorandum of Understanding
MSF	Medecin Sans Frontiers
NACo	National Association of Counties
NASA	National Aeronautics and Space Agency
NCA	National Command Authority (DOD)
NDMOC	National Disaster Medical Operations Center
NDMS	National Disaster Medical System
NDMSOSC	National Disaster Medical System Operations Support Center
NEHRP	National Earthquake Hazard Reduction Program
NEIC	National Earthquake Information Center
NEMA	National Emergency Management Association
NEP	National Exercise Program (ODP)
NEPEC	National Earthquake Prediction Evaluation Council
NGO	Nongovernmental Organization
NIMS	National Incident Management System
NIRT	Nuclear Incident Response Team
NIST	National Institute of Standards and Technology
NMRT	National Medical Response Team
NOAA	National Oceanic and Atmospheric Administration
NPSC	National Processing Service Center
NRC	Nuclear Regulatory Commission
NRCC	National Response Coordination Center
NRP	National Response Plan
NRT	National Response Team
NSEP	National Security Emergency Preparedness
NSF	National Science Foundation
NSSE	National Security Special Event
NVOAD	National Voluntary Organizations Active in Disaster
OCHA	Office for the Coordination of Humanitarian Affairs
ODP	Office for Domestic Preparedness

OEP	Office of Emergency Preparedness, U.S. Public Health Service
OET	Office of Emergency Transportation
OFDA	Office of U.S. Foreign Disaster Assistance
OPA	Office of Public Affairs
OS	Operation Support (OFDA)
OSC	On-Scene Coordinator
OSTP	White House Office of Science and Technology Policy
OTI	Office of Transition Initiatives (BHR)
PACOM	Pacific Command (DOD)
PAHO	Pan-American Health Organization (WHO)
PAO	Public Affairs Officer
PFO	Principal Federal Official
PK/HA	Office of Peacekeeping and Humanitarian Affairs (DOD)
PM	Office of Political/Military Affairs (DOD)
PMPP	Prevention, Mitigation, Preparedness, and Planning (OFDA)
PNP	Private nonprofit
PRM	Bureau of Population, Refugees, and Migration (USAID)
PS	Program Support (OFDA)
PSA	Public service announcement
PSYOPS	Psychological Operations (DOD)
PVO	Private Voluntary Organization
QIP	Quick Impact Project (UNHCR)
RACES	Radio Amateur Civil Emergency Services
RDD	Radiological Dispersion Device
REACT	Radio Emergency Associated Communication Team
REC	Regional Emergency Coordinator
RECC	Regional Emergency Communications Coordinator
RECP	Regional Emergency Communications Plan
RET	Regional Emergency Transportation
RETCO	Regional Emergency Transportation Coordinator
RMT	Response Management Team (OFDA)
ROC	Regional Operations Center
ROE	Rules of Engagement (DOD)
ROST	Regional Operations Support Team
RRT	Regional Response Team
SAC	FBI Senior Agent-in-Charge
SAMHSA	Substance Abuse and Medical Health Services Administration
SAR	Search and rescue
SBA	U.S. Small Business Administration
SCO	State Coordinating Officer
SEARO	South-East Asia Regional Office (WHO)
SFHA	Special Flood Hazard Areas
SFLEO	Senior Federal Law Enforcement Official
SHSP	State Homeland Security Program (ODP)
SIOC	Strategic Information and Operations Center

SITREP	Situation Report
SOCOM	Special Operations Command (DOD)
SOUTHCOM	Southern Command (DOD)
START	Scientific and Technical Advisory and Response Team
TAG	Technical Assistance Group (OFDA)
TOPOFF	Top Officials Terrorism Exercise (biennial)
TRADE	ODP Training and Data Exchange Group
TRANSCOM	Transportation Command (DOD)
UASI	Urban Areas Security Initiative
UN	United Nations
UNDAC	UN Disaster Assessment and Coordination
UNDP	United Nations Development Programme
UNFPA	United Nations Populations Fund
UNHCR	United Nations High Commissioner for Refugees
UNHRD	UN Humanitarian Response Depot
UNICEF	United Nations Children's Fund
US&R/USAR	Urban Search and Rescue
USACE	United States Army Corps of Engineers
USACOM	United States Atlantic Command (DOD)
USAID	United States Agency for International Development
USDA	United States Department of Agriculture
USGS	United States Geological Survey
VMAT	Veterinarian Medical Assistance Team
WB	World Bank
WBG	World Bank Group
WFP	World Food Programme
WHO	World Health Organization
WMD	Weapons of mass destruction
WTC	World Trade Center
ZECP	Zone Emergency Communications Planner

Appendix B
Emergency Management Websites

Category	Organization/Agency	Website URL
Academic	Disasters Roundtable	*Dels.nas.edu/dr/*
Academic	Extension Disaster Education Network	*http://eden.lsu.edu/*
Academic	FEMA Emergency Management Institute	*Training.fema.gov/emiweb*
Academic	George Washington University Institute for Crisis, Disaster and Risk Management	*www.gwu.edu/~icdrm*
Academic	University of Colorado Hazards Center	*www.colorado.edu/hazards*
Academic	University of Delaware Disaster Research Center	*http://www.udel.edu/DRC/*
Academic	University of Wisconsin Disaster Management Center	*http://www.bt.cdc.gov/*
Disaster Information	AlertNet	*www.alertnet.org*
Disaster Information	Avalanche	*www.avalanche.org*
Disaster Information	Center for International Disaster Information	*www.cidi.org*
Disaster Information	Disaster Information Network	*www.disaster.net*
Disaster Information	Disaster News Network	*www.disasternews.net*
Disaster Information	Drought Monitor	*http://www.drought.unl.edu/dm/*
Disaster Information	Earthquake Hazard Program	*http://earthquake.usgs.gov/*
Disaster Information	EPA Oil Spills	*http://www.epa.gov/oilspill/*
Disaster Information	Flood Streamflow Conditions	*http://water.usgs.gov/waterwatch/*
Disaster Information	Global Disaster Alert and Coordination System	*http://www.gdacs.org/*
Disaster Information	Havaria Information Service	*http://visz.rsoe.hu/alertmap/woalert.php?lang=eng*
Disaster Information	National Hurricane Center	*http://www.nhc.noaa.gov/*
Disaster Information	NOAA Watch	*www.noaawatch.gov*
Disaster Information	Pacific Disaster Center	*www.pdc.org*
Disaster Information	Relief Web	*www.reliefweb.int*
Disaster Information	The Disaster Center	*www.disastercenter.com*
Disaster Information	USGS Landslides	*http://landslides.usgs.gov/*

Category	Organization/Agency	Website URL
Disaster Information	Western Disaster Center	*http://www.westerndisaster center.org/*
International	Asian Disaster Preparedness Center	*www.adpc.net*
International	Caribbean Disaster Emergency Response Agency	*www.cdera.org*
International	Interaction	*www.interaction.org*
International	International Committee of the Red Cross	*www.icrc.org*
International	International Federation of Red Cross/Red Crescent Societies	*www.ifrc.org*
International	International Monetary Fund	*www.imf.org*
International	Pan American Health Organization	*www.paho.org*
International	Regional Disaster Information Center	*http://www.crid.or.cr/crid/ing/ index_ing.html*
International	UN Development Programme	*www.undp.org*
International	UN High Commissioner for Refugees	*www.unhcr.ch*
International	UN International Strategy for Disaster Reduction	*www.unisdr.org*
International	UN Office for the Coordination of Humanitarian Affairs	*Ochaonline.un.org*
International	UNICEF	*www.unicef.org*
International	World Bank	*www.worldbank.org*
International	World Bank Hazard Risk Management	*http://www.worldbank.org/ hazards/*
International	World Food Programme	*www.wfp.org*
Journals/Magazines	Australian Journal of Emergency Management	*http://www.ema.gov.au/ajem*
Journals/Magazines	Disaster Prevention and Management	*http://www.emeraldinsight.com/ info/journals/dpm/dpm.jsp*
Journals/Magazines	Disaster Recovery Journal	*http://www.drj.com/*
Journals/Magazines	Government Technology Emergency Management Magazine	*www.emergencymgmt.com*
Journals/Magazines	Journal of Emergency Management	*http://www.pnpco.com/ pn06001.html*
Journals/Magazines	Journal of Homeland Security	*http://www.homelandsecurity .org/journal/*
Journals/Magazines	Journal of Homeland Security and Emergency Management	*http://www.bepress.com/jhsem/*
NGO	Action Against Hunger	*www.actionagainsthunger.org*
NGO	Amateur Radio Disaster Service	*www.ares.org*
NGO	Feeding America	*www.feedingamerica.org*
NGO	American Jewish World Service	*Ajws.org*
NGO	American Radio Relay League	*www.arrl.org*

(Continued)

Category	Organization/Agency	Website URL
NGO	American Red Cross	*www.redcross.org*
NGO	CARE USA	*www.careusa.org*
NGO	Catholic Relief Services	*www.catholicrelief.org*
NGO	Church World Service	*www.churchworldservice.org*
NGO	Habitat for Humanity	*www.habitat.org*
NGO	Humane Society	*www.hsus.org*
NGO	Institute for Business and Home Safety	*www.ibhs.org*
NGO	Islamic Relief Worldwide	*http://www.islamic-relief.com/*
NGO	Mennonite Disaster Service	*http://www.mds.mennonite .net/*
NGO	NVOAD	*www.nvoad.org*
NGO	Oxfam	*www.oxfam.co.uk*
NGO	Public Entity Risk Institute	*www.riskinstitute.org*
NGO	Salvation Army	*www.salvationarmyusa.org*
NGO	Save the Children	*www.savethechildren.org*
State and Local Government	Association of State Floodplain Managers	*www.floods.org*
State and Local Government	Emergency Management Assistance Compact	*www.emacweb.org*
State and Local Government	National Association of Counties	*www.naco.org*
State and Local Government	National Governors' Association	*www.nga.org*
State and Local Government	National League of Cities	*www.nlc.org*
State and Local Government	NEMA	*www.nemaweb.org*
State and Local Government	U.S. Conference of Mayors	*www.usmayors.org*
Terrorism	Two Tigers	*http://www.twotigersonline .com/resources.html*
Terrorism	Council on Foreign Relations: Terrorism	*http://www.cfr.org/issue/135/*
Terrorism	The Terrorism Research Center	*http://www.terrorism.com/*
U.S. Government	FEMA	*www.fema.gov*
U.S. Government	FEMA for Kids	*www.fema.gov/kids*
U.S. Government	Centers for Disease Control	*http://www.bt.cdc.gov/*
U.S. Government	Department of Health and Human Services	*www.hhs.gov*
U.S. Government	Department of Homeland Security	*www.dhs.gov*
U.S. Government	Disaster Help	*www.disasterhelp.gov*
U.S. Government	Environmental Protection Agency	*Epa.gov/naturalevents*
U.S. Government	Environmental Protection Agency Chemical Preparedness and Prevention	*www.epa.gov/ceppo*

(Continued)

Category	Organization/Agency	Website URL
U.S. Government	EPA Environmental Emergencies	*http://www.epa.gov/ebtpages/ emergencies.html*
U.S. Government	Federal Bureau of Investigation	*www.fbi.gov*
U.S. Government	FEMA Disaster Declarations	*http://www.fema.gov/disasters/*
U.S. Government	FEMA HAZUS	*http://www.fema.gov/plan/ prevent/hazus/*
U.S. Government	National Flood Insurance Program	*http://www.fema.gov/business/ nfip/*
U.S. Government	National Interagency Fire Center	*www.nifc.gov*
U.S. Government	National Mental Health Information Center	*http://mentalhealth.samhsa .gov/cmhs/emergencyservices/ default.asp*
U.S. Government	NOAA Northwest Weather and Avalanche Center	*http://www.nwac.noaa.gov/*
U.S. Government	NOAA Satellite and Information Service	*http://www.osei.noaa.gov/*
U.S. Government	Ready.gov	*www.ready.gov*
U.S. Government	Small Business Administration	*www.sba.gov*
U.S. Government	U.S. Coast Guard National Response Center	*http://www.nrc.uscg.mil/ index.html*
U.S. Government	U.S. Department of Agriculture	*www.usda.gov*
U.S. Government	U.S. Department of State Terrorism Information Page	*http://www.state.gov/m/ ds/terrorism/*
U.S. Government	U.S. Fire Administration	*www.usfa.dhs.gov*
U.S. Government	U.S. Secret Service	*www.secretservice.gov*
U.S. Government	USGS Hazards Page	*http://water.usgs.gov/wid/ index-hazards.html*

Appendix C
Ready.gov Citizen Preparedness Recommendations

Step 1—Get a Kit of Emergency Supplies

Be prepared to improvise and use what you have on hand to make it on your own for *at least* three days, maybe longer. Though there are many things that might make you more comfortable, think first about fresh water, food, and clean air. Consider putting together two kits. In one, put everything needed to stay where you are and make it on your own. The other should be a lightweight, smaller version you can take with you if you have to get away.

You'll need a gallon of water per person per day. Include in the kits canned and dried foods that are easy to store and prepare. If you live in a cold-weather climate, include warm clothes and a sleeping bag for each member of the family.

Start now by gathering basic emergency supplies—a flashlight, a battery-powered radio, extra batteries, a first aid kit, toilet articles, prescription medicines, and other special things your family may need. Many potential terrorist attacks could send tiny microscopic "junk" into the air. Many of these materials can hurt you only if they get into your body, so think about creating a barrier between yourself and any contamination. It's smart to have something for each member of the family that covers the mouth and nose.

Plan to use two to three layers of a cotton t-shirt, handkerchief, or towel. Or consider filter masks, which are readily available in hardware stores and are rated based on how small a particle they filter. It is very important that the mask or other material fit your face snugly so most of the air you breathe comes through the mask, not around it. Do whatever you can to make the best fit possible for children.

Also, include duct tape and heavyweight garbage bags or plastic sheeting that can be used to seal windows and doors if you need to create a barrier between yourself and any potential contamination outside.

Step 2—Make a Plan for What You Will Do in an Emergency

Be prepared to assess the situation; use common sense and whatever you have on hand to take care of yourself and your loved ones. Depending on your circumstances and the nature of the attack, the first important decision is deciding whether to stay or go. You should understand and plan for both possibilities.

Develop a Family Communications Plan

Your family may not be together when disaster strikes, so plan how you will contact one another and review what you will do in different situations. Consider a plan where each family member calls, or e-mails, the same friend or relative in the event of an emergency. It may be easier to make a long-distance phone call than to call across town, so an out-of-state contact may be in a better position to communicate among separated family members. You may have trouble getting through, or the phone system may be down altogether, but be patient.

Staying Put

There are circumstances when staying put and creating a barrier between yourself and potentially contaminated air outside, a process known as *shelter-in-place*, can be a matter of survival. Choose an interior room or one with as few windows and doors as possible. Consider precutting plastic sheeting to seal windows, doors, and air vents. Each piece should be several inches larger than the space you want to cover so you can duct tape it flat against the wall. Label each piece with the location of where it fits.

If you see large amounts of debris in the air, or if local authorities say the air is badly contaminated, you may want to shelter-in-place. Quickly bring your family and pets inside, lock doors, and close windows, air vents, and fireplace dampers. Immediately turn off air conditioning, forced air heating systems, exhaust fans, and clothes dryers. Take your emergency supplies and go into the room you have designated. Seal all windows, doors, and vents. Watch TV, listen to the radio, or check the Internet for instructions.

Getting Away

Plan in advance how you will assemble your family and anticipate where you will go. Choose several destinations in different directions so you have options in an emergency. If you have a car, keep at least a half tank of gas in it at all times. Become familiar with alternate routes as well as other means of transportation out of your area. If you do not have a car, plan how you will leave if you have to. Take your emergency supply kit and lock the door behind you. If you believe the air may be contaminated, drive with your windows and vents closed and keep the air conditioning and heater turned off. Listen to the radio for instructions.

At Work and School

Think about the places where your family spends time: school, work, and other places you frequent. Talk to your children's schools and your employer about emergency plans. Find out how they will communicate with families during an emergency. If you are an employer, be sure you have an emergency preparedness plan. Review and practice it with your employees. A community working together during an emergency also makes sense. Talk to your neighbors about how you can work together.

Step 3—Be Informed about What Might Happen

Some of the things you can do to prepare for the unexpected, such as assembling a supply kit and developing a family communications plan, are the same for both a natural or man-made emergency.

However, there are important differences among potential terrorist threats that will impact the decisions you make and the actions you take.

Specific Terrorist Threats

A biological attack is the deliberate release of germs or other substances that can make you sick. Many agents must be inhaled, enter through a cut in the skin, or be eaten to make you sick. A chemical attack is the deliberate release of a toxic gas, liquid, or solid that can poison people and the environment.

A nuclear blast is an explosion with intense light and heat, a damaging pressure wave, and widespread radioactive material that can contaminate the air, water, and ground surfaces for miles around. A radiation threat or *dirty bomb* is the use of common explosives to spread radioactive materials over a targeted area.

Be prepared to adapt this information to your personal circumstances, and make every effort to follow instructions received from authorities on the scene. Above all, stay calm, be patient, and think before you act. With these simple preparations, you can be ready for the unexpected.

Source: www.ready.gov.

Ready.gov Recommendations for Terrorism Preparedness

Biological Threat

A biological attack is the deliberate release of germs or other biological substances that can make you sick. Many agents must be inhaled, enter through a cut in the skin, or be eaten to make you sick. Some biological agents, such as anthrax, do not cause contagious diseases. Others, like the smallpox virus, can result in diseases you can catch from other people.

If There Is a Biological Threat ...

Unlike an explosion, a biological attack may or may not be immediately obvious. Although it is possible that you will see signs of a biological attack, as was sometimes the case with the anthrax mailings, it is perhaps more likely that local health care workers will report a pattern of unusual illness, or there will be a wave of sick people seeking emergency medical attention. You will probably learn of the danger through an emergency radio or TV broadcast, or some other signal used in your community. You might get a telephone call or emergency response workers may come to your door.

In the event of a biological attack, public health officials may not immediately be able to provide information on what you should do. It will take time to determine exactly what the illness is, how it should be treated, and who is in danger. However, you should watch TV, listen to the radio, or check the Internet for official news including the following:

- Are you in the group or area authorities consider in danger?
- What are the signs and symptoms of the disease?
- Are medications or vaccines being distributed?
- Where? Who should get them?
- Where should you seek emergency medical care if you become sick?

During a Declared Biological Emergency ...

1. If a family member becomes sick, it is important to be suspicious.
2. Do not assume, however, that you should go to a hospital emergency room or that any illness is the result of the biological attack. Symptoms of many common illnesses may overlap.
3. Use common sense, practice good hygiene and cleanliness to avoid spreading germs, and seek medical advice.
4. Consider if you are in the group or area authorities believe to be in danger.
5. If your symptoms match those described and you are in the group considered at risk, immediately seek emergency medical attention.

If You Are Potentially Exposed ...

1. Follow instructions of doctors and other public health officials.
2. If the disease is **contagious,** expect to receive **medical evaluation and treatment**. You may be advised to stay away from others or even deliberately **quarantined**.
3. For **noncontagious** diseases, expect to receive **medical evaluation and treatment**.

If You Become Aware of an Unusual and Suspicious Substance Nearby ...

1. Quickly get away.
2. Protect yourself. Cover your mouth and nose with layers of fabric that can filter the air but still allow breathing. Examples include two to three layers of cotton such as a t-shirt, handkerchief, or towel. Otherwise, several layers of tissue or paper towels may help.
3. Wash with soap and water.
4. Contact authorities.
5. Watch TV, listen to the radio, or check the Internet for official news and information including what the signs and symptoms of the disease are, if medications or vaccinations are being distributed, and where you should seek medical attention if you become sick.
6. If you become sick, seek emergency medical attention.

Chemical Threat

A chemical attack is the deliberate release of a toxic gas, liquid, or solid that can poison people and the environment.

Possible Signs of Chemical Threat

- Many people suffering from watery eyes, twitching, choking, having trouble breathing, or losing coordination
- Many sick or dead birds, fish, or small animals are also cause for suspicion
- If you see signs of chemical attack, find clean air quickly.
- Quickly try to **define the impacted area** or where the chemical is coming from, if possible.
- Take immediate action to **get away**.
- If the chemical is inside a building where you are, get out of the building without passing through the contaminated area, if possible.
- If you can't get out of the building or find clean air without passing through the area where you see signs of a chemical attack, it may be better to move as far away as possible and shelter-in-place.

- If you are outside, quickly determine the fastest way to find clean air. Consider if you can get out of the area or if you should go inside the closest building and shelter-in-place.

If You Think You Have Been Exposed to a Chemical …

If your eyes are watering, your skin is stinging, and you are having trouble breathing, you may have been exposed to a chemical.

- If you think you may have been exposed to a chemical, strip immediately and wash.
- Look for a hose, fountain, or any source of water, and wash with soap if possible, being sure not to scrub the chemical into your skin.
- Seek emergency medical attention.

Explosions

If you think there is an explosion:

- Take shelter against your desk or a sturdy table.
- Exit the building ASAP.
- Do not use elevators.
- Check for fire and other hazards.
- Take your emergency supply kit if time allows.

If you think there is a fire:

- Exit the building ASAP.
- Crawl low if there is smoke.
- Use a wet cloth, if possible, to **cover** your nose and mouth.
- Use the back of your hand to feel the upper, lower, and middle parts of closed doors.
- If the door is not hot, brace yourself against it and open slowly.
- If the door is hot, do not open it. Look for another way out.
- Do not use elevators.
- If you catch fire, do not run. Stop-drop-and-roll to put out the fire.
- If you are at home, go to a previously designated meeting place.
- Account for your family members and carefully supervise small children.
- Never go back into a burning building.

If you are trapped in debris:

- If possible, use a flashlight to signal your location to rescuers.
- Avoid unnecessary movement so you don't kick up dust.
- Cover your nose and mouth with anything you have on hand. (Dense-weave cotton material can act as a good filter. Try to breathe through the material.)
- Tap on a pipe or wall so rescuers can hear where you are.
- If possible, use a whistle to signal rescuers.
- Shout only as a last resort. Shouting can cause a person to inhale dangerous amounts of dust.

Nuclear Blast

A nuclear blast is an explosion with intense light and heat, a damaging pressure wave, and widespread radioactive material that can contaminate the air, water, and ground surfaces for miles around. During a nuclear incident, it is important to avoid radioactive material, if possible. Although experts may predict at this time that a nuclear attack is less likely than other types, terrorism by its nature is unpredictable.

If there is a nuclear blast or advanced warning of an attack, take cover immediately, as far below ground as possible, though any shield or shelter will help protect you from the immediate effects of the blast and the pressure wave.

If there is no warning:

1. Quickly assess the situation.
2. Consider if you can get out of the area or if it would be better to go inside a building to limit the amount of radioactive material you are exposed to.
3. If you take shelter, go as far below the ground as possible, close windows and doors, and turn off air conditioners, heaters, or other ventilation systems. Stay where you are, watch TV, listen to the radio, or check the Internet for official news as it becomes available.
4. To limit the amount of radiation you are exposed to, think about shielding, distance, and time:
   - **Shielding:** If you have a thick shield between yourself and the radioactive materials, more of the radiation will be absorbed, and you will be exposed to less.
   - **Distance:** The farther away you are from the blast and the fallout, the lower your exposure.
   - **Time:** Minimizing the time spent exposed will also reduce your risk.

Use available information to assess the situation. If there is a significant radiation threat, health care authorities may or may not advise you to take potassium iodide. Potassium iodide is the same stuff added to your table salt to make it iodized. It may or may not protect your thyroid gland, which is particularly vulnerable, from radioactive iodine exposure. Plan to speak with your health care provider in advance about what makes sense for your family.

Radiation Threat

A radiation threat, commonly referred to as a *dirty bomb* or *radiological dispersion device (RDD),* is the use of common explosives to spread radioactive materials over a targeted area. It is not a nuclear blast. The force of the explosion and radioactive contamination will be more localized. Although the blast will be immediately obvious, the presence of radiation will not be clearly defined until trained personnel with specialized equipment are on the scene. As with any radiation, you want to try to limit exposure. It is important to avoid breathing radiological dust that may be released in the air.

If there is a radiation threat or a dirty bomb:

1. If you are outside and there is an explosion or authorities warn of a radiation release nearby, cover your nose and mouth and quickly go inside a building that has not been damaged. If you are already inside, check to see if your building has been damaged. If your building is stable, stay where you are.Close windows and doors, and turn off air conditioners, heaters, or other ventilation systems.

2. If you are inside and there is an explosion near where you are or if you are warned of a radiation release inside, cover your nose and mouth and go outside immediately. Look for a building or other shelter that has not been damaged, and quickly get inside.Once you are inside, close windows and doors, and turn off air conditioners, heaters, or other ventilation systems.

3. If you think you have been exposed to radiation, take off your clothes and wash as soon as possible.

4. Stay where you are, watch TV, listen to the radio, or check the Internet for official news as it becomes available.

5. *Remember*—to limit the amount of radiation you are exposed to, think about shielding, distance, and time:
   - **Shielding**: If you have a thick shield between yourself and the radioactive materials more of the radiation will be absorbed, and you will be exposed to less.
   - **Distance**: The farther away you are away from the blast and the fallout, the lower your exposure.
   - **Time**: Minimizing time spent exposed will also reduce your risk.

As with any emergency, local authorities may not be able to immediately provide information on what is happening and what you should do. However, you should watch TV, listen to the radio, or check the Internet often for official news and information as it becomes available.

Natural Disasters

Some of the things you can do to prepare for the unexpected, such as making an emergency supply kit and developing a family communications plan, are the same for both a natural or man-made emergency. However, there are important differences among natural disasters that will impact the decisions you make and the actions you take. Some natural disasters are easily predicted, while others happen without warning. Planning what to do in advance is an important part of being prepared.

Find out what natural disasters are most common in your area. You may be aware of some of your community's risks, but others may surprise you. Historically, flooding is the nation's single most common natural disaster. Flooding can happen in every U.S. state and territory. Earthquakes are often thought of as a West Coast phenomenon, yet 45 states and territories in the United States are at moderate to high risk from earthquakes and are located in every region of the country. Other disasters may be more common in certain areas. Tornados are nature's most violent storms and can happen anywhere. However, states located in "Tornado Alley" and areas in Pennsylvania, New York, Connecticut, and Florida are at the highest risk for tornado damage. Hurricanes are severe tropical storms that form in the southern Atlantic Ocean, Caribbean Sea, Gulf of Mexico, and eastern Pacific Ocean. Scientists can now predict hurricanes, but people who live in coastal communities should plan what they will do if they are told to evacuate.

Source: www.ready.gov.

Appendix D
A Day in the Life of Homeland Security

Today, U.S. Customs and Border Protection agents will:

- Process over 1.1 million passengers arriving into our nation's airports and seaports
- Inspect over 57,006 trucks and containers, 580 vessels, 2,459 aircraft, and 323,622 vehicles coming into this country
- Execute over 64 arrests
- Seize 4,639 pounds of narcotics in 118 narcotics seizures
- Seize an average of $715,652 in currency in 11 seizures
- Seize an average of $23,083 in arms and ammunition and $467,118 in merchandise
- Deploy 1,200 dog teams to aid inspections
- Make 5,479 predeparture seizures of prohibited agricultural items
- Apprehend 2,617 people crossing illegally into the United States
- Rescue three people illegally crossing the border in dangerous conditions
- Deploy 35,000 vehicles, 108 aircraft, 118 horses on equestrian patrol, and 480 all-terrain vehicles
- Utilize 238 remote video surveillance systems, each system using one to four cameras to transmit images to a central location, and maintain the integrity of 5,525 miles of border with Canada and 1,989 miles of border with Mexico

Today, Transportation Security Administration employees will:

- Screen approximately 1.5 million passengers before they board commercial airlines

Today, the Federal Law Enforcement Training Center will:

- Provide law enforcement training for more than 3,500 federal officers and agents from 75 different federal agencies

Today, the Office for Domestic Preparedness will:

- Disburse millions of dollars to states and cities across the country

Today, U.S. Coast Guard units will:

- Save 10 lives and assist 192 people in distress
- Protect $2.8 million in property
- Interdict 14 illegal migrants at sea
- Conduct 109 search and rescue cases
- Seize $9.6 million of illegal drugs
- Respond to 20 oil and hazardous chemical spills
- Conduct 50 port security patrols
- Conduct 20 homeland security air patrols
- Board two high-interest vessels
- Escort eight vessels (i.e., cruise ships or high-interest ships) in and out of port
- Maintain over 90 security zones around key infrastructure in major ports or coastal areas
- Educate 502 people in boating safety courses

Today the U.S. Citizenship and Immigration Services will:

- Provide information and services to approximately 225,000 customers in one of its 250 field locations
- Respond to 75,000 calls to its 1-800 customer service number that helps to assist its customers navigate the immigration process
- Naturalize approximately 1,900 new citizens
- Process approximately 19,000 applications for a variety of immigration-related benefits

Today, U.S. Immigration and Customs Enforcement agents will:

- Make 217 arrests on immigration-related violations
- Make 41 arrests on customs violations
- Remove 407 criminal aliens and other illegal aliens
- Investigate 12 cases involving unauthorized employment threatening critical infrastructure
- Participate in 24 drug seizures resulting in the seizure of 5,311 pounds of marijuana, 774 pounds of cocaine, and 16 pounds of heroin
- Make seven currency seizures, totaling $478,927
- Make grand jury appearances resulting in the indictment of a combination of 32 people and companies
- Launch 20 vessels in support of marine operations protecting the territorial seas of Puerto Rico, South Florida, the Gulf of Mexico, and Southern California
- Fly 25 surveillance flights supporting criminal investigations in Puerto Rico and the continental United States
- Disseminate 80 criminal investigative leads to field offices
- Review 1,200 classified intelligence cables; protect over 8,000 federal facilities
- Screen over one million federal employees and visitors entering federal facilities
- Make six arrests for criminal offenses on federal property
- Intercept 18 weapons from entering federal facilities to include firearms, knives, and box cutters, and deploy federal air marshals to protect the skies

Today, Department of Homeland Security Information Analysis and Infrastructure Protection employees will:

- Distribute four information bulletins or warning products to critical infrastructure about vulnerability assessments, risk reduction, and protective measures
- Receive and review 500 cyber security reports from Internet security firms, government organizations, private companies, and foreign governments
- Review more than 1,000 pieces of intelligence from the intelligence community and law enforcement agencies

Today, the U.S. Secret Service will:

- Protect high-profile government officials including the president, the vice president, visiting heads of state, and former presidents
- Provide protection to traveling protectees in 17 different cities
- Screen over 4,000 people entering protective sites
- Examine 1,500 protective intelligence reports to assess potential threats to protectees
- Complete 11 protective intelligence investigations to assess potential risk to protectees from individuals or groups
- Open over 90 new cases involving financial and electronic crime, identity theft, counterfeiting, and personnel security investigations
- Prevent over $6 million in financial crime losses to the American public and seize (on average) $172,000 in counterfeit currency

Today, DHS Science and Technology employees will:

- Engage the best and brightest minds—along with the most advanced technologies—through three distinct Centers of Excellence, which enlist academics, businesses, and scientists as partners with government to boost our efforts to develop an enduring national research capability in homeland protection
- Develop and implement technical standards for chemical, biological, radiological, and nuclear countermeasures
- Deploy radiation sensors to detect the illicit transport of radioactive materials and experiment with capabilities to similarly protect our cities
- Receive approximately 27 new homeland security technology proposals from large and small businesses
- Receive an average of six homeland security technology proposals submitted via the science .technology@dhs.gov e-mail address

Today, Federal Emergency Management Agency (FEMA) employees will:

- Improve the effectiveness of 220 fire service personnel through courses offered by FEMA's National Fire Academy
- Help protect 1,000 students at risk for tornadoes by providing their school administrators with information about how to properly construct tornado shelters

- Provide 4,000 people with volunteer opportunities to help better prepare their communities through Citizen Corps at its website, *www.citizencorps.gov* (the site receives 36,000 hits per day)
- Help save $2.7 million in damages from flooding across the country through the department's flood plain management
- Spend $10.6 million to help communities respond and recover from disasters
- Help protect an additional 104 homes from the devastating effects of flooding through flood insurance policies issued by the National Flood Insurance Program
- Help 224 Americans recover from disasters by providing direct federal disaster relief assistance in the forms of low-interest loans, unemployment insurance, crisis counseling, and temporary housing
- Distribute $45,243 to state and local governments through FEMA's Emergency Management Performance Grants to help develop, maintain, and improve their emergency management capabilities
- Distribute $51,506 through FEMA's Community Emergency Response Team grants to help state emergency managers initiate, organize, train, and maintain teams of citizens who are qualified to assist in responding to disasters
- Provide an average of $917,808 in grants to America's fire departments through the Assistance to Firefighter Grant program and distribute (on average) $221,917 through FEMA's Emergency Operations Center grants to state governments to help them develop and improve emergency management facilities
- Distribute (on average) $218,493 through FEMA's Interoperable Communications Equipment grants to help develop and support communications interoperability among first responders and public safety emergency officials.

Source: Department of Security Results Agenda—August 2004.

Glossary

Adjutant General An administrative military officer charged with managing military assets in a particular state, primarily those of the National Guard. Many Adjutant Generals are also charged with managing the state's emergency management resources, though this association has diminished over time.

After-action report A document that summarizes any problems or capability deficiencies that arose in the response to a disaster event and provides possible explanations and solutions for organization learning purposes.

Avalanche A mass of ice or snow that moves downhill at a high velocity.

Blizzard A prolonged shortage of available water, primarily due to insufficient rain and other precipitation, or because exceptionally high temperatures and low humidity cause a drying of agriculture and a loss of stored water resources.

Building codes Regulations enacted by state and local governments that provide the requirements for design and construction of buildings in a given jurisdiction.

Business continuity planning The act of developing a plan by which the survival of an operation of a business is maintained despite the consequences sustained due to emergency or disaster losses (direct or indirect).

CBRN weapons The broad family of weapons that include chemical, biological, radiological, and nuclear agents and that have the potential to bring about an extraordinary degree of deaths, injuries, and property destruction.

Civil defense The discipline dealing with protecting civil society from threats.

Coastal erosion A loss of land bordering a body of water.

Complex humanitarian emergency A humanitarian crisis in a country or region where there is total or considerable breakdown of authority resulting from the internal and/or external conflict and that requires an international response that goes beyond the mandate or capacity of any single agency.

Continuity of Operations Plan (COOP) A planning document that outlines the actions that must be taken to ensure that governmental or organizational services and activities (including business operations) do not cease during emergency or disaster contingencies and that identifies the individuals or agencies responsible for those actions.

Coordinating organization Associations of NGOs that coordinate the activities of hundreds of preregistered member organizations to ensure response with maximized impact.

Critical infrastructure Infrastructure components that are essential for the normal functioning of society.

Dam failure The sudden breach of a river water containment wall, known as a dam, which results in a sudden and uncontrolled downstream rush of water and debris.

Department of Homeland Security The federal departments charged with protecting the United States from future terrorist attacks, reducing the nation's vulnerability to terrorism and minimizing the damage from potential terrorist attacks and natural disasters.

Developing nation A self-applied title typically used to describe countries with lower economic, social, nutritional, and other scores on common development indices.

Disaster communications strategy Provides timely and accurate information to the public in all four phases of emergency management.

Disaster Recovery Center   A satellite component of the Joint Field Office; provides a central facility where individuals affected by a disaster can obtain information on disaster recovery assistance programs.

Disaster   An event that exceeds the emergency response and recovery capabilities and resources of the agencies and officials responsible for its management in one or more critical area of response or recovery.

Donor agency   Private, national, or regional organizations whose mission is to provide the financial and material resources for humanitarian relief and subsequent rehabilitation.

Drill   A controlled, supervised method by which a single disaster management operation or function is practiced or tested.

Earthquake   A sudden, rapid shaking of the earth's crust caused by the breaking and shifting of rock beneath the earth's surface

Emergency management/response personnel   Includes federal, state, territorial, tribal, substate regional, and local governments; NGOs; private sector organizations; critical infrastructure owners and operators; and all other organizations and individuals who assume an emergency management role. (Also known as *emergency responder*.)

Emergency management   The discipline dealing with risk and risk avoidance.

Emergency operations plan   An ongoing plan for responding to a wide variety of potential hazards.

Emergency support function   The coordination mechanism to provide assistance to state, local, and tribal governments or to federal departments and agencies conducting missions of primary federal responsibility.

Expansive soil   Soils and soft rock that tend to swell or shrink because of changes in moisture content.

Extreme cold   Periods of colder than normal conditions exhibiting a range of negative consequences (as dictated by the particular area and economy faced with the cold conditions).

Extreme heat   Temperatures that hover 10°F or more above the average high temperature for the region and last for several weeks.

Federal Coordinating Officer (FCOs)   Appointed to manage the federal resources during a disaster, their primary mission is to coordinate the timely delivery of federal assistance to state and local governments, individual victims, and the private sector.

Federal Emergency Management Agency (FEMA)   The federal agency responsible for federal policies, programs, and actions to mitigate, prepare for, respond to, and recover from all hazards.

First responders   Fire, police, and emergency medical technicians.

Flood   An overabundance of water that engulfs normally dry land and property, which may be caused by a number of factors, including heavy rainfall, melting snow, an obstruction of a natural waterway, and other generative factors.

Full-scale exercise   A scenario-based event that seeks to create an atmosphere that closely mimics an actual disaster.

Functional exercise   An exercise that tests and practices response capabilities by simulating an event to which responsible officials must respond.

Hail   Frozen atmospheric water that falls to the earth.

Hazard identification   The process undertaken to analyze sources of danger that may or may not lead to an emergency or disaster. Hazard identification is the foundation of all emergency management activities.

Hazard   A source of danger that may or may not lead to an emergency or disaster and is named after the emergency/disaster that could be so precipitated.

Hazardous materials   Substances that can pose a threat to the environment or health if accidentally or intentionally released.

Hazards-risk management   A process by which individuals, communities, and countries deal with the hazard risks they face.

Homeland Security Advisory System   A five-color coded terrorism risk alert and warning system maintained and issued by the Department of Homeland Security to communicate with governments, the private sector, NGOs, the public, and other stakeholders.

Homeland Security Presidential Directive Presidential directives are executive orders issued by the president of the United States that have security implications and legal authority. Presidents have used a range of terminology for these directives; the HSPD was the moniker of choice for the George W. Bush administration.

Hurricane A tropical storm with winds that have reached a sustained speed of 74 miles per hour.

Incident command system Establishes a set of planning and management systems that helps agencies responding to a disaster to work together in a coordinated and systematic approach.

Incident Commander The individual responsible for all incident activities, including the development of strategies and tactics and the ordering and release of resources. The IC has overall authority and responsibility for conducting incident operations and is responsible for the management of all incident operations at the incident site.

International financial institution Organizations comprised of national governments that provide loans for development and financial cooperation throughout the world.

International organization An organization with global presence and influence.

Joint Field Office (JFO) The primary federal incident management field structure. The JFO is a temporary federal facility that provides a central location for the coordination of federal, state, tribal, and local governments and private sector and nongovernmental organizations with primary responsibility for response and recovery.

Joint Information Center The central point for coordination of emergency public information, public affairs activities, and media access to information about the latest developments in a disaster.

Land subsidence The loss of surface elevation caused by the removal of subsurface support; it ranges from broad, regional lowering of the land surface to localized collapse.

Landslide An uncontrolled movement of relatively dry rock, soil, or debris down a slope.

Land-use planning A process that is applied within communities to determine how the community will grow and develop. It includes a number of strategies that support mitigation such as ordinances, easements, flood plain management, acquisition annexation, historic and environmental reviews, setbacks, and subdivision controls.

Lateral spread The downward and outward spreading of large quantities of accumulated earth or other materials due to gradual hydrologic and gravitational forces.

Mass movement The horizontal or lateral movement of large quantities of physical matter.

Mitigation A sustained action to reduce or eliminate the risk to people and property from hazards and their effects.

Mudflow (or debris flow) A water-saturated river of rock, earth, and other debris that is drawn downward by the forces of gravity.

National Incident Management System A set of principles that provides a systematic, proactive approach guiding government agencies at all levels, nongovernmental organizations, and the private sector to work seamlessly to prevent, protect against, respond to, recover from, and mitigate the effects of incidents, regardless of cause, size, location, or complexity, in order to reduce the loss of life or property and harm to the environment.

National Processing Service Center (NPSCs) Receive calls and process applications from disaster victims who need assistance. The NPSCs are central to the success of the applicant telephone registration process and the FEMA Helpline. The advantage of the centralized NPSC system is that the centers can be staffed within five hours after the president declares a national disaster.

National Response Framework A guide to how the nation conducts all-hazards response.

Natural hazard A hazard that exists in the natural environment and poses a threat to human populations and communities.

New media Social media outlets such as YouTube, Facebook, and Twitter.

Nongovernmental organization The general term for an organization made up of private citizens, with no affiliation with a government of any nation other than the support from government sources in the form of financial or in-kind contributions.

Preparedness   A state of readiness to respond to a disaster, crisis, or any other type of emergency situation.

Private voluntary organization   An organization that is nonprofit, tax-exempt, and receives at least a part of its funding from private donor sources.

Recovery   The development, coordination, and execution of service- and site-restoration plans; the reconstitution of government operations and services; individual, private sector, nongovernmental, and public assistance programs to provide housing and to promote restoration; long-term care and treatment of affected persons; additional measures for social, political, environmental, and economic restoration; evaluation of the incident to identify lessons learned; postincident reporting; and development of initiatives to mitigate the effects of future incidents.

Risk   A measure of the likelihood that a hazard will manifest into an actual emergency or disaster event and the consequences should that event occur.

Rockfall   When masses of rock or other material detach from a steep slope or cliff and descend by free-fall, rolling, or bouncing.

Safe room   An area within a larger structure that is designed to withstand the wind and debris forces of a major tornado.

Severe winter storm   When extremely cold atmospheric conditions coincide with high airborne moisture content, resulting in rapid and heavy precipitation of snow and/or ice.

Situation report   A report that provides information regarding the nature and scope of an incident, the estimated human and economic damages, and what recovery measures are underway.

Sovereignty   The recognition of political authority characterized by territory and autonomy.

State coordinating officer   When the president makes a major disaster declaration, he shall request that the governor of the affected state designate a state coordinating officer for the purpose of coordinating state and local disaster assistance efforts with those of the federal government.

Storm surge   A mass of water that is pushed toward the shore by the force of an oncoming storm or other force.

Structural controls   Physical constructed measures taken to control the impacts of hazards such as levees, culverts, groins, and seawalls.

Tabletop exercise   A discussion-based activity wherein officials practice components of or the full activation of the emergency response plan within the confines of a controlled, low-stress meeting environment.

Technological hazard   Hazards that exist as a result of technological innovation and human development.

Terrorism   The use of force or violence against persons or property for purposes of intimidation, coercion, or spreading faith in order to attain political, religious, or ideological goals.

Thunderstorm   A meteorological event generated by atmospheric imbalance and turbulence caused by unstable warm air that rises rapidly, heavy moisture, and upward lift of air currents that can bring a combination of heavy rains, strong winds, hail, lightning, and tornadoes.

Tornado   A rapidly rotating vortex or funnel of air extending groundward from a cumulonimbus cloud.

Tropical cyclone   A low-pressure area of closed-circulation winds that originates over tropical waters.

Tropical storm   A warm-core tropical cyclone in which the maximum sustained surface wind speed ranges from 39 miles per hour to less than 74 miles per hour.

Tsunami   A wave or series of waves generated by a mass displacement of sea or lake water.

Unified Command   A process that all participating agencies can use to improve overall management whether their jurisdiction is of a geographical or functional nature.

Volcano   A break in the earth's crust from which molten rock exits from below the surface.

Wildland fire (or wildfire)   A large, often out-of-control burning of trees, fallen wood, detritus, and other debris in uninhabited or sparsely inhabited forest or grasslands.

Zoning   Involves the regulation of the use and development of real estate. Zoning regulations and restrictions are used by municipalities to control and direct the development of property within their borders.

References

After-Action Report on the Response to the September 11 Terrorist Attack of the Pentagon, July 2002. Titan Systems, Inc., Washington, DC.

American Red Cross. Disaster Operations Center Visitor's Guide.

Bagli, C.V., January 29 2002. Seeking safety, downtown firms are scattering. New York Times, p.A-1.

Bakhet, O., June 1998. Linking Relief to Development. UNDP Rwanda.

Ballard, M., February 8 2007. Officials urge federal role in hurricane insurance. The Advocate Online.

BBC News, May 8, 2008. Burmese Blog the Cyclone. <http://news.bbc.co.uk/2/hi/asia-pacific/7387313.stm/>.

Bowman, S., Willis, C., 2003. We Media: How Audiences are Shaping the Future of News and Information. The Media Center at the American Press Institute.

Burke, R., 2000. Counter Terrorism for Emergency Responders. CRC/Lewis Publishers, Boca Raton, FL.

Burma News, May 13, 2008. Burmese Journals Face Restriction on Cyclone Coverage. <http://myamarnews.blogspot.com/2008/05/burmese-journals-face-restrictions-on.html/>.

Carafano, J.J., 2007. U.S. Thwarts 19 Terrorist Attacks Against America Since 9/11. Heritage Foundation November 13. <http://www.heritage.org/Research/HomelandDefense/bg2085.cfm>.

Catone, J., October 26, 2007. Online Citizen Journalism Now Undeniably Mainstream, ReadWriteWeb. <http://www.readwriteweb.com/archives/online_citizen_journalism_mainstream.php/>.

Center for Disaster Management and Humanitarian Assistance. NGOs and Disaster Response Who Are These Guys and What Do They Do Anyways? Available at: <www.cdmha.org/ppt/%20presentation.ppt/> n.d.

Congress Daily, February 2, 2007. Estimated Price Tag of Security Causes Stir. Government Executive Magazine, Federal Briefing.

Congressional Research Service, December 15, 2006. Federal Emergency Management Policy Changes after Hurricane Katrina, a Summary of Statutory Provisions. Available at: <http://www.fas.org/sgp/crs/homesec/RL33729.pdf/>.

Cooper, G., October 3, 2007. Burma's Bloggers Show Power of Citizen Journalism in a Crises. Reuters Alert Net. <http://www.alertnet.org/db/blogs/30708/2007/09/3-134022-1.htm/>.

Coppola, D., 2006. Introduction to International Disaster Management. Elsevier, Burlington, MA.

Coppola, D., Harrald, J.R., Yeletaysi, S., 2004. Assessing the Financial Impacts of the World Trade Center Attacks on Publicly Held Corporations. The Institute for Crisis, Disaster, and Risk Management. The George Washington University.

Coyle, D., 1969. The United Nations and How It Works. Columbia University Press, New York.

Department of Defense, CCRP. The Complex Process of Responding to Crisis. Available at: <www.dodccrp.org/ngoCh2.html/> n.d.

Department of Homeland Security, 2007. DHS Proposed Budget 2008. Available at: <http://www.dhs.gov/xlibrary/assets/budget_bib-fy2008.pdf/>.

DHS Office of the Inspector General, 2005. Audit of FEMA's Individuals and Households Program in Miami-Dade County, Florida, for Hurricane Frances, OIG-05-20. Available at: <http://www.dhs.gov/xoig/assets/mgmtrpts/OIG_05-20_May05.pdf/>.

Emergency Management Institute. 2001–2002 Catalog of Activities, Emmitsburg, MD. Available at: <www.fema.gov/>.

Erickson, P. A. Emergency Response Planning for Corporate and Municipal Managers.

Federal Emergency Management Agency Office of the Inspector General, January 1993. FEMA's Disaster Management Program: A Performance Audit after Hurricane Andrew. H-01-93. FEMA, Washington, DC.

FEMA, March 1997. Report on Costs and Benefits of Natural Hazard Mitigation. FEMA, Washington, DC.

FEMA, May 1997. Partnerships in Preparedness, a Compendium of Exemplary Practices in Emergency Management, Vol. II. FEMA, Washington, DC.

FEMA, October 1998. FEMA Emergency Information Field Guide (condensed). FEMA, Washington, DC.

FEMA, April 1999. Federal Response Plan. FEMA, Washington, DC.

FEMA, January 2000. Partnerships in Preparedness, a Compendium of Exemplary Practices in Emergency Management, Vol. IV. FEMA, Washington, DC.

FEMA, 2001. International Technical Assistance Activities of the United States Federal Emergency Management Agency. FEMA, Washington, DC.

FEMA, 2007, February 7, Homeland Security Establishing New Advisory Council, press release.

FEMA, 2007. Catalog, Emergency Management Institute. Available at: <http://training.fema.gov/emiweb/emicourses/emicatalog.asp/>.

FEMA. Web site <www.fema.gov/>.

FEMA, August 2007. National Incident Management System: FEMA 501/Draft August 2007. FEMA, Washington, DC.

Ferrara, L., October 2, 2007. AP's 'NowPublic' Initiative. Remarks at the Associated Press Managing Editors' Conference, Fast Forward to the Future. <http://www.j-lab.org/apme07notesp5.shtml/>.

Flynn, K., September 13, 2001. After the attack: the firefighters; department's cruel toll: 350 comrades. New York Times Section: National Desk.

Fox News, December 27, 2009. Suspect Charged in Thwarted Terror Plot Aboard Detroit-Bound Jet. <http://www.foxnews.com/story/0,2933,581180,00.html/>.

Gandel, S., March 4, 2002. Consultants push wall street to leave; downtown's losses are huge, but some companies shrug off fears, concentrate workers in midtown. Crain's New York Business, 1.

Gilbert, A., March 2002. Out of the Ashes. Information Week Available at: www.informationweek.com/story/IWK20020104S0008.

Gilbert, R., Kreimer, A., 1999. Learning from the World Bank's Experience of Natural Disaster Related Assistance. The World Bank, Washington, DC.

Gillmor, D., 2006. We the Media: Grassroots Journalism By the People, For the People. O'Reilly Media Inc.

Gillmor, D., Hattotuwa, S., 2007. Citizen Journalism and Humanitarian Aid: Boon or Bust? ICT for Peacebuilding <http://ict4peace.wordpress.com/2007/07/30/citizen-journalism-and-humanitarian-aid-bane-or-boon/>.

Glaser, M., October 25, 2007. California Wildfire Coverage by Local Media, Blogs, Twitter, Maps and More. MediaShift <http://www.pbs.org/mediashift/2007/10/the_listcalifornia_wildfire_co_1.html/>.

GlobalCorps. OFDA's Evolving Role. Available at: <www.globalcorps.com/ofda/ofdarole.html/> n.d.

Global Voices Online. Myanmar Cyclone 2008. <http://www.globalvoicesonline.org/specialcoverage/myanmar-cyclone-2008/>.

Grimmett, R., 2006. 9/11 Commission Recommendations: Implementation Status. Congressional Research Service, Report RL33742.

Hattotuwa, S., 2007. Who is afraid of citizen journalists? Communicating Disasters, TVA Asia Pacific and UNDP Regional Centre in Bangkok.

Hawley, C., March 20, 2002. Globalization and Sept. 11 Are Pushing Wall Street off Wall Street, Analysts Say. Associated Press State and Local Wire, February 1, 2002, State and Regional Section, in Lexis-Nexis Universe: World Trade Center, Firm and Tenant.

Hedges, C., October 1, 2001. Monday counting losses, department rethinks fighting every fire. New York Post.

Hollis, M., February 14, 2007. Florida calling for catastrophe fund. Los Angeles Times, part A, 17.

Houston, A., October 22, 2001. Crisis communications: the readiness is all: how the red cross responded. PR Week, p.13.

Houston, A., November 5, 2001. Crisis communications: confused messages spur switch to sole spokesman. PR Week, p.11.

Intergovernmental Panel on Climate Change, 2001. Special Issues in Developing Countries. Available at: <www.ipcc.ch/pub/tar/wg2/340.htm/>.

International Monetary Fund, 2001. IMF Emergency Assistance Related to Natural Disasters and Post-Conflict Situations: A Factsheet. <www.imf.org/external/np/eexr/facts/conflict.htm/>.

Karter, M.J., 2008. Fire Loss in the United States 2008. National Fire Protection Association. Fire Analysis and Research Division, Quincy, MA.

Kettl, D.F., September 2005. The Worst is Yet to Come: Lessons from September 11 to Hurricane Katrina. Fels Institute of Government. University of Pennsylvania.

Laituri, M., Kodrich, K., 2008. On Line Disaster Response Community: People as Sensors of High Magnitude Disasters Using Internet GIS. Colorado State University.

Madison County, North Carolina. Multi-Hazard Plan for Madison County.

Mancino, K., 2001. Development Relief: NGO Efforts to Promote Sustainable Peace and Development in Complex Humanitarian Emergencies. Interaction, Washington, DC.

May, A.L., 2006. First Informers in the Disaster Zone: The Lessons of Katrina. The Aspen Institute.

Maynard, K. Healing Communities in Conflict: International Assistance in Complex Emergencies. Available at: <www.ciaonet.org/book/maynard/maynard07.html/> n.d.

McKinsey & Company, August 19, 2002. Improving NYPD Emergency Preparedness and Response. Author.

Mileti, D.S., 1999. Disasters by Design: A Reassessment of Natural Hazards in the United States. John Henry Press, Washington, DC.

Mitchell, J.K., et al., 1999. Crucibles of Hazard: Mega-Cities and Disasters in Transition. United Nations University Press, New York.

National Association of Counties, August 2004. Counties and Homeland Security: Policy Agenda to Secure the People of America's Counties. Available at: <www.naco.org/programs/homesecurity?policyplan.cfm/>.

National Emergency Management Association, October 1, 2001. White Paper on Domestic Preparedness. NEMA, Washington, DC.

National Emergency Management Association, June 2002. NEMA Reports on State Homeland Security Structures. Available at: <www.nemaweb.org/ShowExtendedNewscfm?ID=171/>.

National Fire Protection Association, 2006. Fire Loss in the U.S. during 2005. NFPA Report. Available at: <http://www.nfpa.org/assets/files/PDF/OS.fireloss.pdf/>.

National Governor's Association (NGA), August 2002. Center for Best Practices. Issue Brief.

National Governors Association (NGA), February 5, 2007. Letter to Senator Leahy and Senator Bond. Available at: <http://www.nga.org/portal/site/nga/menuitem.cb6e7818b34088d18a278110501010a0/?vgnextoid=edd8b31eb2990110VgnVCM1000001a01010aRCRD/>.

National Interagency Fire Center, 2009. Fire Information – Wildland Fire Statistics. NIFC Website. <http://www.nifc.gov/fire_info/lg_fires.htm/>.

Natsios, A.S., 1997. U.S. Foreign Policy and the Four Horsemen of the Apocalypse. Praeger Publishers, Westport, CT.

New York Magazine, 2009. Death, destruction, charity, salvation, war, money, real estate, spouses, babies, and other September 11 statistics. Website: <http://nymag.com/news/articles/wtc/1year/numbers.htm/>

NOAA, 2006. The Northeast Snowfall Impact Scale (NESIS). Available at the NOAA Web site <http://www.ncdc.noaa.gov/oa/climate/research/snow-nesis/>.

Office for the Coordination of Humanitarian Affairs, 2005. OCHA Organigramme. Available at: <http://ochaonline.un.org/webpage.asp?site=organigramme/>.

Office for the Coordination of Humanitarian Affairs. Information Summary on Military and Civil Defence Assets (MCDA) and the Military and Civil Defence Unit (MCDU). Available at: <www.reliefweb.int/ocha_ol/programs/response/mcdunet/0mcduinf.html/> n.d.

Office for the Coordination of Humanitarian Affairs. Coordination of Humanitarian Response. Available at: <www.reliefweb.int/ocha_ol/programs/response/service.html/> n.d.

Office of Domestic Preparedness, 2007. ODP Grant Programs. Available at the U.S. Department of Justice Web site <http://www.ojp.usdoj.gov/odp/>.

Office of Homeland Security. State and Local Actions for Homeland Security, July 2002. Available at: <www.whitehouse.gov/homeland/stateandlocal/>.

Oklahoma Department of Civil Emergency Management, 1997. After Action Report, Alfred P. Murrah Building Bombing. Lessons Learned. Author.

Otero, J., October 22, 2001. Congress, Administration Examines Emergency Communications Systems. Nation's Cities Weekly, p.5.

Pan American Health Organization. Natural Disasters: Protecting the Public's Health. PAHO Scientific Publication No. 575, n.d.

Powell, M., Haughney, C., February 25, 2002. A towering task lags in New York, city debates competing visions for rebuilding devastated downtown. Washington Post, p.A03. Available at: www.washingtonpost.com/ac2/.../A22040-2002Feb16?language=printe.

Ranganath, P., 2000. Mitigation and the Consequences of International Aid in Postdisaster Reconstruction. Centre d'Etude et de Cooperation Internationale.

Rendleman, J., October 29, 2001. Back online, despite its losses, verizon went right back to work restoring communications services. InformationWeek available at www.informationwee.com/story/IWK2001105S0017.

Reuters, November 20, 2009. US Government Liable for Katrina Damage. ABC Local. <http://www.abc.net.au/news/stories/2009/11/20/2748195.htm?site=local/>.

Rincon, J., May 16, 2008. Myanmar: citizen videos in cyclone Nargis aftermath. Reuters Global News Blog <http://blogs.reuters.com/global/tag/burma/>.

Robertson, C., April 7, 2010. Suspense Builds Over Census for New Orleans. NY Times. <http://www.nytimes.com/2010/04/08/us/08orleans.html/>.

Salomons, D., 1998. Building Regional and National Capacities for Leadership in Humanitarian Assistance. The Praxis Group, New York.

SBA, 2009. FY2009 Annual Report on Disaster Assistance. <http://www.sba.gov/idc/groups/public/documents/sba_homepage/serv_da_annual-report_2009.pdf/>.

Select Bipartisan Committee to Investigate the Preparation for and Response to Hurricane Katrina, February 15, 2006. A Failure of Initiative: Final Report of the Special Bipartisan Committee to Investigate the Preparation for and Response to Hurricane Katrina. Government Printing Office. <http://www.gpoaccess.gov/congress/index.hmtl/>.

Senate Committee on Homeland Security and Governmental Affairs, 2006. Hurricane Katrina: A Nation Still Unprepared. Available at: <http://hsgac.senate.gov/_files/Katrina/ExecSum.pdf/>.

Shirky, C., 2008. Here Comes Everybody: The Power of Organizing Without Organizations. The Penguin Press.

Site One. History of the Red Cross. Available at: <www.siteone.com/redcross/anniv.htm/> n.d.

Smith, L.R. Lessons Learned from Oklahoma City: Your Employees … Their Needs, Their Role in Response and Recovery. Available at: <www.recovery.com/>.

Southern African Regional Poverty Network. Least Developed Countries of the Disaster Profiles. <www.savpn.org.za/relsites.php?site=2/> n.d.

Stabe, M., October 25, 2007. California Wildfires: A Round Up. OJB Online Journalism Blog, <http://onlinejournalismblog.com/2007/10/25/california-wildfires-a-roundup/>.

Strohm, C., February 5, 2007. Homeland Security Budget Generous to Customs, Border Agency. Government Executive.

Strohm, C., February 6, 2007. Proposed Cuts to First Responder Grants Draw Fire. Government Executive.

Town of Boone, North Carolina, July 1999. All Hazards Planning and Operations Manual. Author, Boone, NC.

Townsend, F. F., February 2006. The Federal Response to Hurricane Katrina Lessons Learned. The White House.

Tsunami Education a Priority in Hawaii and West Coast States, June 2001. Bulletin of the American Meteorological Society, p. 1207.

UN Rwanda. The United Nations Development Programme in Rwanda. Available at: <www.un.rw/UNRwa/UNDP.shtml/> n.d.

United Nations Development Programme, 1995/96. Further Elaboration on Follow-up to Economic and Social Council Resolution 1995/96: Strengthening of the Coordination of Emergency Humanitarian Assistance. Available at: <www.undp.org/erd/archives/executiv.htm/> (accessed 10–14, 03–97).

UNDP, May 2001. Disaster Profiles of the Least Developed Countries. United Nations, New York.

UNDP. About ERD. Available at: <www.undp.org/erd/about.htm/> n.d.

UNDP. Building Bridges Between Relief and Development: A Compendium of the UNDP in Crisis Countries. Available at: <www.undp.org/erd/archives/bridges.htm/> n.d.

UNDP. The Disaster Reduction and Recovery Program: An Introduction. Available at: <www.undp.org/erd/archives/brochures/drrp/main.htm/> n.d.

UNDP. Reintegration and Rehabilitation. Available at: <www.undp.org/erd/randr.htm/> n.d.

UNDP. Strengthening National Disaster Management. Available at: <www.undp.org/erd/archives/brochures/drrp/countries/Botswana.htm/> n.d.

UNDP. The United Nations Development Programme Mission Statement. Available at: <www.undp.org/info/discover/mission.html/> n.d.

UNDP. Vulnerability Reduction and Sustainable Development. Available at: <www.UNDP.org.in/dmweb/> n.d.

UNDP. Working for Solutions to Crises: The Development Response. Available at: <www.undp.org/erd/archives/bridges2.htm/> n.d.

United Nations, May 8, 2001. General Assembly Economic and Social Council. United Nations, New York.

U.S. Agency for International Development, 1996. Rebuilding Postwar Rwanda: The Role of the International Community. Available at: <www.usaid.gov/pubs/usaid_eval/ascii/pnaby212.txt/>.

U.S. Agency for International Development, 1998. Field Operations Guide for Disaster Assessment and Response, Version 3.0. USAID, Washington, DC.

U.S. Agency for International Development, 2000. OFDA Annual Report 2000. USAID, Washington, DC.

U.S. Agency for International Development, 2009. USAID Seeing Results in Tsunami Reconstruction. USAID Website. <http://www.usaid.gov/locations/asia/tsunami/>.

U.S. Army. About NGOs. Available at: <http://call.army.mil/fmso/ngos/indtroduction.html/> n.d.

U.S. Conference of Mayors, December 2001. A National Action Plan for Safety and Security in America's Cities. Available at: <www.usmayors.org/uscm/home.asp/>.

U.S. Department of State. Bureau of Population, Refugees, and Migration. Available at: <www.state.gov/g/prm/> n.d.

VIPs, Disaster Service Calls May Get Priority, November 26, 2001. The Daily Yomiuri [Tokyo], The Yomiuri Shimbun, p. 1.

Wagner, M., October 24, 2007. Google Maps and Twitter Are Essential Resources for California Fires. Information Week <http://www.informationweek.com/blog/main/archives/2007/10/google_maps_and.html/>.

Walsh, E., September 12, 2001. National response to terror; FEMA leads effort; borders tightened. Washington Post, p.A-1.

Washkuch, F., May 20, 2008. Relief Groups Turn to Twitter Amid Crises. PR Week, <http://www.prweekus.com/Relief-groups-turn-to-Twitter-amid-crises/article/110368/>.

Waugh Jr., W., 2000. Living with Hazards—Dealing with Disasters: An Introduction to Emergency Management. M.E. Sharpe, New York.

Wax, A.J., Diop, J.C., March 11, 2002. Return to Downtown; Office Leases Are Being Signed Again, but Revival Will Take a While. Newsday, p.D13.

Wireless System Improves Communications. American City and County, August 2001.

Whoriskey, P., February 20, 2007. Florida's big hurricane gamble. Washington Post, section A. p.A02.

World Bank, April 2000. Assistance to Post-Conflict Countries and the HIPC Framework. Available at: <www.imf.org/external/np/hipc/2001/pc/042001.htm/>.

YouTube <http://www.youtube.com/user/AfterNargisYgn/>.

Zevin, R., August 2001. Tapping Web Power in Emergencies. American City and County.

Index